CALIFORNIA
jews

AVA F. KAHN & MARC DOLLINGER, EDITORS

CALIFORNIA
JEWS

BRANDEIS UNIVERSITY PRESS

Waltham, Massachusetts

BRANDEIS UNIVERSITY PRESS

An imprint of University Press of New England

www.upne.com

© 2003 Brandeis University

First Brandeis University Press paperback edition 2011

All rights reserved

Manufactured in the United States of America 5 4 3 2 1

ISBN for the paperback edition: 978-1-61168-219-9

University Press of New England is a member of the Green Press
Initiative. The paper used in this book meets their minimum
requirement for recycled paper.

For permission to reproduce any of the material in this book,
contact Permissions, University Press of New England,
One Court Street, Suite 250, Lebanon NH 03766;
or visit www.upne.com

Library of Congress Cataloging-in-Publication Data

California Jews / Ava F. Kahn & Marc Dollinger, editors.

p.   cm. — (Brandeis series in American Jewish history, culture,
and life)

Includes bibliographical references and index.

ISBN 1-58465-060-5 (cloth : alk. paper)

1. Jews—California—History. 2. California—Ethnic relations.
I. Kahn, Ava Fran. II. Dollinger, Marc, 1964–   III. Series.

F870.J5C36 2003

979.4'004924—dc21   2003010132

BRANDEIS SERIES IN
AMERICAN JEWISH HISTORY, CULTURE, AND LIFE

Jonathan D. Sarna, Editor

Sylvia Barack Fishman, Associate Editor

For a complete list of books that are available in the series, visit www.upne.com

Leon A. Jick, 1992
The Americanization of the Synagogue, 1820–1870

Sylvia Barack Fishman, editor, 1992
Follow My Footprints: Changing Images of Women in American Jewish Fiction

Gerald Tulchinsky, 1993
Taking Root: The Origins of the Canadian Jewish Community

Shalom Goldman, editor, 1993
Hebrew and the Bible in America: The First Two Centuries

Marshall Sklare, 1993
Observing America's Jews

Reena Sigman Friedman, 1994
These Are Our Children: Jewish Orphanages in the United States, 1880–1925

Alan Silverstein, 1994
Alternatives to Assimilation: The Response of Reform Judaism to American Culture, 1840–1930

Jack Wertheimer, editor, 1995
The American Synagogue: A Sanctuary Transformed

Sylvia Barack Fishman, 1995
A Breath of Life: Feminism in the American Jewish Community

Diane Matza, editor, 1996
Sephardic-American Voices: Two Hundred Years of a Literary Legacy

Joyce Antler, editor, 1997
Talking Back: Images of Jewish Women in American Popular Culture

Jack Wertheimer, 1997
A People Divided: Judaism in Contemporary America

Beth S. Wenger and Jeffrey Shandler, editors, 1998
Encounters with the "Holy Land"; Place, Past, and Future in American Jewish Culture

David Kaufman, 1998
Shul with a Pool: The "Synagogue-Center" in American Jewish History

Roberta Rosenberg Farber and Chaim I. Waxman, editors, 1999
Jews in America: A Contemporary Reader

Murray Friedman and Albert D. Chernin, editors, 1999
A Second Exodus: The American Movement to Free Soviet Jews

Stephen J. Whitfield, 1999
In Search of American Jewish Culture

Naomi W. Cohen, 1999
Jacob H. Schiff: A Study in American Jewish Leadership

Barbara Kessel, 2000
Suddenly Jewish: Jews Raised as Gentiles

Jonathan N. Barron and Eric Murphy Selinger, editors, 2000
Jewish American Poetry: Poems, Commentary, and Reflections

Steven T. Rosenthal, 2001
Irreconcilable Differences: The Waning of the American Jewish Love Affair with Israel

Pamela S. Nadell and Jonathan D. Sarna, editors, 2001
Women and American Judaism: Historical Perspectives

Annelise Orleck, with photographs by Elizabeth Cooke, 2001
The Soviet Jewish Americans

Ilana Abramovitch and Seán Galvin, editors, 2001
Jews of Brooklyn

Ranen Omer-Sherman, 2002
Diaspora and Zionism in American Jewish Literature: Lazarus, Syrkin, Reznikoff, and Roth

Ori Z. Soltes, 2003
Fixing the World: Jewish American Painters in the Twentieth Century

David Zurawik, 2003
The Jews of Prime Time

Ava F. Kahn and Marc Dollinger, editors, 2003
California Jews

Naomi W. Cohen, 2003
The Americanization of Zionism, 1897–1948

To the generations

who have come before and

those to follow.

To Rebecca and Shayna,

Sixth Generation California Jews

CONTENTS

Foreword *by Moses Rischin* *xi*

Acknowledgments *xvii*

INTRODUCTION
"The Other Side" *1*
    Ava F. Kahn and Marc Dollinger

CHAPTER 1
The Challenge of Family, Identity, and Affiliations *17*
    Bruce Phillips

CHAPTER 2
Joining the Rush *29*
    Ava F. Kahn

CHAPTER 3
Early Synagogue Architecture *40*
    David Kaufman

CHAPTER 4
Through the Lens of Latino-Jewish Relations *57*
    Steven Windmueller

CHAPTER 5
Jewish Space and Place in Venice *65*
    Amy Hill Shevitz

CHAPTER 6
"Kibbutz San Fernando" *77*
    Na'ama Sabar

CHAPTER 7
Ketubot of the Golden State *87*
    Robert Saslow

CHAPTER 8
Jewish Leaders and the Motion Picture Industry *95*
    Felicia Herman

CHAPTER 9
Civil Rights and Japanese American Incarceration *110*
    Ellen Eisenberg

CHAPTER 10
Jews and Catholics Against Prejudice *123*
    William Issel

CHAPTER 11
From Minyan to Matriculation *135*
    Lawrence Baron

CHAPTER 12
120 Years of Women's Activism *143*
    Ava F. Kahn and Glenna Matthews

CHAPTER 13
The Counterculture *154*
    Marc Dollinger

CHAPTER 14
Contemporary Art Glass *167*
    David and Michelle Plachte-Zuieback

CHAPTER 15
Shlomo Bardin's "Eretz" Brandeis *151*
    Bruce J. Powell

Contributing Authors *185*

Bibliographical Essay *187*

Index *189*

FOREWORD

After four decades of California living, teaching, and scholaring, I have been dubbed among others a bicoastal American Jewish historian. It is a persona that I find especially plausible, at this time, even riveting, in helping me to begin to explain the distinctive perspective that I may be said to have brought to the study of California Jews.

As one who acquired his credentials considerably earlier than has the contributing company to this collection of venturesome essays, this historian brings with him a prospect deeply conditioned by what might be called a previous incarnation. A native New Yorker, in 1962 he had just become the first historian to write of New York in some depth during the era of the Great Jewish Migration. It also happened to be a banner year for California, and he and his wife helped make it so. In 1962 California would surpass New York, the first state in the nation in population for nearly a hundred and fifty years. It already had outdistanced the Empire State as the prime destination for immigrants. Like many new Californians in those boom years of heaviest internal migration and spectacular growth, we felt almost restively impelled at that time to search out the wellsprings for a new equilibrium that would subsume past, present, and future and do justice to the pluralistic impulses that variously colored our responses to our great adventure in newness and the greatest joint adventure of our lives.

To reflect upon the past on such personal terms after the passage of forty years is a daunting challenge that I fear I may not quite be able to meet. But let me try.

In the summer of 1962, in response to an invitation to me to accept a one-year appointment at the UCLA History Department, replacing Donald B. Meyer, an old friend teaching American social and intellectual history during his sabbatical, my wife, Ruth, and I migrated to Los Angeles from Cambridge, Massachusetts. In a new age of jet air transportation, we opted to travel by train. The physical state in which Ruth found herself in the early weeks of her first pregnancy, the attractions of an old-fashioned scenic transcontinental journey with stopovers at Chicago and Denver along the way, and the economies of rail baggage rates were determinative. Just a few months earlier, *The Promised City: New York's Jews 1870–1914* had been published by the Harvard University Press and reviewed by John Higham in the Sunday *New York Times*. In short order my signature work was to establish my reputation as an American, a Jewish, and an immigration and ethnic historian, and not before long as an urban historian in an incipient subfield. But positions for one with my indeterminate unconventional profile were few for the expansive new priority years for history departments were only beginning to break. Yet I was very fortunate to find myself in California at a critical juncture in American higher education when the University of California was fully emerging as the nation's pacesetter and model "multiversity."

A second year appointment further enhanced my sense of the extraordinary dynamism of that new university colossus, a prototype of what Daniel Bell was soon to call, no less, "the paramount institution" in "post-industrial society" and of the free-flowing vitality and the incipient cosmopolitanism that was becoming emblematic of Los Angeles as it abruptly sallied forth as the "avant-garde showcase of a brave new world." When on a quick plane trip East in October 1962 upon the death of my father-in-law, I was handed a thinnish copy of the *New York Times*, its new Western Edition published in Los Angeles by the nation's foremost newspaper, I sensed that it signaled the coming to California before long of a higher national American journalism. Clearly New York's best was to prod the *Los Angeles Times* led by its remarkable young editor and former Olympic-class shot putter, Otis Chandler, to transform that dullish daily, noted primarily for its unrivalled advertising lineage, into a paramount force in national and international newspaperdom.

In a burst of rational exuberance and agog with the perception that he was living at the vortex of the classic epic of internal migration conventionally called the epic of the

West, this historian of immigration asked students in his senior research seminar in 1963 and 1964 to prepare family histories. Addressing the general theme, "Southern California: Frontier of the Mid-twentieth Century," the students were to give major attention to the human migration process itself, whether shaped by internal migration or emigration from abroad or both. In their papers that process was to be documented from a wide variety of select public and family records extending as far back as chance, time, and sheer ingenuity would permit. "California in the past year has become the first state in the nation," read the opening passage of the research assignment. "California has eclipsed New York, the nation's most populace state for one hundred and fifty years. This is a remarkable development. In 1850, California with 92,000 inhabitants, was equal in population to Delaware. In 1900 with 1,485,00 inhabitants, it was equal in population to Arkansas. In 1920, with 3,425,000 inhabitants, it was equal in population to Missouri. Today with a population of 17,500,00 inhabitants, it has no equal. And since 1950, seventy per cent of the 7,000,000 state population increase has come in southern California, where we live." In response, Jane Mitchell, an older student, responded with an incisive eloquence that this immigration historian had never encountered before: "Becoming an American is a spiritual journey, " she wrote.

Every group in America—Irish, Jewish, Southern, or Japanese—feels that its experiences as a group have set it off from the rest of America. We speak of first, second, and third generation Americans, but we never think of applying these terms to New Englanders or Southerners. My people have lived in the South for more than two hundred years. There were Mitchells in the House of Burgesses and the Revolutionary Conventions before the War with England. There were Elmores from Virginia who fought with Greene's men in South Carolina and saw Cornwallis surrender at Yorktown. Yet I am the first American in my family. It seems symbolic that all groups, no matter how different, have to go through the same experience to become Americans. We must love and hate our group, be ashamed and proud of our past; be nostalgic for home, yet strive to be free. Sometimes it seems Americans not only had to create America, they had to create Americans.

Changing one's location in space does not change one's identity; it is the experiences one finds there. For me California was a step into the world, and my experiences there have made me an American.

For us in 1964, our second step into the American world state of California was to take us from the prototypical dispersed futuristic suburb-metropolis of Los Angeles and UCLA to the incomparably appointed dense environs of legendary San Francisco and to San Francisco State. So different were these two urban centers and educational institutions in so many of their aspects, that we felt blessed to be able to entertain so unpremeditated an exposure to alternative possibilities for everyday living and for being able to experience so dramatically and immediately upon coming West two such strikingly contrasting vital California worlds.

For the Rischins, old San Francisco had the appeal almost of an urban idyll. Close by, the tone, texture, and tempo of life for us were set by the new campus site at the city's semi-rustic semi-marine southwestern edge. There the Metropolitan Life's almost new garden-tower apartment housing complex, a model elementary school, the plain-faced college without a solitary old building or a remotely inspired new one, and Stonestown, a state of the art shopping mall deliberately blended together in what seemed almost intimate adjacency to form an immediately welcoming if sanitized microcosm devised especially for new faculty. With a human geography facilitating both open access and assured fixity new residents were invited to settle among the spheres of the public, the private, and the in-between.

At State, my appointment on my own terms to teach American immigration and ethnic as well as urban history, perhaps one of the first historians in the country to teach both, guaranteed that we would remain Californians. Despite repeated efforts to persuade this historian to accept positions elsewhere, he knew that for his wife, three daughters, Sarah, Abigail, and Rebecca and himself, the resplendent totality that was San Francisco would allow us all to sustain the equilibrium that we cherished.

At a time of unprecedented growth in faculty hiring, State hummed with ambitious and gifted newcomers. The innovative School of Creative Arts, especially, already had acquired an enviable national reputation. With the School's renowned program, San Francisco State was attracting students and faculty from near and far, stirred by its disproportionately rich offerings in art, music, dance, theater, and film, as well as in the creative writing workshop opportunities in the School of Humanities. On being assigned an office directly opposite the writer Herb Wilner, I promptly learned that his eminent colleagues, the officemates, Kay Boyle and Wright Morris, represented "a unique event in the world's history of higher education. There was not a single college degree between them but between them were more than fifty books they have written." If our more conventional History Department could not quite point to such productivity, it too represented accomplishment of a high order. The business historian, Gerald T. White, author of the history of the Standard Oil Company of California, who was denied the right to publish his second volume; John L. Shover, the agricultural and labor historian; and the Iranian-born and Lebanon-educated Vartan Gregorian, who was about to complete his Stanford doctoral study of modern Afghanistan and was teaching Middle East and modern Russian history, would do honor to any university faculty in the world. If something of an open secret, our department also was gaining a reputation for attracting able graduate students and was to stand second only to UCLA and Berkeley in the number of graduate degrees in history granted in the state of California.

Above all, these were the embattled 1960s. Already greeting us from across the Bay was the burgeoning student Free Speech Movement, led by twenty-two-year-old Mario Savio, its most lyric voice, fresh from the civil rights Mississippi Freedom Summer Project. To Mario, Clark Kerr's Berkeley, just rated "the best balanced distinguished university" in the nation, a mite ahead of Harvard, had failed abysmally. No one was to assail the University more vehemently than did he. In "Operation of the Machine," his most electrifying jeremiad, Mario was to cry out: "There is a time when the operation of the machine becomes so odious," that it "makes you sick at heart, that you can't take part, can't even tacitly take part; and you've got to put your bodies upon the gears and upon the wheels, upon the levers . . . And you've got to make it stop!" Exactly twenty years later, to fulfill the American history requirement for graduation, Mario, about to receive his Bachelors' Degree in Physics at State with highest honors was to enroll in my class, his last, for credit/no-credit, remaining unrecognized by a new generation of undergraduates, as well as by a few re-entry older women students, even though his name was read on the roll-call and also appeared in the index of their history text.

By 1968 and 1969 when the race revolution and the Vietnam War had ripped our nation apart, San Francisco State, with its record four-month long student protest strike, led by the Black Students' Union and the Third-World Liberation Front and culminating in the founding of the first College of Ethnic Studies, along with the faculty union strike, would secure for State unequaled international notoriety. Fortunately, for a part of that time, my Fulbright-Hays appointment at the University of Uppsala liberated me and my family from sharing in the daily ordeal facing us right across the street from our home. Regarded as an expert on the subject, I was to keep David Riesman, that master scholar of "our secular cathedrals," as he referred to our universities, informed of doings across the way and subsequently at Uppsala, and there, also, to comfort visiting conscience-ridden American university administrators, driven to summon police to their campuses. By comparison, the Swedish student refrain that went "Ukaz, mukaz, and pukaz" (edict, medict, and pedict), which I heard on board a train on the way to lecture at Lund, mockingly calling for educational reform, from what I could make out, seemed utterly tame and remote from the American scene.

Then there were the daunting imperatives of the scholar-historian and none were more obsessive than mine. Some months before our departure for California, encouraged by my wife, I resolved to do a biography of Abraham Cahan (1860–1951), however mammoth in its parameters, no matter what. To do justice to that enigmatic American Jewish world figure, editor of the *Jewish Daily Forward*, now appearing as a weekly in three editions in his three languages—English, Yiddish, and Russian—and avatar of the golden era of Yiddish journalism, I was determined to move quickly before it was too late in order to track down the dispersed venerables who knew Cahan, even if I was not yet conversant with the best historical literature critical to asking the right questions, not to speak of Cahan's immense epistolary and newspaper record. Fortunately for me, on learning of my UCLA appointment, the astute labor economist, Theresa Wolfson, reminded me that in Los Angeles there lived the retired brilliant *Forward* labor journalist, Harry Lang (1888–1970), an all-round newspaper man and Cahan maven without peer. Clearly, California was for me, and Lang was to prove to be the very best and most ebullient of the scores of live witnesses whom I would interview in the years ahead. Immediately essential, too, and made feasible by a Guggenheim Fellowship in 1966 was a visit to Israel as well as to

London, Amsterdam, Vienna, Leningrad, Moscow, and, of course to Cahan's Vilna, where we might behold some of the stopping places in his life, examine special manuscript collections, and meet informants who might further assist us. In Jerusalem an interview with the President of Israel, Zalmon Shazar, proved especially rewarding, but a crippling all too familiar stomach misery prevented me from keeping my date with David Ben Gurion at Sdeh Boker in the Negev. Only years later, after taking part in a conference there, would I at last spend a Chanukah week tracking down key Hebrew passages in the monumental Ben Gurion diaries documenting his relations with Cahan.

Yet the Cahan biography, if that titanic figure and his world were to receive their just desserts, I knew, if not fully as yet, would call for prodigious research in non-English language and other recalcitrant often barely legible sources that would have to be identified, explored, decoded, translated and assimilated. In addition, crucial problems in American, Jewish, European, and Russian history, language, literature, and culture were still waiting to be addressed for the first time by a superbly equipped newer generation of scholars. The Cahan biography was not to be a quickie. Only dogged incrementalism would enable me to do credit to that big life.

In any case, the 1960s could not wait. Concurrent with my Cahan biography, it was incumbent upon me to pursue my interests in immigration, ethnic, and urban history with which my recognized scholarship self-evidently had been identified. With the passage of the Immigration and Nationality Act of 1965 immigration history was acquiring a new vitality, prompting a fresh generation of scholars to address every aspect of the subject. And it was my good fortune to be among them. In the years ahead as a member and officer of the new Immigration History Society, a founder of the *Journal of American Ethnic History,* a member of the advisory board of the Immigration History Research Center at the University of Minnesota, as well as of the Statue of Liberty-Ellis Island Centennial Commission, I was able to keep in close touch with developments in the whole field. In 1969, my Fulbright-Hays lectureship at the University of Uppsala also gave me the opportunity to participate in the ongoing research seminar of the Migration Research Project on Swedish immigration to the United States, focusing with matchless precision on the role of the country of origin rather than on the country of destination.

My own migration initially to southern California, as I have noted, had inspired me almost immediately to begin to investigate the western and the California migration experience, a subject that surprisingly, I was to learn, never quite had been addressed before. In the *Journal of American History* of June 1968, I attempted to do so in "Beyond the Great Divide: Immigration and the Last Frontier," followed in February of 1970 by a paper that I delivered at Stanford entitled, "Immigration, Migration, and Minorities in California," subsequently published in the *Pacific Historical Review* and in a volume of essays reappraising California history where comparisons between the California and New York experiences were particularly germane and reflected my bicoastal bent.

As a mainstream American historian who had infused the New York Jewish immigration story into the American canon, I also aspired to do likewise for the West and California. Yet, notably absent in California and the West until the 1960's was a Jewish museum, archive, and library dedicated to acquiring and preserving the California and western Jewish historical record and promoting its understanding and dissemination within a larger context. Thanks to our good timing, just shortly before we came to San Francisco, the Jewish educator, Seymour Fromer, had begun to put together the foundation blocks for what became the Judah L. Magnes Memorial Museum and its Western Jewish History Center, named after the West's first American-trained rabbi, who in 1925 became the first chancellor and later president of the Hebrew University in Jerusalem. At Fromer's invitation, I agreed to join him as Director of the WJHC and to accept the challenge for advancing our knowledge of American Jewish history in a new direction that would serve critical communal and intellectual needs. We succeeded. In the course of over three decades, with barely adequate resources, the Western Jewish History Center in conjunction with the Magnes Museum was to acquire a national and international reputation and to become America's first accredited Jewish museum. To this historian fell the task of overseeing the preparation of three California bibliographies by Sara Cogan and the WJHC *Guide to Archival and Oral History Collections* prepared by Ruth Rafael, advising oral historians and the authors of histories of Temple Emanu-El, the Concordia Argonaut Club, and many others, and organizing the first conferences on Western Jewish history in Berkeley and then in Denver, as well as the international symposium during the Lebanon war, commemorating the life and legacy of Judah Magnes, and editing the important books that emerged from these events. An invitation to edit The *Jewish Legacy and The German Conscience, Essays in Memory of Rabbi Joseph Asher*, led me to immerse myself in a project that proved profoundly preceptive for an American historian ever alert to critical European issues. Last but not least, Ava F. Kahn's *Jewish Voices of the California Gold Rush: A Documentary History, 1848–1880,* appearing in 2002 in the Wayne State University Press's American Jewish Civilization series, co-edited by Jonathan Sarna and myself, most fittingly commemorated the fortieth anniversary of the Magnes Museum and the WJHC.

In our time the epic of California Jews also took a new direction for the Rischins. The rise of the dissident movement in the 1960s and 1970s in the Soviet Union created a swelling new tide of Russian-Jewish immigrants. Reminiscent of the pioneer migrations of the 1880s to America and to Palestine, it swept its way into the center of our lives. To us, the initial momentum for our compelling interest in Russia went back to October 1957, when the Soviet Union launched the first artificial earth satellite, the redoubtable Sputnik I, to orbit the earth. Marking the advent of the Space Age, it also helped to launch America's modern Russian language programs. Two years later, newly married, the Rischins settled in Cambridge, Massachusetts, where lo and behold, one early September evening, Professor Leon Twarog, then of Boston University, standing at center stage in Harvard's formidable Sanders Theater, heartily greeted a class of a few hundred students newly enamoured with the Russian language. Looking out over the heads of the curious-faced learners before him, and repeatedly belting out "Chto eto?" (What is this?) "Eto stol!" (This is a table) Twarog proceeded to enjoin us all to belt it back to him. In one voice we roaringly obliged. Along with a great majority of that first night crowd, I regrettably was soon forced to drop out. But Ruth was converted. Thanks to Sputnik I and Professor Twarog, she was on her way to becoming a notable scholar of Russian language and literature with special attention to its Jewish dimension. Our subsequent move to Los Angeles and then most auspiciously to San Francisco was to enable her to enroll in the then unique Russian in Russian program directed by the gifted Yuri Sorokin, a former prisoner both of the Nazis and the Soviets, who during the strike turmoil in 1969 tragically succumbed to a heart attack at age fifty-four. After receiving her M.A. at SFSU and raising our three daughters, Ruth was to earn her doctorate in Slavic Languages and Literatures at the University of California at Berkeley.

Ruth's subsequent original work as a scholar and translator from the Russian was to range from the rendering into English under the literary pseudonym, Ranne Moab, of *Confession of a Jew,* Leonid Grossman's biography of the notorious Avram Kovner, the legendary atheist and epistolary companion of Fyodor Dostoevsky, to a series of seminal dialogical articles focusing on the late nineteenth- and twentieth-century entry of Jewish writers into Russian drama and literature. Among these have been studies of Vladimir Solovyov and Naum Naumov; Maxim Gorky, Chaim Nakhman Bialik and Semyon Dimanshtein; Ivan Bunin and Semyon Yushkevich. More precipitously, Ruth's meticulous scholarship thrust her into the public arena. When Russia appeared in San Francisco in the early 1970's as represented by the new Russian immigration, she was joyously welcomed into the free public American world of Russian culture. At Temple Emanu-El, at the College of Judaic Studies, and later at San Francisco State, she was to teach courses in Russian and Slavic literature on the Jew as Cosmopolitan, Jews in the Land of Solzhenitsyn, and Jews, Literature and the State, never offered before, to the very newest Americans as well as to old-line Californians.

With her linguistic, literary, and artistic talents, resonating to the challenge, she was emboldened to conceptualize, structure, and develop a series of unusual cultural events. Early on, the Magnes Museum exhibit, entitled "Twelve from the Soviet Underground," introduced the free world to the art of the Russian-Jewish dissident movement by displaying the paintings and sculptures of artists, who had clandestinely exhibited their works at an apartment in Leningrad in November 1975 and then in Moscow. Smuggled out of Russia by emissaries of the Bay Area Council on Soviet Jewry, a color film of the original exhibit was made in May 1976 into a full-size set of art reproductions for the Magnes exhibit. In this international exchange, Ruth served as interpreter, translator and cultural ambassador. The following year, enlisting the talents of Russian emigres in the Bay Area, Ruth introduced to California Jews a new awareness of the pioneering role played over a century earlier by the world-renowned Anton Rubinstein in the development of Russia's musical culture. In November 1976, "Anton Rubinstein Comes to America: A Russian-Jewish Festival," was held at Stanford's Dinkelspiel auditorium, generously supported by the Los Altos Jewish community. Over a decade later, an exhibit prepared by the Magnes Museum commemorated the sixtieth anniversary of the performance of Solomon An-sky's classic, *The Dybbuk,* by the Temple Players of Congregational Emanu-El, directed by Nahum Zemach, exiled founder of the famed Habima Hebrew Theater. For its landmark exhibit program, Ruth contributed succinct essays describing and analyzing the Temple Players' production, the hugely successful Pasadena Playhouse production that followed, the original Habima production in Moscow in 1922, *The Dybbuk* on the world stage, and the intense but doomed Soviet Jewish theater of the 1920s. In sum, Ruth had recovered for contemporaries diverse idioms in Russian-Jewish culture and projected them into the public domain. Somewhat similarly, in a curious turn, Los Angeles born Michael Tilson Thomas, the new composer-conductor of the San Francisco Symphony and grandson of Yiddish theater idols, Boris and Bessie Tomashefsky, has shown himself to be the most sophisticated musical educator among his contemporaries.

Tilson Thomas, by his own re-readings of works in the Russian and Russian-Jewish musical tradition, has brought among others the less well-known Jewish-themed compositions of Dmitry Shostakovich to the attention of a clamorous Bay Area public.

The story that I have sketched here of how I became a California Jew is a narrative intended to induce a new measure of equipoise in the writing of our history in the opening years of the twenty-first century. Hopefully, my retrospective and the other essays in this volume will help a new generation of historians of America's and California's now more than a million Jews to amplify and redefine those experiences along comparative lines that radiate outward to the larger world as well as inward to the Jewish one. In that way, surely, will we advance the capacity of the historian to construct an agenda appropriately designed to our precarious times.

—Moses Rischin

ACKNOWLEDGMENTS

California Jews represents the collective efforts of many individuals and organizations committed to telling the story of this state's Jewish communities. Phyllis Deutsch, history editor at Brandeis University Press, first proposed this project and has been its guiding light from beginning to end. Professor Jonathan Sarna, chair of Near Eastern and Judaic Studies at Brandeis University and series editor for this book, helped direct us on this scholarly journey just as he has been a source of constant support and encouragement to so many in the field of American Jewish history. The professional staff of the Autry Museum of Western Heritage in Los Angeles organized and sponsored a one-day symposium, "California Jews: From Generation to Generation," that brought together many of our contributing authors and allowed us to introduce this project to the larger community. We would like to extend particular thanks to Autry executive director and CEO John L. Gray and others of the Autry's wonderful staff including: James Nottage, Scott Kratz, Sandra Odor, Kathryn Radcliffe, Evelyn Davis, and Meredith Hackleman. Susan Morris, director of the Judah Magnes Museum in Berkeley, opened the museum and its archives to this project. Longtime Magnes community volunteer Mary Hoexter guided us through the archives of the Western Jewish History Center. Lawrence Baron, founder and president of the Western Jewish Studies Association, recommended the editors for this volume and continues to raise the profile of California Jewish history within the academy. Dr. Moses Rischin, professor of history at San Francisco State University and the dean of California Jewish history, took an interest in this project from the very start, offered his wisdom and experience on a variety of historical questions, and graciously agreed to author the foreword to this book.

We would also like to thank the American Jewish Historical Society for sponsoring our session on California Jews at the January 2002 American Historical Association national conference held in San Francisco. The staffs of many libraries and archival institutions helped us gather the photographs and images for this book. Susanne Kester, Marcie Kaufman, Kathryn Radcliffe, and Adele Burke offered assistance at the Skirball Cultural Center. Sally Hyam and Abigail Yasgur opened the archives of the Jewish Community Library of Los Angeles. Stephen Sass made the Southern California Jewish Historical Society's gems available. Gladys Sturman and David Epstein offered material from the archive of *Western States Jewish History*. Ben Ailes photographed the cover and many of the book's other images. We would also like to thank and acknowledge the following individuals and organizations for permitting us to reprint images from their collections: Bill Aron, Dion Aroner, Ruben Arquilevich, Beatrice Boykoff, Vivien Braly, Hasia Diner, Lenore and Malin Dollinger, Yehudit and Reuven Goldfarb, Howard Harawitz, Irene and Howard Levine, Carole Martin, Don May, Kathy and Bruce Pither, David and Michelle Plachte-Zuieback, Robert Saslow, Dorothy and Richard Schwartz, Ira M. Sheskin, the American Jewish Historical Society, Susan Snyder of the Bancroft Library, the Brandeis-Bardin Institute, Congregation Mishkon Tephilo, *The Daily Aztec* at San Diego State University, the Huntington Library, the Jewish Community Library of Los Angeles, the Jewish Historical Society of Los Angeles, Lipinsky Institute for Judaic Studies Archive, Rose Jewish Studies Reading Room, Love Library, San Diego State University, Sears Historical Library, Los Angeles County Museum of Natural History, Oakland History Room, Oakland Public Library, San Francisco History Center of the San Francisco Public Library, the Seaver Center for Western History Research, Aaron Kornblum of the Western Jewish History Center.

Gretchen Anderson, division dean of social sciences at Pasadena City College, arranged a leave of absence that enabled Marc Dollinger to focus on *California Jews*. Milton Brown, a New Yorker by birth and Californian by choice, helped place the experience of California Jews into a larger national perspective. Bruce Schulman offered his insightful perspective on various parts of the manuscript while Marci

Dollinger continues to make all of this possible. Most of all, Mordechai and Leah Dollinger deserve great praise for electing "the other side" and offering their descendants a bright future in the Golden State.

Ava F. Kahn also thanks her family for settling in California, the land where her father said, "orange juice fell from the sky." Both Ruth Haber and Mitchell Richman read drafts of parts of this manuscript, and their time, consideration, and comments made this a better work. Mitchell Richman, the relief historian, is especially singled out for his continual support. Phyllis Deutsch first proposed this project and has been its guiding light from beginning to end.

CALIFORNIA
JEWS

EMIGRATION TO
CALIFORNIA !

Do you want to go to California? If so, go and join the Company who intend going out the middle of March, or 1st of April next, under the charge of the California Emigration Society, in a first-rate Clipper Ship. The Society agreeing to find places for all those who wish it upon their arrival in San Francisco. The voyage will probably be made in a few months.— Price of passage will be in the vicinity of

ONE HUNDRED DOLLARS !
CHILDREN IN PROPORTION.

A number of families have already engaged passage. A suitable Female Nurse has been provided, who will take charge of Young Ladies and Children. Good Physicians, both male and female go in the Ship. It is hoped a large number of females will go, as Females are getting almost as good wages as males.

FEMALE NURSES get 25 dollars per week and board. SCHOOL TEACHERS 100 dollars per month. GARDNERS 60 dollars per month and board. LABORERS 4 to 5 dollars per day. BRICKLAYERS 6 dollars per day. HOUSEKEEPERS 40 dollars per month. FARMERS 5 dollars per day. SHOEMAKERS 4 dollars per day. Men and Women COOKS 40 to 60 dollars per month and board. MINERS are making from 3 to 12 dollars per day. FEMALE SERVANTS 30 to 50 dollars per month and board. Washing 3 dollars per dozen. MASONS 6 dollars per day. CARPENTERS 5 dollars per day. ENGINEERS 100 dollars per month, and as the quartz Crushing Mills are getting into operation all through the country, Engineers are very scarce. BLACKSMITHS 90 and 100 dollars per month and board.

The above prices are copied from late papers printed in San Francisco, which can be seen at my office. Having views of some 30 Cities throughout the State of California, I shall be happy to see all who will call at the office of the Society, 28 JOY'S BUILDING, WASHINGTON ST., BOSTON, and examine them. Parties residing out of the City, by enclosing a stamp and sending to the office, will receive a circular giving all the particulars of the voyage.

As Agents are wanted in every town and city of the New England States, Postmasters or Merchants acting as such will be allowed a certain commission on every person they get to join the Company. Good reference required. For further particulars correspond or call at the

SOCIETY'S OFFICE,
28 Joy's Building, Washington St., Boston, Mass.

Propeller Job Press, 142 Washington Street, Boston.

INTRODUCTION

"THE OTHER SIDE"

AVA F. KAHN & MARC DOLLINGER

In the late nineteenth century, a Jewish resident in the small Romanian town of Husch received a letter from a friend in America. "If you want to be poor all your life," the writer explained, "go to New York." Otherwise, he admonished, "go to the other side," meaning California, where the 1848 discovery of gold in the Sierra Nevada foothills unleashed a massive migration from Europe, Asia, and the eastern United States.

For many Jews, California became the Promised Land. Besides its potential wealth, California physically resembled the land promised to the children of Israel. This was clear to Jews of all political persuasions. Mordecai Noah believed that California was the biblical Ofir (spelled with an "f" instead of the traditional Ophir to demonstrate that all its letters were contained in "California").[1] Anti-Zionist California congressman Julius Kahn, who grew up among the gold miners in Mokelumne Hill, called San Francisco his Jerusalem.[2]

On the other side of the political spectrum, Henrietta Szold, in a 1915 article in the *American Jewish Year Book*, explained how some young Jewish colonists traveled to California to study agriculture. She believed that "their attainments can only benefit Palestine, seeing that California resembles it so closely in climate, geological formation, and agricultural problems and advantages, while surpassing it in prosperity and technical progress."[3] In reverse, just a few years later Justice Louis Brandeis called the land of Israel "a miniature California."[4] Californians also identified their landscape with the biblical land. The leadership of San Francisco's Reform Congregation Sherith Israel went even further, envisioning the Golden State as their new Promised Land. In 1904 they commissioned a stained glass window to adorn their new sanctuary at California and Webster streets. Recalling the classical biblical story of

Moses delivering the Ten Commandments to the Jews, the synagogue created a new image for posterity: Moses descending with the tablets from El Capitan into California's own Yosemite Valley. According to this new California-centered scripture, still on display in Sherith Israel's sanctuary (and on the cover of this book), the Israelites have been redeemed in North America's only remaining glaciated valley.

Since California became a state in 1850, its Jewish history has challenged conventional assumptions about American Jewish life. Jewish immigrants to California took advantage of its physical environment, ethnic diversity, and cultural distinctiveness to fashion a form of Judaism unique in the American experience. California's varied landscape offered its Jewish inhabitants access to impressive harbors, stunning beaches, fertile farmland, and magnificent deserts. On the social scene, California Jews enjoyed rapid integration into the mainstream and unprecedented access to political power a generation earlier than their New York co-religionists. They thrived in the multicultural mix, redefining the classic black-white racial binary by forging relations with Chinese Americans in San Francisco and Latinos in Los Angeles. In a state hailed as the nation's trendsetter, California Jews created new forms of Jewish expression and helped define popular interpretations for millions of Americans across the country.

California Jews represents a grand new historiography with essays composed by a new generation of scholars immersed in the academic work of the last thirty years and committed to bringing the California Jewish experience into the world of contemporary historical debate. While scores of books detail the New York Jewish immigrant experience, few address the important, though exceptional, experiences of Jews in California and the

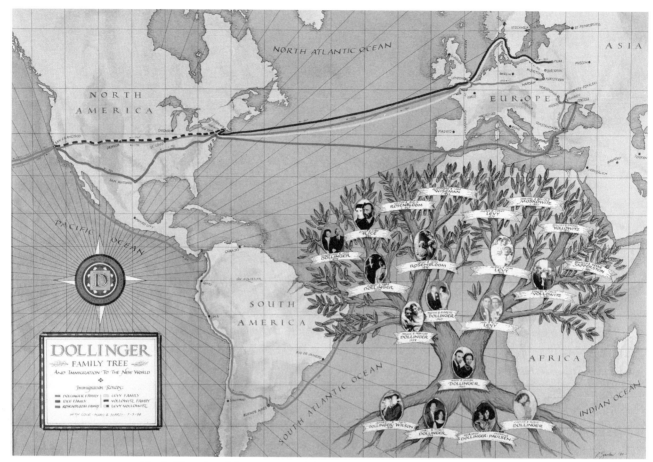

The Dollinger Family's Journey to California, by Robert Saslow (Also see color plate.)
Courtesy of Malin and Lenore Dollinger.

West. This volume is the first to look at a variety of topical issues that have shaped California Jewry over its one-hundred-and-fifty-year history. Its fifteen chapters explore the state's rich contributions to the American Jewish experience and push the scholarship forward.

The authors take advantage of the plentiful primary documents and images that have to this point remained largely hidden. They have sought out the records of California Jewish life in the Western Jewish History Center of the Judah Magnes Museum, the Bancroft Library, the American Jewish Archives, the American Jewish Historical Society, and in synagogue and private collections that describe letter-by-letter, newspaper-by-newspaper much of California's Jewish history. Besides these collections, the authors have taken advantage of the *Western States Jewish Historical Quarterly* (now *Western Jewish History*), which has since 1968 published primary documents and articles that have brought California and the Western Jewish history out of the archives and into the light.

California Jews is organized roughly by theme and chronology and is designed to introduce readers to a variety of interesting and important historical issues. This is as much a project of historiography as history. It includes, for the first time, the voices of women as well as men, the stories of large cities and small towns, and examples of California Jewish failures, not just success stories. We focused particular attention on once-taboo subjects, including Jewish reaction to Japanese incarceration and Latino-Jewish relations.

Our understanding of the California Jewish experience grows as much from our generational outlook as it does from our geographic perspective. Our historiographic perspective grows from our own experiences as California Jews. These have informed our acculturation to America and guided our movement into the organized Jewish world. As scholars of American Jewish history, we have struggled throughout our academic careers to understand the exceptionalism of our California Jewish lives and to educate our colleagues about how it contradicts many

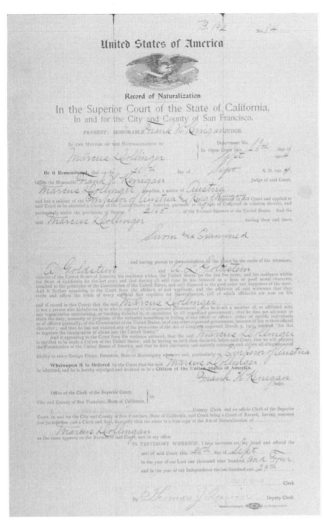

Naturalization Certificate of Marcus (Mordechai) Dollinger.
Courtesy of Marc Dollinger.

Dollinger family had journeyed through Chile and on to Panama where, joined now by their Chilean-born son Michael, they boarded the steamship *Colima* for the trip to San Francisco.

As part of their Americanization process, many Jewish immigrants elected to shed their old-world Yiddish names. In Albert Dollinger's diary he recounts how he and several of his friends Americanized their names:

> Just about this time an "epidemic" of "name changing" broke out among the boys in our neighborhood.
>
> One of the boys whose name was "Yonkella" something or other (I don't remember what his last name was). We called him Jake or Jakey, which he didn't mind too much, but his mother would always come out of the house, calling at the top of her voice, "Yonkella," which seemed to humiliate him very much.
>
> Most of us had similar troubles, not only with our parents calling us by our Yiddish names, but others in the neighborhood, making fun of us and trying to imitate, and finally ending up in calling us "Sheeny" or "Iky."
>
> A group of about ten of us boys got together and agreed that the only solution to the problem was not to fight them, as we had been doing, but to Americanize our names, thereby establishing our American rights.
>
> We were sitting on the front steps of Yonkella's house, so it was only natural for us to help him choose another name. One of the boys came up with a bright idea. Didn't the Swedes or Norwegians pronounce their "J"s as "Y"? Why not change "Yonkella" to "Johnkella"? "Wait a minute," one of the boys said, and taking a piece of paper, he wrote in large letters, "Johnkelly. How does that look and sound?"
>
> Poor Yonkella was so overcome he was almost in tears. He rushed in the house calling for his mother, and explained to her that all she had to do when calling his name was to say Johnkelly. She tried to repeat it as he dictated, and after the third or fourth try, a smile broke out on her face, and said, "Johnkelly, dat's a good Yiddish, American, Irisher name. My own Johhnykel." And henceforth, he was known to us as "John Kelly."

assumptions born of the New York City experience. Part of a new generation of scholars born and raised in the West, we are committed to defining the contours of California Jewish life and demonstrating how it enriches our understanding of the American Jewish experience as a whole.

It was Marc Dollinger's great-great grandfather Mordechai (later Marcus) Dollinger, an immigrant from Husch, Romania, who received the letter advising him to go to the "other side." Resisting the larger trend that brought most eastern European Jewish emigrants to New York City, Mordechai and his wife Leah headed first to Istanbul and then to Marseille, in the south of France. Boarding a ship for the New World, Mordechai, Leah, and their two young children Emma and Ya'akov (later Albert) sailed to South America, where the family briefly settled in Baron De Hirsch's New Palestine Colony in Argentina. By 1890, the

Just about this time an "epidemic" of "name changing" broke out among the boys in our neighborhood.

One of the boys whose name was "Yonkella" something or other (I don't remember what his last name was) we called him Jake or Jaky, which he didn't mind too much, but his mother would always come out of the house, calling at the top of her voice "Yonkella", which seemed to humilate him very much.

Most of us had similar troubles, not only with our parents calling us by our Yiddish names, but others in the neighbourhood, making fun of us and trying to imitate, and finally ending up in calling us "Sheeny" or "Iky".

A group of about ten of us boys got together, and agreed that the only solution to the problem, was not to fight them, as we had been doing, but to Americanize our names, thereby establishing our American rights.

We were sitting on the front steps of Yonkella's house, so it was only natural for us to help him choose another name. One of the boys came up with a bright idea. Didn't the Sweeds or Norwegian pronounce their "J" was "Y"? Why not change "You kella" to "John-kella"! "Wait a minute", one of the boys said, and taking a piece of paper, he wrote in large letters, "John Kelly". "How does that look and sound?"

Each of us, in turn read out loud "John Kelly" and we all liked what we saw and heard.

Poor Yankella was so overcome he was almost in tears. He rushed in the house calling for his mother, and explained to her that all she had to do when calling his name was to say Johnkelly. She tried to repeat it as he dictated, and after the 3rd or 4th try, a smile broke out on her face, and said "Johnkelly, dat's a good Yiddish, American, Irisher name. My own Johnykel." And henceforth he was known

to us as "John Kelly".

Then there was a boy whose name was Jake Silverman or Silverstein, I don't remember which. He became "John Silver".

There where quite a few Rosenbergs, and not all of them related. One became Joe Ross. 2 brothers Rosenberg, one liked Rosen, and the other liked Berg. Out of 3 Rosenbergs we had 3 others, Ross, Rosen, and Berg.

Changing our first names was a problem, as we all wanted to retain our first initial. Oscar Goldblatt became "Oliver" Goldblatt. Meyer Goldfarb, became Meyer Gold, Solomon something or other, became Sam. Moisha Hyman became "Mush". Some of the fellows liked to add middle names. Henry Goldstein became "Harry Gordon Goldstein". His brother Meyer, liked "Mark Goldie". Morris Edlin, was henceforth known as "Edward M. Edlin". I don't remember all of the name changing that went on. Some of the fellows had parental trouble about their own names and had to drop them. I did not have that kind of trouble, for the simple reason, that I did

I had no problems. Emma, who had changed her own name, some years before, from "Boba" to Emma, and Joe, where the only ones of the family who knew it. I, as well as some of the other boys, practiced on writing new Signatures. I had half a dozen which I liked. here are a few A.D., A.J. Dollinger, Albert Dollinger, Albert J. Dollinger.

We corresponded almost weekly, so as to get used to writing our new names at the bottom of the letter. I began receiving all kinds of mail, as I had answered a few little ads in magazines

Diary entry from Albert Dollinger, circa 1895.
Courtesy of Marc Dollinger.

Wedding photograph of Albert and Sara Dollinger,
December 31, 1905, San Francisco.
Courtesy of Marc Dollinger.

Then there was a boy whose name was Jake Silverman or Silverstein, I don't remember which. He became "John Silver."

There were quite a few Rosenbergs and not all of them related. One became Joe Ross. Two brothers Rosenberg, one liked Rosen, and the other liked Berg. Out of three Rosenbergs we had three others, Rose, Rosen, and Berg.

Changing our first names was a problem as we all wanted to retain our first initials. Older Goldblatt became "Oliver" Goldblatt. Meyer Goldfarb became Meyer Gold. Solomon something or other, became Sam. Moisha Hyman became "Mush." Some of the

fellows liked to add middle names. Henry Goldstein became "Harry Gordan Goldstein." His brother Meyer liked "Mark Goldie." Morris Edlin, was henceforth known as "Edward M. Edlin." I don't remember all of the name changing that went on. Some of the fellows had parental trouble about their new names and had to drop them. I did not have that kind of trouble, for the simple reason that I did tell my parents. I had finally been able to teach my mother to call me "Abe" instead of "Alter" so I wasn't taking any chances. All my mail came addressed to "A. J. Dollinger." So when I changed my name to "Albert Jerome Dollinger," I had no problems. Emma, who had changed her own name some years before, from "Boba" to Emma, and Joe, were the only ones of the family who knew it. I, as well as some of the other boys, practiced on writing new signatures. I had half a dozen which I liked. Here are a few: [signatures followed, see page 5, lower right]

We corresponded almost weekly, so as to get used to writing our new names at the bottom of the letter. I began receiving all kinds of mail, as I had answered a few little ads in magazines.

The family's maternal branches mirrored the settlement patterns of many California Jews. Isaac and Leah Rosenbloom moved first from Poland to London before deciding on a life in San Francisco. In 1907, following the traditional route across the north Atlantic to Ellis Island in New York Harbor, the Rosenblooms immediately boarded a train for the cross-country trek to California. Emile and Toba Raitsits (later Rice) sailed from Europe to Galveston, Texas, in 1877, some thirty years before Jacob Schiff would inaugurate his famous, "Galveston Project" to encourage Jewish immigrant settlement in the West. The family's arrival in San Francisco turned tragic in 1911 when Emile became one of the city's first drunk-driving fatalities.

Ava Kahn's family also barely set foot on New York soil. Her maternal grandmother Rose Schneider, born in the village of Rovno (Wolyn), left Russia as a small child and traveled with her parents, Fannie and Hyman, to Chicago in 1902. There Kahn's maternal great-grandparents joined the thriving Jewish community on the southside. Chicago would become the home of her father's family, which also had roots in eastern Europe. Her father's grandparents settled in South Chicago where Moses Aaron Kahn, Ava Kahn's great-grandfather, became the perennial

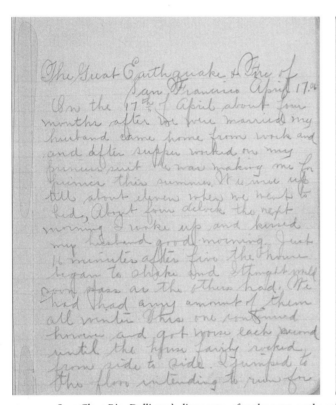

*Business card for Bert (Albert Jerome) Dollinger's acting school,
San Francisco, 1906–1907. Jewish immigrants and their children
learned Shakespeare, acting, and "voice culture" in order to show
their integration into California and American cultural life.
Courtesy of Marc Dollinger.*

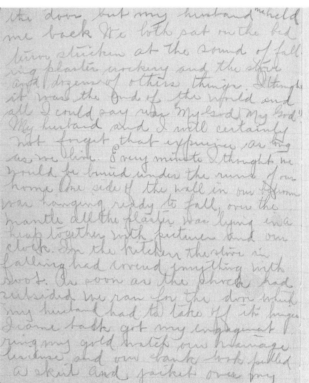

Sara Clara Rice Dollinger's diary entry after the great earthquake and fire, San Francisco, 1906. Courtesy of Marc Dollinger.

The Great Earthquake and Fire of San Francisco April 17, 06: On the 17th of April about four months after we were married my husband came home from work and after supper worked on my princess suit he was making me for picnics this summer. We were up till about eleven when we went to bed. About four o'clock the next morning, I woke up and kissed my husband good morning. Just 16 minutes after five the house began to shake and I thought [we] would soon pass as the others had. We had had many amount of them [earthquakes] all winter. This one continued however and got worse each second until the house fairly rocked from side to side. I jumped to the floor intending to run for the door but my husband held me back. We both sat on the bed, terror stricken at the sound of falling plaster, crockery, and the stove and dozens of other things. I thought it was the end of the world and all I could say was "My God My God." My husband and I will certainly not forget that experience, as long as we live. Every minute I thought we would be buried under the ruins of our home. One side of the wall in our bedroom was hanging ready to fall, over the mantle all the plaster was lying in a heap together with pictures and our clock. In the kitchen, the stove in falling had covered everything with soot. As soon as the shock had subsided, we ran for the door which my husband had to take off its hinges. I came back, got my engagement ring, my gold watch, our marriage license, and our bank book, pulled a skirt and jacket over my night dress and we hurried across the street. Sara Clara Rice.

Emile Rice, San Francisco, circa 1900.
Courtesy of Malin and Lenore Dollinger.

Toba Rice, San Francisco, circa 1900.
Courtesy of Malin and Lenore Dollinger.

president of the Orthodox Agudath Achim-Bikur Cho-lim synagogue.

Kahn's parents did not meet in Chicago, however, but in Los Angeles, where her father, along with thousands of other migrants came to California in search of the post–World War II prosperity. The Jewish population of Los Angeles grew by in leaps and bounds after the war, more than doubling its prewar numbers.[5] Ava's maternal aunt and uncle also joined this migration. Her mother and father first met when Beatrice came west to visit her newly married twin-sister in California. After their November nuptials, Kahn's parents, like so many other former midwesterners, joined with native Californians in attending California's most widely known winter event, the Tournament of Roses Parade. Kahn grew up as a Californian, "back East" was Chicago, while New York held no family memories at all. Both Dollinger and Kahn, fifth- and second-generation Californians' history mirrors that of many other Californians as well as of many other California Jews.

The thirty-first state emerged as one of the nation's most diverse, known for its history of immigrants and migrants. California's indigenous peoples were forced off their lands first by Spanish settlers, then by the arrival of Chinese, South American, and European gold miners. With the strength of Catholic missionaries throughout the state, eastern-style Protestantism did not dominate California, permitting a more rapid and inclusive immigrant acculturation process.

Moses Aaron Kahn, circa 1900
Courtesy of Ava F. Kahn and Dorothy and Richard Schwartz

Wedding of Ava's maternal grandparents, Rose Schneider and Leo Mondschein, circa 1920. From left to right: Rose and Leo Mondschein, Charlie Mondschein, Lil Schneider (flower girl), Anne Schneider (maid of honor).
Courtesy of Ava F. Kahn.

Bea and Marvin Kahn, 1948.
Courtesy of Ava F. Kahn.

Kahn with parents and grandparents.
Courtesy of Ava F. Kahn.

Ketubah created by Ava F. Kahn and Mitchell A. Richman for their Berkeley wedding, featuring image of Lake Tahoe. Courtesy of Ava F. Kahn and Mitchell A. Richman. (See also color plate.)

California Jews struggled with many of the same issues faced by Jews in other parts of the country. Working class, Orthodox immigrant Jews wrestled with their wealthier Reform-movement German American co-religionists for control of civic life. Prejudice and discrimination against Chinese and Japanese Americans, while not directed at the Jewish community, still presented serious challenges to a community committed to equal protection. The process of Americanization, while defined in a different geographic context, still drove the issues of intermarriage, assimilation, and identity to the forefront of Jewish communal debate.

But the diversity of California's population helped define both the place of California's Jews in society and the development of California Judaism. California's Jewish history starts with the gold rush, which brought adventure seekers, both Jews and Gentiles, from every part of the world. With such a rapid growth rate characterized by the intermingling of many different national groups, Jews integrated quickly into the ever-changing culture. California's unique history encouraged Jews to construct ethnic identities that differed from many of their co-religionists from the East, South, and Midwest. While first- and second-generation eastern European immigrants struggled to gain a foothold in New York City life, economic success came to many Jews in the burgeoning cities of gold rush California as they opened stores to outfit the hopeful miners. Jewish immigrants to the eastern seaboard arrived in the United States familiar only with their own customs, while many California Jewish arrivals, having already spent time away from their native lands, were more cosmopolitan by the time they reached the West Coast. Some had lived briefly in South America, England, or in the eastern or midwestern United States before settling near the Pacific Coast. Many had already become accustomed to other cultures, the English language, and to

AVA F. KAHN AND MARC DOLLINGER

Personal account of the 1899 California-Stanford Football "Big Game." For many immigrants, spectator sports emerged as an important agent of American acculturation. In the San Francisco Bay Area, the annual college football rivalry between the University of California, Berkeley, and Stanford University provided Jewish immigrants an avenue to the social mainstream. This selection, from a turn-of-the-century handwritten monthly journal, Equality, written by a group of Jewish immigrant boys, captures one of the first Cal-Stanford "Big Games." Courtesy of Marc Dollinger.

American life, so that when they settled in California they integrated much more quickly, enjoyed the privileges of civil equality, and built communities that incorporated their California surroundings with Jewish traditions.

From the nineteenth century when the gold rush drew Jews West, to the twentieth century when the climate brought Jews to the Golden State for their health and movie production, California's physical environment has helped determine the prosperity of California Jewry. Life was shaped by the abundant natural resources of the state, its ideal climate, and picture-postcard mountains, deserts, and seas. While immigrants headed to New York and the eastern seaboard often heard stories of American streets paved with gold, some new arrivals to California came to search for the elusive precious metal itself.

California's physical environment, whether in Yosemite Valley, San Francisco Bay, or the desert climate of southern California, has become powerful in all interpretations of California history. In environmental terms, gold produced the first relationship that new immigrants had with the land in what historian Patricia Nelson Limerick calls an "intersection of ethnic diversity with property allocation."[6] California's wealth came from its natural minerals, and from a climate that was a boon to agriculture and tourism alike. For the state's Jewish population, the landscape helped to form a new ethnic and social identity.

When Jews first arrived during the gold rush, they began to establish their own and specially California Jewish culture.[7] Jews arriving in San Francisco experienced little antisemitism and enjoyed almost immediate access to power. Southern California Jews, though few, helped establish the motion picture industry, one of the greatest and longest-lasting Jewish contributions to the American cultural scene. The cultural environment encouraged California Jews to follow paths distinct from their eastern coreligionists, defying many assumptions about the American Jewish experience. Jews in California tended to vote Republican while East Coast Jews were Democrats. They formed the nucleus of the American Council for Judaism, the nation's leading anti-Zionist Jewish group. Their material culture, whether represented in synagogue architecture, ritual objects, or artistic representations, often reflected the California environment and its more permissive popular culture. Interfaith dialogues tended to join Catholics and Jews more often. While many Jewish immigration stories describe the interaction of the Jewish settler with an already established city or town, California

Jews often migrated during a community's early settlement and were not seen as interlopers. Indeed, as the historian John Higham has noted, pioneer status created opportunities for Jews to develop significant institutions and relationships with other ethnic groups. All were newcomers.

The intersection of California and Jewish history forged a distinctive California Judaism unparalleled in other parts of the nation. Building upon the state's diversity, unique physical attributes, and cultural openness, California Jews positioned themselves as creators of both secular and religious institutions. They built cities and towns and helped shape some of the most important social innovations in American life. This book chronicles their journey.

According to sociologist and demographer Bruce Phillips, California Jews, though few, were integral to the development of the American West. For Phillips, whose provocative observations form this book's first chapter, the California Jewish experience was "not only geographically distinct, but in many ways entirely different from the Jewish experience in the Northeast and Midwest." Analyzing synagogue affiliation rates, residency patterns, communal ties, and intermarriage levels, Phillips demonstrates the particular and sometimes troubling impact of California's diverse climate on its Jewish residents.

The second chapter of *California Jews* features a new interpretation of the gold rush. As chapter author Ava Kahn points out, "Jewish men and women living in the small villages and the large cities of the Americas, Europe, and even Australia, caught gold fever." This was the beginning of California's Jewish diversity that shaped Jewish life in the cities of California as well as in the state as a whole. With "Joining the Rush," Kahn demonstrates how Judaism persisted during the first chaotic years of the gold rush and how the men and women who kept it alive became part of the foundation of the state's Jewish community. During this "time of adventure and turmoil in places where many would surmise that Jews would quickly assimilate and Judaism would not survive, both often thrived." As Kahn explains, "By the 1870s, San Francisco's Jewish population had reached sixteen thousand. . . . The rush for gold brought Jews to the West, and whether they first made their homes in the mining communities or in the port city itself, all added to the multi-textured Jewish community." The first settlers built a "substantial community structure," becoming "the progenitors of today's diverse Jewish and secular communities."

Not only did California Jews create communities for generations to come, they built impressive buildings to publicly announce their presence. For American Jewish historian David Kaufman, synagogue architecture reveals important, and often overlooked, insights into the diverse lives, beliefs, and acculturation patterns of California Jews. In both Los Angeles and San Francisco, nineteenth- and early twentieth-century Jews focused their religious identities around their local synagogues, which often became splendid architectural wonders. "Though little supported by their religious tradition, and often derided as exhibiting an "edifice complex," Kaufman writes, "American Jews nonetheless attach great importance to the building of synagogues." Architects, working with rabbis and lay leaders, designed and built houses of worship that reflected the unique cultural expressions of California Jews. For Kaufman, styles of synagogue construction revealed "the pioneering spirit of the forty-niners, the enterprising spirit of urban commerce, the democratizing spirit of American citizenship, the liberalizing spirit of Reform Judaism, and the civilizing spirit of Jewish tradition."

As California's diverse population inspired Jews to build coalitions with a variety of ethnic and religious groups, and influenced by the state's strong Hispanic presence, some of California's early Jews learned Spanish before English. In southern California, Latinos proved the most numerous and historically important ethnic group, encouraging early Los Angeles Jewish leaders to forge political alliances that would prove critical in a number of local public policy decisions. Significantly, Angelenos called their city's first rabbi "Padre."

As Steven Windmueller explains in chapter 4, "Through the Lens of Latino-Jewish Relations," Jewish political activism in L.A. challenges many commonly held assumptions about inter-ethnic relations. With a population reaching 40 percent by 2000, Latinos in Los Angeles have emerged as the city's largest and most important voting bloc. Faced with the emergence of these new political leaders, the rise of identity politics, and the influence of church-based social ideas, L.A. Jews have realized that their future is inextricably linked to California's original settlers.

Calling on his career in both Jewish communal leadership and academic life, Windmueller points to the important changes in the urban centers of Los Angeles and the nation. While Jews traditionally have gained power in urban politics through direct engagement, Los Angeles Jews' political activism has been by more indirect means. With the growth of both Orthodox Judaism and Jewish Republicanism in southern California, Windmueller notes, the city's Jews will also have to renegotiate their timeworn assumptions about the primacy of secular Jewish liberalism. If Los Angeles will be seen as the new archetype of inter-ethnic relations, then perhaps, as Windmueller concludes, we are "witnessing in Los Angeles, and maybe elsewhere in this nation, a Jewish disengagment from its historic legacy" as urban America's leading catalyst for social reform.

These changes can also be witnessed in settlement patterns. Geography proved critical for Jews who integrated the beaches of southern California, the geologic finds of the Sierra foothills, and the natural harbors of San Francisco into their religious identities. In chapter 5, religious studies professor Amy Hill Shevitz locates many important and unique manifestations of California Jewish culture in her study of the Golden State's once-canaled city, "Jewish Space and Place in Venice." Focusing on California's unique cultural history, Shevitz examines the Venetians' propensity for constant renewal and reinvention. In a city "where geography and culture, California place and the California state of mind, converge in special ways," three generations of Jews mediated the influences of a beach locale, the often carnivalesque atmosphere of the city's boardwalk, and their own religious and spiritual needs. What began as a novel experiment for a small group of eastern European immigrant Jews in turn-of-the-century Venice, California, evolved into a thriving center for Jewish community life that counted parishioners from much of Los Angeles' west side. Venice, Shevitz tells us, "demonstrates the ability of place—even an idiosyncratic and seemingly alien style of place—to refresh communal and individual Jewish lives."

California's allure as the New Zion reached beyond America's borders to the Jewish people's national homeland. As professor of Jewish education Na'ama Sabar learned, many former kibbutzniks left Israel to venture to Los Angeles in search of a better life. "I was astounded to discover," Sabar explains in chapter 6, "how many Israelis who had been born and raised on a kibbutz now chose to live in L.A." In "Kibbutz San Fernando," Sabar reports on conversations she conducted with twenty-six former kibbutzniks as she examined why her subjects left kibbutz, what they thought of life in California, and whether they entertained thoughts of returning to their native land.

Sabar observes powerful connections between the California Israelis and the lessons they learned during their years on kibbutz. Once they arrived in southern California, the new immigrants sought out fellow former kibbutzniks and created a powerful subculture. With poor English skills, the need for transportation and a job, as well as the anxiety that typically accompanies such a long-distance move, the new arrivals emulated many of the kibbutz' communitarian values by coming to the aid of their fellow ex-patriots. With little formal education and unbearable work hours, many of Sabar's interviewees longed for the socialist lifestyle of their youth. Their immigrant experience, Sabar notes, proved even more difficult for women, who almost unanimously lobbied their husbands or boyfriends to return to Israel. After examining these former kibbutzniks, Sabar concludes, "the inescapable conclusion is that they are emigrants rather than immigrants." While they left Israel and the kibbutz, they "have not really arrived in America. Their discourse is that of sojourners, their language is Hebrew, and their dreams are of Israel."

Perhaps equally separate from the general Jewish community were the moguls of Hollywood. According to Felicia Herman, traditional analyses of Jewish Hollywood overlooked the critical role played by the city's Jewish organizational leadership. "The story of the Jewish moguls," Herman writes in chapter 8, "is not the only story of Jews and the motion picture industry." In "Jewish Leaders and the Motion Picture Industry," Herman argues that "a host of Jewish communal leaders were active within the industry" but chose to act with relative anonymity. At a time when antisemites used Jewish influence in Hollywood to advance their larger claims of a Jewish cabal, Jewish leaders elected to keep their dealings with the industry quiet and out of the public eye."

With domestic antisemitism skyrocketing in the late 1930s, pressure built on President Roosevelt to join the European war against Hitler. Los Angeles Jewish organizational leaders, hobbled by fear and anxiety, urged the Hollywood moguls to accept Jewish communal oversight during the production of films about Jews or Jewish themes. Officials from the Anti-Defamation League, the National Community Relations Advisory Council, and the Los Angeles chapter of the Jewish Community Committee joined together and became, in Herman's estimation, the most influential Jewish communal voices within the film industry for decades. Quite apart from the high-profile work of Jewish movie executives, the quiet efforts of Jewish organizational leaders helped protect the Jewish public image by preventing the many types of film content that might reflect negatively upon Jews.

Historian Ellen Eisenberg carries Herman's discussion of antisemitism and California culture through the war years. For Eisenberg, the need to defend Jews against antisemitism at home and abroad complicated efforts to protect U.S. citizens of Japanese descent from President Roosevelt's infamous Executive Order 9066, which led to the exclusion of Japanese Americans from the West Coast defense zone and to their incarceration in camps in the interior. California Jewish reactions to the internment of Japanese Americans inspired heartbreaking dilemmas for Jews: how could American Jews reach out to their co-religionists facing persecution in Europe and not stand against the denial of constitutional rights to their fellow citizens at home?

In research that began in her home state of Oregon and continues now to the south, Eisenberg concludes that the "California Jewish community was notably silent." While Eisenberg is careful to note that California Jewish organizations and leaders did not endorse incarceration, they still "failed to defend Japanese Americans." At a time when the U.S. Supreme Court and even the national leadership of the American Civil Liberties Union (ACLU) supported mass internment, American Jews might be forgiven for their indifference. Yet, as Eisenberg concludes, "faced with a conflict between fighting prejudice and supporting the war effort that was so critical to the very survival of the European brethren, the California Jewish community deemed the war effort a higher priority."

California's postwar climate inspired Jewish leaders to redefine conventional notions of inter-ethnic relations and local political culture. While the rise and fall of the black-Jewish alliance dominates most historical writing on Jewish involvement in the civil rights movement, Professor of history William Issel discovered powerful connections between Bay Area Jews and Catholics. In chapter 10, "Jews and Catholics against Prejudice," Issel demonstrates how the city's tradition of religious tolerance played a role in shaping the nature of Jewish and Catholic participation in the civil rights movement in the 1940s and 1950s.

While Issel acknowledges that early postwar San Franciscans did not welcome racial diversity, gays, lesbians, or political radicals any more than did the rest of urban America, he did discover a well-deserved civic reputation for religious tolerance. Catholic and Jewish leaders joined in a centrist liberal critique of Bay Area life that led them to join forces on a host of civil rights issues. Issel cautions against reading these historical developments as a narrative of the golden age of interfaith cooperation, but still concludes that the Catholic-Jewish union prepared the ground for an expansion of interfaith cooperation, as well as for further legislative victories at the state and local levels during the 1960s.

These interreligious and interethnic coalitions throughout the state of California helped Jews forge a distinctive culture founded upon the state's singular history. In San Diego, Jewish residents enjoyed a dramatic population explosion in the postwar years and the concomitant growth of its local university's Jewish studies program. For Jewish studies professor Lawrence Baron, those impressive demographic changes challenged the community's Jews and its local state-run university to reinvent themselves. The history of San Diego State University (SDSU), Baron discovered, paralleled the most important developments in the larger history of Jews in California and distinguished his hometown in several important ways.

In its early years, San Diego offered Jewish women access to higher education and careers in teaching. By the early twentieth century, SDSU embraced an Orthodox Jewish professor and, with a few exceptions within the fraternity and sorority system, extended Jewish students equal opportunity free of antisemitic discrimination. In the postwar years, the GI Bill sent thousands of new students to college and inspired a massive surge of Jewish enrollment at SDSU and throughout the nation. For Baron and many other Jewish studies professors, the challenge of such dramatic growth inspired development of impressive new campus-based Jewish education and political activism. Chapter 11, "From Minyan to Matriculation," surveys Jewish life in San Diego from its nineteenth-century origins to contemporary on-campus debates over Jewish studies, multiculturalism, and the Jewish community's "town-gown" relationship.

The relationship between the university and the Jewish community was not a new one, however, for in Berkeley, where the first campus of the University of California was built, the symbiotic relationship was longstanding. Glenna Matthews and Ava F. Kahn suggest in chapter 12, "120 Years of Women's Activism," "much of the success of Jewish women in California is due to the state itself," especially the opportunity to attend the University of California at Berkeley tuition-free. As early as the 1920s, Florence Prag Kahn (not related to the author) demonstrated the strength and possibilities for Jewish women in California politics. According to Matthews and Kahn, many Jewish women attribute their political activities to their "Jewish upbringing," and believe that their political actions were influenced by their "ethnic identity." "Many felt the need to work for a better society." The postwar years marked the beginning of a generations-long California Jewish focus on women in politics. The election of two California Jewish women to the United States Senate in 1992 capped an impressive "year of the woman" in American national politics. For Jewish Californians, though, high political office was not the only field of innovation.

Marc Dollinger's "The Counterculture" surveys the creation of a distinctive California Jewish political culture during the pivotal years of American social protest. Expanding his earlier work on American Jewish liberalism, Dollinger traces the journey of young California Jews as they became disenchanted with secular protest and turned inward toward Jewish-centered issues. Reared during the civil rights struggles of the 1950s and early 1960s, young California Jewish activists defied conventional assumptions about wealth, education, and political persuasion, critiquing the very system that had so recently welcomed them into the all-American middle-class suburbs. Some protested the hearings of the House UnAmerican Activities Committee when it met in San Francisco while others marched with local hotel workers on strike for better wages. When students launched the Free Speech Movement (FSM) and the anti-war movement that followed, Jews joined with impressive numbers.

By the late 1960s, though, California Jews retreated from many of the social protest movements they helped found and turned instead to activism within the Jewish communal world. With the rise of black nationalism and Israel's victory in the 1967 Six Day War, Jewish protesters faced an impossible dilemma: how to continue their social reform activism among a community of activists who had espoused both anti-Israel and antisemitic sentiments. Disillusioned with secular politics, Dollinger concludes, many Jews applied the lessons of the California counterculture to Jewish religious life. Women pressed for ordination in the rabbinate, *havurot* (small group worship) grew in response to the perceived indifference of California synagogues, and a new generation of theologians reinterpreted Jewish understandings of a host of social issues.

Many of these California educational, theological, and especially geographical, influences came together in the founding of Brandeis Camp Institute by Shlomo Bardin in 1947. Inspired by the Danish folkschool movement, the American summer camp, and the Israeli kibbutz, Bardin, as instructed by Justice Louis Brandeis, built a camp–learning center where American Jews could learn about their culture in a nondenominational environment. In "Shlomo Bardin's 'Eretz' Brandeis," educator Bruce Powell argues that Bardin chose southern California because he saw in the people of Los Angeles in 1947 "a willingness to pioneer . . . unlike the deeply rooted East Coast Jews." Bardin found people in L.A. "willing to take a chance, to build, to dream, to plant their own unique roots." A land of sunshine for year-round programs, a supportive community, and a geography that physically resembled Israel, the Promised Land, provided Bardin a permanent home for his new educational endeavor.

This volume is further enhanced by the addition of two photo essays that capture different styles of California Jewish art. As a form of expression rooted in the distinctive visual elements of California Jewish life, these images dramatically convey the depth and meaning of California Judaism. Chapter 7, "Ketubot of the Golden State," features the original wedding contracts of artist Robert Saslow. For prospective brides and grooms, the landscape,

symbols, and sites of California often figure prominently in their ketubah designs. Seven of his most revealing California ketubot are featured here. For Michelle and David Plachte-Zuieback, Jewish stained glass artists from northern California, art has imitated life. A survey of their twenty-year artistic career reveals larger trends in California Jewish life. Born of the secular counterculture, the Plachte-Zuiebacks eventually returned to more active involvement in the Jewish community. A photo essay featuring eight of their windows chronicles that journey.

NOTES

1. Jonathan D. Sarna, *Jacksonian Jew: The Two Worlds of Mordecai Noah* (New York: Holmes & Meier, 1981), 137.

2. *Emanu-El*, San Francisco. February 14, 1919, pp. 10–11.

3. Henrietta Szold, "Recent Jewish Progress in Palestine," *American Jewish Year Book 1915–16*, p. 81

4. Jonathan D. Sarna, "The Greatest Jew in the World since Jesus Christ: The Jewish Legacy of Louis D. Brandeis," *American Jewish History* (spring–summer 1994), p. 360.

5. Deborah Dash Moore, *To the Golden Cities* (New York: The Free Press, 1994) 23.

6. Patricia Nelson Limerick, *The Legacy of Conquest* (New York: W.W. Norton, 1987), 27.

7. For primary accounts of this period see Ava F. Kahn, *Jewish Voices of the California Gold Rush: A Documentary History 1849–1880s* (Detroit: Wayne State University Press, 2002).

CHAPTER I

THE CHALLENGE OF
FAMILY, IDENTITY, AND AFFILIATIONS

BRUCE PHILLIPS

Introduction

Though few in number, Jews were integral to the development of the American West. Their acceptance by fellow citizens was a result of the Jewish contribution to the development of their communities and of the ethos of individualism that grew out of life on the sparsely settled frontier. More than a century later differences persist between the West and the other regions of the United States for Jews and the general population alike. For Jews, as for non-Jews, there are differences in the affiliation patterns, religious identification, and marriage between the West and the other regions. Among Jews, some of these patterns applied mostly to California, while others applied mostly to the other western states, and still others were equally characteristic of both California and the rest of the western states. Patterns that distinguish California Jews and Jews in other western states from the rest of American Jewry are reflections of the larger culture of the West. Similarities between California and the rest of American Jewry not shared by Jews in other western states signal a new phase for California Jews: the maturation of Jewish communities such as San Francisco and Los Angeles.

California Jews share with other western states Jews a regional history that is not only geographically distinct, but in many ways entirely different from the Jewish experience in the Northeast and Midwest. At the end of the twentieth century, the Jewish population of the West differed demographically from the rest of American Jewry. In this essay I present a sociological history that stresses how the Jewish experience in the western states has been qualitatively different from that in the Northeast and Midwest. Jews in the East were numerous, residentially concentrated, and socially separate from the majority population.

By contrast, Jews in the West were small in number, geographically dispersed, and extensively integrated within the communities around them. This essay examines the demographic differences between California Jews, other western states Jews, and Jews in the Northeast, Midwest, and South and considers possible connections between the Jewish historical experience in the West and contemporary patterns of Jewish communal involvements in that region in general, and California in particular.

The Jewish Economic Role in California

The Los Angeles city directory of 1880 listed 103 Jewish businesses. By 1890, 80 percent of Jews were in white-collar occupations, more than double the percentage of non-Jews. Jews were heavily clustered in dry goods and the food, beverage, and tobacco trades. Of the forty-four Jews holding clerical and sales positions, thirty-eight worked in stores. Los Angeles Jews dominated those areas of trade in which they engaged. Jews owned five of Los Angeles' seven tobacco stores, and three of the four booksellers and stationers were Jews. The owners of the city's only house furnishings and crockery stores were Jews as well.

As proprietors and merchants, Jews were important community builders throughout California in three highly visible ways. First, they were a stabilizing influence both by their persistence and by their economic activity. The kinds of enterprises in which they were engaged were in themselves emblematic of, and therefore contributed to, a sense of permanence and stability in settlements that had grown up overnight. Second, Jews were active boosters of their communities, introducing a range of civic and economic improvements. Third, they reinvested the capital they accumulated as merchants in new ventures,

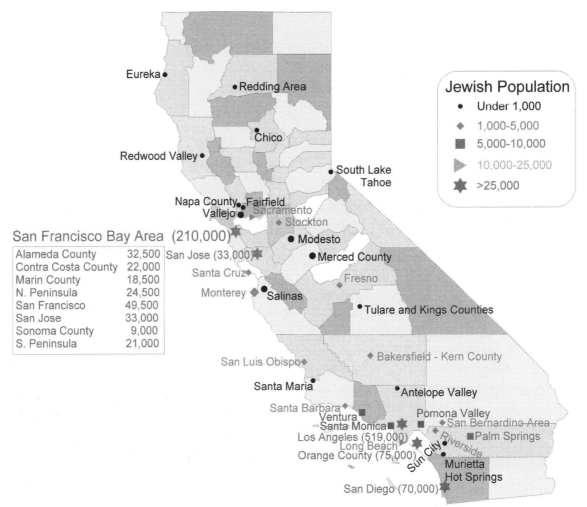

Jewish Population

●	Under 1,000
◆	1,000-5,000
■	5,000-10,000
▶	10,000-25,000
★	>25,000

San Francisco Bay Area (210,000)

Alameda County	32,500
Contra Costa County	22,000
Marin County	18,500
N. Peninsula	24,500
San Francisco	49,500
San Jose	33,000
Sonoma County	9,000
S. Peninsula	21,000

Courtesy of Ira M. Sheskin. Data derived from American Jewish Year Book, 2000.

thereby broadening and diversifying the local economies of their towns.

Nineteenth-century Los Angeles was an unstable settlement, with constant migration in and out. Los Angeles Jews, however, were more stable residents than non-Jews. As proprietors they had staked their future on Los Angeles, and moving away would mean starting over. In addition, Jews were less likely to be unmarried or living on their own but lived in extended families with parents: 21 percent of Los Angeles Jews in 1880 lived in households of nine or more persons, compared with only 9 percent of non-Jews.

The economic endeavors of Jewish merchants brought order and stability to the frontier in several ways. The brick buildings they erected created a sense of permanence in towns filled with easily conflagratable wooden structures. Their creation of local banking systems contributed to California's economic growth. And in the ab-

sence of a formal banking system in remote frontier settlements, Jewish merchants often provided it.

I. W. Hellman, who would become one of the premier bankers of California, began as a Los Angeles dry goods merchant who held gold for miners when they came into town. Fearing that one of the miners could easily accuse him of stealing or simply rob him, he purchased gold dust at the current exchange rate instead of keeping it in his safe. He would deposit the money in his own bank, and the miners could draw from it by writing checks that would be honored as long as the money lasted. Hellman eventually incorporated as the Farmers and Merchants Bank; he later became president of the Wells Fargo Bank, still one of the most prominent in California.

Pioneer Jews also invested in agriculture, ranching, mining, and transportation. These ventures contributed to California's economic diversification. Mining was the single most important reason for the expansion of the

BRUCE PHILLIPS

western frontier in the nineteenth century, and Jews were involved in every aspect of it. Some Jews came West as prospectors, while others became miners indirectly by advancing money and provisions to prospectors in return for either a share in the discoveries or first option to purchase the claim. Adolph Sutro, a self-taught mining engineer who would later become mayor of San Francisco, was responsible for several western mining innovations, including a four-mile tunnel into the Comstock Silver Lode in Nevada, which took thirteen years to complete.

Los Angeles Jews were active in land development that would transform the small town into an important city. Charles Jacoby, Louis Lewin, and Herman Silver developed the area that would one day become Boyle Heights, Los Angeles' first authentic Jewish neighborhood.

As the leading merchants in town, Jews were the most likely to stay to help those towns grow. When Jewish businesses began to flourish the owners found they had no reason to leave. As permanent citizens they began to think of government as a tool for community growth. They organized chambers of commerce, expanded the school systems, and pushed for roads, railroads, and federal subsidies to advance their towns' interests.

Railroad access was a necessity for growth and prosperity in the far West. Rail lines were the link to eastern population and markets that would bring prosperity to the towns they came through, and Jews were among the leading negotiators to bring the railroads to their towns. Solomon Lazard, I. W. Hellman, and Harris Newmark were honored by their fellow citizens for their role in bringing the railroad to Los Angeles when they were sent as part of the delegation to drive the golden spike that joined the westward and eastward tracks of the Southern Pacific.

Civic Leadership

The acceptance, even prominence, of Jews on the frontier is evident in the prominent role they played in the political life. Jewish political involvement came about in three phases: local civic leadership, local office, and state and national offices.

Realizing their economic stake in the political stability of the growing communities of the West, Jews, like other merchants, became prominent in local politics early on. Los Angeles Jews organized a local militia that kept order before there was a formal police force.

Emigrant Jews came from Europe with civic as well as business experience, and were an important part of a proto-government of the frontier. Jews had come from communities in Europe that were well structured and democratically governed, giving them governance skills in the same way that many had arrived with mercantile skills. Jewish merchants typically ran the local post office. Because they were both stable and accomplished record keepers, Jews were often called upon to keep track of land and mining claims. As Harriet and Fred Rochlin noted, "In the earliest and most frantic days on the frontier, this service was often the first—and occasionally the one—semblance of government in a settlement."

Jewish merchants also played a leading role in creating the civic order of many a western town. When Los Angeles was incorporated as an American city in 1850, Morris Goodman, a member of the first city council, urged that the city establish a police force. When nothing happened, he and Solomon Lazard along with other Jewish pioneers served on a vigilante force. (As quoted in the Rochlin's *Pioneer Jews*, even after a police force was established, Los Angeles was still known for exhibiting "the most lawlessness west of Santa Fe.") In 1870, Emil Harris was appointed to the police department, rising to the level of chief of police only eight years later. He brought a great improvement in police work and he is best remembered for preventing an anti-Chinese riot in Los Angeles in 1871. His likeness appears in a mural at the Los Angeles Police Academy.

Los Angeles Jews were ardent boosters of their community. Solomon Lazard, the first president of the Los Angeles Board of Trade (1873–1876), and M. J. Newmark and I. W. Hellman were the first to initiate the development of San Pedro (thirty miles to the south of the city) as the Port of Los Angeles. Hellman organized the first street railway in 1883, explaining that: "I am now in a position to benefit and improve the city." Harris Newmark (son of M. J. Newmark), at his own expense, edited and printed a pamphlet promoting the new city of Los Angeles at the Philadelphia Centennial Exhibition in 1876.

Jews As State Leaders

Jews were also active at the state level in California. I. W. Hellman of Los Angeles served as a regent of the recently founded University of California in 1881. In 1886 he thought about but declined a seat in the U.S. Senate. In San Francisco, Charles DeYoung, a crusading reformer, started the *Daily Morning Chronicle,* which later became the *San Francisco Chronicle*. His career in public service was cut short by an assassin angry about DeYoung's political coverage. Julius Kahn represented the San Francisco district in the U.S. Congress from 1898 to 1902 and 1904 until his death in 1924, when his wife Florence Prag Kahn was elected to his seat (see chapter 12).

As the new century dawned, the wide range of political opportunities for Jews grew attenuated. As corporations gobbled up increasingly large sections of far western commerce and industry, the Jewish merchant was less prominent, and Jews left small towns for urban centers. They were no longer personally known in the community as they had been. Those that did continue in politics were usually from the very affluent pioneer families who were well entrenched in entrepreneurial circles.

Growth of the Jewish Population in the West in the Twentieth Century

Over the course of the twentieth century both the Jewish population and the American population migrated from the Northeast and Midwest to the West and South. In the early part of the century, the Jewish population was far more concentrated in the Northeast than the American population as a whole, but was on the way to catching up by century's end.

Chart 1 compares the distribution of the American and Jewish populations at the beginning, middle, and end of the twentieth century. In 1920, Jews were underrepresented in every region of the United States except the Northeast. In 1920, 70 percent of the Jewish population lived in the Northeast, as against 28 percent of the American population as a whole. Within the Northeast, Jews were three times as likely as the population as a whole to live in the Mid-Atlantic states, which contains the large Jewish communities of New York and Philadelphia. The proportion of both populations in the western states was very small in 1920, but Jews were only one-third as likely as other Americans to be living in this region by the first quarter of the century. The gap was even wider between the general and Jewish populations in the South. Almost a third of all Americans resided in the southern states, as compared with only 7 percent of Jews.

The Midwest ("North Central Region" for the U.S. Census) had the second largest concentration of Jews in 1920. Although Americans as a whole were more likely to live in this region than were Jews (32 percent versus 20 percent),

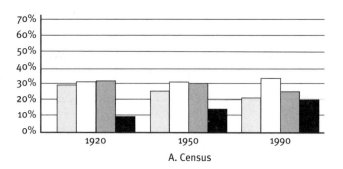
A. Census

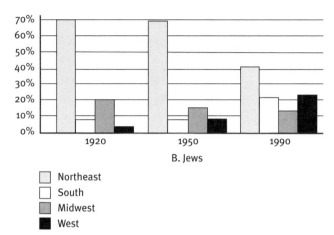
B. Jews

Northeast
South
Midwest
West

CHART 1: *Regional Distribution of the Jewish and General Population, 1920–1990*

Jews were less underrepresented in this region than in the West and South. The gap between the Jewish and general population was not uniform in the Midwest.

The East North Central Division (Wisconsin, Michigan, Illinois, Indiana, and Ohio) accounted for 16 percent of American Jews, close to the 20 percent of the American population as a whole residing in this census division in 1920. Much of its Jewish population was living in the major Jewish population centers of Cleveland, Detroit, and Chicago.

By contrast, Jews were only a third as likely as other Americans to be found in the Great Plains states of the West North Central Division (North Dakota, South Dakota, Nebraska, Kansas, Missouri, Iowa, and Minnesota). While there were important Jewish communities to be found here, as in Kansas City and St. Louis, for example, these communities had Jewish populations that were much smaller than in Detroit and Chicago.

By mid-century Jewish population grew at a faster rate than the population as a whole. The proportion of all Americans living in the western states grew by 50 percent between 1920 and 1950, while the proportion of Jews living

BRUCE PHILLIPS

in the West tripled over the same time period. Within the West, the proportion of Jews living in the Pacific Division (California, Washington, Oregon, Hawaii, and Alaska) quadrupled due to the huge Jewish population increase in California. In 1920 there were about 30,000 Jews living in both San Francisco and Los Angeles. Between 1920 and 1955 the San Francisco Jewish population grew substantially, from 30,000 to 51,000. Even more impressive was Jewish population growth in Los Angeles, which had reached 272,000 by 1950, almost a tenfold increase over this thirty-year period. By 1955 Los Angeles, with a Jewish population that had swelled to 320,000, replaced Chicago as the second largest Jewish community in the United States.

The overall population of the Midwest declined as the West grew, and the migration from the Midwest to California that took place in the 1920s and 1930s has been elegantly documented by Carey McWilliams, who also assessed the cultural impact of this midwestern migration on the Golden State. Jewish population decline in the Midwest between 1920 and 1950 was greater than for the population as a whole. The proportion of all Americans living in the Midwest declined by 10 percent, while the proportion of Jewish population declined by 25 percent. The proportion of both the Jewish and general populations in the Northeast and South remained stable during this thirty-year period. Thus, the growth of the West for both Jews and all Americans was in part the story of Midwest migration.

The postwar redistribution of both the Jewish and general populations was a move from the Rust Belt to the Sun Belt. Between 1950 and 1990, the United States population grew by 63 percent but the Northeast and Midwest regions grew at only about half that rate (29 percent and 34 percent, respectively). Conversely, the population of the South and West grew at higher rates than the country as a whole following World War II. The South grew by 81 percent between 1950 and 1990, and the West by 148 percent. The slowest growth rates were in the middle of the country: the North Central Division, the East South Central Division in the South, and the Middle Atlantic Division in the Northeast.

Much of the growth that took place in the West and South during the period 1950–1990 occurred after 1970. Between 1950 and 1990 the population of the West grew by over twenty-two million persons, and almost half (47 percent) of this growth occurred between 1970 and 1990. Between 1970 and 1980, the South increased by 20 percent

and the West by 24 percent. Within the West, the fastest growing states since 1975 have been in the Mountain division.

Jewish population change in the postwar period mirrored and even amplified that of the general population. By 1990, the proportion of Jews living in the Pacific states was one-third higher than the proportion of the general population found in this division. During this same time period the proportion of Jews living in the South (22 percent) grew to equal the proportion living in the West (24 percent). This growth was concentrated in two divisions of the South. The proportion of Jews living in the South Atlantic States was about the same as among the general population, due almost entirely to the Jewish population growth in Florida. The proportion of the Jewish population found in the West South Central division, though small (3 percent) had nonetheless tripled since 1950, due mostly to the growth of the Texas Jewish population centers of Dallas and Houston.

Barry Kosmin, who directed the 1990 National Jewish Population Survey, has analyzed the growth rates of Jews and all Americans on a regional basis. Adjusting for differences in Jewish and American growth, Kosmin compared the Jewish and overall rates of growth for each state for the fifty-year period between 1930 and 1980. The states in which the Jewish population grew faster than the state's overall population were all in the South and West. In descending order, these were: Arizona, Nevada, Hawaii, Florida, New Mexico, California, Georgia, and the District of Columbia. Kosmin and his co-researchers attributed this "Jewish overgrowth" to economic factors. Jewish population growth took place in states with growing economies: "We suggest that the Jewish 'overgrowth,' that is, the rate of increase in the Jewish population beyond that of the general population, occurred precisely in those areas of the country that were experiencing the greatest economic development."

Between 1920 and 1950, the proportion of Jews living in the Northeast had hardly changed at all. Throughout the first half of the twentieth century, this region consistently accounted for two-thirds of the American Jewish population. Between 1950 and 1990, however, the mid-Atlantic states saw population declines for both the Jewish and non-Jewish populations, but the Jewish population decline was double that of the population as a whole. The proportion of all Americans who lived in the mid-Atlantic states declined by a quarter from 20 percent to 15 percent. By contrast, the Jewish population share found in the mid-Atlantic states declined nearly by half, from 61 percent of all Jews in 1950 to 34 percent of all Jews in 1990. Between 1980 and 1989 alone, the mid-Atlantic States saw 402,000 Jews leave the Northeast. Interestingly, the Jewish population in New England gained Jewish population in the 1980s, thanks in part to the "Massachusetts Miracle" of economic growth touted by Governor Michael Dukakis in his unsuccessful run for president.

The Jewish population of the Midwest also experienced continued decline in the second half of the twentieth century. The Jewish population of the North Central Division peaked in 1937 at just under a million (768,000), and then declined steadily to 648,000 by 1990. The proportion of Jews in the Midwest decreased by half, from fewer than 20 percent in 1937 to just over 10 percent in 1986. By the mid-1960s as many Jews lived in the West as lived in the Midwest and by 1990 almost twice as many Jews lived in the western states as in the midwestern states. Cities such as Cleveland and Chicago saw huge population losses. Between 1955 and 1990 the Chicago Jewish population declined from 350,00 to 260,000 and the Jewish population of Cleveland decreased from 85,000 to 65,000.

Regional Differences

The 1990 National Jewish Population Survey reveals that there is a contemporary sociological parallel to the historical differences described above. Special tabulations were prepared for this analysis that separate data for California from the rest of Western states Jewish population.

One important difference is the impact of continuous Jewish migration on the makeup of the Jewish population in Western states. The proportion of local "natives" is substantially lower in the West and South than in the Northeast and Midwest. Chart 2 shows the proportion of the Jews in each region who were born in the state of current residence. Over 60 percent of all Jews living in the Northeast and Midwest were born in the state of current residence. By contrast, only 42 percent of California Jews were born in California.

The proportion of natives is lowest in the South, largely because of migration to Florida in the 1980s. This is evident in chart 3, which presents the percentage of the Jewish population "locally born" as reported in local Jewish population surveys. Florida cities that have experienced recent Jewish growth such as Sarasota, Orlando,

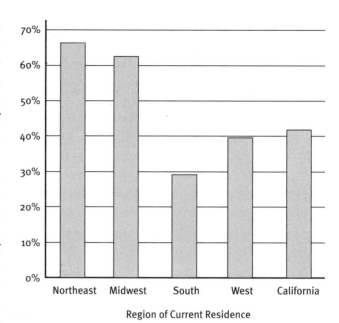

CHART 2: Percent of Jews Born in the State of Current Residence, NJPS 1990

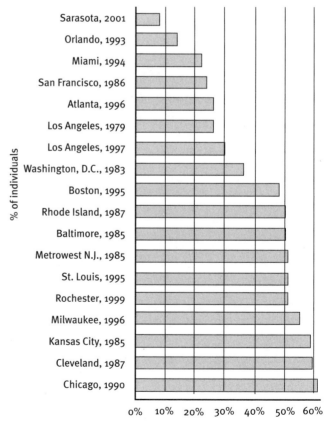

CHART 3: Percent of Jewish Population Locally Born

BRUCE PHILLIPS

and Miami have the lowest proportions of locally born Jews. The growth of South Florida Jewry in recent decades has largely been from the Northeast (especially New York and New Jersey, leading to the popular observation, "The farther south you go in Florida, the farther north you get.") Atlanta, too, has experienced a sizeable migration from the Northeast, and is now popularly described as "the most northern city in the South." In Atlanta, as in Florida, only a relatively small percentage of Jews are locally born. The same is true for Los Angeles and San Francisco where less than a third of all Jews were locally born. Unlike Florida, however, the Jewish migration to California has taken place during half a century. Thus, the proportion of locally born Jews in Los Angeles was lower in 1979 than in 1997. The percentage of locally born Jews was even lower in the Los Angeles Jewish Population Survey of 1953.

COMMUNAL PARTICIPATION

For both Jews in particular and Americans in general, migration has been found to weaken community participation because affiliation is a late step in the process of "settling in." Moreover, Jewish migrants arrive anonymously in their new communities, and have the option of remaining unknown to the organized Jewish community. Thus, one would expect that the regions with the highest percentages of recent migrants would have the lowest rates of affiliation with synagogues and Jewish organizations. But this is only partially true.

SYNAGOGUE AFFILIATION

The Northeast and Midwest, as expected, have the highest rates of synagogue membership. Based on the extent of migration just described, the South should have

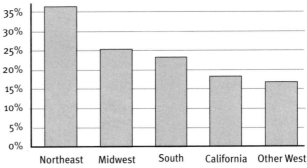

CHART 5: Synagogue Affiliation Among Married Couples with Children, NJPS 1990

the lowest rate of synagogue affiliation—but it doesn't. Jews in California and other western states have the lowest rate of current synagogue membership and also are less likely than southern Jews to have been a synagogue member in the past.

Family cycle is another variable strongly associated with synagogue membership: every local Jewish population survey has found that synagogue membership is most prevalent among married couples with children. Perhaps the higher rate of synagogue membership in the South relative to California and the West is explained by differences in the prevalence of married couples with children. But chart 5 shows this is not the case. Looking only at households that are composed of a married couple with children under eighteen at home, synagogue membership is lowest in California and the other western states.

Similar evidence is available by comparing individual Jewish communities in the West with data available for communities in the Northeast, South, and Midwest (charts 6, 7, and 8). If family structure explained regional differences between California and the western States and the other regions, then Jewish communities with the highest proportions of married couples with children should also have the highest rates of synagogue affiliation. Chart 6 compares data from three Jewish population surveys in the West (Denver, Los Angeles, and San Francisco) with six Jewish population surveys in the South. With the exception of Orlando, the Jewish communities of the South all have higher rates of synagogue affiliation than the three Jewish communities in the West. However, these six southern Jewish communities do not have the highest proportion of married couples with children. Compare Los Angeles, for example, with Sarasota, Florida. The proportion of married couples in children in Los Angeles is more than

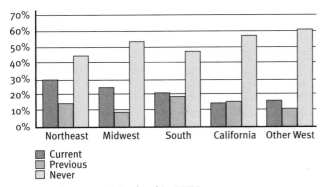

CHART 4: Synagogue Membership, NJPS 1990

Legend:
- Current
- Previous
- Never

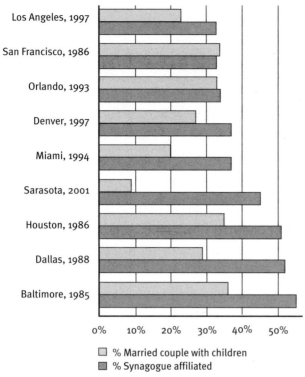

CHART 6: Synagogue Affiliation and Family Status, West and South

CHART 7: Synagogue Affiliation and Family Status, West and Northeast

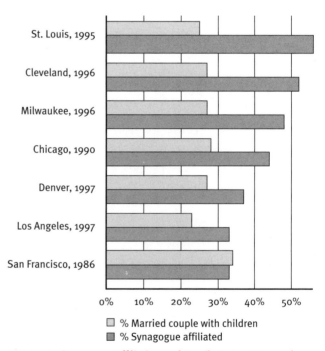

CHART 8: Synagogue Affiliation and Family Status, West and Midwest

twice that of Sarasota, but the synagogue affiliation rate in Sarasota is 1.5 times as high as in Los Angeles. Comparing Los Angeles with Dallas and Houston is similarly instructive. As compared with Los Angeles, both of these Texas Jewish communities have much higher rates of synagogue affiliation but only marginally higher proportions of two-parent families.

Chart 7 makes a similar comparison with regard to the Northeast. Denver, Los Angeles, and San Francisco have the lowest rates of synagogue membership as compared with four Jewish communities in the Northeast for which data are available (Boston, Rhode Island, New York, and Metrowest in New Jersey), but they have comparable or even higher proportions of married couples with children. The comparisons between Denver, Los Angeles, and San Francisco and the four midwestern Jewish communities shown in chart 8 (St. Louis, Cleveland, Milwaukee, and Chicago), are even more dramatic. San Francisco and Chicago both have about 250,000 Jews. San Francisco has 6 percent more families with children than has Chicago, but the synagogue affiliation rate in San Francisco is 11 percent lower than in Chicago. Denver and St. Louis have comparably sized Jewish populations and almost identical percentages of fami-

lies with children, but the synagogue affiliation rate in St. Louis is almost 28 percent higher than in Denver.

There is strong evidence both at the national and community level to conclude that region itself is associated with synagogue membership. Additional evidence for this regional hypothesis is available from data about non-Jews.

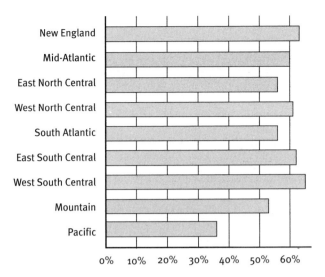

NORTHEAST
    New England = NH, VT, MA, RI
    Mid Atlantic = NY, PA, CT, NJ
MIDWEST
    East North Central = WI, MI, IL, IN, OH
    West North Central = ND, SD, NE, KS, MO, IA, MN
    South Atlantic = WV, VA, NC, SC, GA, FL
SOUTH
    East South Central = KY, TN, AL, MS
    West South Central = OK, TX, AR, LA
WEST
    Mountain = MT, ID, WY, UT, NV, CO, NM, AZ
    Pacific = WA, OR, CA, HI, AK

CHART 9: Church Membership by Census Division, 1980

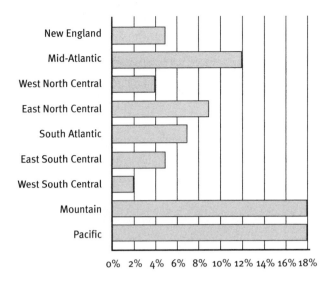

NORTHEAST
    New England = NH, VT, MA, RI
    Mid Atlantic = NY, PA, CT, NJ
MIDWEST
    East North Central = WI, MI, IL, IN, OH
    West North Central = ND, SD, NE, KS, MO, IA, MN
    South Atlantic = WV, VA, NC, SC, GA, FL
SOUTH
    East South Central = KY, TN, AL, MS
    West South Central = OK, TX, AR, LA
WEST
    Mountain = MT, ID, WY, UT, NV, CO, NM, AZ
    Pacific = WA, OR, CA, HI, AK

CHART 10: Percent Never Attending Church, 1980

Sociologists studying American religion have argued that the West, rather than the South, is the region that is religiously distinct. Even though the South is known as the "Bible Belt," the church membership rates shown in chart 9 reveal that the South is not all that different from the Midwest and Northeast. On the other hand, the church membership rates in Pacific and Mountain States are the lowest in the United States. Similarly, the percentage of Americans who never attend church (shown in chart 10) is significantly higher in the Mountain and Pacific states than in the rest of the United States.

For this reason, sociologists Rodney Stark and William Sims Bainbridge have dubbed the West the "Unchurched Belt." They have observed that "something about the far West is clearly inhospitable to churches, and this is not a new phenomenon. When we examine reliable data on church membership rates collected by the U.S. Census near the turn of the century, we find things then like they are now." One source of this non-affiliation is the legacy of individualism in the West. Another source is the gendered demography of the West. As Rodney Stark has dis-

cussed in *The Churching of America,* the disproportionate ratio of men to women on the frontier made it difficult for the mainstream churches to set down roots. Conversely, the "wide-open" culture of the West that gave birth to the counterculture of the 1960s (see chapter 13) has also been distinctly fertile soil for the growth of "new age" religious movements.

OTHER AFFILIATIONS

Federation giving is an excellent indicator of communal cohesion. First, federations have to know about Jews in order to solicit them. Communities in which Jews stay invisible will have lower rates of federation giving. Further, the primacy of the local federation as reflected in federation giving says a lot about the presence of that "central address" in the Jewish community. Federation giving is lowest among western states Jews living outside California, and second lowest among California Jews (chart 11). The picture of Jewish organizational affiliation is similar: Jews in California and the western states are the least likely to belong to a Jewish organization (chart 12).

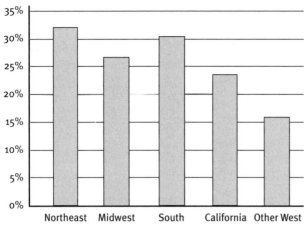

CHART 11: Household Contributed to Local Federation, NJPS 1990

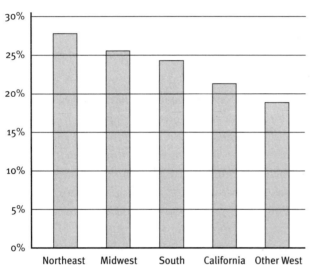

CHART 12: Household has at Least One Jewish Organizational Membership, NJPS 1990

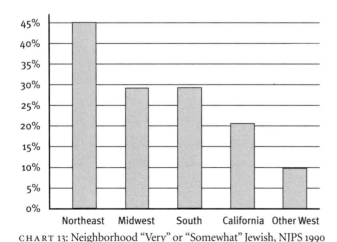

CHART 13: Neighborhood "Very" or "Somewhat" Jewish, NJPS 1990

The kinds of neighborhoods in which Jews live also differ by region. Jewish respondents in the Northeast were by far the most likely to have reported that they live in a neighborhood that is "very" or "somewhat" Jewish. Conversely Jews in California and other Western States were the least likely to live in neighborhoods that were either very or even somewhat Jewish (chart 13).

Two Cultural Differences

The culture of the West is reflected among Jews in multiple ways, and two examples are given here. California Jews, in keeping with both their local and national reputation, are by far the most likely to describe themselves as "very liberal" (chart 14). Research on religious demography has shown that Americans in the western states are the most likely not to identify with any religious denomination or with a "new age" religion. Chart 15 shows that this is true for Jews as well. More Jewish households in the western states outside of California identified with a religion other than Judaism or with no religion at all than identified with one of the four established movements within Judaism. In this regard, California much more resembles the Northeast than it does the rest of the western states. This finding suggests that synagogue affiliation and religious self-identification are independent dimensions. Chart 16 focuses on the relative presence of the major movements within each region. This does not refer to the type of synagogue to which the household belongs, but rather, the denomination with which the respondent indicated that the household identified. Again, California more resembles the other regions than it does the other western states. The similarity of California to the other regions in terms of denominational identification highlights the impact of regional culture on synagogue affiliation.

INTERMARRIAGE

The final regional difference considered—intermarriage—is in many ways the most dramatic. The Jewish parentage of the respondent provides a retrospective estimate of the relationship between region and intermarriage. Respondents born in the Northeast, followed by the Midwest, are by far the most likely to have had two Jewish parents. Respondents born in Los Angeles, other western cities, and the South are much more likely to have only one Jewish parent (chart 17). These findings are consistent with

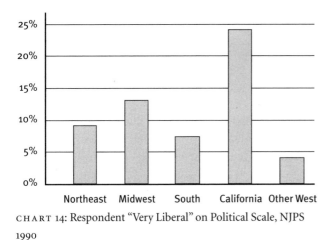

CHART 14: Respondent "Very Liberal" on Political Scale, NJPS 1990

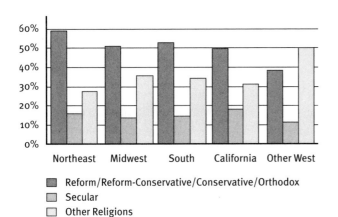

■ Reform/Reform-Conservative/Conservative/Orthodox
□ Secular
□ Other Religions

CHART 15: Denomination of Household by Region

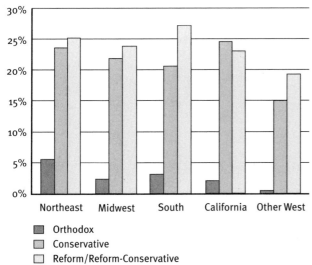

■ Orthodox
■ Conservative
□ Reform/Reform-Conservative

CHART 16: Denominational Breakdown of Household by Region, NJPS 1990

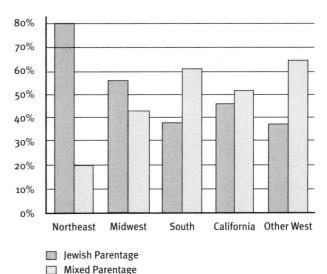

■ Jewish Parentage
□ Mixed Parentage

CHART 17: Jewish Parentage by Region of Birth for Respondent, NJPS 1990

the "mixed race" data from the 2000 Census. Americans of mixed race (i.e., mother and father are of different races) are most prevalent in the West. Both the Jewish parentage and mixed-race findings are consistent with the individualist culture of the West in which communal pressures tend to be trumped by individual predilections.

As is already clear, American Jewry has experienced extensive migration, and intermarriage is associated with the pattern of regional migration. The Jews least likely to have intermarried were born in and have remained in the Northeast. Conversely, the Jews most likely to have intermarried were born in and have remained in the West. Jews who were born and still reside in the South were the next most likely group to have intermarried. Jews who migrated to the West and South also have low rates of intermarriage, because they were migrating from the Northeast and Midwest. We would expect them to reduce the overall rate of intermarriage in the West and South. The (1990) rates of intermarriage shown in chart 19 suggest that this is in fact true. The rates of intermarriage in the South, Midwest, and California are fairly close. The two regions that stand out the most are the western states outside California (with a high rate of intermarriage) and the Northeast (with a singularly low rate of intermarriage.) This suggests that California may be becoming more "mainstream" with regard to intermarriage even as the rest of western states' Jewry becomes less like the rest of American Jewry.

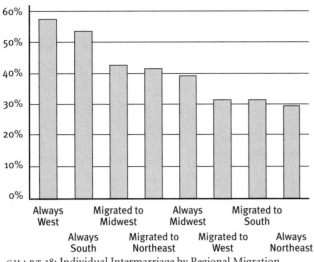

CHART 18: Individual Intermarriage by Regional Migration Pattern, NJPS 1990

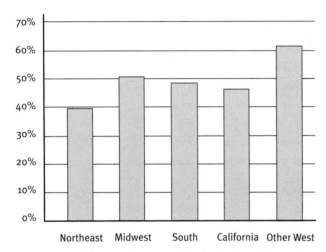

CHART 19: Couple Rate of Intermarriage by Region of Current Residence, NJPS 1990

Conclusion

Much analysis lies ahead for the sociological understanding of California and western Jewry. The analysis here in no way exhausts the variables available for analysis from the 1990 National Jewish Population Survey. Within another year or so the data from the 2000 Survey will be available. Social scientists will be able to assess the persistence of the interregional differences described above. The availability of data for individual communities from the National Jewish Data Bank under the auspices of the United Jewish Communities and the City University of New York challenge sociologists to look not only at regional and state differences, but communal differences as well both within and across regions. Social scientists who accept those research challenges would be well advised to keep some history books close by.

CHAPTER 2

JOINING THE RUSH

AVA F. KAHN

News of the gold rush spread like wildfire across the United States and throughout the world. Jewish men and women living in the small villages and the large cities of the Americas, Europe, and even Australia caught gold fever. In San Francisco and in little mining towns, Jews built their homes and businesses next to Yankees, Scots, Italians, and Germans. California Jewry's birth and development held prominence on the world stage. Word of the growing Jewish community at the Golden Gate even reached Jerusalem. A little more than ten years after San Francisco's first minyan gathered, the elders of Jerusalem sent an embassy to the United States seeking support for their poor. Due to the thirty-first state's worldwide reputation, the elders addressed their appeals to all Jews "residing in peace in all the States of gracious America and the magnificent State of California."

The elders of Jerusalem were correct in their assumptions, for, in fact, California was different from most places in the Union. Jews played significant roles in creating the cosmopolitan port city of San Francisco along with the many communities that suddenly dotted California's foothills and riversides. Jewish men and women became part of the hundred thousand migrants who sought their fortunes in the eight crowded gold rush counties. By 1860 as many as ten thousand Jews had left their homes, and frequently their families, to join the hunt for prosperity in California's mining towns and growing cities.[1]

During this time of adventure and turmoil in places where many would surmise that Jews would quickly assimilate and Judaism would not survive, both often thrived. In a short time, kosher bakeries and boarding houses, synagogues and day schools, Jewish newspapers and merchandise stores became community institutions. Because of this substantial community structure, families with strong Jewish identities became the progenitors of today's diverse Jewish and secular communities. Contemporary letters, diaries, and newspaper articles recount how Jews first learned of the gold rush and how and why they founded communities on the Pacific shores and in the small mining towns. This essay explores the birth and development of the early San Francisco Jewish community from its gold rush infancy to its maturity in the 1870s.

Like the Irish, German, French, and Chinese adventurers who came to California, most Jews arrived on the West Coast as part of a chain or family migration. Usually, one brother arrived and set up a business. When he was ready to expand to another town or enlarge his business a relative came from the East or Europe to help out. In this way, families and friends from the same homelands settled together in the Golden State.

All were not treated equally. The Chinese, Indians, and Hispanics were made scapegoats, blamed for thievery and economic downturns. Although their personal lives were not restricted as they had been in Europe, where in some German states including Bavaria the number of Jewish marriages was regulated, Jews at times faced discrimination and limitations. Especially egregious were the Sunday Laws that unfairly kept their businesses closed two days a week if they observed the Jewish Sabbath. On the other hand, many Jews succeeded and were recognized throughout the region.

Everyone knows the Horatio Alger story of Levi Strauss who, like many others, made his living as a merchant in San Francisco. But unlike others he went on to manufacture and retail a unique product—copper-riveted denim jeans—now known throughout the world. This chapter tells the story of his milieu using the voices and experiences of lesser known Jews who were present during the birth and adolescence of this community, men and women who came west to gamble on the potential of the newly settled region. Noted historian Moses Rischin, in his trail-blazing chapter in *Jews of the American West* (Wayne State University Press, 1991), observed that as the mining era waned in the 1870s, Jews represented a remarkable 7 percent to 8 percent of the population of San Francisco. This was a higher percentage than in any other city west of New York. These unknown men and women created a vibrant and lasting Jewish community.

First News of the Gold Rush

The *Alta California*, a San Francisco newspaper, mentions in its issue of June 18th, the formation of a Jewish Benevolent Society.

—*Occident,* September 1850

Read throughout the nation, *The Occident,* a prominent Jewish newspaper published by Isaac Lesser in Philadelphia, announced the formation of Jewish life in the far West to the eastern Jewish community. Now men and women living in New York, Philadelphia, and Charleston knew they would find other Jews when they reached the West Coast. The same was true for the Jews of Europe, for news of the excitement was translated into many languages and published in the principal Jewish newspapers of England and the Continent. The *Allgemeine Zeitung des Judenthums* (General Journal of Judaism) in Leipzig, the *Jewish Chronicle* of London, and the *Archives Israelite* of Paris all carried news of the budding Jewish communities. Along with news of the gold strikes, descriptions of Jewish life in the far-off region were a stimulant for leaving home. Some of these stories came from the new immigrants themselves, as they sent letters to family, friends, and Jewish journals telling of their experiences and their new lives in the Golden State. All at home wanted to know what to expect in California and wondered especially if Judaism would survive in this remote land.

One young man who helped to answer that question for the Jews of England was Samuel H. Cohen. A native of London, Cohen reached San Francisco in 1851 and reported to his sister at home that one could in fact live as a traditional Jew in the young San Francisco. Because of the general interest in the subject, the *Jewish Chronicle* of London published his letter in full. Cohen wrote:

We have Kosher meat, a burial-ground, and a synagogue which was formed, three days before Passover, by twelve single young men and one married man. We have now forty-two members, principally English, and we have some old married men to lead us the correct way. Our form of prayers is that of the Great Synagogue [of London] ... Mr. Isaacs, of Brown's Lane, baked the matzos for Passover, with whom twelve of us youngsters passed the festival. I do not think that the Jews in any part of the world could have kept the Passover more strictly than we did, and I am happy to say he intends to keep a Kosher house all the year round, so that we shall be enabled to eat lawful meats.

You might imagine how well this news was received in London by young Jewish men and their parents alike, for it proved that it was possible to be an observant Jew even in this new El Dorado. There must have been a large demand for kosher-for-Passover foods, for Isaacs from London, like Cohen, hired an assistant to help him bake Matzoth. Indeed an advertisement in Alexander Iser's *The California Hebrew and English Almanac for the year 5612* [1851–1852] states that Isaacs, now a baker on Bartel Street near Broadway, will "Board over Passover at a moderate charge." In addition to B. Adler's kosher meat shop and Mark Isaacs' kosher bakery, there were at least two kosher boarding houses, one run by E. Alexander on Battery street, near Washington Street and another, owned by Mr. Rubenstein on Montgomery Street between Pine and Bush, which advertised, "Meals at all hours, and at moderate charges."

The German *Allgemeine Zeitung des Judenthums* told its readers of life in the West, noting in July 1851 that "two congregations were formed" in San Francisco. In France, the *Archives Israelite* frequently corresponded with a journalist and fellow countryman, Daniel Levy, who stated, in a letter published in the journal in 1855, "Among all the areas in the world, California is possibly the one in which the Jews are more widely dispersed. I do not know of one village, one hamlet, one settlement of any kind, either in the North, mining area, or the South, the region of Ranchos, where they have not established themselves." This was all good news for those considering leaving their homes in Europe and the eastern United States to travel to the far Pacific shores.

They Came West

Making the decision to travel to California was one thing; actually making the trip involved much planning and fortitude. Some made up their minds to venture to California while in Europe and came almost directly to the Pacific Coast, while others only knew that they wanted to come to the United States and then, after months or years, elected to make the trip west. Before the East and West coasts were united by rail in 1869, the overland journey was usually made by slow moving wagon trains, while sea voyages from the East Coast either went around the Horn or crossed Central America at an isthmus.

Because most European Jews were familiar with sea travel and were starting from the eastern seaboard, sea voyages were usually chosen over a long overland trip; but, a few took the treacherous overland route, including Louis Sloss, who would help to found both the Sacramento and San Francisco Jewish communities. Born in 1823 Bavaria, Sloss came to the United States in 1845 and settled in Kentucky. With news of the gold rush, he headed for St. Louis. There, for a fare of two hundred dollars, he joined a wagon train west. After much hardship he left the company with two companions and continued to Sacramento on horseback. He arrived in 1849, in time to be counted as one of the few Jewish "forty-niners."

The land route was also chosen by Fanny Brooks and her new husband Julius who had arrived at New York's Castle Garden just in time to hear of a new wondrous gold find announced in every newspaper. In 1854, after a short time in New York, the new immigrants from Breslau took the railroad west to join a wagon train. Many believe that Fanny Brooks was the first Jewish woman to cross the plains. The seventeen-year-old bride learned how to bake bread on an open fire and guide a two-mule covered wagon across the prairies. On the plains, Brooks socialized with women of different nationalities, an experience that helped prepare her for multi-ethnic California. The family's final destination was Timbuktu, a small, unglamorous mining hamlet, where they sold goods to miners. Most Jews journeyed to California by ship. Some sailed around the Horn of South America from the east coast of the United States, which took over four months. While others traveled by ship to the east coast of Central America, disembarking at the Isthmus of Panama or Nicaragua, crossing to the West Coast using a combination of small sailing boats and mules and foot travel, and continuing by steamer to San Francisco, which took from five to eight weeks, depending on the reliability of ships at the Pacific shore. Frequently, passengers were forced to stay at the Isthmus for weeks because the ships destined for San Francisco were usually late or damaged at sea. On the ships and on land, Jews found each other and shared kosher meals, observed Jewish holidays, and established lasting friendships. For some, the crossing was easy and they enjoyed a pleasant trip. Others, however, vowed never to travel by ship again; many of the ships were old and the rush for gold had called some into service that should have been retired years before. In 1852, one out of ten sea passengers to San Francisco died before seeing the Golden Gate. Nevertheless, it was by steamer that most Jews reached California. Some even bragged about the speed of the trip. A young Eugene Meyer (whose son would become publisher of the *Washington Post*) on his way to clerk in a San Francisco store, was exuberant at having made the trip from New York to California across the Isthmus in only twenty-four days.

Although a few Jewish families journeyed to gold rush San Francisco, most of the first Jews to reach the Pacific were young men, and often their only companion on the long voyage was their merchandise: European clothing, cloth, and everyday necessities to be sold when they reached the muddy unpaved streets of the nascent San Francisco.

The Founding of the Jewish Community

Jews arriving in California sought each other out; they formed benevolent societies and considered establishing a permanent congregation. In a merchant's wood-framed-tent store on September 22, 1849, the first Jews of San Francisco gathered to celebrate High Holiday service. Observing different customs, the men could not agree to form a single congregation. In 1851, during the same spring week, two congregations—Emanu-El and Sherith Israel—wrote constitutions. Although both were Orthodox, with women seated separately from men, and both hired a *shochet* to slaughter their meat according to kosher laws, each congregation wanted to establish practices that were familiar to their members from birth. Conducting services largely in German, the majority of Emanu-El's membership were Bavarians, along with American Sephardim and French Jews. Sherith Israel, although known as the Polish congregation, had a diverse membership with congregants from England, Poland, Posen, Russia, and the eastern and southern United States. Showing connections to the New

Fanny Brooks with children, circa 1859.
Courtesy of the Bancroft Library, University of California, Berkeley (1992.0&7 pic).

York Jewish community, both Emanu-El and Sherith Israel congregations named themselves after that city's leading German and Sephardic congregations, and they simulated the eastern congregations' competitve spirits. Members of both congregations often left San Francisco for months or years to establish stores or businesses in other parts of the West before returning home to the "city."

Though few Jews became miners, Jewish men and women played consequential roles in the development of San Francisco, Sacramento and in the surrounding mining towns. Not only were they town founders and active community leaders, but they brought Jewish religious and social life wherever they went. Although not all Jews were observant, even in the small towns they established Jewish community life. They celebrated the holidays of the Jewish calendar, took part in social activities, and performed nec-

AVA F. KAHN

Port of San Francisco, 1852, from a sketch by George W. Casilear.
George Victor Cooper, American artist, and John Cameron, American lithographer.
Courtesy Bancroft Library, University of California (BANC PIC 1963.002:0994:01—A).

essary life-cycle events, including marriage, circumcision, bar mitzvah and proper burial.

In the first years of the gold rush, Jews joined others to quickly construct towns and hamlets. Often these towns went up overnight with unstable buildings and equally unstable economies. Jews did not know if the towns and Jewish communities they were forming would last generations or if they would be gone within decades.

By virtue of their experience in Europe and the eastern United States as merchants, many young Jews had the knowledge and the skills to supply miners and other town residents with clothing, boots, hats, and other essentials. Because of established family chains between Europe, the eastern United States, San Francisco, and the mining areas, they were able to bring goods to market. This was especially important when that market was located in a small rustic mining camp.

Mining Towns

Although San Francisco's Jewish community offered religious and fraternal associations, and a community-at-large with opera, theater and social clubs, it was some-

times hard to make a living there. Most of the men who gathered in San Francisco in the 1850s for High Holiday services were merchants or clerks. Many were products of chain migrations, with a brother, uncle, cousin, or friend staying on the East Coast or in Europe sending merchandise west, while the young Californian set up shop. Those who could afford it stayed in San Francisco, while those who could not compete in the crowded market went off to the mining camps and interior towns, where there were fewer stores and the accommodations were often marginal. In 1852, half of California's population lived in the eight gold rush counties. Few Jews who went to the interior mined for gold. Most clerked in or owned small stores. There, too, Jews often established a family chain between supply towns and the smaller camps. Henry Cohn, a young immigrant from Germany, minded a store in Poker Flat, for example, while his relatives owned a store in the slightly larger town of Saint Louis. The goods for both stores were brought in by mule train from Marysville, having come up-river from San Francisco.

To observe Jewish traditions, men often rented halls from the Masons or the Odd Fellows to use for holiday worship. Of the mining towns, only Jackson and Placerville built synagogues, and few owned Torah scrolls, borrowing them when needed from larger towns. Of all the foothill mining communities, Nevada City, seventy miles northeast of Sacramento, stood out as a Jewish social and religious center. In the fall of 1850, a year after gold was discovered in its hills and rivers, the town had a population of six thousand; it soon became home to many Jewish merchants and their families. There, far removed from the port city of San Francisco, families held Jewish ceremonies, often closing their businesses on the Sabbath and religious holidays. One such family was that of Aaron Baruh. A native of Landau in Bavaria, Baruh arrived in Nevada City in 1852 after spending two years in New Orleans. In the foothill town he married Rosalie Wolfe and opened a series of stores, from a clothing store with his brother, Herman, to a grocery store, and finally to a liquor store. Families including Baruh's with his seven children observed kosher laws and marked their homes with *mezuzot*. Baruh made Nevada City his home for over fifty years and was often the center of its Jewish community, serving as an officer in its many fraternal societies, including the B'nai B'rith. These associations were community member's business and social networks, and their connection to the outside world—B'nai B'rith, for instance, had a national membership and Kesher Shel Barzel (Band of Iron) had international chapters. Through these organizations, their correspondence, and Jewish newspapers, mining town residents learned about Jewish life outside of the foothills, and Jews as far away as the east coast learned what it was like to live in a California gold rush town.

In 1852, merchant Aaron Rosenheim wrote to Isaac Leeser, editor of the *Occident,* describing the Yom Kippur services held that year in Nevada City's Masonic Hall, since everyone wanted to know of the survival of Jewish practice and how Jews were treated in such remote locale:

> [T]he room was appropriately furnished and the Ceremonies conducted with dignity and ability, the Room was crowded with Visitors, who were anxious to visit our ceremonies. Among the visitors were the first Citizens of the place, the Judges of Courts, &c, and all expressed their entire satisfaction at our ancient and holy ceremonies and proceedings which were conducted with profound respect.

As was common throughout the United States, the Jewish community of Nevada City welcomed prominent non-Jews to their services and social events. Jews were usually recognized as hard-working and patriotic new citizens. Most people admired them for their ability as businessmen, especially in the often isolated gold camps, and for their adherence to tradition in a time of chaos. There were some, however, who viewed them as what historian Jonathan Sarna calls the "mythical Jew," the Jew they had read about in their Bibles and talked about as a stereotype. This image often diverged from the Jew they knew from the dry goods store who was their neighbor.[2] The stereotype made its way into print in several fashions. The most common was to characterize local Jews as fitting a global, and derogatory, image. In 1852 James H. Carson, a reporter for the *San Joaquin Republican* in Stockton reinforced this stereotype when he described Jews as "unwashed-looking, slobbery, slipshod individuals." But although antisemitism did exist, it did not for the most part affect the way individual Jews were treated by their neighbors. One trait most appreciated was that they took care of their co-religionists and rarely sought public assistance.

When the Nevada Hebrew Society was born, most of the Jewish community became members. The association met twice a week as a benevolent society, helping the sick, establishing a consecrated Jewish cemetery, and burying the dead. Far from friends and family, community members willingly undertook the responsibility and obligation for attending to each other's needs.

Caring for the young was equally important, as the whole community witnessed the growth of family life. Jewish practices were observed in Nevada City the same way they were observed in San Francisco. Written under the banner of "local affairs" in the *Nevada City Journal* of December 11, 1857 was an article of special interest to both the Jewish community and its neighbors:

> Circumcision.—We were induced to witness the rite of circumcision at the house of a Jewish friend, on Wednesday. The officiating priest [*sic*] was the Rev. Mr. Laski of San Francisco. The ceremony consisted of first lighting a couple of candles, putting on of hats by the whole company present, procuring a glass or two of wine, and reading a portion of Hebrew. Second, introduction of the child, nipping in the bud, and a short ceremony of reading. Third, partaking of hospitalities, more reading which was all Hebrew to us, and adjournment.

The author advised "those curious in such matters . . . to obtain further information by seeing for themselves, or

Aaron and Rosalie Baruh, circa 1870s.
Courtesy of the Searls History Library, Nevada City, California.

consulting a rare old book a part of which is said to have been written by Moses." Jews were just one ethnic group in a town that was home to dozens. All were inquisitive about each others' practices, and most were treated with respect. Jews wanted to show others that they had a dignified form of worship. The *mohel*, Samuel M. Laski, was a frequent visitor to Nevada City, as he was also a *shochet* who came once a year to slaughter meat so that the Jewish community could enjoy a kosher Passover.

Nevada City Jews were also known for their extensive social life. As early as the 1850s the Jewish merchants had built substantial wooden homes, with men and women making their own entertainment. In addition to their fraternal and benevolent societies, they formed the Eureka Social Club. Because of its sizable Jewish community, as many as seventy members during its most populous years, the town held many social activities. According to an article in San Francisco's *Hebrew*, 1868 was an especially festive year for Nevada City:

There is probably not another town in California, aside from San Francisco and Sacramento, where the Hebrew element exercises a greater influence. . . . The club gave one masquerade ball last winter, and a subscription dance ball on Thanksgiving evening, both of which were highly successful and the latter particularly surpassed anything of the kind ever before witnessed in this city.

This type of entertainment was popular, drawing both the Jewish and non-Jewish members of the community to the parties.

Attracting men from the smaller camps, these events in the mining and supply towns gave Jews a way to affiliate with other Jews and Judaism. More importantly, the larger cities of San Francisco and Sacramento were key to preserving Jewish life in the mining region. Seeking wives, men traveled to the cities with larger Jewish populations. Although San Francisco was mainly a community of

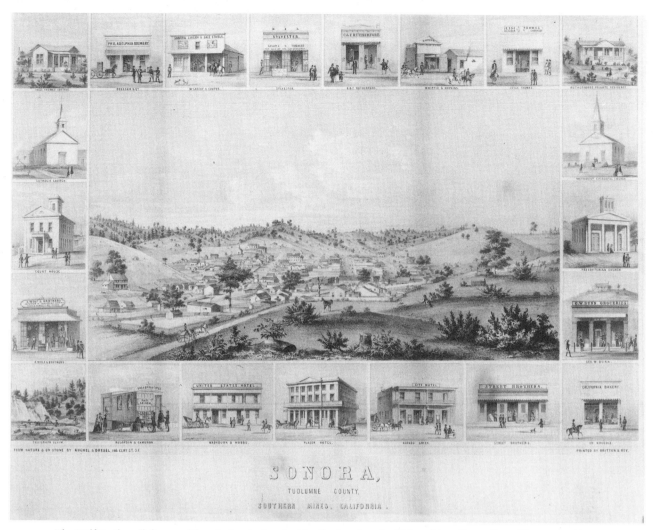

The Wolf Brothers (left, second from bottom) advertised "well selected stock of Miners' Supplies, India Rubber Coats, d[itto].
Boots Oil Cloth Suits." (Sonora Herald, June 11, 1853). Sonora Tuolumne County, Southern Mines, California [1854] lithograph.
Kuchel & Dresel, artist, lithographer, and publisher. Britton & Rey printer.
Courtesy of the Bancroft Library, University of California (1963.002:0906—D)

young men, Jewish women did accompany their fathers and brothers west soon after the discovery of gold. During a trip to San Francisco in 1851, Emanuel Linoberg, a resident of the mining community of Sonora, courted and married Pauline Meyer. As recorded in Sherith Israel's minute book, Pauline and Emanuel were married in the newly founded congregation, and Emanuel brought his bride back to his home in the rustic foothill mining community.

One of Sonora's first non-Mexican settlers, Linoberg first came to the Sierra Nevada from his native Poland in 1849 at age thirty-one. Sonora, the county seat, was called the Queen of the Southern Mines. Founded in 1848 by Mexicans from the State of Sonora, it was incorporated by American settlers in 1851, after the non-citizen miners' tax pushed the Mexicans off their claims. Like most Jews in the mining regions, Linoberg was a merchant. The enterprising young man owned the Tiende Mexicano, a large store on the corner of Sonora's main street. But unlike most, Linoberg was more than a merchant—he owned a mule train to bring in supplies to his store, an entertainment hall, and a gold mine. He also served the medical needs of the miners; with a doctor, he operated a "Russian Steam Bath," which advertised that it could cure anything from gout to rheumatism.

But business was not the only thing on Linoberg's mind. Although not yet citizens of the United States, new immigrants filled volunteer and elected offices in their

AVA F. KAHN

new home towns. Jews in mining towns were volunteer firemen, served on juries and as political party delegates, and were elected to local governments. Linoberg served on Sonora's first town council and participated in the political, business, and religious affairs of the new town.

Jews in mining towns were not isolated from the outside world. They contributed money for the relief of the Jewish community after Sacramento floods, for support for the poor Jews of Jerusalem, and for building synagogues in the larger towns. Most gained their knowledge of the outside world from letters from family members and from the California and national Jewish newspapers. Men like Linoberg debated religious and civic issues. Writing to Rabbi Isaac Mayer Wise in Cincinnati, the editor of the *American Israelite*, Linoberg strongly advocated Reform Judaism, declaring: "I fully approve of your advocacy of Reform. Orthodox suited time past, but reform suits times of progress. . . ." Traditional Jews and those leaning toward Reform Judaism were members of Jewish communities in mining towns and big cities alike; but though there were many opinions in the mining towns, the small numbers of men could sustain only one congregation.

Linoberg became the first president of the Hebrew Congregation of Sonora, and five years after his own marriage his home served as the wedding site of another Sonora couple. As the community grew, Jewish women came to the mining towns with their merchant brothers and fathers. It was no longer necessary for single men to venture to San Francisco to find a bride and a minyan; by then in most towns there were more than the required ten Jews for worship.

In addition to small congregations and benevolent societies, Jewish men in mining towns joined fraternal organizations, some with other Jews only, and others that were community-based. These organizations served social and business purposes, allowing men to gather, share club rituals, and exchange the news of the day as well as help fellow brothers in times of need. In the mining towns these fraternal relationships were often called upon. As Linoberg was a founding member of Sonora's Masonic Lodge, its members were part of his extended family. When he died suddenly at age forty, he was buried in Sonora's Jewish cemetery, his funeral attended by the Masons, Odd Fellows, the fire department, and the Hebrew Benevolent Society, as well as by many of the citizens of Sonora. After Emanuel's death his wife, Pauline, married his brother, Louis. It is traditional for a Jewish man to take care of his

Emanuel Linoberg (1818–1858) gravestone, Jewish Cemetery, Sonora, California. Decorated with a grieving woman and child, the gravestone displays to all that he died at a young age. Photo by Ira Nowinski. Courtesy of the Western Jewish History Center, Judah Magnes Museum.

widowed sister-in-law, but the reason for this union is unknown. The new couple with Emanuel and Pauline's two children went down from the mining country to make their home in the larger community of San Jose.

Although Emanuel Linoberg succeeded in business, he might just as easily have failed, for a merchant's profits depended on miners' ability to continually find gold in the hills and streams that surrounded the gold rush towns. For some merchants, business failure led to tragedy. In one distressing incident, Selig Ritzwoller, the owner of a money-losing store in Sonora, committed suicide, leaving behind a wife and children. In his suicide note, written in German, Ritzwoller appealed to his friends and neighbors and to the San Francisco Hebrew Benevolent Society to care for his survivors.

Temple Emanu-El, San Francisco, 1867.
Courtesy of the San Francisco History Center, San Francisco Public Library.

More typical of life in Sonora is the story of Caroline and Philip Selling. In 1853 they were living in a tent that was also their store. When it burned to the ground, they lost all of their merchandise and all their personal possessions, valued at $8,000. The next day a meeting was held by all in town. A miner took off his hat and requested that everyone put in a little gold dust so that the Sellings could buy what they needed to survive.

End of the Rush

Gradually, as the gold rush economy dried up and Jews could no longer support themselves in the mining towns, they moved on. Jewish worship ended in many of the mining towns in the late 1870s and 1880s, when congregations disbanded as their members left for other places. Most Jews made their way to the growing, cosmopolitan San Francisco. Others continued to look for new opportunities in the mining regions of Nevada, Colorado, and Alaska, as well as in the burgeoning communities along the Northwest Coast and commercial centers of the Southwest. Michel Goldwater (grandfather of Senator Barry Goldwater), a failed merchant in Sonora, found wealth in Phoenix, while the son of Sonora's Phillip and Caroline Selling, Ben Selling, became a leader of Portland's Jewish community. In southern California, the Jewish community in Los Angeles was growing, and Jews lived in communities large and small thoughout the region.

By the 1870s, San Francisco's Jewish population had reached sixteen thousand. The city supported four major congregations and several smaller ones, a host of benevolent societies, fraternal organizations, women's associations, an orphanage and home for the aged, and several Jewish newspapers. The rush for gold brought Jews from Europe and the eastern and southern United States to the Pacific shores, and whether they first made their homes in

AVA F. KAHN

the mining communities or in the port city itself, all added to the multitextured Jewish community. Men who had been members and leaders of Jewish mining-town communities now joined congregations Sherith Israel, Emanu-El, Beth Israel, Ohabai Shalome, and others to create a permanent Jewish presence in the city of San Francisco and throughout California. When travelers arrived in San Francisco by ship, one of the first buildings to come into view was Temple Emanu-El. Its hilltop prominence reflected the place of Jews as founders and builders of the state and of a new Jewish community.

Directory of Sources

Many of the documents quoted in this chapter are reproduced and discussed in Ava F. Kahn's *Jewish Voices of the California Gold Rush: A Documentary History 1849–1880* (Detroit: Wayne State University Press, 2002). Also see Kahn's edited volume *Jewish Life in the American West: Perspectives on Migration, Settlement, and Community* (Heyday Books, Berkeley, 2003/Autry Museum of Western Heritage, 2002). To learn more about Jews in gold rush country see: Robert E. Levinson, *The Jews in the California Gold Rush* (Berkeley: Commission for the Preservation of Pioneer Jewish Cemeteries and Landmarks of the Judah L. Magnes Museum, 1994); Susan Morris, *A Traveler's Guide to Pioneer Jewish Cemeteries of the California Gold Rush* (Berkeley: Commission for the Preservation of Pioneer Jewish Cemeteries and Landmarks, Judah L. Magnes Museum, 1996); Rudolf Glanz, *The Jews of California, from the Discovery of Gold until 1880* (New York: self-published, 1960); Fred Rosenbaum, *Visions of Reform: Congregation Emanu-El and the Jews of San Francisco, 1849–1999* (Berkeley: Judah L. Magnes Museum, 2000). An interested reader should also consult back issues of *Western States Jewish History,* a journal dedicated to Jewish life in the West and especially California.

For those who wish to read contemporary works, I suggest: I. J. Benjamin, *Three years in America, 1859–1862,* translated by Charles Reznikoff (Philadelphia: Jewish Publication Society of America, 1956) and *Western Jewry: An Account of the Achievements of the Jews and Judaism in California,* including eulogies, biographies, and "The Jews in California" by Martin A. Meyer (San Francisco: Emanu-El, 1916), which has recently been republished by Henry Hollander, a San Francisco bookseller.

The Western Jewish History Center of the Judah Magnes Museum in Berkeley, California, and the Bancroft Library on the Berkeley campus are excellent sites for gold rush research. The Bancroft has finding aids on-line. Printed aids on the subject include: Ruth Kelson Rafael, *Western Jewish History Center: Guide to Archival and Oral History Collections* (Berkeley: Western Jewish History Center, Judah L. Magnes Memorial Museum, 1987); Sara G. Cogan, *The Jews of San Francisco and the Greater Bay Area, 1848–1919,* an annotated bibliography (Berkeley: Western Jewish History Center, Judah L. Magnes Memorial Museum, 1973); Sara G.Cogan, *Pioneer Jews of the California Mother Lode, 1849–1880,* an annotated bibliography (Berkeley: Western Jewish History Center, 1968) and Louis J. Rasmussen, *San Francisco Ship Passengers List* vol. IV. (Colma, California: S.F. Historical Records, 1970).

NOTES

1. Based on contemporary figures, these population numbers vary considerably. See Jacob Rader Marcus, *To Count a People: American Jewish Population Data, 1585–1984* (Lanham: University Press of America, 1990), 20.

2. Jonathan D. Sarna, "The 'Mythical Jew' and the 'Jew Next Door' in Nineteenth-Century America," in David A. Gerber, *Antisemitism in American History* (Urbana: University of Illinois Press, 1986), 58.

CHAPTER 3

EARLY SYNAGOGUE ARCHITECTURE

DAVID KAUFMAN

Though little supported by their religious tradition, and often derided as exhibiting an "edifice complex," American Jews nonetheless attach great importance to the building of synagogues. This is no less true in California as elsewhere, and the following survey of early synagogue architecture in the Golden State will demonstrate it amply. Of the manifold reasons for this uncharacteristically Jewish interest in architecture, a number may be suggested by the metaphors we use to describe the synagogues we build. The most obvious source of the synagogue-building impulse is religious devotion and, certainly, the practice of Judaism requires provision of an adequate house of worship—in keeping with its devotional aspect, we tend not to call it a house per se, but more often, a "temple." (Of late, the Yiddish diminutive "shul"—formerly reserved for Orthodox synagogues—has begun to replace the English term, indicating the synagogue's assigned role as the last preserve of Jewish tradition.) Conversely, another key factor spurring synagogue construction is the pervasive religiosity of American society—where every good citizen attends religious services—and hence American Jews eagerly build a "church" of their own, the synagogue thereby serving as a vehicle of acculturation and integration. Yet another essential explanation is the importance of forming community through the establishment of religious, educational, and social "centers"—a need especially salient for Jewish settlers on the frontiers of American life. It has even been suggested that we sometimes build synagogues in response to antisemitism, that is, as a sort of spiritual "sanctuary" offering protection from a hostile environment.

While all these have validity, one other reason stands out above all, one that has no descriptive metaphor save the very graphic images of the buildings themselves. It is this: Jews are enormously proud to have become a full participant in and prominent part of American society and want to both advertise the fact and lend it further support. The building of synagogues achieves this dual goal nicely—call it, "conspicuous construction." The physical concreteness of the buildings marks the Jewish presence on the American landscape as nothing else can. Built to last, ostensibly permanently, and designed to impress Jews and the general public alike, these monuments make a powerful statement of American Jewish success—a multiple success, insofar as it conveys images of religious vitality, social acceptance, economic achievement, and historic "arrival." With these structures, American Jews announce their arrival in both Jewish time and American space. Jews often reflect on their long journey through history—witness, for example, the ancient Jewish prayer, *she-hechianu* (thanking God for preserving us to this day). Jews also commonly celebrate their establishment in the modern world and are especially grateful for the experience of "making it" in America. Such are the American Jewish values expressed in the construction of a new synagogue.

Before reading on, the reader is invited to take a quick test: flip through the following pages, looking at the multiple images of California synagogues. Then ask yourself: how does it make you feel? What is your visceral reaction to seeing these historic structures? The answer, especially if you are yourself an American Jew, should provide some indication of the reason they were built. As they did for nineteenth-century California Jews, the buildings speak to us of the presence of Jewish life. Vibrant echoes from the past, they simply say, "Jews were here." That carved-in-a-tree-trunk sentiment is the essence of Jewish history, is it not? It most certainly is the essence of our review of California's historic nineteenth-century synagogues. We will proceed chronologically, concentrating on the first half-century of synagogue construction in the state, a period which has left all too few surviving synagogue structures intact. Instead, most exist only in old photographs and illustrations buried in archival repositories and synagogue histories, awaiting discovery by the Jewish collective memory.

We begin in the year 1854, during the antebellum years of American history, midway between the gold rush and the Civil War. Exactly two hundred years earlier, the first Jewish community in North America had appeared in what was then New Amsterdam. The Jewish population remained small throughout the colonial and federal periods, but immigration picked up steam in the first half of the nineteenth century and the westward movement of American Jewry began. Communal and institutional development followed soon thereafter. In 1854, Judah Touro became the first American Jewish philanthropist through his generous bequests to Jewish communities around the country; and in the same year, Rabbi Isaac Mayer Wise moved to Cincinnati to launch his crusade to create a truly American Judaism. Among Wise's strategies was the publication of a new Jewish newspaper, *The American Israelite,* which then estimated the nationwide Jewish population at a hundred thousand souls, their community organized into some eighty congregations. By 1854, Jews had settled in thirty-six states, including California, Oregon, Utah, and Washington.

In California, Jews had arrived with the gold rush and settled the northern boom towns of Marysville, Sonora, Columbia, Nevada City, Placerville, Stockton, Jackson, and Mokelumne Hill. Each of these towns would soon see the founding of a Jewish cemetery, congregation, or other Jewish organization. Some even managed to create a makeshift space for a synagogue. The pioneer Jewish community of Sacramento, for example, converted a church edifice, purchasing a prefabricated wooden structure from the Methodist church in June of 1852. It was called "the first synagogue west of the Rockies"; and it was, until consumed by fire just a few months later. The honor of building California's first two "permanent" synagogue structures—both in 1854—would fall instead to the fastest growing Jewish community in California—San Francisco.

San Francisco, the gateway city of the state, became home to the most prominent Jewish community of the nineteenth century. An organized community came into being following the gold rush, and the first religious services were held in the fall of 1849. At the high holiday services of the following year, the Yom Kippur sermon was delivered by twenty-nine-year-old Lewis Franklin who exhorted his co-religionists: "I ask you, shall there be no temple built to Israel's God?" They would heed his call. As early as 1851, the mostly young, immigrant businessmen who formed the nascent congregation announced themselves "desirous of building a house of worship," and began raising the necessary funds. In April of that year, ethnic rivalry led to the formation of separate congregations: Emanu-El and Sherith Israel. Nevertheless, plans to build proceeded apace—in fact, they may even have been spurred by the growing competition between them. For Emanu-El, $1,500 was raised that first year, and after a delay caused by the disastrous fires of that period, another $20,000 was pledged in November 1853. It is worth noting that these fundraising meetings were public affairs, and that the success of their efforts was attributed to "the liberality of our fellow-citizens." That winter, under the leadership of new president Henry Seligman, then only twenty-five years old, Congregation Emanu-El purchased a lot on Broadway, between Powell and Mason Streets, 63 feet by 137 feet, and costing $4,500. The neighborhood was situated just to the west of the central business district of San Francisco, and was rapidly developing into the residential area of preference for most Jews of the city. There was little surprise when Sherith Israel purchased a lot on Stockton Street for its new synagogue, just two blocks away. The first Jewish neighborhood of San Francisco may be seen in the accompanying illustration, conveying some of the flavor of the period and prominently displaying the rather substantial "Broadway Synagogue" of Congregation Emanu-El (figure 1).

Construction for the new Emanu-El synagogue commenced in June 1854, supervised by builder John Daniels, architects William Crane and Thomas England, and the building committee of the congregation—who stated at the time, "by the help of Almighty God, we purpose consecrating by Roshoshanah next." Following the plans of its architect, Miner Frederic Butler, Sherith Israel began its building process a few months later; construction proceeded quickly and the structure was completed in just one month, in time to dedicate the building on September 8. Emanu-El would hold its opening ceremony just six days later, on the fourteenth of the month. Both synagogues were consecrated by the city's first rabbi, Julius Eckman, and both stood open for the high holidays of that year. Though born of an ethnic split just three years

Figure 1. Aerial view of Emanu-El, San Francisco, built 1854. Courtesy of Western Jewish History Center, Judah Magnes Museum.

earlier, the German Emanu-El and the Polish Sherith Israel commissioned remarkably similar buildings (figures 2, 3). Both were medium-sized, three-storied rectangular brick buildings—the all-brick Emanu-El measured 65 by 78 feet and sat approximately 800, whereas the brick-fronted Sherith Israel was somewhat smaller, seating 400; and both were given façades designed in provincial Gothic style, exhibiting gabled façades punctuated by ornate pinnacles and arched windows and doorways. They differ in a number of details—especially Emanu-El's picturesque double stoop—yet the overall impression is one of similitude. While divided internally, the nascent Jewish community of San Francisco presented a united front to the outside world.

Still, the choice of the Gothic revival for the new synagogues' architecture raises a number of questions. The Gothic style is most often associated with the religious architecture of Christian Europe. In most other Jewish communities around the world, the Gothic was eschewed as an appropriate synagogue style for this very reason—it looked "too Christian." How then, to explain this choice made by early California Jews? (One might object that members of the community would have had nothing to

do with the stylistic choice, and that it would have been the decision of the architect alone. True, most people tend not to be architecturally sophisticated; yet everything we know of synagogue politics, building committees, and American Jews' concern with their public image suggests that at the very least, the congregational leadership would have assented to the design only after due consideration.) By accepting this most churchly look, the Jews of San Francisco indicated the religious basis of their new American community. Rather than stress their ethnic foreignness, they built ecclesiastic chapels reassuring in their familiarity to fellow churchgoing San Franciscans. Another possibility, with opposite implications, is that the style was influenced by immigrant Catholics, who built similar versions of the historical cathedral style. In this scenario, the German and Polish Jews were simply identifying with their fellow ethnics. Either explanation still begs the question of Californian exclusivity from other Jewish communities. How is it, when both San Francisco congregations chose names emulating prominent synagogues in New York, no attention was paid to the architectural precedents of other American synagogues? The best answer, perhaps, is that the decade of the 1850s was still early in the history of

DAVID KAUFMAN

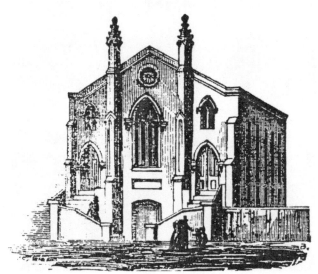

Figure 2. Emanu-El, San Francisco, built 1854.
From Rachel Wischnitzer, Synagogue Architecture in the United
States. *Courtesy of the Jewish Publication Society of America.*

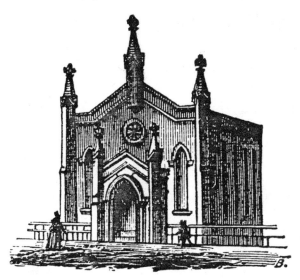

Figure 3. Sherith Israel, San Francisco, built 1854.
From Rachel Wischnitzer, Synagogue Architecture in the United
States. *Courtesy of the Jewish Publication Society of America.*

Figure 4. Reim Ahuvim, Stockton, built 1855.
Courtesy of Western States Jewish History Archive.

American synagogue architecture, and thus any choice of style was necessarily experimental. The experiment would bear fruit with the next major synagogue in San Francisco.

But first, other California synagogues would hew more closely to general trends. In 1851, the Jews of Stockton organized a congregation called Reim Ahuvim (also spelled Ryhim Ahoovim), meaning "beloved friends." Four years later, in the summer of 1855, they prepared to build a synagogue. It was to be located on riverfront property donated by the town's founder, Captain Charles Weber, and

would be built entirely of wood, for the cost of $3,500. Unlike its predecessors in San Francisco, it was designed in a neo-colonial style with a more American look (figure 4)—complete with wooden fence, shuttered windows, clapboard siding, and most conspicuously, a prominent arcaded steeple. With perhaps a nod to the year-old synagogues in the big city, the corners of the gable were adorned with Gothic-type turrets; nevertheless, the overall effect was that of an ordinary country church. Above the gabled doorway, and enclosing the central circular window, was inlaid a double arch, evoking the twin tablets of the Ten Commandments—the only indication of the Jewish purpose of the building, and a subtle one at that. This early California synagogue was certainly beloved by its congregation. When later inundated with water by the overflow of the river, it was rescued by moving the entire structure to a new location rather than rebuilding anew. The original building was relocated yet again when the congregation finally built a new synagogue in 1905, and has survived, at least in part, being designated a Stockton Historical Landmark in 1983.

A more instant landmark was created in San Francisco with the construction of a second home for the Emanu-El congregation. As early as 1860, the congregation foresaw the need for larger accommodations. In his annual address, President Heinrich Seligmann pointed to "the great growth of our congregation," and thus raised "the necessity of providing a house of worship adequate for all." He continued: "It is clear that in a short time our synagogue will not be large enough for our needs, and I take the liberty of urging you to select soon a suitable plot of ground." By 1864, the Broadway synagogue was put up for sale, a new site purchased, an architect hired, and work begun on what historian Moses Rischin, in his *Jews of the American West,* would call "the West's most renowned Jewish edifice."

The new synagogue, henceforth to be called "Temple," was big, ornate, and above all, impressive. Built from 1864 to 1866, the extraordinary structure immediately became a physical landmark on the skyline of the city, an architectural landmark of the entire West Coast, and an historic landmark in the annals of California Jewry. The new Temple Emanu-El was built for the ages—it is truly lamentable, therefore, that having barely survived the great earthquake of 1906, it no longer stands today. Yet its striking image, preserved in numerous photographs and illustrations from the era, testifies to a remarkable moment in the history of California's Jews (figure 5). Covering its dedication in March of 1866, the newspaper correspondent for the *Daily Alta California* gushed,

> In point of architectural beauty and grandeur the synagogue not only surpasses all churches in the State, but excels the great majority in the United States, ranking nearly every synagogue extant. It is a chaste and elegant ornament to our country, and reflects credit on California talent in its construction, and does honor to the taste and liberality of our Jewish fellow-citizens.

The congregation had begun planning in earnest for a new synagogue just ten years after erecting its earlier building on Broadway. In June 1864, a projected expenditure of $134,000 was approved by the board, and a cornerstone was laid on the new site on Sutter Street in October of that year. By the time of its completion one and a half years later, the cost would be close to $200,000—nearly

Figure 5. Emanu-El's 1866 synagogue, San Francisco. Courtesy of Western States Jewish History Archive.

ten times the amount spent on the first synagogue. The *arriviste* members of Emanu-El had risen economically in dramatic fashion, and would now demonstrate their success for all to see. The congregation's able historian, Fred Rosenbaum, notes that "the Sutter Street temple was part of the boom in synagogue construction throughout America in the 1860s, as German Jews everywhere seemed to reach a new level of wealth and acculturation and demanded elegant edifices to house their growing congregations." Regarding Emanu-El, he adds: "the grand scale of the Sutter Street temple indicated that a Jewish commercial elite had crystallized in San Francisco as well—and within a shorter time than anywhere else."

And the scale was grand indeed. The building's footprint measured 78 feet in width and 120 feet in length, and its sanctuary sat no fewer than eight hundred on the main floor and four hundred in the galleries. The interior must have awed those who came to worship, as it was "one of the largest vaulted rooms ever constructed in California, 53 feet across, 97 feet long, and 50 feet from the floor to the highest keystones" (figure 6). The most lasting impression was created by the two towers of the exterior façade, both reaching 176 feet into the sky (about fifteen stories), and capped by bronze-plated bulbous domes. Together with the building's location atop a San Francisco hill, the distinctive towers guaranteed that Temple Emanu-El was a conspicuous feature on the skyline of the city—it would

DAVID KAUFMAN

Figure 6. Interior of Emanu-El, San Francisco, 1866.
From Jacob Voorsanger, The Chronicles of Emanu-El.
Courtesy of Western States Jewish History Archive.

be sighted from ships in San Francisco Bay and was even visible to hikers across the Bay in the Berkeley Hills. By reaching for the sky, the new monument fulfilled the aspirations of its builders—the same expressed by temple builders since ancient times—to show the world the power of their faith. Yet the "faith" displayed by the San Francisco Jews was based upon more than a sense of spiritual rectitude; it now evinced as well a hard-won belief in their own ability to prevail materially in the new American homeland.

The design of the new Temple Emanu-El communicated still another set of messages (figure 7). Unlike the earlier building, we know that the choice of a stylistic scheme was well thought through by the architect, William Patton. The English Patton was trained by the most famous Gothic revivalist of the time, Sir Gilbert Scott, and made his reputation as a church architect. He had designed another synagogue in San Francisco—Ohabai Shalome (a more conservative offshoot of Emanu-El), described as "an elegant and substantial brick structure"—and was also well known as the architect of Thomas Starr King's Unitarian church, built in 1863. Both were designed in the familiar style of a Gothic church. For Emanu-El, however, Patton declared himself freed of any stylistic constraint, intending to invent a truly Jewish style of architecture. Since no such historical style existed, he instead combined a variety of traditional motifs and integrated the whole through the use of Jewish imagery. The building was Gothic in overall form and engineering, though built of brick rather than the traditional stone. At the same time, it also incorporated Romanesque round archways and Orientalist onion domes. The structure was furthermore plastered with Jewish symbols—Stars of David inlaid in numerous locations on the façade and in the tracery of its stained glass windows, and the Ten Commandments perched prominently atop the gable. It has even been suggested that the domes were meant less to evoke the Orient than the *rimmonim,* or "pomegranate capitals" adorning a

Figure 7. Emanu-El, San Francisco, 1866.
From Jacob Voorsanger, The Chronicles of Emanu-El.
Courtesy of Western States Jewish History Archive.

Torah scroll. Whether true or not, it is unquestionable that William Patton's intent—and hence the intention of the congregation—was to create an identifiably Jewish building, demonstrating in no uncertain terms the acceptance of Judaism in America. As the immigrant architect himself stated at the cornerstone laying ceremony, the new temple would reflect what was most "admirable in this wonderful age, and in this wonderful land . . . that cosmopolitan freedom of thought and toleration of opinion that treats all civilized men and women as equal."

The new Temple Emanu-El was thus both a statement of American freedom and Jewish pride—and combining the two was the emergent movement of Reform Judaism, an expression of "Jewish freedom," as it were, and a religious orientation embodied by the architecture as well. New Reform temples were then about to sprout throughout the country, and the pathbreaking Emanu-El of San Francisco was joined by two other prominent models, Cincinnati's Bene Yeshurun of 1866 and New York's Emanu-El of 1868—likewise leaders in the new movement for a progressive American Judaism. The former structure, also known as the "Isaac Mayer Wise" or "Plum Street" Temple, was designed in the Moorish Revival style, its picturesque mosque-like appearance meant to evoke the Golden Age of Spanish Jewry. The New York building was a more restrained combination of the Gothic and the Moorish styles, as designed by America's first two Jewish architects, Henry Fernbach and Leopold Eidlitz. All three were monumental structures clearly intended to herald a new era in Jewish history and a new phase in the development of Judaism.

Similarly, the interior of the buildings provided a new kind of congregational space for a new style of Jewish worship. Like its parallels across the country, the sanctuary of Emanu-El of San Francisco was filled throughout with family pews, the whole space illuminated through stained-glass windows, "cloth[ing] it with that subdued and holy light which always tends to the promotion of sincerity in religious worship." The *Daily Alta California* also noted the novel arrangement of the *bimah:* "The reading-desk, pulpit, and ark, as is the custom of the Reformed Jewish Church, are united, and located in front of the recess of the north end of the building." No separate platform highlighting the centrality of the Torah was thought necessary in this auditorium for song and sermon; and no eastward orientation to Jerusalem was required for this new Temple in a new Zion, America. Further emphasizing the frontal arrangement of the sanctuary, above the *bimah* appeared lavishly appointed loft spaces for the choir and grand organ, providing the musical accompaniment to the revised service. Together, these innovations communicated a new form of Judaism, one well suited to the hospitable environment of nineteenth-century America.

Hence Patton's design for Emanu-El was seen as a complete success, lauded as "a true creation of genius." Standing majestically on its Sutter Street site, the "Temple on a hill" served the prospering congregation through four decades—until, tragically, it was nearly destroyed in the great earthquake of 1906. Though the congregation pledged to rebuild the cherished edifice, the reconstruction would neglect to include the famous towers. As such, the building never regained its former glory and was abandoned by the congregation altogether in the 1920s. But for well over a generation, the Temple Emanu-El of 1866 reigned over the San Francisco skyline as a powerful declaration that both Jews and Judaism had arrived in the West. It would also be impossible to ignore as a model for other California synagogues yet to be built.

A number of such "responses" to Emanu-El were put up during the 1870s, both in new Jewish communities around the state and in San Francisco itself. At the start of the decade, Emanu-El's rival congregation, Sherith Israel, followed suit with a new building of its own. Located at the corner of Post and Taylor Streets, the new synagogue appears in a contemporary photograph as a more ornate version of the earlier synagogues for Emanu-El and Sherith Israel (figure 8). Built of brick and stone, it was again a rectangular box of a building, festooned with Gothic ornament, and surmounted by eight pinnacles (four to each side tower). The Polish congregation was not quite as affluent as the German Emanu-El, and hence creating another grand gesture was not in the offing. Yet atop the tower pinnacles are miniature, encrusted onion domes—surely a small gesture toward the example of the neighboring Sutter Street temple. Likewise, the photograph reveals the Stars of David inset into the arched windows alongside the building. Emanu-El had been one of the first synagogues in America to employ this now common Jewish symbol (the Baltimore Hebrew Congregation of 1845 is believed to have been the first), and its influence would be felt in synagogue design for the next century and more. Interestingly, an interior photograph of Sherith Israel's sanctuary in 1901 (figure 9). highlights not Jewish symbols, but rather, the regalia of American patriotism—the

Figure 8. Congregation Sherith Israel,
San Francisco, Post and Taylor, 1870.
Courtesy of Western Jewish History Center, Judah Magnes Museum.

Figure 9. Interior of Sherith Israel, San Francisco, built 1870.
Courtesy of Western Jewish History Center, Judah Magnes Museum.

occasion was the assassination of President McKinley, reminding us once again of the dual purpose of the American synagogue: not only to celebrate Judaism, but also to consecrate Americanism.

Another synagogue of 1870 reveals the trend of employing the Jewish symbolism of the Star of David most dramatically. The Bickur Cholim synagogue of San Jose was dedicated in August 1870 at the northeast corner of Third and San Antonio Streets (figure 10). When the Jews of San Jose erected a new synagogue for their congregation, Bickur Cholim (referring to the original purpose of the society—"visiting the sick"—but later renamed Emanu-El), they rejected the Gothic in favor of Romanesque, the favored architectural style for modern synagogues throughout central Europe, as well as for many throughout the United States. Some contemporary examples of Romanesque Revival American synagogues include New York's B'nai Jeshurun of 1851 and Rodeph Shalom of 1853, Philadelphia's Mikveh Israel of 1860 and Keneseth Israel of 1864, New Orleans' Temple Sinai of 1872, Chicago's Sinai Temple of 1876, and many more through the 1880s and 1890s. The San Jose synagogue must be seen therefore as part of a greater trend, further demonstrated by the rather noticeable Star of David window highlighting its façade.

Our survey now moves to Southern California, with the first synagogue of Los Angeles. The city's founding congregation, B'nai B'rith, was established in July of 1862. For the first several years of its existence, religious services were led by members of the congregation and were held in various rented quarters; but in 1869, a rabbi was employed and a building campaign begun. At a meeting held on March 10 of that year, reported the *Los Angeles Star,* "the ladies of the congregation assembled for the purpose of devising means to raise funds to purchase a lot and erect a suitable church building." Under the leadership of President Joseph Newmark and Rabbi Abraham Wolf Edelman, the women succeeded in their enterprise. In August of 1872, a cornerstone was laid at a downtown site on Fort Street (today's Broadway) between Second and Third Streets, and the new synagogue was dedicated exactly a year later. It was designed by one of the first architects in Los Angeles, Ezra F. Keysor, who gave the young congregation yet another California synagogue "of Gothic formation and adornment" (figure 11).

Unlike the preceding buildings, the B'nai B'rith synagogue of 1873 lacked any explicit Jewish symbolism on its exterior. In lieu of Stars of David, Keysor bedecked the

DAVID KAUFMAN

Figure 10. Bickur Cholim, San Jose, built 1870.
Courtesy of Western States Jewish History Archive.

shows B'nai B'rith on Fort Street and three neighboring churches (figure 12). The closest, the First Presbyterian Church, was on the same block—a significant fact in itself, reflecting religious amity in the developing city. Its design is English-inspired Gothic Revival, and the large structure is dominated by a majestic spire atop the corner tower. A block beyond the Presbyterian church can be seen Saint Vibiana's Roman Catholic Cathedral, designed in an Italianate Renaissance Revival style by none other than Ezra Keysor. Clearly different from both the "English" Presbyterian church and the "Italian" Catholic church, the design for B'nai B'rith may have been inspired by central European historical styles thought to be appropriate for a Jewish house of worship. Especially in Keysor's two "church" designs, the contrast of building styles demonstrates the architect's intention to create a distinctive look for his Jewish clients. It may be helpful here to quote architectural historian David P. Handlin:

> In seeking an appropriate image for a place of worship, every religion and denomination had to engage in a self-conscious search for an architecture that was not only identified with its history but also allowed for a fresh and compelling interpretation. This task was probably most difficult for American Jews. Their attempt to find an appropriate image for the synagogue epitomized a condition that was general to all nineteenth-century architecture in that they had no obvious precedent to which to turn.[1]

And so it might be best to see Keysor's anomalous design for B'nai B'rith as part of an ongoing experiment in American synagogue architecture—parallel to the continued attempts to define an appropriate style of American Judaism, and indeed, of Jewish life in America on the whole.

Another enigmatic design appeared in 1878 with the new synagogue for the First Hebrew Congregation of Oakland. On November 18, 1875, a group of eighteen enterprising young Jewish immigrants—from points of origin as diverse as Prussia, Alsace, Poland, Hungary and Bavaria—met in Nathan Rosenberg's cigar store to establish a congregation. By the following January a lot was purchased for a new synagogue and surely construction would have commenced soon thereafter had not an economic depression intervened. As soon as recovery was in sight, however, a wooden structure was put up for the sum of about $8,000. Located at the corner of Fouteenth and Webster Streets, it was dedicated on August 15, 1878. The outlook for the fu-

façade with five-pointed stars instead, one in the central window and one surmounting the finial above. This may seem puzzling given the precedents of earlier years and the fact that the new Los Angeles synagogue served an Orthodox congregation, certainly proud of its Jewish identity. We might nonetheless expect to have seen the influence of the Reform Temple Emanu-El, especially since the Los Angeles congregation had sent representatives to San Francisco to request monetary aid in its endeavor ($1,000 was pledged). The architect must not have been among the delegation. Apparently, the architecture of Los Angeles' first synagogue was just that—the first civic statement by the fledgling Jewish community, and its timid design reflected that insecurity.

At the same time, it must be noted that Keysor provided them with a synagogue distinctly unlike contemporary church buildings in Los Angeles. An aerial view of 1885

Figure 11. B'nai B'rith, Los Angeles, built 1873.
Courtesy of Western States Jewish History Archive.

Figure 12. Aerial view of B'nai B'rith, Los Angeles, 1885.
Courtesy of Western States Jewish History Archive.

Figure 13. First Hebrew Congregation, Oakland, built 1870.
Courtesy of the Oakland Public Library, Oakland History Room.

ture was optimistic, as the Jewish community of Oakland was still relatively small yet the new synagogue was large enough to seat five hundred worshippers. Though it stood for less than a decade (tragically, it burned down in 1885), its architectural design was striking and worth recalling (figure 13).

Like most other founding congregations of a city (for example, B'nai B'rith of Los Angeles), the First Hebrew Congregation of Oakland was Orthodox from its inception. Unlike the pioneer synagogue of Los Angeles, however, its design was progressive in every way, indicating some measure of influence from its neighbor across the bay. Like Emanu-El, its design incorporated Stars of David throughout the façade and onion domes capped its roof towers. Yet departing from the Emanu-El model, its domi-

nant scheme was not Gothic but some combination of Moorish (see its keyhole windows and insets) and Renaissance Revival (see its grand double staircase and entryway). The overall effect is an appearance far more exotic and picturesque than its San Francisco cousin. Since we have only an ink drawing of the 1878 building, it is hard to know its coloration; but based on the exquisite detail of the façade and the fact of its wooden construction—it would therefore have been painted—we may assume that it was as colorful in life as it was in conception. Unfortunately, the 1886 building that replaced it had none of the poetry of the original, though it did still exhibit onion domes on its roof.

In general, the 1880s was a slow period in the history of the California synagogue; no buildings of architectural

Figure 14. Beth Shalom, San Leandro, built 1888.
Courtesy of Western States Jewish History Archive.

significance were constructed during the decade. Yet ironically, the two small synagogues erected at the end of the decade are two of the few that still exist today. In September 1888, the Jewish congregation of San Leandro dedicated its new synagogue on Chumalia Street (figure 14). It was a modest wood structure, resembling a private house more than a public institution, and was denoted as a synagogue only by the Ten Commandments plaque set above the doorway and the words "Temple Beth Sholom" emblazoned on the doorframe. The building served as a small-town synagogue for sixty-five years, and in 1970 was moved to the present site where it was converted to use as a clubhouse for the youth of the congregation. It now merits distinction as the oldest surviving synagogue structure in California.

A close second oldest is the 1889 building of San Diego's early congregation, Beth Israel. Having dedicated their new synagogue on September 25 of that year, its members were justifiably proud of the attractive redwood edifice (figure 15). Though costing only $3,500 to construct, it exhibited distinctive architectural detailing. Its rectangular front was punctuated by several circular portals containing Star of David windows; and atop the gable was prominently displayed the twin tablets motif. The congregation endured

DAVID KAUFMAN

Figure 15. Beth Israel, San Diego, built 1889.
Courtesy of Western States Jewish History Archive.

some difficult times when forced to rent out the synagogue to various church groups and eventually sold the property in 1926. In 1978 the building was designated a historic site and was consequently moved to Heritage Park in San Diego's Old Town, a "living museum" of nineteenth-century buildings.

A third surviving synagogue building of the period stands in San Francisco itself—the Ohabai Shalome synagogue of 1895, perhaps the masterpiece of the genre under discussion (figure 16). Founded in 1864, Ohabai Shalome was the aforementioned offshoot of Emanu-El, created in opposition to the reformist tendency of the parent congregation. Its membership consisted of Jews from both Eastern and Western Europe, and its religious stance would remain conservative. By the 1890s, the congregation was ready to erect its own grand temple; still in rivalry with Emanu-El, however, any possible architectural in-

fluence was bound to be attenuated. While responding competitively with an equally grandiose and unique design, the 1895 Bush Street Synagogue of Ohabai Shalome was a clear departure from its famed predecessor.

As designed by architect Moses J. Lyon, the building was a fanciful collage of disparate styles and details. With unabashed eclecticism, Lyon combined round-arched doorways and windows (Romanesque) on the ground floor, with a quatrefoil arcaded porch (Venetian Gothic) on the second level, with horseshoe arches and onion domes (Moorish) on the towers above. Between the towers was set a pinnacled roof structure resembling a miniature triumphal arch whose sole purpose, it seems, was to frame the Ten Commandments at its heart. The all-redwood façade was unified through the use of alternating bands of color—characteristic of both the Venetian Gothic and Moorish revival styles. The inventive look was said to be in

Figure 16. Ohabai Shalome, San Francisco, built 1895.
Courtesy of Western Jewish History Center, Judah Magnes Museum.

Figure 17. Ohabai Shalome, sanctuary interior, 1906. Confirmation
ceremony was delayed until October because of the earthquake.
Courtesy of Western Jewish History Center, Judah Magnes Museum.

the "Sephardic" or "Mediterranean" style, referring both to the Venetian/Moorish-derived architecture and to the diasporic roots of European Jewry. Like William Patton before him, Moses Lyon had attempted to create a "Jewish" style of architecture.

Ohabai Shalome remained at its Bush Street location for nearly forty years, until changing demographics forced the disbanding of the congregation. The neighborhood had become San Francisco's "Japantown," and the building was sold for use as a Japanese Zen Buddhist Temple. Designated a city landmark in 1976, the building became the subject of a legal battle between the Japanese American Religious Federation (JARF), nobly intending to convert the building into senior housing for local residents, and a Jewish group headed by architect Felix Warburg. Warburg's concern was the preservation of Jewish architectu-

ral history, and his group's intention was to fully restore both the exterior and interior (figure 17) of the structure and ultimately to create a new institution: the Bush Street Synagogue Cultural Center. Its stated purpose was to "educate community residents about Jewish life, while fostering tolerance and understanding." As of this writing, the San Francisco Development Agency has awarded the property to the JARF, but Warburg is sanguine that they have agreed to honor his preservationist agenda and hopes to have access to the former sanctuary in the evenings for public programs and tours.

The final two buildings in our survey were both designed by one of the first Jewish architects in California—Abraham M. Edelman, son of the pioneer rabbi of Los Angeles. As a youngster, the future architect was likely present during the construction of the first B'nai B'rith synagogue in 1873, and it requires little stretch of the imagination to link the experience to his later choice of profession. He certainly spent much time in the original structure, contemplating its form and function, and thereby preparing, knowingly or not, for his career as a synagogue architect.

In 1884, Rabbi Edelman resigned the pulpit in the face of mounting pressure to reform the congregation. Following the progressive trend, the congregation continued its rapid growth and began in the 1890s to look for a new location—a site was soon found at the corner of Ninth and Hope Streets. Abraham Edelman (the younger) was commissioned to design the new structure, and on September 6, 1896, the B'nai B'rith congregation dedicated its second synagogue edifice, which served the community until the

Figure 18. B'nai B'rith, Los Angeles, 1896.
Courtesy of Western States Jewish History Archive.

move to Wilshire Boulevard in 1929. The building was substantially larger than the earlier structure, and its architecture far more pleasing (figure 18). Edelman was well aware of the Moorish Revival trend upstate and elsewhere and incorporated the distinctive bulbous domes of the style in his design for B'nai B'rith. The rest of the building was a well-executed example of the Romanesque Revival style, highlighted by an outsized Star of David rose window. While housed in this attractive building, the congregation joined the Union of American Hebrew Congregations in 1903 and installed Edgar Magnin as rabbi in 1915. Though the congregation has survived to the present day (renamed the Wilshire Boulevard Temple), the historic building sadly has not.

Just after the turn of the century, Abraham Edelman would design a second synagogue in Los Angeles. A smaller, wood-constructed version of B'nai B'rith, it served a new congregation named Beth Israel (est. 1892). Located on Olive Street in the Bunker Hill section of downtown Los Angeles, the new synagogue was dedicated on April 13, 1902 (figure 19). Until its demise in 1940, it was fondly known to

its congregants (and to other Los Angeles Jews) as the "Olive Street Shul"—the familiar Yiddish term *shul* indicates a new religious and cultural orientation: the Orthodox Judaism characteristic of East European Jews. The 1902 building, erroneously called "the first Orthodox synagogue in Los Angeles" (recall that B'nai B'rith had been Orthodox at its inception), is significant more as a harbinger of the Jewish immigrant wave soon to hit California.

In the twentieth century, the overwhelming majority of American Jews would descend from the Yiddish-speaking regions of Russia, Poland, and Rumania; and in this regard, Beth Israel was the pioneer. But the historic structure has more to tell us concerning the mindset of these early California Jews. Arriving in a state with few traditionalist enclaves, the only institutional model they found was the Reform temple, B'nai B'rith. Though its religious style was abhorrent to the new arrivals, its level of social acceptance and political integration in the new society was, quite the contrary, to be prized. How to repeat the success of their predecessors? The recent immigrants went about the process of learning English and learning

Figure 19. Beth Israel, Los Angeles, built 1902.
Courtesy of Western States Jewish History Archive.

lowing year, the great earthquake struck and Emanu-El was forced to reconstruct its historic temple. Also damaged by the quake was a synagogue just in the process of being built for Congregation Beth Israel; construction was begun again and the building completed in 1908. The First Hebrew Congregation of Oakland was renamed Temple Sinai and in 1914 made a dramatic statement with a new building designed by Jewish architect G. Albert Lansburgh. The 1920s saw a boom in synagogue construction throughout the state, as indeed throughout the country. But that subject must await another opportunity. Our brief review of the nineteenth-century synagogue architecture of California has fulfilled its purpose—demonstrating the pervasive drive to erect physical monuments to the Jewish spirit. In its Californian context, that spirit encompassed the pioneering spirit of the forty-eighters, the enterprising spirit of urban commerce, the democratizing spirit of American citizenship, the liberalizing spirit of Reform Judaism, and the civilizing spirit of Jewish tradition—all captured in the extraordinarily eclectic architectural legacy recovered in these pages.

NOTES

1. Handlin, David P. *American Architecture* (1985), p. 91.

new civic practices with equal aplomb; and the new synagogue they built may be seen in this vein as well. Certainly not intended to emulate the Reform temple religiously, it was nonetheless intended to emulate its status as a proper, American synagogue. While Abraham Edelman had provided the imitative design, the Orthodox Jews of Olive Street moved into their new congregational home with pride in their arrival and great aspirations for the future—exactly the sentiments of generations of American Jews before them.

In the years to come, many of the same congregations continued to build newer, bigger, and better synagogues. In 1905, Sherith Israel of San Francisco replaced its 1870 building with a monumental domed structure. In the fol-

DAVID KAUFMAN

CHAPTER 4

THROUGH THE LENS OF
LATINO-JEWISH RELATIONS

STEVEN WINDMUELLER

Over the next decade Latinos will emerge as America's largest minority community, with a population in excess of thirty million, representing 25 percent of this nation's citizens. In Los Angeles, Latinos already account for over 40 percent of this city's population. While many observers of the American Jewish scene have identified the black–Jewish alliance as paramount, California Jews understand that their future is inextricably linked to the state's original settlers. Beyond L.A., the growth of Latino influence within this society will fundamentally change the inter-group relations construct of America.

This notion of ethnic succession has defined the landscape of urban politics, and in this context, the process of gaining access to power has shaped how groups perceive themselves and their relationships to other communities and the larger society. Certainly for Jews their entry into the landscape of America's cities was linked to the challenge of understanding how the intricacies of power and influence would unfold in this society. Organizing themselves and, in turn, engaging other ethnic and racial groupings helped to frame and launch American Jewry's passion for political activism. In the end a core axiom of Jewish influence involved the principle that for this community to gain access to power in an urban context, it would have to coalesce with other key constituencies. This model was reflected in the formation of the African American–Jewish alliance that would play a major role in shaping urban politics.

The story of Los Angeles reflected this same scenario, as Jews found an opportunity over the past half-century, with blacks and others, to help form coalitions and promote political consensus, and in turn achieve a level of significant influence and power. In the process of building these connections, a type of social contract linking Jews to the city's social and political infrastructures evolved. Today,

however, the City of the Angels is entering a new period in its development, and with these changes are major challenges to the future role and place of the Jewish community in the urban landscape of Los Angeles. With the emergence of new contenders for political influence in this city, primarily Latinos but also an array of other new immigrant ethnic constituencies, these factors will create a profound political fallout for the Jewish community as well as impact and shape how Jews in Los Angeles will perceive themselves.

Over the past half-century, Jews achieved direct power by electing their own to political office; as a result of the changing character of this city, Jews will gain power through indirect channels, petitioning others to act on their behalf. Similarly, an increasing number of those Jews who are being elected today and in the future to public positions are more likely to be less connected to the Jewish communal establishment than their predecessors, due in part to the weakening of these communal institutions. In light of these political and demographic changes, the future of Jewish power in L.A. appears to be at best uncertain.

The new realities of Los Angeles, dictated by demographics and economics, will bring Latinos to power more rapidly than perhaps the Jewish community or others could have fully understood or appreciated. In this transition of group influence and power, the issues remain open as to how this succession of power will occur and what role Jews will play in this unfolding story. Unlike the story of the black–Jewish experience, with its rich and complex legacy, there are a host of unknown factors that will influence and define this new Los Angeles coalition.

What is equally striking is the changing character of the Jewish community itself, involving the emergence of a growing and influential presence of a new class of Jewish immigrants from non-Western, non-liberal societies, who do not share the same intensity for urban engagement. Clearly, Jews from the former Soviet Union, Iran, and elsewhere view their communal and civic responsibilities from within a different cultural frame. Their focus, reflective of their communal experiences with antisemitism, is centered principally on Jewish security and identity.

One of the keys to the Jewish urban story has been the level of personal investment and social connection that in the past linked certain Jews to the urban community. For many of these Jews their own sense of Jewishness was defined through the lens of intergroup relationships. More recently, however, the passion and consensus that once defined the politics of Jewish urban social activism seem at best weakened and in disarray, giving way to a growing separation from the "outside" world, in turn, replaced by a renewed internal focus on Jewish interests.

The implications of these new realities, both the changing political dynamics of Los Angeles and the disengagement of Jews from their social contract with this urban center, may not only have significant impact on the political standing of the Jewish community in Los Angeles but also reflect a pattern of Jewish disengagement from the American urban agenda. In order to understand the importance of these developments, it is necessary to understand what is happening in Los Angeles, as a barometer of what will occur in this nation's major cities over the decades ahead.

L.A. must be seen as the new Ellis Island, where more than one-third of its residents are immigrants. One hundred and forty languages can be heard on the streets of Los Angeles, while six hundred religious traditions are observed within L.A. County. As a result of these dramatic developments a new political environment is also forming, which will affect the Jewish community of this city.

Latinos and Jews, either as partners or as competitors, may well define the city's future. Collectively these constituencies account for nearly 40 percent of the Los Angeles vote. Yet, we are witnessing two communities at very different points in their American sojourn. One community has already moved through its American ethnic urban adventure; the other, with its significant immigrant population, is embarking on that trail of discovery and adjustment. It is sobering to note that Latinos today constitute over 40 percent of this city's population and already number more than ten million residents in California. This community is seen both as the fastest growing segment of new home owners and small business entrepreneurs. Over this same time frame, this emerging community will articulate a shared political vision, deliver significant voters to its expanding base of political leaders and future candidates, and create the necessary grassroots infrastructures in order to meet its communal priorities.

The organized Jewish community, among others, historically viewed urban politics along racial boundaries; with the influx of new immigrants to this nation's major urban areas, an alternative model has emerged, framed around multiculturalism and the politics of diversity. This reformulation of the urban landscape will challenge the existing political elites to examine the old notions of coalition and partnership. Latinos, as the most dominant community within this new sector of diversity, will seek to exercise their growing influence in gaining access to the centers of power. Accordingly, we are witnessing in L.A., and in cities across this country, a civic transformation of profound and historic implications as these "new Americans" empowered by their numbers and encouraged by their emerging leadership seek their place at the tables of dialogue and decision making. These events will have a significant effect on the political and social systems of our communities, challenging and changing institutional culture and representation.

Correspondingly, the old notions of bilateral relations, featuring, for instance, blacks and Jews, may give way in the future to a "selective engagement" model where constituencies will randomly move in and out of coalition arrangements with others. This type of "engagement politics" operates on a different community organizing principle, consisting of pragmatic leaders and floating constituencies, allowing groups to convene around specific interests for given periods of time.

For Jews, this emerging Latino presence evokes the dual images of discomfort and respect. Jews observe a community of significant numbers of young families, for the most part poor, undereducated, and in certain situations undocumented. But this growing community has fostered as well a compelling image of being hard working, family focused, religiously connected, and educationally committed.

For Latinos, their perceptions of Jews, if any exist at all, are in part framed by their current economic encounter, principally in an employee-employer relationship. It may be defined as well by images of Jews and Judaism created through traditional teachings of the Church, by media

STEVEN WINDMUELLER

Soviet Jewry protest march led by U.S. Senator Alan Cranston, then L.A. city councilman, Tom Bradley (later the mayor), and L.A. Jewish Federation Council vice-president Albert A. Spiegel. From the Archives of the Jewish Community Library of Los Angeles.

images of Jewish wealth and power, and the belief by many of Jewish influence within Hollywood and its power within the entertainment industry. And it is through these different lenses that certain ideas have been formed regarding the perceptions of each community about the other.

The realities associated with intergroup relations and political alliances are that communities need not be in the same place in order to interact with one another. This thesis suggests that coalitions can be formed around shared agendas and the endorsement of candidates who are supported by diverse constituencies. Blacks and Jews defined the urban landscape for much of the last half of the twentieth century. With the exception of the eight years of the Riordan mayoralty, that pattern held true in Los Angeles, especially during the tenure of Mayor Tom Bradley.

Alliances are born around securing the common ground and a willingness to share power but can give way to conflict over these very same considerations. The Alacon-Katz contest for the state senate seat in the San Fernando Valley in 1998 served as a case study of heightened intergroup tension and a test of group power, as Joel Kotkin observed in "The Real Issues," in the *Jewish Journal*, December 1998. During that contest, charges and counter-charges were made by both campaigns involving the imposition of ethnic references and personal attacks. The Katz campaign was accused of circulating inflammatory materials while at the same time Richard Alacon refused to disavow a letter circulated by his political allies labeling Richard Katz "an immigrant hater." In the end, Katz lost a closely fought election, as significant numbers of Latinos rallied to support their

Campaign flyer for Richard Katz, Los Angeles mayoral race, 1993.
Courtesy of the Skirball Cultural Center, gift of Nate Brogin.

candidate. Some analysts have suggested that, in these types of scenarios when "identity (ethnic-based) politics" replaces coalition-based campaigns, there is little room for reasoned debate and cross-community participation. The effect of these types of election campaigns is to leave all sides feeling angry, with each element believing that they were the aggrieved party.

There exists the possibility that in a future L.A. mayoral election we could witness a Latino-Jewish contest for power. Regardless of whether such a scenario emerges, one gets the impression in L.A. that there is an emerging tone of confidence among Latinos that "this is our time" and "this is our city."

Whether exploring the possibilities of a Latino-Jewish coalition or the potential for intergroup conflict, we need to address two sets of paradigms: one focuses on the pragmatic realities that might inhibit this relationship, while the other seeks to examine the prospects for building such a linkage. Four characteristics make up each of these visions. For this pragmatic outlook, the following ideas would seem to be significant.

First, the impact of old-world theology and contemporary church social policy could limit Jewish access and the potential for political and communal connections. Some immigrants from Central America view Jews through this lens of traditional church teachings. Further, in survey data, one can document Latinos' opposition to abortions and their support of government vouchers for parochial education, positions endorsed by the church, yet opposed by the major public policy institutions of the Jewish com-

munity and a majority of Jews. In addition, there is a growing body of evidence suggesting a shift in Jewish voting patterns is taking place, especially with local elections. This was documented in the Riordan mayoral elections and by the evidence of Jewish support for the San Fernando Valley secession movement, as Gregory Rodriquez observed in "No Exodus," in the *Los Angeles Buzz,* September 1998. These political realities can create additional barriers between the two constituencies.

As understood within the black-Jewish context, there is the presence within certain circles of the Latino community a strain of "identity" or separationist politics, which rejects coalitional relationships, especially with existing white power elites. Similarly, the "legitimacy of corporate ethnic group" rights has become a significant and divisive factor today in American politics. It will affect and cloud the ties between these two communities, as Latinos seek to pursue their interests through the prism of group entitlement, focusing on affirmative action initiatives and bilingual programs that do not resonate well with most Jews. Correspondingly, a significant segment of the Los Angeles Jewish leadership remains less focused on collective political or intergroup interests and more concerned with internal considerations. These factors may limit the opportunities for coalition building.

Thirdly, the case against such a coalitional arrangement is further made by the fact that Jews are not considered a "community of color," placing them outside the boundaries of the emerging new centers of power. Peter Langman in his engaging text, *Jewish Issues in Multiculturalism,* asks "why non-Jews have not included Jews in the multicultural framework." Langman notes a number of reasons, namely that Jews are seen as an assimilated non-minority, as economically privileged, as part of the white majority, as members of a religion, and as a community whose oppression is not known or always understood or recognized.

Finally, the reality of "place" and "space" suggests that these two communities are demographically and economically at different points in their development and transformation within this society, creating yet further barriers and possible tensions between the two communities. The average age of a Latino born in Los Angeles County is fifteen years; at the same time, we should note that 20 percent of Jews in Los Angeles are over seventy years of age. The "mean age" for L.A. Jews is forty-eight; for Latinos it is twenty-six. Similarly, the two communities are situated at the polar ends of the social-economic scale. While Latinos

STEVEN WINDMUELLER

dominate geographically East L.A., the east San Fernando Valley, and parts of South Central Los Angeles, Jews have migrated to the west side of the city and to the west San Fernando Valley. These communities rarely intersect by age, economic status or residency. Further, in contrast to the model of an overorganized and highly centralized Jewish community system, Latinos have been struggling with the issues of institutional coordination.[1]

In interviews with Latinos and Jews regarding this "pragmatic frame," one can pick up comments from both communities that reflect this resistance to engagement. A Latino interviewee noted that Jews have too much power and needed to share it with the emerging groups in L.A. Another commented, "while I don't wish to offend you, it is clear that your day in this city is over." Similarly, some Jews were also not certain that engaging Latinos would be politically beneficial, arguing that this community had "yet to prove that it could deliver" while another Jewish contact suggested that Latinos "didn't respect us, so why invest so much attention to them?"

While the four principles outlined above suggest the potential for problems in the framing of such a connection, a second set of characteristics focuses on the potential opportunities for a Latino-Jewish relationship. These four ideas might be described as the "romantic" frame.

Once again religion enters this scenario, but here one can find the potential for linkages around shared ideas about community as well as a social justice agenda. Certain Latino values parallel Jewish ones. These include *familialismo* (the centrality of family); *personalismo* (good character); *espiritualidad* (spirituality); and *colectivismo* (collectivism). These concepts, while drawn from one cultural source, resonate with many communities and traditions. Similarly, recent voting patterns and polling data suggest an overwhelming convergence between Latinos and Jews around educational policy, immigrant services, and social justice interests, along with mutual connections to the Democratic party.

Secondly, land and peoplehood offer unique points of intersection. We are examining here two transnational peoples—one whose history is for the most part a diaspora story, the other is engaging in this outbound journey for the first time. For Jews, this sojourn into the world has been about religious freedom and social acceptance; for Latinos, depending on their nation of origin, it could well be economic, or possibly political, even at times religious. Linkages to one's homeland is a shared experience for

most Diaspora peoples, and so too for Jews and Latinos. Similarly, the centrality of culture represents a powerful force within both communities and in some measure a bridge between these two worlds. The following poem about the power of memory, written by a Latino, can easily be appreciated in a Jewish context as well:

> Remember
> Who, how
> Remember who you are.
> How did I get here?
> Remember your descendants.
> Remember who you are,
> Even when there's prejudice
> Of who
> And what you are.
> Remember.[2]

The development of shared communal systems represents a third theme. While these communities are clearly at fundamentally different points in their institutional development, there are a significant number of agencies within the Latino community based on Jewish models or reflective of similar values and purposes. These organizational models include the *landsmanschaft*-type institutions providing needed social services for neighborhoods and communities.[3] Similar to the Israel-based institutions operated by the Jewish community, Latinos have created fundraising structures that have developed extensive economic and social ties to native villages in Mexico and Central America, involving the support of specific projects in the "homeland" country.[4] Locally, Latinos, drawing upon the model of the Jewish Federation's United Jewish Fund, have established a community-wide umbrella structure, the United Latino Fund, to underwrite community services. MALDEF (Mexican-American Legal Defense Fund) and other civil rights and social justice entities also reflect organizing patterns similar to those found in the Jewish community.

A shared history within Los Angeles suggests another point of significant linkage. Mythologies develop around past events and shared moments in time. Yet they help to contribute to images that feed and foster a romantic and positive association with the "other." The two communities in the mid-part of this last century "shared" East Los Angeles, and more specifically the Boyle Heights corridor as their common ground, building networks of friendships, participating together in the early stages of the civil rights

Solicitation for donations,
Jewish Home for Wayfarers, Boyle Heights, 1935.
Courtesy of Western States Jewish History Archive.

Advertisment for Levi Strauss in Spanish, 1926.
Courtesy of Skirball Cultural Center, gift of Levi Strauss Co.

struggle, and creating education and business connections. These earlier linkages resonate today as possible models for a shared future.

There are always individuals or "connectors" who can and do move more easily between communities, function as interpreters of information, and provide opportunities for interaction. Jews from Latin America can serve as valuable liaisons between these two cultures. The keys to building new points of interaction between these communities will be the expansion of these relationships.

In the end, what does the potential for a new alliance mean to the Jewish community and to individual Jews, as citizens of Los Angeles? When exploring other examples of intergroup relationships, we can find that such associations define at least for some their Jewish connection. Certain Jewish activists have found in their interaction with other communities a mirror into their own histories. In

this context they have on occasion taken on the case of the "other," equating the pain and victimization of these communities to their own people's suffering, just as others have attempted to minimize the distress faced by other groups, as not being equated with the pain associated with the Jewish experience in history. In these patterns of both "acceptance" and "rejection" their own sense of Jewishness can be affirmed or, conversely, minimized.

In the past, the Jewish community was perceived in certain settings as more interested in building such connections than were the potential partner communities. For a segment of Jewish activists, their own identity was sustained and strengthened through their participation in intergroup politics. The process of building or promoting these relationships represented a powerful incentive for such Jews regarding their own sense of doing "good" or creating "tikkun olam." As a result, there was the tendency to observe in some scenarios an uneven relationship in which the Jewish community tended to give more to a partnership than may have been welcomed or offered by

STEVEN WINDMUELLER

the other constituency. This created an unspoken imbalance and at times a silent discomfort on the part of others in these associations.

Examining the various intergroup models, one cannot help but recognize the intensity and scope of these past Jewish encounters with other cultures and communities. In the twentieth century, Jews helped to shape how urban communal and political affairs were managed in America's cities. Understanding the value of alliances and intergroup associations, Jews created an infra-structure of agencies, services, and programs dedicated to this task.

As noted earlier, the Jewish stake in social activism, community affairs, and public advocacy has markedly diminished. While some activists and institutions seek to continue this tradition of community engagement through community-based projects, many Jews no longer focus on the issues and relationships associated with the urban agenda. Without being a part of the city scene, Jews may not be able to achieve the same level of influence that has marked the past half-century. For Jewish self-interests, if not for the general welfare of this society, these neighborhood relationships and coalition partnerships are essential to the broad and extensive national and international concerns that remain significant and critical to the American Jewish enterprise. For one cannot gain access to power devoid of community-based relations. As a result, the forging of a Latino-Jewish connection could renew for L.A. Jewry its passion for urban coalition politics. Each of these communities today may require the other in order to shape and influence intergroup cooperation and to gain political power in the city. Latinos and Jews, in many ways, each represent multiple communities, not only by nationality and culture but also by generation. Further, these are the two American constituencies whose identities and self-definitions are shaped both by different nationalities and the power of religious ideology.

At a time when Jewish institutions are searching for ways to engage disaffected and unaffiliated Jews, the message and meaning of community activism offers an arena for significant participation while affording individuals an opportunity to encounter the Jewish social justice tradition. For the welfare of America's cities combined with the activist imperative that has inspired and transformed Jews in the past, the forging a Latino–Jewish relationship is an imperative.

We are witnessing in Los Angeles, and maybe elsewhere in this nation, a Jewish disengagement from its historic urban legacy. The price of this Jewish disconnection from city and community affairs is simply too significant for such a transition of responsibility to be acceptable. Latinos and other communities are dependent on the Jewish communal enterprise to be at the tables of decision making, assisting and promoting models of institutional cooperation, interethnic programming and political advocacy. The American Jewish story can be told through multiple lenses.

Clearly a most significant and powerful one is this urban encounter. As L.A. emerges as the prototype of the contemporary urban center, with its diversity of cultures and the uncertainties of its political and social foundations, the critical concerns for its citizens, Jews included, will be the quality of its civic, religious, and political leadership, the success of its educational enterprise, and the viability of its changing globally based economy. Jewish communities do not function in a vacuum; they are bound to the urban setting. In the American context, Jews are identified with cities, and in turn, cities are linked to the contributions made by its Jewish residents.

In the twenty-first century, Jewish identity will be shaped by multiple social forces. Jewish civic engagement will represent one of these avenues of expression. As some Jews struggle to find venues by which they can "make" Judaism meaningful and vital to their lives, the environment of the city will afford such activism. In some measure the challenges and the opportunities posed by the new L.A. immigrant cultures has the possibility of stimulating a renewal of Jewish social engagement.

In the end, will Jewish leadership in Los Angeles be prepared to articulate the case for a recommitment of resources to the renewal of an urban encounter? At the same time, the test will be whether Jews will find a receptive civic environment where Latinos and others will be ready to embrace this community should it seek to re-engage.

Directory of Sources

For additional information on Latinos and Jews, see my article entitled: "A Framework for Hispanic-Jewish Relations" in the *Journal of Jewish Communal Service* 68, 3 (spring 1992) 224–226; also my complete study, which can be found on the John Randolph and Dora Haynes Foundation web site: http://www.haynesfoundation.org. For an excellent introduction to the issues of urban politics and minorities, see *Racial Politics in American Cities* (second ed.), Rufus P. Browning, Dale Rogers Marshall, and David

H. Tabb, eds. (New York: Addison Wesley Longman, 1997), especially, Raphael Sonenshein's chapter, "The Prospects for Multiracial Coalitions: Lessons from America's Three Largest Cities," pp. 261–276; F. Chris Garcia, *Pursuing Power: Latinos and the Political System* (Notre Dame University Press, 1997); Deborah Dash Moore, *To the Golden Cities: Pursuing the American Jewish Dream in Miami and Los Angeles* (New York: Free Press, 1994); Wayne Winborne and Ranae Cohen, eds., *Intergroup Relations in the United States* (New York: National Conference for Community and Justice, 1998).

See also Peter Beinart's article in the *New Republic* (August 11–18, 1997), "New Bedfellows: The New Latino-Jewish Alliance." Gregory Rodriguez's articles in the *Los Angeles Times*, including "The Impending Collision of Eastside and Westside" (August 3, 1997) and "Politics in a Civic Vacuum," (January 24, 1999), are especially helpful. Readers might wish to also see Gary Greenebaum and Arturo Vargas, "Jews, Latinos Need to Forge Coalition, Not Engage in Conflict," in the *Los Angeles Times* (July 1, 1998). The writings of Joel Kotkin on this subject are also of value; see for example his article in the *Los Angeles Jewish Journal* entitled "The New Class Conflict" (June 19, 1998). The materials produced on Latinos by the Tomas Rivera Policy Institute of Claremont, Calif. (http://www.trpi.org) are especially impressive.

NOTES

1. Armand Navarro, "The Post-Mortem Politics of the Chicano Movement," in *Perspectives in Mexican American Studies* 6 (University of Arizona, 1977), 67.

2. Renato Rosaldo, "Cultural Citizenship, Inequality, and Multiculturalism," in *Latino Cultural Citizenship*, Rina Benmayor, ed. (Boston: Beacon Press, 1997), 35.

3. Jose Amaro Hernandez, *Mutual Aid for Survival* (Malabar: Robert Krieger, 1983), 84.

4. Xandra Kayden, "The Mexican American Community in Los Angeles" (unpublished monograph), 11.

CHAPTER 5

JEWISH SPACE AND PLACE IN VENICE

AMY HILL SHEVITZ

"Place is an organized world of meaning. . . . Abstract knowledge about a place can be acquired in short order
if one is diligent. The visual quality of an environment is quickly tallied if one has the artist's eye.
But the 'feel' of a place takes longer to acquire. It is made up of experiences,
mostly fleeting and undramatic, repeated day after day and over the span of years."[1]

Southern California has always held, in the white American imagination, the power to help people remake themselves. In the same way as they imposed a tropical paradise on an arid landscape, Americans infused life there with a dream of infinite renewal, drawing migrants from around the world into the project.

Among experienced migrants, Jews are historically preeminent. Judaism's adaptability has created great synthetic civilizations in contexts as varied as ancient Babylonia, medieval Spain, premodern Poland, and twentieth-century New York City. Linking to the American experience, Judaism has thrived also—in different ways—in Los Angeles. For Southern California's propensity for reinvention can invigorate as well as sap Judaism; it can boost Jewish creativity as well as undermine traditional behavior. One idiosyncratic example is the history of the reinvention of Jewish community in beachside Venice, where geography and culture, California place and the California state of mind, converge in special ways in a colorful milieu.

Venice has always been a place in which the romantic and the bizarre are intertwined. Some seventy years ago, an "old-timer" observed, "Venice was a collection of gorgeous excesses. Potted palms and pennants lined the streets in constant celebration—of what I was never sure—and the architecture was the grandest, an intricate blend of Italian columns, porticos and balustrades, only slightly marred by the presence of guess-your-weight machines." At the end of the twentieth century, public officials do battle with those who, in the spirit of true Americanism, defend the

people's right to sell obscene T-shirts, read palms, swallow fire, and let their pit bulls run free on Venice's famous beach boardwalk, which runs from upscale Santa Monica on the north to upscale Marina Del Rey on the south. Venice cannot even really be classified as "downscale." In many respects, it just operates on a different scale entirely—some would say in a parallel universe. Over the years, this quirky place has been home to different communities of Jews, communities established through years of "fleeting and undramatic" experiences in an ever-changing environment. These communities have coalesced in different times in contexts that were created by shifting variables related to aspects of "place," including the actual physical setting of the beach, the social value put on that setting (and the social class implications for residents), the politics of the relationships among the city of Los Angeles' constituent parts, and American Jews' understandings of the notion of "sacred space."

Venice was the brainchild of Abbott Kinney, a transplanted Easterner who made his money in tobacco and settled in California in the late 1870s. Kinney, like other Victorians, was attracted to the dream of California, to a vision replete with romantic images unavailable elsewhere in the United States: the grandeur and tragic dignity of the Spanish/Indian past, the potential for a fresh new take on the classical world of the Mediterranean (a comparison invited by geography and weather), and the Edenic promise of the "Garden of the World." His artistically inclined

Ocean Front Walk, 1922, "Main Street" for Jewish Venetians.
Courtesy of the Seaver Center for Western History Research, Los Angeles County Museum of Natural History.

peers excavated and repackaged the past into sad novels of lost Indian heroines and gallant Spaniards and into the stylized material culture of the Arts and Crafts movement.

Kinney was, in California historian Kevin Starr's *Inventing the Dream,* "perhaps the most conspicuous Southern Californian of his type and generation . . . the entrepreneur-philanthropist in whom self-serving sagacity and an otherworldly, slightly eccentric humanitarianism coexisted in creative tension." His calling was to create a place for the dream of California; in this endeavor, he blended the imaginativeness of image making and the hard-headed business of real estate development. Kinney's master plan was a residential and resort town with the physical atmosphere of the Mediterranean and the cultural life of upper- and middle-class Victorian America: a sort of upscale Disneyland cum Chautauqua. In 1900, he

began construction of "Venice of America" in an unincorporated area south of the city of Santa Monica. It was an elaborate layout of hotels, residences, amusement piers and theatres, featuring Italianate architecture and fifteen miles of canals. It opened formally in 1905.

Unfortunately, Kinney's cultural interests and aspirations overreached those of his potential constituency, but with true entrepreneurial flexibility, he abandoned his fantasies to concentrate on recreational possibilities. If the place couldn't be "Venice of America," then at least it could be "Coney Island of the West." In the '10s and '20s, when, in Carey McWilliams's words, Los Angeles was "a great circus without a tent," Venice gained tremendous popularity as a weekend and summer destination for the working and middle classes, especially Angelenos. In an earlier business partnership, Abbott Kinney had helped develop a recreational pier in Ocean Park, in adjacent Santa Monica. Other piers were built north along the shore from Abbot Kinney's Venice pier; in the early '20s there were eight amusement piers along two miles of beach in Venice and Ocean Park. Hordes of people left the hot and crowded city to park their beach umbrellas on the cool—if crowded—seashore.

In the early twentieth century, the city of Los Angeles slowly began a territorial expansion. This expansion accelerated rapidly in the 1920s, as migration boomed. Los Angeles County gained one and a quarter million migrants during that decade, and unincorporated areas of the county were swallowed up through annexation. Some incorporated areas also agreed to consolidation, and in 1925, after twenty years of independence, Venice became part of the city of Los Angeles. It was one of the city's last large acquisitions. But though Venice was technically in the city, it was not truly of the city proper. Epitomizing recreation and leisure, Venice maintained a sense of being a different sort of place, despite the fact that many of the canals were soon filled in. (Not only were they were deemed unsanitary, they were inconvenient—more car parking was needed!)

Venice was, in both the popular and Bakhtinian senses, a carnival. Proper citizens who would never drive their Model T's more than twenty miles per hour jumped on an aptly-named roller coaster for a "Race Through the Clouds." Responsible businessmen and homemakers cast planning aside and consulted palm readers. They could eat at a restaurant constructed to look like a pirate ship or dance in a spacious hall hung with Chinese lanterns. Wealthy Angelenos had since the 1870s trekked to summer houses near the shore, but this was a new phenomenon. It was a mass experience.

In this slightly unreal setting, fifteen miles from the center of the city of Los Angeles, a small Jewish community began to grow in the early decades of the century.

In 1900, there were only about twenty-five hundred Jews in Los Angeles' population of 102,000. Most were veterans or descendants of the mid-nineteenth-century immigration of central European Jews to the United States, and by the turn of the century, they were settled, acculturated, and prosperous. A number were quite wealthy and prominent in social and civic affairs. Many were American-born—even native Angelenos—and were related to one another through networks of interlocking family ties. There was only one well-established synagogue, Reform congregation B'nai B'rith, and no noticeable residential clustering.

But Los Angeles' Jewish population was growing rapidly. Between 1880 and 1914, more than two million Jews from eastern Europe, especially the Russian Empire, immigrated to the United States. Around the turn of the century, Jews from this mass migration began to trickle into southern California. Few came to California directly from Europe. Rather, they had spent some time in other American cities, usually in the Northeast and upper Midwest. Max Vorspan and Lloyd Gartner, historians of Los Angeles Jewry, describe this "newer type" of Jewish immigrant as "likely to be an acculturated European immigrant or his grown sons who had some resources and [who] were allured by Los Angeles' economic opportunities and not indifferent to its climate."

These East European Jews settled first in neighborhoods just to the north and east of downtown. By the 1920s the center of Jewish population and cultural life settled decisively in Boyle Heights, a newly developed neighborhood several miles east of downtown Los Angeles. In 1920, about two thousand Jewish families lived in Boyle Heights; by 1930, there were more than ten thousand.

It was a largely working-class community—both blue- and white-collar—with an infrastructure of merchants, and it provided increasing diversity to the Los Angeles Jewish scene. In 1900, Los Angeles had, in addition to Reform congregation B'nai B'rith, only a few small, loosely organized new Orthodox congregations struggling to stay afloat. By 1920, there were ten full-fledged synagogues with their own buildings, serving twenty thousand Jews in a city of slightly more than half a million population. By 1930, as the city used annexation to grow by leaps and bounds, there were more than thirty synagogues for a Jewish population of seventy thousand in a general population of one and a quarter million.

Venice's Jews were peripheral to the urban immigrant East European concentration in Los Angeles proper but shared many of its demographic characteristics. A look at a sample from the 1920 census reveals that three-quarters of Venice's Jewish heads of household, including married women living with their husbands, were foreign-born. The majority of these were Russian; some named a specific place of origin such as Bessarabia, Odessa, Kiev, or Grodno. There were also natives of Austria-Hungary, Rumania, and Poland. Most of them were young couples in their twenties, thirties, and forties, with young and teenage children.

One-third of those born in the United States were natives of New York. Yet many immigrants were also, presumably, significantly acculturated, for more than 80 percent had already been in the United States for more than twenty years. Their sojourns on the way to California had taken them through a variety of American settings, several in the East (New York, Pennsylvania) but also in the Midwest (Ohio, Illinois, Wisconsin, Missouri) and the West (Colorado, Oregon). Several families of Russian origin came down from Canada. Interestingly, several families had lived in Nebraska in (at least) the 1890s; probably they were either an extended family or a group of friends who migrated to California together. At least some families lived for a time in Boyle Heights before moving to Venice. It would be hard to determine how many Jews settled in Venice after spending time there as vacationers, but by the early 1920s there were several hundred permanent Jewish residents. Wealthy Jewish Angelenos had summered in the chic hotels and rustic cabins of Santa Monica since the late nineteenth century, but they were not the ones who moved to Venice.

Similar to most East European Jewish immigrants elsewhere in the United States at the time, Venice Jews were primarily working class and small-scale merchants. Fully one-fourth of a sample from the early 1920s owned or worked in groceries, bakeries, or restaurants. Fifteen percent were tailors and about 10 percent sold clothing. Only a few had occupations unique to their setting, for instance, an actor, a few musicians, a property manager for a motion picture studio. The Bloom brothers ran a concession stand on the Windward Avenue Pier, and Ignatz Lowenberg described himself as a "huckster," presumably also working on the amusement pier. For the most part, however, Jews in Venice helped provide the commercial and service infrastructure that supported the amusement industry.

In many ways, the Venice Jewish community was typical of other east European immigrant Jewish settlements. But the physical space in which Venice Jews worked, lived, and developed their community was unique, and the allure of the ocean was evident. Geographer Yi-Fu Tuan observed that among the definitions of place is "whatever stable object catches our attention. As we look at a panoramic scene our eyes pause at points of interest. Each pause is time enough to create an image of place that looms large momentarily in our view." The Venice Jewish community emerged with a distinct oceanward orientation. In the early 1920s, two-thirds of Jewish households in Venice and Ocean Park were located within three blocks of the beach. All were within three-quarters of a mile.

Almost all of Venice's Jews lived at or very near their places of business, so the beach was both residential and work space. It also encompassed their religious space: the Orthodox congregation Mishkon Tephilo, founded in 1918, and several *shtieblach* (very small synagogues) were located within three blocks of the oceanfront in Venice's north beach. So were several kosher butchers and kosher bakeries; it was necessary to go to the larger Boyle Heights shops only on special occasions. The beach community's distance from the center of gravity of Jewish Los Angeles was accentuated by the fact that few Jews lived in between; West Los Angeles and Santa Monica had few Jews.

The boardwalk along the beach, known officially as Ocean Front Walk, was Main Street to Jewish Venetians. The cultural importance of Main Street, writes historian Richard Francaviglia, in *Main Street Revisited*, is as "a setting in which social dramas unfold: Main Street is essentially a stage upon which several types of human dramas are performed simultaneously, each character or actor in the drama having a designated role (e.g., consumer, merchant, designer) that is dependent on his or her relationship to the 'set.'" Venice Jews played out their role as merchants on a Main Street that was literally a stage: a fantasy construction, partly with the atmosphere of another time and place, a place for pretending, for carnival.

They also played out Jewish roles on this Main Street. Before Congregation Mishkon Tephilo had its own building, it held High Holiday services and other meetings in a rented hall on Fraser Pier in Ocean Park. After the building was erected in 1922 (a few blocks from Fraser Pier), Fannie Klein still set up her table on Ocean Front Walk in advance of the holidays to distribute tickets for seating at services. When the congregation ran out of chairs at these services, young men borrowed benches from the beach. The beach as Jewish Main Street was the arena for important community interactions—and, of course, gossip. The frustrated president of Mishkon Tephilo tried in vain to control it; at a congregational board meeting, he firmly "requested the Members not to hold discusions [*sic*] about the Congregation on the Ocean Front Walk but all pro's or againsts to be brought to the Meeting." One doubts his admonitions were effective.

AMY HILL SHEVITZ

Frasier Pier in Ocean Park, 1913. Congregation Mishkon Tephilo first met for High Holiday services in rented rooms on the pier. Courtesy of the Henry E. Huntington Library.

This first configuration of the beach as Jewish space lasted into the 1930s. Through that period, Venice's Jews remained generally of the same socioeconomic class as those catered to by the mass entertainments of the amusement piers, that is, primarily working- and lower-middle-class. Its second generation was still comprised primarily small merchants. But gradually, Jews also moved into the amusement-pier business. In 1947, at least one-third of the concessions on the Ocean Park Pier were owned by Jews. Though many of the concessionaires did not live in the Ocean Park–Venice area, their activity bound Jews even closer to an idiosyncratic regional sub-economy determined by geography.

Another beach-related development occurred after World War II, when the Venice boardwalk took on a new configuration as intense Jewish space. During the Great Depression, retired Jews of modest means, mainly eastern European immigrants, had begun to settle in Venice and Ocean Park. Some were from Los Angeles; others came from elsewhere, often to be near children in California. By 1950, says historian Deborah Dash Moore in *To the Golden Cities,* Ocean Park and Venice's north beach "emerged with a new identity as a Jewish area with a handful of synagogues and kosher bakeries and butcher shops." Although its aspect was different, there was—with due respect to Moore—nothing unprecedented about this Jewish identity. In fact, the existence of a permanent Jewish community, with a core of institutions (synagogues, kosher butchers and restaurants, and so on) was no doubt a positive factor in these Jews' decisions to come to Venice. As a result of this migration, there was overlaid on the permanent working- and lower-middle-class Jewish population of Venice, a new,

Mishkon Tephilo Sisterhood poses for a group portrait in 1948 in the sanctuary of the congregation's first synagogue.
Courtesy of Temple Mishkon Tephilo.

generally working- and lower-middle-class, Jewish retirement community.

It was this retirement community that was immortalized in anthropologist Barbara Myerhoff's 1977 film and 1978 book *Number Our Days*. Myerhoff pursued her research mainly within the walls of the Israel Levin Center, a recreational and educational center for elderly Jews that opened on the north end of the Venice boardwalk in 1964. Although in the early 1960s there may have been, Myerhoff claims, as many as ten thousand elderly Jews in Venice and Ocean Park, by the time she did her research in the 1970s, there were only about four thousand. Virtually all of these Jews were born in eastern Europe, had come to the United States as children, and were thus bound together by a common historical experience and a common language, Yiddish.

Myerhoff described how the boardwalk functioned as Jewish space for these resident retirees: "Collective life was and still is especially intense in this community because there is no automobile traffic on the boardwalk. Here is a place where people may meet, gather, talk, and stroll, simple but basic and precious activities that the elderly in particular can enjoy here all year round." Boardwalk culture was highly structured, with the retirees clustering in subgroups. The "organization Jews," members of the senior center, gathered on benches just outside the Levin Center. Those who preferred to pass their days playing poker and Mah-Jongg gathered ritually at designated benches and tables to meet their opponents. A group of Old Left radical Jews would periodically spend time distributing Marxist literature and haranguing passersby to sign petitions for leftist causes.

Esther Kite Schwartzman enjoying Venice beach, 1939.
Courtesy of Hasia Diner.

All of this activity—like the activity of the permanent Venice Jewish community of the 1920s—was geographically circumscribed. Myerhoff found that an area of about five miles along the oceanfront, running inland by about a mile, constituted "the limits of the effective community" of the retirees. As with the Jews of the 1920s, it was the boardwalk that served as Main Street, in Myerhoff's analogy, "a village plaza, a focus of protracted, intense sociability."

But Myerhoff's subjects lived in a different sort of Venice than did the community of the 1920s. A series of wrenching changes had altered the profile of the neighborhood dramatically. The main amusement pier, at the

end of Windward Avenue, was demolished by the city in 1947, and suddenly the south end of Venice was deserted. Games of chance were closed in 1950, eliminating some crime but also some vitality. Losing its original rationale and rejecting, with suspicion, the city's offers of urban redevelopment, Venice soon became a low-rent haven.

The Ocean Park Pier in the city of Santa Monica, which was close to where most Venice Jews lived, was renamed Pacific Ocean Park in 1958 and remained a viable venture into the late 1960s. By then, newer sorts of entertainments had cut into the amusement piers' business. Venice was also seriously affected by Santa Monica's decision to bring urban renewal to Ocean Park, at Venice's northern border. Beginning in 1965, beachfront buildings were cleared out in favor of new high-rise apartments, though much of the cleared land remained vacant for a decade.

In the mid-1960s, Venice reached its nadir of urban depression. The large number of Jewish retirees masked the gradual exodus of Jewish families and young people. The constituency of all of Venice's Jewish institutions became older and older. Congregation Mishkon Tephilo had joined the Conservative movement in 1952, part of a wave of defections from "old-fashioned" Orthodoxy. But it was hardly representative of the sort of modernity typified by postwar Conservative Judaism: Yiddish, not English, was the lingua franca, even for the rabbi's Saturday morning sermons, into the early 1960s.

Some of the younger (that is, middle-aged) leaders of the congregation proposed selling their oceanside building, since the location was no longer desirable to them. Complained one member (who successfully led opposition to the sale), "They wanted to move anyplace, anyplace away from the beach." The center of gravity of Los Angeles' Jewish community exhibited in the postwar years a strong geographic shift to the west; large, wealthy congregations built new structures in fashionable areas of the Westside. This shift had already deposited enough Jews in Santa Monica to create the base for an organized community there for the first time in the 1940s. But the shift westward, and then northward to the San Fernando Valley, bypassed Venice.

Eventually, Santa Monica's urban renewal paid off, as luxury apartments and condominiums cropped up along the cleaned-up, now beautifully maintained beach. Just over the city line in Venice, it was a different story. Venice's revival was based on the evolution of Ocean Front Walk into a new sort of amusement area, an "unstructured

Jewish retirees, among the subjects of Barbara Myerhoff's study, relax outside the Israel Levin Center, 1979.
Copyright Bill Aron.

midway," as one local observer described it. The Beats of the 'fifties and the artists and hippies of the 'sixties, who moved to Venice for cheap rents, cheap drugs, and minimal social pressure, created a mystique which in the 1970s made the carnival of unconventional behavior into a tourist trap.

For a while, the intense *Yiddishkeit* of the elderly Jewish retirees coexisted uneasily with the carnival atmosphere of Venice Beach. Meyerhoff described the scene one afternoon in the mid-1970s: "An impromptu steel band had formed in front of the [Levin] Center. A dozen or so adolescents were banging exultantly on congo and bongo drums, garbage can lids, and wine bottles under a fragrant cloud of marijuana. . . . Winos, rousted from their benches by the crowds, muttered and shuffled along, avoiding the [police] squad car that cruised by dispersing the band, which regrouped as soon as it passed." The old folks aggressively defended their use of boardwalk space against the hordes of young, careless bicyclists and roller skaters.

As the Jewish retiree community gradually evaporated through death and displacement, Venice's Jewish scene experienced another transformation. An erratic gentrification began in the mid-1970s, and now Venice exhibits an unusually broad socioeconomic and ethnic diversity of residents. Today, Venice Beach sometimes seems to exist solely *pour épater le bourgeois*—and the bourgeois flock to the crowded Ocean Front Walk to submit themselves to it.

Yet somehow, the beach continues to be renewed as Jewish space, if on a more modest level. Though its clientele is much smaller, the Israel Levin Center, whose existence looked precarious when Myerhoff researched her book, still offers a full range of social, religious, and educational programs for Jewish elderly, directed by a full-time social worker. (The center's survival was secured in large part because of the attention the book itself received.) The center's building was badly damaged in the 1994 Northridge earthquake but was soon rebuilt and freshly painted with a brightly colored Chagall-esque mural adorning its northwest corner.

The small beachside Orthodox synagogues that served first the immigrants and then the retiree community have virtually disappeared. The exception is one that got a new lease on life in the mid-1970s as the result of a split within Conservative congregation Mishkon Tephilo. A group of young Jews who had moved to Venice became active in the congregation. This group, led by writer Michael Med-

ved, instigated what Medved frankly called "a 'mini-plot' that made him president [of the congregation] and put his supporters in nineteen of twenty-one seats on the board of directors." However, Medved and his colleagues were *baalei tshuva*—Jews who became Orthodox after liberal or non-observant upbringings—and their agenda at Mishkon Tephilo reflected their growing attraction to orthodoxy. Ironically, this agenda scared and antagonized the other major segment of the congregation, the elderly. One kvetched, "Those young people wanted to go back to more traditional ways . . . sometimes it was just hard to swallow, as if our grandparents became resurrected or [as] if . . . the ghosts of the past came back and said you have to do it this way."

The nouveaux Orthodox soon decamped to the moribund Bay Cities Synagogue on the boardwalk and successfully mounted a coup there, renaming it the Pacific Jewish Center. They also embarked on an ambitious plan to create an intensive and totally Jewish community for themselves in Venice–Ocean Park, referring humorously to their project as the "commotion by the ocean."

PJC members soon began to make joint purchases of apartment buildings so that they could live near each other and, in accordance with Jewish law, within walking distance of the oceanfront shul. A school for members' children was inaugurated. Eventually, ten families bought lots on Ozone Street in Ocean Park, not far from the Venice border, and built single-family homes, in effect creating a insular, religiously observant neighborhood de novo. The Ozone Street development's initial success was aided by regional real estate trends and by its members' own professional financial successes. Members moving to the area got in "on the ground floor" as property prices rose; they built larger, more expensive houses than the neighborhood average.

PJC's experiment in creating community was uniquely suited to its Jewish ideals. If "[p]lace is an organized world of meaning," the *baalei tshuva* consciously and deliberately created place from the meaning of their religious commitments. Rather than acquiring "the 'feel' of a place . . . [through] experiences, mostly fleeting and undramatic, repeated day after day and over the span of years," they took available space and made it Jewish space, creating the "feel" through shared behaviors and communal ties. The physical construction of their Orthodox community mirrored their construction of an Orthodox personal religious identity. It was no coincidence that this happened

Congregants from the Orthodox Bay Cities Synagogue (later renamed Pacific Jewish Center) share space on the Venice boardwalk, late 1970s.
Copyright Bill Aron.

in Venice, away from the "establishment" Orthodox institutions with which many *baalei tshuva* were still a little uncomfortable, and away from middle-class Jewish neighborhoods that might very well have been uncomfortable with them.

For about ten years, the PJC community grew and thrived. Between 1979 and 1987, there were reportedly sixty-five weddings, suggesting both numerical growth and increased stability through family formation. But by the late 1980s, growth stalled. In 1995, one insider suggested that the community was shrinking because of the availability of other viable Orthodox communities: "Ten years ago it [PJC] was the only place for *baalei tshuvah*. [But now] the Pico/Robertson area [a densely Jewish neighborhood of Los Angeles] offers more diversity."

In addition, serious religious and power struggles strained and finally rent the community, destroying its communal cohesiveness and its financial base. The rabbi who provided unusually strong guidance in the early years moved to another city, and the community school's property in Venice was sold, though the synagogue remains open on the boardwalk. As early as 1980, one journalist had foreseen the possibility of schism. But if the PJC community did not entirely fulfill its promise of a new sort of synthesis of American and Jewish cultures, it still vividly represents possibilities and actualities of personal and communal renewal in a continually reconstructed environment.

Conservative congregation Mishkon Tephilo has managed to stabilize, and even get a new lease on life, since the 1970s. In part, this is because Venice has benefited from an increase in Jewish population on Los Angeles' Westside generally. The increase was smaller in Venice than in nearby areas such as Marina del Rey and Pacific Palisades, which are significantly wealthier; also, a high percentage of Jews in Venice are intermarried and/or unaffiliated. But other factors have helped create a promising synergy.

Above all, since the mid-1980s, Mishkon Tephilo has developed a reputation as an eclectic, idiosyncratic congregation in touch with important new spiritual currents in the contemporary Jewish scene, yet grounded in traditional practice. In 1989, it set a milestone as the first Conservative

AMY HILL SHEVITZ

Members of Congregation Mishkon Tephilo observe the Rosh Hashanah custom of Tashlich
(symbolically tossing away one's sins into a body of water) at Venice Beach, fall 2000.
Copyright Carole Martin.

congregation in the West led by a woman rabbi, Rabbi Naomi Levy, from the first ordination class of the Conservative seminary, New York City's Jewish Theological Seminary, to include women. By virtue of the precarious finances and communal divisions that inhibited the congregation from moving, Mishkon Tephilo now can claim significance as the oldest Westside congregation continuously in the same location.

Ironically, Mishkon Tephilo's survival is also a function of the decline of the neighborhood synagogue in non-Orthodox American Judaism. Only about one-sixth of the congregation's membership lives in Venice. The plurality—40 percent—live throughout Santa Monica (not primarily in areas adjacent to Venice) and another one-quarter live in various neighborhoods of West Los Angeles. A new community based on a common approach to Judaism, rather than physical proximity, transcends arbitrary markers of place for shared psychic space, a shared commitment and shared religious style. Observing how

people use space, sociologists have expanded the definition of "sacred space" to include "those socially and culturally constructed environments [like residential neighborhoods and shopping areas] that are not necessarily associated with explicitly holy or religious events or objects . . . the social spaces in which religious communities live and exist [which] have a sacredness that, although not explicitly holy, is nevertheless essential to those communities." The creation of communities across space diminishes the centrifugal force of geographic centers like the traditional Los Angeles Jewish neighborhoods of Fairfax and Pico-Robertson; the goods from their plethora of Jewish grocery and specialty stores are available to nonresidents within a short drive.

It somehow seems appropriate that a distinctive Jewish style has now developed in the creative free-for-all and nonchalant hipness of Venice. Challenging many conventional notions, Venice also presents challenges to conventional notions of Jewish life. In Southern California, Jewish self-perceptions confront a new physical geography of sun and sand and a new psychic geography of pleasure and relaxation. Over the years, American Jews generally have become more comfortable with inhabiting that psychic terrain, though not without some difficulty. For most of the twentieth century, American Jews have concentrated in northern, especially northeastern, cities, particularly New York, and, as David Rieff points out, "*schadenfreude* has always been the Northeast's middle name." A Bostonian, driving past Venice Beach, articulated this mindset. Even as she admired (and enjoyed) the sun and the warmth, she exclaimed, "How is it possible to be a serious Jew here?!" Serious Jewishness, after all, means suffering—as in old Russia, so too here.

Venice Jewish life has always challenged this presumed disconnection between Jewishness and physical enjoyment. Like PJC's "commotion by the ocean" slogan, Mishkon Tephilo emphasizes its beachside location in its publicity—"the cool shul by the sea"—and includes a photo of a beach scene on its web page. Inside the synagogue, above the front door, is a carved plaque with the traditional Jewish blessing to be made on seeing the ocean: "Blessed are you, Lord, ruler of the universe, who made the great sea." In the summer, the congregation has regular Havdalah services on the beach on Saturday night, ushering out the Sabbath under the stars by which Jews reckon the end of the holy day. After the all-night study session that inaugurates the holiday of Shavuot, an early morning service is held on the beach. Congregants taking a break from Shabbat morning services hang out on the portico to catch the ocean breeze and a glimpse of the water. Passing a coffee shop on his way to Shabbat services, the rabbi, in his distinctive gray homburg, is greeted pleasantly by a generically scruffy young man with a throaty, "Shabbat shalom, dude."

For eighty years, Venice has been a viable, if changing and occasionally unstable, environment for Jewish communal life. That resiliency bodes well for the future, especially as that Jewish communal life continues to reflect the creativity, informality, and openness of the beach community. The power of place can regenerate community and, like waves washing over the seashore, this process of community renewal seems likely to continue in Venice. A model of American Jewry's balance of continuity and change, Venice demonstrates the ability of place—even an idiosyncratic and seemingly alien style of place—to refresh communal and individual Jewish lives.

Directory of Sources

The Jewish community of Venice has been best known through Barbara Myerhoff's book about Jewish retirees, *Number Our Days* (1978). Myerhoff's interest, however, was her subjects' age and Jewishness, rather than their locale per se. Deborah Dash Moore's insightful and very readable book, *To the Golden Cities: Pursuing the American Jewish Dream in Miami and L.A.* (1994), puts the retirement community into its regional and historical context. Another good source about Los Angeles Jewish life generally is *History of the Jews of Los Angeles* (1970) by Max Vorspan and Lloyd Gartner.

The literature about the "idea" of Los Angeles is vast, ranging from Carey McWilliams's pioneering works such as *Southern California: An Island on the Land* (1946) to Mike Davis's dark *fin-de-siecle* musings in *City of Quartz* (1990). A particularly fine contribution is William Alexander McClung's *Landscapes of Desire: Anglo Mythologies of Los Angeles* (2000). Kevin Starr's colorful histories of California in various eras are also important to understanding Southern California's uniqueness; *Inventing the Dream: California through the Progressive Age* (1985) describes the processes that made possible such a place as Venice.

NOTES
1. Yi-Fu Tuan, *Space and Place: The Perspective of Experience* (Minn.: University of Minnesota Press, 1977).

AMY HILL SHEVITZ

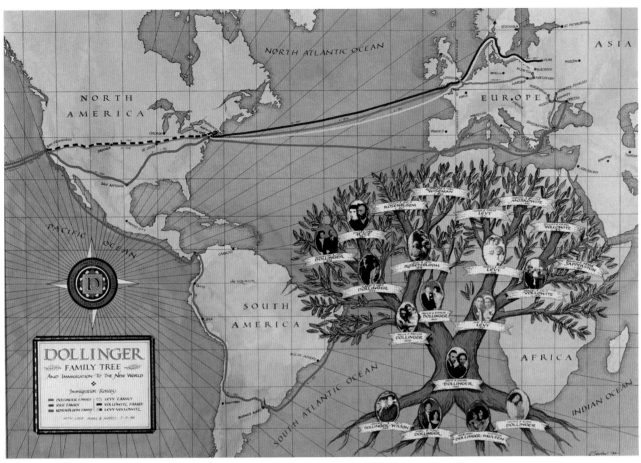

Plate 1. The Dollinger family's journey to California, by Robert Saslow.
Courtesy of Malin and Lenore Dollinger.

Plate 2. Ketubah created by Ava F. Kahn and Mitchell A. Richman for their Berkeley wedding featuring images of Lake Tahoe.
Courtesy of Ava F. Kahn and Mitchell A. Richman.

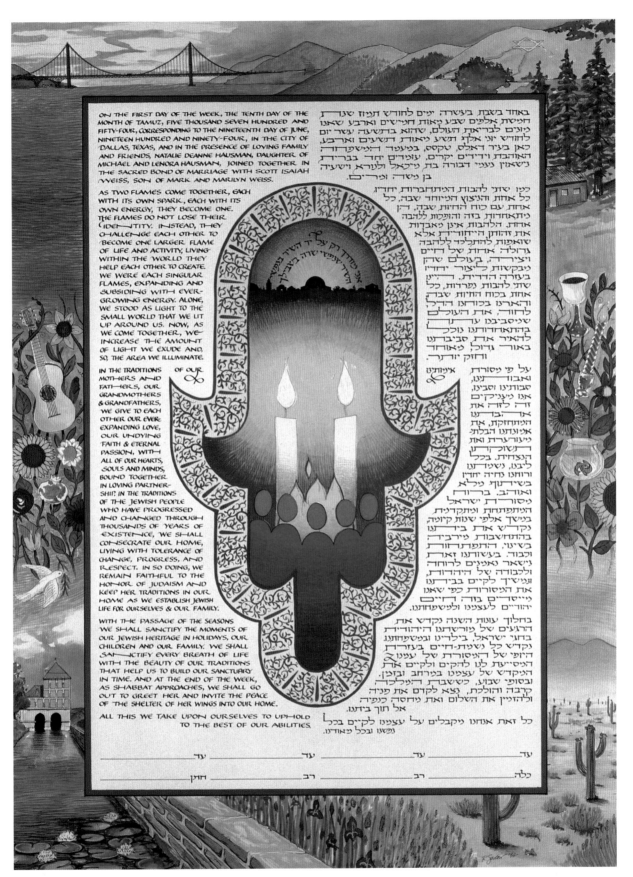

Plate 3. Wedding ketubah of Natalie and Scott Hausman-Weiss, June 19, 1994,
featuring images of San Francisco's Golden Gate Bridge and UAHC Camp Swig, Saratoga, California.
By Robert Saslow.

Plate 4. Wedding ketubah of Vivien Braly and Ruben Arquilevich, October 9, 1994,
featuring images of the northern California coast, Big Sur, Camp JCA-Shalom in Malibu.
By Robert Saslow.

באחד בשבת שמונה ימים
להדש אלול שנת חמשת אלפים ובצע מאות
חמשים ושמונה לבריאת העולם למנין שאנו מונים כאן בוקס הוליווד, קליפורניה
החתן חיים חיים בין בן דוד וגולה לאה   הכלה לאה בת ראובן וגיא רחל
אמר לכלה לאה בת ראובן בן דוד וגולה לאה   היי לי לאשה כדת משה וישראל ואני אוקיר
ואכבר אותך כדרך בני ישראל המוקירים   אוקיר ואכבד אותך כדרך בנות ישראל
המוקירות ומכבדות את אנשיהן וביראה   וכיבדים את נשיהם באמונה וביושר.

החתן חיים בין והכלה לאה הבטיחו הדדית זה לו לאשאו להשיג את המטרורת
הבאות מאך חיים המשותים: להגיע לגלוי לב הדדי אשר יאפשר להם פעולה בשלימות
בהחאבקעדהם בתהראשותים ובהרגיותיהם, להיות עדים פתוחים האחד לכל צרכי השני, לשאון להגיע
להגשמה הדדית של צרכי השכל רוחיו חומן הגופ ופנפש, להתחזק ולהנציר את נחלת היהדרית ונם ישראל
בביתם בחיי משפחתם ובקשריהם וחברתיהם.

המשאים האלו אושרו גם-כן על ידי השלטונות האזרחיים בקליפורניה והכל שריר וקים.

חתן _____ עד _____ כלה _____ רב _____

ON THE FIRST DAY OF THE WEEK, THE EIGHTH DAY OF THE MONTH OF ELUL, FIVE THOUSAND SEVEN
HUNDRED FIFTY-EIGHT YEARS SINCE THE CREATION OF THE WORLD, CORRESPONDING TO THE TWENTY-NINTH
DAY OF AUGUST, NINETEEN HUNDRED NINETY-EIGHT HERE IN WEST HOLLYWOOD, CALIFORNIA.

THE BRIDE, LINDA ELLEN SCHACK, DAUGHTER OF   THE GROOM, KEVIN BRADLEY KAISERMAN, SON OF
GLORIA AND RALPH SCHACK, PROMISED THE GROOM,   JOYCE AND DONALD KAISERMAN, PROMISED THE BRIDE,
KEVIN BRADLEY KAISERMAN, SON OF JOYCE AND DONALD   LINDA ELLEN SCHACK, DAUGHTER OF GLORIA AND RALPH SCHACK,
KAISERMAN, YOU ARE MY HUSBAND ACCORDING TO THE   YOU ARE MY WIFE ACCORDING TO THE TRADITION OF MOSES
TRADITION OF MOSES AND ISRAEL, I SHALL CHERISH YOU   AND ISRAEL, I SHALL CHERISH YOU AND HONOR YOU, AS IS
AND HONOR YOU, AS IS CUSTOMARY AMONG THE DAUGHTERS   CUSTOMARY AMONG THE SONS OF ISRAEL WHO
OF ISRAEL WHO HAVE CHERISHED AND HONORED THEIR   HAVE CHERISHED AND HONORED THEIR WIVES IN
HUSBANDS IN FAITHFULNESS AND INTEGRITY.   FAITHFULNESS AND INTEGRITY.

THE BRIDE LINDA AND THE GROOM KEVIN HAVE ALSO PROMISED EACH OTHER TO STRIVE
THROUGHOUT THEIR LIVES TOGETHER TO ACHIEVE AN OPENNESS WHICH WILL ENABLE THEM TO SHARE THEIR THOUGHTS,
THEIR FEELINGS AND THEIR EXPERIENCES, TO BE SENSITIVE AT ALL TIMES TO EACH OTHER'S NEEDS; TO ATTAIN
MUTUAL EMOTIONAL, PHYSICAL, AND SPIRITUAL FULFILLMENT; TO WORK FOR THE PERPETUATION OF JUDAISM
AND OF THE JEWISH PEOPLE IN THEIR HOME, IN THEIR FAMILY LIFE, AND IN THEIR COMMUNITY ENDEAVORS.

THIS MARRIAGE HAS BEEN AUTHORIZED ALSO BY THE CIVIL AUTHORITIES OF THE STATE OF CALIFORNIA.
IT IS VALID AND BINDING.

BRIDE _____ GROOM _____

WITNESS _____ RABBI _____ WITNESS _____

Plate 5. Wedding ketubah of Linda Schack and Kevin Kaiserman, August 29, 1998, featuring images of Yosemite Valley.
By Robert Saslow.

Plate 6. Wedding ketubah of Annette Taub and Terrance Stinnett, June 29, 1991,
featuring images of Mount Diablo, northern California.
By Robert Saslow.

Plate 7. Wedding ketubah of Sari Scherer and Joel Poremba, October 26, 1996, inspired by their love of the Los Angeles Dodgers. By Robert Saslow.

Plate 8. Thirty-third anniversary ketubah for Irene and Howard Levine, June 10, 1994, featuring images of California grapes.
By Robert Saslow.

Plate 9. Hurwitz residence, Beverly Hills, 1978. This work focused on the theme of bougainvillea flowers and is typical of the floral style the Plachte-Zuiebacks developed during their early days in Willits. Courtesy of Michelle and David Plachte-Zuieback.

Plate 10. Signer residence, Beverly Hills. Completed in 1984 for the home of a Hebrew Union College professor and rabbi, this forty-eight-inch-square panel bears the inscription, "Yesh M'ayin" (literally, "something from nothing"), a term describing a medieval theory of the origin of the Universe.
Courtesy of Michelle and David Plachte-Zuieback.

Plate 11. One of many windows created by campers at UAHC Camp Swig, "Jewish Identity" expresses the individual creativity
of more than 150 young people. This composition represents a view of the giving of the Ten Commandments at Sinai
as seen from beneath the fringes of a tallit while the first shema illuminates the landscape.
Courtesy of Michelle and David Plachte-Zuieback.

Plate 12. Lopati Chapel, Valley Beth Shalom, Encino, 1992. This symbolic composition on the theme "It is a tree of life to them who hold fast to it" consists of fifteen stained glass panels, two sandblast-carved ark doors, and two eternal lights. Courtesy of Michelle and David Plachte-Zuieback.

Plate 13. Study at Valley Beth Shalom, Encino, 1997. A pomegranate, symbol of the Torah, splits open and spills books, including a page of Talmud and a Hebrew alphabet, dotted with honey to make learning sweet. The Talmud page was rendered by silk screening high-fire glass enamels directly onto the glass before firing them in the kiln. Painted dichroic glass creates the seeds within the pomegranate. Courtesy of Michelle and David Plachte-Zuieback.

Plate 14. "Divine Spark," Congregation Beth Am, Los Altos Hills, California, 1999. Lightning occurs when the heavens touch the earth. In this interpretation of Redemption and the splitting of the Red Sea, lightning flashes, a pillar of cloud looms, and a rolling sea separates. Sound ripples the crackling atmosphere in a moment of elemental power. In the open position, set for worship, a new stained glass setting is created, representing the elements of Revelation: earth, fire, air, and water. Six hundred-thirteen dichroic stars are spread, like sparks, from the tips of the flame that is a letter shin. It is the cauldron of creation, the tip of Mount Sinai, an image of the presence of God. Courtesy of Michelle and David Plachte-Zuieback.

Plate 15. Back of "Divine Spark," Congregation Beth Am, Los Altos Hills.
The three-dimensional Character of this installation is evident when viewed from the exterior.
The desert rock of Sinai and the elemental shin-shaped flame stand out against the background of lightning and darkness.
Courtesy of Michelle and David Plachte-Zuieback.

Plate 16. "Eretz (land of) Brandeis!"
Courtesy of Hannah R. Kuhn, photographer.

Plate 17. One of Bardin's dreams, the "House of the Book," on the Brandeis-Bardin campus, dedicated on July 22, 1973. Designed by Sidney Eisenshtat, its dedication plaque reads: "'Come ye and let us go up to the mountain of the Lord,' ancient words of Isaiah and Micah."
Courtesy of Hannah R. Kuhn, photographer.

CHAPTER 6

"KIBBUTZ SAN FERNANDO"

NA'AMA SABAR

As a matter of fact, here we've also created our own little kibbutz. —Nir

Soon after my arrival in Los Angeles, I was astounded to discover how many Israelis who had been born and raised on a kibbutz now chose to live in L.A. The source of my astonishment was twofold. First, emigration from Israel is generally discouraged. Although much more acceptable in recent years than in the 1960s and 1970s when emigrants were scorned, the practice is still disparaged. Second, the kibbutz society, which these emigrants chose to abandon, was referred to until the early 1980s as utopia, paradise and a dream.[1]

The phenomenon of Israelis living abroad exemplified by former kibbutzniks such as Nir reflects a complex picture. It is difficult to grasp the personal outlook of individuals without having close contact with them. This chapter attempts to present that personal view of what is happening in Los Angeles against the background of one of the best-known of the communal frameworks—the Israeli kibbutz.

Background: The State of Israel

In 1948, the State of Israel was established as the fulfillment of the Zionist dream and in response to the Holocaust. But even after more than half a century of independence, the permanence of the state is not assured. People are essential for survival. Israel invests enormous resources to recruit newcomers from around the world. Immigrants are called *olim,* those who ascend. Emigrants are called *yordim,* those who descend. Although less so in recent years, the term "yordim" still carries the negative connotation of deserters. Consequently, deciding to live outside of Israel is not an easy step for an Israeli. Apologetic and filled with guilt, many do not openly declare their intention to emigrate.

The Kibbutz

The kibbutzim were created more than ninety years ago by immigrants from Eastern Europe to implement the Zionist national ideal of creating a homeland for the dispersed Jewish nation, while upholding the socialist values of equality, political and economic democracy, and social justice. Kibbutzim comprise fewer than 3 percent of the total Jewish population in Israel today. There are 260 kibbutz communities in existence, with a population of about 120,000. They vary in size from newly founded settlements with forty adult members to older settlements with over a thousand members and three or four generations. Most kibbutzim have between two hundred and four hundred members. The kibbutz has always been functionally, socially, intellectually, and culturally influential upon Israeli society.

Physically, a typical kibbutz is a collection of small, one- or two-story houses surrounded by lawns and gardens, interconnected by paths. A central dining room serves as a meeting place for members at mealtimes and for general meetings and entertainment in the evenings. The children's houses (sleeping quarters and classrooms for the elementary school) are grouped near the members' homes. The industrial area is generally located farther from the living quarters, often near the road leading to the kibbutz.

The kibbutz, a direct form of democracy, is governed by a general assembly, which convenes weekly and is responsible for electing a network of committees. The committees have the authority to run day-to-day life. Yet, in its sovereignty, the general assembly expresses the basic democratic principles of equality of influence among kibbutz members and of the authority that resides in the collective as a whole.

Education has the highest priority in the kibbutz budget. In fact, the kibbutz investment per capita in education is the highest in Israel (where education is second in priority only to security but far lower in budget). Kibbutzim have even established their own institutions of higher learning that offer vocational training.

In spite of the large financial investment in education, pupils in the kibbutz schools are described as academic underachievers. For many years the kibbutz educators' disdain for competition was reflected in the schools' de-emphasis of academic achievement. Sports and other nonacademic pursuits were and still are emphasized. At the same time, the belief that the kibbutz form of life is preferable and superior to all other forms is instilled in the youngsters from the early stages of life.

On the kibbutz, the peer group remains constant from infancy to high school graduation. An individual's deviation from proper behavior or neglect of duty comes immediately to the attention of the rest of the group. "Public opinion" within the group becomes the most important source of power in the child's life from primary school onward. Since the peer group plays a very important role in the individual's life, social success and status are much more important for the child on the kibbutz than for a child outside.

In recent years, Israeli society as a whole has undergone a change from a pioneering culture to a more materialistic, westernized society. In addition, since 1984, the Kibbutz movement has experienced a severe economic crisis, which has led many kibbutz members to the conclusion that the kibbutz will be unable in the future to provide all "the good things" in life. As a result, many of the kibbutzim have modified their basic principles and the kibbutz is becoming less collective in its philosophy than the original tenets prescribed. Add to this the constant security problems that have made relentless demands on all citizens, together with the unique competing pressures of individual versus collective on the kibbutz, and it is perhaps natural that a new attitude—accepting, rationalizing, and partially justifying emigration—has developed among young kibbutz members.

The second and third generations appear to be free of the ideological ties that kept their parents on the kibbutz. The kibbutz founders, coming from Europe, generated commitment to a life according to a rigorously defined set of principles. For their children, however, the kibbutz is a taken-for-granted world that is theirs by birth rather than by choice. Even when, as adults, they choose their parents' kibbutz as their home, it is not the same choice their parents made, nor can it be expected to be. Indeed, today, for many different reasons more than 50 percent of kibbutz-born children choose either not to become, or not to remain, members of any kibbutz. For them, the kibbutz is a fact of life, the place they were born, not an ideal for which to fight. Perhaps naturally, they ask themselves if the kibbutz is the best place for them to grow and develop as adult individuals.

Given all these considerations, it is a disappointing reality, and to some extent a crisis for the kibbutz founders, to see many hundreds of young people, aged twenty-five to forty, leaving the Promised Land. These emigrants, as well as their peers who have remained on the kibbutz, are the end products of a unique society. In light of this situation, it is fair to ask what has happened to the wayward children of the kibbutz. At this point, my aim is to better understand, interpret, and explain the reasons and motives of the individuals who chose to live in Los Angeles, abandoning both the socialist and Zionist tenets of the kibbutz.

Kibbutzniks in Los Angeles

Initially, I had difficulty establishing contact with the kibbutzniks in Los Angeles. I attempted to reach them by phone and heard all sorts of excuses as to why they could not meet with me. When I finally met with my first informants, however, they helped me make the next contacts. I conducted personal, intensive interviews in Hebrew with twenty-six kibbutzniks between the ages of twenty-four and forty who had been born and raised on a kibbutz. They had been living in the United States from two to ten years, and currently in Los Angeles. I also spoke at length with others whom I met by chance at kibbutzniks' social functions in which I participated or just in Hebrew-speaking neighborhoods. All together, I interviewed—in varying degrees of intensity—close to fifty former kibbutz members.

Five of the kibbutzniks I interviewed intensively were female; ten were single (with or without partners). Of the married participants, five were married to non-Israelis (whom they met either in Israel or in the United States), and two-thirds had children.

Each interview, recorded both in writing and on tape, lasted several hours and covered the informant's family, childhood, schooling, military service and experiences from the time they arrived in the United States until the time of the interview (the end of 1988). I was interested in the decisions they had had to make as well as hearing about their difficulties and successes.

Interviews were conducted at the home of the interviewee, except for three cases, where two interviews were held at the participants' businesses and one other in a coffee shop because the informant felt his apartment was too small. I also managed to extensively interview one ex-kibbutznik on his native kibbutz. He had taken a year off from his business in L.A., and brought his American wife and two infants to his kibbutz, just "to clear [his] head of worries and do some thinking." Naturally, all the names I use in referring to informants are fictitious, and only the kibbutz movement affiliation, and not the kibbutz, is disclosed.

The interview topics included: the process of settling in L.A.; employment opportunities; their affinity to Zionism and Judaism; why they left Israel; how they feel about living in L.A., and why they stay.

LIVING ARRANGEMENTS AND
THE PROCESS OF SETTLING

Most of the kibbutzniks came to the United States without any intention of staying; they came to spend part of a year off that they receive from the kibbutz sometime after their military service. During their travels, when the need for money arose, they took on odd jobs, and some got "stuck," as they put it. They found it easy to find work and housing in Los Angeles. The climate is similar to that of Israel, as is the informality, and many Israelis live nearby. The commercial phrase, "Nice 'n Easy," works for them, so they stay.

L.A.'s ex-kibbutzniks have a very effective informal network to help new arrivals. Lodging is provided upon arrival, if needed, as well as help in finding a job or getting a car. They also help each other with loans for business ventures and housing, professional advice, and connections. As Ilana said, "The collective responsibility we were brought up with on the kibbutz, the cooperation and solidarity, are implemented here in L.A. where we see to it that the ex-kibbutzniks have an easier transition into this new culture. . .". On the other hand, they do not encourage their peers to emigrate. At a social gathering, Yohai mentioned a friend who had phoned from Israel inquiring about life in L.A. but said that he had told him how "it is not all milk and honey in L.A." Yohai was concerned about "what will happen to [Israel's] future if everyone asserts his personal freedom."

Most ex-kibbutzniks live in one of two areas, the San Fernando Valley and West Hollywood. The latter is a rather run-down neighborhood but the kibbutzniks live on the better streets. Both areas are generally less expensive than other parts of L.A. Most of my meetings with the kibbutzniks took place in the San Fernando Valley, a part of greater Los Angeles where many Israelis, including former kibbutz residents, live. It's a developing area that promises employment. The population is young, mainly middle-class, and, compared to the better neighborhoods of L.A., the prices here are reasonable and the dream of a single house with a lawn and a barbecue in the back yard is within reach, much sooner than in Israel. From the interviews I learned that the desire to gain economic status is among the major motives for emigration; it is therefore no wonder that for kibbutzniks the fastest way to demonstrate newfound "wealth" is to buy a house. Kibbutzniks are also attracted to the area by those who came before them; living in an area where there are other *yordim,* many with some kibbutz experience, lessens the sense of alienation and provides a source of mutual support. Thus the move from the kibbutz to a suburb that imparts a sense of community eases the culture shock they experience in their transition from the kibbutz to a totally foreign culture.

The kibbutzniks socialize almost exclusively with other Israelis, mainly ex-kibbutzniks. Often during my interviews the phone would ring. The informant would pick up the phone and automatically say *"qen"* (meaning yes and used as hello) in Hebrew, on the apparent assumption that only Hebrew speakers would be calling. Still, social gatherings are much less frequent than they would be in Israel due to the long, intensive working day and the distances. A cultural change is occurring where money is replacing friendship. This seems to be the unexpressed reality of the ex-kibbutzniks in L.A.

A few of the kibbutzniks came to the States with their families, but most have deferred starting a family for economic reasons. Most wait until age thirty to thirty-five to marry or live with their Israeli mates. Only two-thirds of the married people I interviewed had children of any age, very few of whom had been born in the States. On the kibbutz there is strong social and parental pressure to marry; their Israeli peers, with rare exceptions, are married and have at least two or three children at a comparable age. Ella, who stays here with misgivings, described the pressure on the kibbutz: "You don't know what it means to come to the dining room on Friday evening for dinner without a boyfriend. At the age of twenty-three they looked at me with such pity, I hated going to the dining room."

EMPLOYMENT OPPORTUNITIES,
INCOME, AND EDUCATION

Theories of social mobility in the Western world present two common roads to upward social mobility: through higher education leading to higher professional status, or through success in business. The ex-kibbutzniks have chosen the latter path. In L.A., however, I met only one obviously wealthy kibbutz businessman. The rest live modestly considering their relatively good incomes. In most cases they spend very little, both because a modest standard of living is a value of their upbringing and because many feel a lack of economic security. "I don't feel secure even though I make much more than I need," was often stated. This may be natural for people who found themselves facing economic concerns for the first time. Unlike many other young people in the modern world, they had never heard their parents worrying about how they would make ends meet, since on the kibbutz the economic burden is shared. Many of the businessmen among my informants described the constant high pressure they lived under and the worries they had. Guy, who I met during his "year off" from L.A. said, "Only when I took off and went back to my kibbutz did I realize how in L.A. I was never really relaxed or relieved of my worries. Will I meet my bank payments? And what will happen if not?"

With respect to their economic status and the professional and educational training, this group differs greatly from non-kibbutz Israeli emigrants in the United States. The latter have been described as among the wealthiest of all immigrants to the United States and many have professional training and careers. Neither of these characteristics is true for the majority of ex-kibbutznik emigrants. Almost all came with no more than one thousand dollars (if they weren't in debt), and had completed, at most, twelve years of schooling, except for two women who had gone on to higher education.

Almost all the informants work in nonprofessional jobs, such as construction, gardening, maintenance, sales, or technical work. One reason is their lack of systematic training and another is that working in the United States is different. Many start as employees in another ex-kibbutznik's business. After about two years, more than half of those who plan to stay try to open their own businesses, usually one similar to the one in which they had previously worked and often with a loan from friends. In L.A., more than ten former members of one kibbutz opened up a joint real estate business. Informants indicate that there are usually fewer hard feelings over competition in business than there would be in Israel because L.A. is so big and "there is room for all competitors."

"There is enough work for any kibbutznik who wants to come and work here," Shai, who employs 150 people including some kibbutzniks, told me. "They are hard workers, have respect for all types of work, have extensive previous work experience, are industrious, ready to put in long hours of work if needed, modest in their demands other than salary and are resourceful. These are virtues they acquired in their kibbutz upbringing which serve them well here," says Shai.

Almost all my informants work long days, many leaving their homes at 7:00 A.M. and not returning before 8:00 or 9:00 P.M. Very few work only five days a week and some work seven days a week if a client needs them. Gil's case is illustrative. When I tried to make an appointment with Gil, who worked as a contractor for home improvement and was the most difficult interviewee to reach, he said, "Although I come home around 8:00 P.M., I may go out again if a client calls me. I can make a tentative appointment with you on Sunday, November 27th at 2:00 P.M. on condition that I am not called." Gil told me that the first time in four years that he had had a Thanksgiving meal with his family was the week before. This strong drive to work and save money is further illustrated by Guy, who commented to another ex-kibbutz friend: "What are we doing here? This is a 'work camp'; we just work and watch our savings grow. What else do we have here? I'm tired of it, I'll take off and go to my kibbutz for the year and then see what's what." Their peers who remained on the kibbutz work only about forty-five hours during a six-day work week. Coming home around 4 P.M., relieved of household or economic worries, the kibbutz member can then devote a great deal of time to his children, to hobbies, or to furthering his own education.

Eight of the more veteran interviewees came to the United States as professionals: four teachers, one agronomist, two technical engineers, and one with incomplete engineering training. The teachers, except for one who works in Jewish education, do not have credentials to teach what they do. Fewer than a third of the interviewees, mainly women, attended classes in the United States, including English classes to improve their command of the language.

In many cases, the ex-kibbutzniks' command of English is very poor, especially their reading and writing. Only one of my informants completed a degree and later became a CPA. Another, who had received technical training in Israel, has pursued a bachelor of arts degree over a long period. "Who can afford it when you have to make a living and care for a family and children?" asked Gil, who was perceived by his fellow kibbutz members to be exceptionally talented and who came to L.A. five years ago with his American-born wife, intending to begin his studies. "If I were on the kibbutz now I would probably have gotten an engineering degree long ago and would be working in the kibbutz factory. Here, I don't have the time or the economic security to take up studies, and I am not even sure that I need to."

THE KIBBUTZNIKS' AFFINITY TO RELIGION AND ZIONISM

My informants' perception of their link to Judaism and Zionism is rooted in the antagonism of the early Zionist movement to traditional Jewish Diaspora life. The early Jewish settlers, and among them the founders of the kibbutzim, set as their goal the creation of "a new Jew" who viewed physical work as the highest ideal. Apparently, the founding members have been too successful in their attempt to eliminate the "old Jew." Years later, Oved, who was raised on a secular kibbutz, observed that "the founding members of the kibbutz revolted against the religion and traditions of their parents and Judaism, and, with the work ethic weakening, there was an ideological vacuum and nothing to fill the spiritual gap."

This gap is especially disconcerting to emigrants who are no longer physically residing in Israel, where by virtue of living in the country they belong to the Jewish people. As a result, they are now faced with a perplexing longing for Jewish roots. On all the visits I paid to married couples, I noticed Jewish religious articles such as candlesticks, a mezuzah, or a Hanukah menorah.

The former members of religious kibbutzim observe neither the Jewish holidays (not even Yom Kippur) nor the ritual precepts. Hedva, who was brought up on a religious kibbutz and is married with two daughters, noted that "as a couple we don't observe the Sabbath or keep a kosher kitchen but we don't mix meat and milk. That's in our blood." However, she sends her daughters to a religious kindergarten so that "they receive the basic Jewish elements that we got." Oren (who was single when I interviewed him) observed that he was "completely cut off from religion. I don't even observe the basic traditions." Regarding the symbols of Judaism, he said that a person who was once religious and abandoned it "has no need of these identifying signs which have lost all value for him. On the other hand, somebody who was never religious and grew up in a secular and even anti-religious atmosphere searches for his roots and ties because without them he feels anchorless." Izzy agrees, saying that "I only have a mezuzah on my door because it was given to me. I wouldn't have put one up otherwise. I don't feel the need and it's not important to me."

On the other hand, the secular ex-kibbutzniks range in their religious behavior from those who send their children to religious Jewish schools and are themselves members of the synagogue, to those who work on Yom Kippur. Naomi, who was raised on a secular kibbutz, said that "before the Yom Kippur War, I didn't know that people fasted on Yom Kippur. People on my kibbutz worked as usual." It is perhaps interesting to note that in L.A., Naomi does seek a link to religion. This is expressed in her conscientious lighting of the Hanukah candles for the first time in her life.

On nonreligious kibbutzim, religious observance of holidays was initially replaced by secular (usually agriculturally linked) celebrations, and, with the establishment of the State of Israel, supplemented by secular holidays such as Independence Day. Most of the secular ex-kibbutzniks I interviewed in L.A. observe the holidays together with friends in a typical festive meal but they no longer have the cultural content that the kibbutz used to provide, nor the religious tradition to which they were never exposed.

Though the former members of religious kibbutzim don't observe religious precepts, their ultimate commitment to Israel seems to result from their upbringing and the priorities that are inbred. All three expressed their feelings about Israel without being asked. Hedva admitted to having "a real problem with my life here. I won't say I'm against people leaving Israel, because everyone has the right to live where he pleases, but I do believe in Israel and Zionism. I personally believe that my place is there. I keep hoping to go back." Oren mentioned that his parents still believed that he would return to Israel, and he agrees. "I also believe that I'll be back," he said, "We were mainly educated to religious precepts and the importance of settling the country, and I think that it is these which will cause me to return to Israel." Izzy reflected the same attitude when he said that his education "had a strong Zionist foundation. My parents had no problem with my leaving the kibbutz or the orthodoxy. My leaving the country is harder on them." Oren's parents seem to have the same attitude, as Oren's girl friend Naomi pointed out. She compared her parents, who typify the secular reaction, with Oren's, saying that "my parents told me that they didn't care where I lived as long as I was happy." She criticized Oren's parents for not supporting him, as hers did, by telling him that they wanted him to be happy, but in Israel.

It is not surprising that some secular ex-kibbutzniks expressed the feeling that had they been brought up in a stronger religious background they wouldn't be in L.A. Oved summed up this feeling: "If I were religious, I wouldn't be here. If I had received a religious education, I wouldn't be living here."

WHY THE KIBBUTZNIKS LEFT AND
WHY THEY REMAIN IN L.A.

A majority of the informants justify the lengthening of their stay by mentioning the economic, social, and personal freedom they have discovered in the United States. They find that they can very soon buy a car, something no individual on the kibbutz has. On the kibbutz, cars are available to serve people when they need them, like all other communal property. Cars in Israel are very expensive: the smallest Subaru, 1,000 cc, costs about $22,000. So their eyes grow wide when they see their fondest dream, a car, becoming a reality within weeks of their arrival, and when many of their other materialistic desires become realized.

Some justify their life in the United States by saying, "we were born into the kibbutz; it was not our choice as it was our parents' or grandparents'. Our parents did a great deal for the society and the country but they did not prepare us for our economic future. It is time that we did

something for ourselves. We can do it here since the system here works for you and not against you as it often does in Israel. For example, the high income tax, the bureaucracy, and the military reserves that call you when you are just starting something new. We don't have fathers in Tel-Aviv who can help us start a business. Our fathers can give us only moral support since they do not have any private financial means."

On the kibbutz, they did things mainly with the group or on behalf of the group. They were bound to the kibbutz's decisions regarding their own future plans, for example regarding further studies. "If only they had let me study to be a physical education teacher when I asked to, I wouldn't be here today," confessed Ella. "But their approval came after I made up my mind to travel. I got a small inheritance from my grandmother and that enabled me to leave Israel." Leaving Israel and leaving the kibbutz is often used synonymously.

In L.A. the ex-kibbutzniks discovered their own value. Even those who had been considered shy, academically average, or social misfits found satisfaction in this test of their own worth. They can express their individuality and enjoy being financially compensated for their efforts and abilities. They like the responsibility they have and the feeling that they can handle business matters successfully. According to the interviewees, assuming responsible functions is beyond reach for young people on the kibbutz as long as their parents' generation is still healthy and fully active. On the kibbutz, options are limited and there is a long waiting list for challenging jobs. "And besides, every decision needs the assembly's approval." These ex-kibbutzniks seem to prefer a meritocratic society, one with incentives and compensations. Many feel that the kibbutz' pursuit of equality has resulted in many people becoming parasites. "We are responsible for whatever happens to us here, you get what you are worth. You pay for your own mistakes and gain from your own successes," says Gil.

I often heard the following statement: "I like proving myself with no one knowing what I do or how successful I am." For this reason, many of the kibbutzniks rejected the idea of living elsewhere in Israel. "The country is so small. If I fail in the city, everyone on my kibbutz will know about it and will judge my departure." "If I did in Tel-Aviv what I do here," says Yohai, who is a simple laborer, "it would be considered a disgrace and I'd barely earn my living. Don't forget that I don't have a profession to come back to if I fail [this statement was repeated often], so I can't afford to fail and start from scratch again." Many of them say that they will return once they have an economic base.

Many of them love the anonymity they find for the first time. "On the kibbutz you live in a pressure cooker," they told me. "If you have not lived there you cannot understand it. You see the same people all the time, they know what you are going to say and you know their reactions before they even utter a word." Yet, in L.A. these ex-kibbutzniks seek mostly other ex-kibbutzniks for social contacts and seem to need this secure, socially tight framework. This simultaneous love of anonymity and the need to seek the fellowship of other kibbutzniks seems to be part of the conflicting forces that control their social behavior. They want to escape from the kibbutz, but are pulled by their socialization into kibbutz life when they form a strong social network in L.A.

HOW KIBBUTZNIKS FEEL ABOUT LIVING IN L.A.

All my informants except for one said, often without even being asked, "I will never feel that this is my home, I'll always be a stranger here. People are cold to each other. I miss my family and miss my friends in Israel. I have convenience here but I do not have a home." Others expressed the same feeling by saying, "We have a high standard of living, but a low quality of life."

Many informants referred to their families in Israel as warm and supportive, and missed them immensely. Very often I noticed kibbutz newsletters and open letters from home that looked as if they had been read over many times. Many of the interviewees expressed longing for their families (more so among the female interviewees), their culture, and the landscapes of their childhood. A few even missed the military reserves which in itself comprises a subculture in Israel.

Only a few of the informants saw themselves as leaders in their childhood or youth. The majority perceived themselves as average both socially and academically. A few viewed themselves as shy or searching for themselves or as misfits with respect to their peers, particularly if they were younger than the other children in their group. On the kibbutz, when one age group doesn't have enough children of the same age, the group may include children who are two years apart. Despite this, almost all the interviewees described their childhood on the kibbutz as "enchanted" or "the dream of any child." One explanation may be that most of the interviewees were good at some type of sport, an area highly fostered by the kibbutz in contrast to the lack of emphasis given to academic areas. One can easily achieve high peer recognition and status by excelling at sports and by readiness to contribute to the group. At the same time, academic performance may be average or below average. Many informants could not resist comparing their childhood and their children's by saying, "I wish my children could have a childhood like on the kibbutz."

Zeev, who came to L.A. alone ten years ago to find a job and an apartment before bringing his family, lived for a time on the beach in an effort to save money. After getting settled, he gradually rose to a position of responsibility in an industrial firm. He proudly showed me his home in the San Fernando Valley, in a new but remote development. He expresses his conflicting emotions when he says, "From the point of view of work and self-fulfillment and creativity, I do produce and see things being created. However, there is a price the family pays and the children pay; they are hurt. I have built up my own career. I am constantly at war with myself and thinking about those around me."

Many of the single informants, and those who were married and childless or parents of very young children, commented that they could not imagine their children growing up in L.A. They hope to establish a financial base and then return to Israel. "Isn't it every one's dream to go back to Israel when he makes enough money?" asked Adiv naively.

All the Israeli girl friends or wives of the kibbutzniks I interviewed, except for three, regardless of whether they themselves were kibbutzniks, did not like staying in the United States, and would have returned home "yesterday." "Just give me two hours to pack and we can sail," says Adina to her husband Zeev who loves his work immensely but misses Israeli life. This unhappiness of the women is pervasive. It is even more striking if one considers the fact that women on the kibbutz have always been subordinate to men (in spite of the founding premise of gender equality) and many are frustrated because of the limited range of jobs available to them on the kibbutz.

Only three of the ex-kibbutzniks originally came to L.A. because their non-Israeli spouses did not like living on the kibbutz. These ex-kibbutzniks felt their spouses deserved "some time" in their "home environment." However, this "time" extended much beyond the kibbutznik's wish, to a point now where it means either staying or breaking up the family.

Leaving Israel and living in L.A. was not an easy subject for the participants to discuss. For many, the decision to live away from the kibbutz (and Israel) was far from resolved in their minds and hearts. Throughout the interviews, many ex-kibbutzniks mentioned their lack of feelings of guilt without my having addressed the issue. They often said, "We did to our parents [left them behind] what our parents did to their parents when they left the Diaspora." The difference is that their parents left for ideological reasons while they left for materialistic ones. Their denials of guilt reflected their need to define the term *yored*, in relation to who is leaving whom. That is, is it Israeli society that has created the conditions that cause them to leave, or is it just the point they have reached in their lives when they made the decision to do what is best for themselves? I often noticed that many still perceive leaving the kibbutz as betrayal.

The main difficulty some informants had to overcome was making the actual decision to leave the kibbutz. Leaving behind aging parents, friends with whom you had shared literally everything, and, mainly, a way of life toward which your upbringing was geared and aimed, were serious problems. The kibbutz and Israel were one to these people who did not know any other form of life. The military was their first encounter with the existence of Israel's other social strata.

Consequently, once a decision was made to leave the kibbutz, leaving Israel itself didn't seem to be a real crisis. This nondistinction between leaving the kibbutz and leaving Israel was especially true for those who come from the kibbutzim of the secular, left-wing Shomer HaTsair movement. On these kibbutzim in particular, the superiority of the kibbutz form of life was overinstilled in the youngsters. In some of their educational institutions, as Nira said, "the children could not even express the shortcomings of kibbutz life as they encountered them. You had to accept the teacher's attitude or you were a rebel." "I hated writing all those essays on why the kibbutz was the best form of life," said Guy. It seems that the idea of leaving the kibbutz and living elsewhere in Israel, which should be a natural option for people who were born into the kibbutz without choice, isn't a natural option for many of the kibbutzniks I met. The only exceptions are the few ex-kibbutzniks from the religious kibbutzim who had a clear sense of the place of Israel in their expressed priorities. They said clearly that settling in Israel comes before the kibbutz or the religion and that their own case was an ex-

ception. For most others, it seems that emigrating to the United States is an easier alternative.

After listening to the interviewees it was clear to me that each one had his case and his reasons. But while I was talking with them I noticed that two themes seemed to stand out more than others. First, many were looking for a challenge and for personal success, which they did not feel was possible in the kibbutz and, for some, not even in the army. This need for personal success is also found in the second, and to me, more striking theme: an outcry for individual recognition and freedom. It is hard to determine how much of their new-felt success was due to prior motivation and how much of it was a product of acculturating American values. Yet, since hardly any of them had planned to live in the States for a long period, it seems that they were carried away by the economic success they encountered.

An interesting question is why the kibbutzniks in L.A. choose business as their path of social mobility rather than education, as do many of their Israeli peers. Is their lack of drive for education related to the stress on equality rather than excellence in education prevalent in the kibbutz educational institutions? Or is it just this particular group of ex-kibbutzniks for whom advanced studies are not important? Several factors may provide insight into why these ex-kibbutzniks prefer to seek success through work rather than education. Kibbutzniks needed much more intrinsic motivation to become serious students because the school atmosphere was not always studious. In the participants' view, having a good time, *qeff* in Hebrew, was very important during their educational upbringing. High achievement was not encouraged as it was outside the kibbutz. The drive for excellence in studies was not one of their school's goals and the ones who excelled did so in spite of the atmosphere. Also, the regular work assignments given to school youths often interfered with their formal studies. These young people were trained to be industrious, to do any kind of job, and to have a strong work ethic. In view of their self-perception and their backgrounds, it may well be that these ex-kibbutzniks strive for success in an area where they feel best prepared, work, rather than searching for what may be more uncertain options opened up through education.

To a great extent, many of the young ex-kibbutzniks living in L.A. are uneducated in the modern sense. For some, their poor English is a handicap. But because they live in their own subculture, they manage to get along with Hebrew and only a little English. Even though many of the

NA'AMA SABAR

interviewees are carpenters, plumbers, and carpet layers, they view themselves as distinct from the American working class, whom they look down upon. Although they are uneducated, they view themselves as intelligent and very resourceful. These people are daring and, once they decide to stay in L.A., they search for ways to exercise free enterprise.

The personal achievement and financial success kibbutzniks find in the United States appears to satisfy a need. On the kibbutz, it is the group's rather than the individual's achievement that is stressed. In a non-kibbutz family, the parents search for areas of success for their children and help them through encouragement and reinforcement, whereas the kibbutz system expects its educators to be effective socializers and to inculcate kibbutz ideology. Parents have a secondary place in socializing and rely much more on the educators who may not always attend to all the children's needs as parents would.

I did, however, meet a few kibbutzniks who had experienced success in almost all facets of their performance on the kibbutz. They were in L.A. for different reasons. Gil, who was known as a leader of his kibbutz, said he wanted to be relieved of the burden of being a role model which he had always had to play. "It's time I was myself. Here I am anonymous. Here I can get light-headed at parties and be serious at work. I like the idea that everyone gets what he deserves. On the kibbutz, a few people carry the burden and most have it easy. People don't care about public property. An appliance, for example, can be returned in poor condition although it was received in perfect condition. People will keep on getting what everyone else gets in spite of their carelessness. There are no punitive steps." Another who also experienced success throughout his upbringing as well as during his military service was Zvi. "I did all that the kibbutz could offer me and it wasn't enough. I needed a challenge. I also felt the need to get away from the hardships caused by my having to encourage and support my parents whenever there were problems." So Zvi came with a wife and three children, with no guarantee of work or support, and found a challenge.

Regarding the significance of the repudiation of Diaspora existence, it appears that the generation that participated in the establishment of the State of Israel equated the Diaspora with the "shtetl," with ghettoes, and with oppression of Jews. In the minds of most *Sabras* today, the Diaspora is associated with the characteristic trimmings of ultra-Orthodoxy—the black clothing, the beards and the sideburns. They cannot understand it in terms of the modern world, democracy, freedom, or choice. It is even more difficult for these young Israelis to relate it to the American scene where so many respected institutions and well-known celebrities bear Jewish names. This misinterpretation of the reality of the Diaspora is even more pronounced among secular kibbutzniks who as yet do not have to face the dilemmas involved in bringing up children in a foreign culture among people of very different religions. It takes time for them to realize that they are not as free as they had initially thought themselves to be, that they are not in their land, and that what they have given up is national pride, political independence. and a real home as the price for living in the American Diaspora.

The kibbutzniks in L.A. have created a closed social network that encourages continued ties with their kibbutz in Israel. Maintaining their identity as kibbutzniks, within the framework of social ties with other kibbutzniks, is part of their tendency to be culturally isolated and establish only weak ties with the American, and even with the Jewish, community. They make no effort to adopt American customs or lifestyle, but stick to what is familiar to them from their homes. Their ties with the surrounding society are distant and alienated, while those within the social network are close to the point of clingingness. The selfless collectivism and practical orientation of the kibbutz upbringing, which lay at the very center of the nation-building ideology of Zionism and Israel, made at least some kibbutzniks ill-suited to function in contemporary Israeli society. Yet, paradoxically, their dense ties allow kibbutzniks to function quite well in super-individualistic, capitalistic Los Angeles, and still adhere to their home values. It turns out that the network helps the first generation of kibbutznik immigrants to cope on a daily basis, but their close attachment to it increases their insularity and their isolation from American society.

After examining these former kibbutzniks, the inescapable conclusion is that they are emigrants rather than immigrants. These kibbutzniks have left Israel and the kibbutz, but they have not really arrived in America. Their discourse is that of sojourners, their language is Hebrew, and their dreams are of Israel.

Directory of Sources

Extensive interviews with the former kibbutzniks who appear in this chapter and other aspects of their lives in

California can be found in my book, *Kibbutzniks in the Diaspora* (SUNY Press, 2000). Israeli emigrants to the United States have interested scholars since the phenomenon began. Some of the researchers who have examined this issue are Zvi Sobel (*Migrants from the Promised Land,* Transaction Books, 1986), Moshe Shokeid (*Children of Circumstances: Israeli Emigrants in New York,* Cornell University Press, 1988), and David Mittelberg (with Zvi Sobel, "Commitment, Ethnicity and Class Factors in Emigration of Kibbutz and Non-Kibbutz Population from Israel," *International Migration Review* 24 [4], 1990, 768–782). In the U.S., Steve Gold has investigated Israeli immigrants in several studies, among them, "Israelis in Los Angeles" (the Susan and David Wilstein Institute of Jewish Policy Studies, 1992); "Nascent Mobilization in a New Immigrant Community: The Case of Soviet Jews in California" (*Research in Community Sociology* 2 (1992), 189–211); "Israeli Immigrants in the U.S.: The Question of Community" (*Qualitative Sociology* 17 [4] 1994, 325–363); and with Bruce Phillips' "Israelis in the United States" (In D. Singer and R. A. Sheldon, eds., *The American Jewish Yearbook,* Vol. 96, The American Jewish Committee, 1996) 51–101. Major works on the kibbutz include Melford E. Spiro, *Kibbutz: Venture in Utopia* (Shoken, 1963) and, more recently, David Mittelberg, *Strangers in Paradise: The Israeli Kibbutz Experience* (Transaction Books, 1988). Yuval Dror has published a number of studies on kibbutz education.

NOTES

1. Based on my book, *Kibbutzniks in the Diaspora* (New York: SUNY, 2000).

CHAPTER 7

KETUBOT OF THE GOLDEN STATE

A PHOTO ESSAY FEATURING THE
ORIGINAL DESIGNS OF ROBERT SASLOW

The *ketubah,* or Jewish wedding contract, originated in the first century B.C.E. as a legal document ensuring the bride certain rights within the marriage. Over the centuries, the ketubah has evolved from its original legalistic purpose to its current place as a celebrated work of Jewish wedding art. Especially in the last thirty years, brides and grooms have commissioned unique ketubot (plural of ketubah) with artwork that reflects their upbringing, courtship, and vision for the future.

Born and raised in Los Angeles, ketubah artist Robert Saslow began his professional career directing the art program at the Union of American Hebrew Congregation's Swig Camp Institute for Living Judaism in the Santa Cruz Mountains south of San Francisco. His artwork combines the traditional Jewish elements of the ketubah with many California Jewish influences. On the pages that follow, you will find Saslow's unique California Jewish artistic style illustrated with images of San Francisco's Golden Gate Bridge, the rocky landscape of Big Sur, the Napa Valley winegrowing region, and the natural beauty of Yosemite Valley. With California's physical geography Saslow has integrated images and symbols particular to the personal stories of bride and groom, creating an original illustrated manuscript that reflects a broad spectrum of California Jewish experiences. (See also the color plates.)

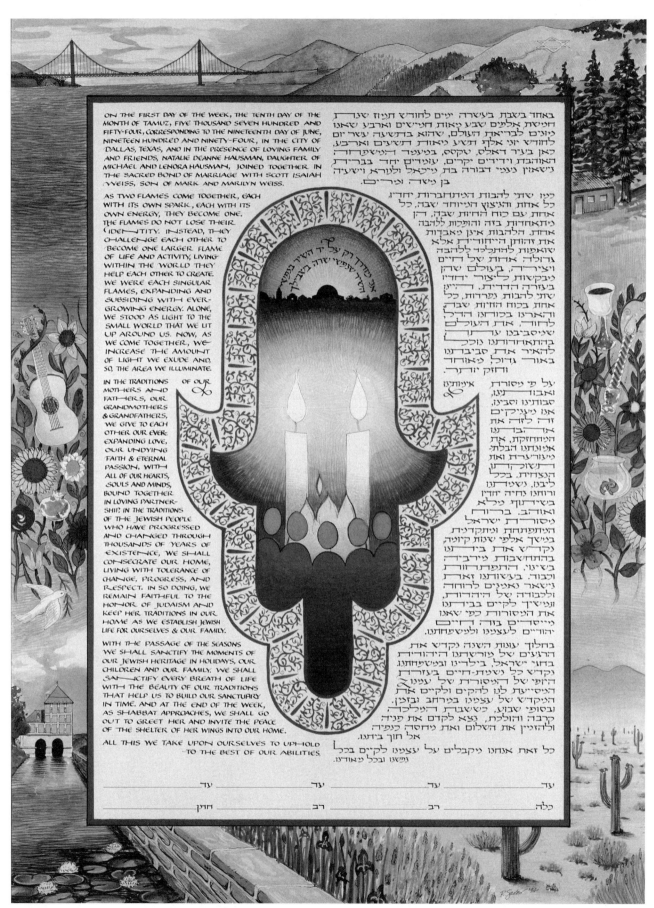

ON THE FIRST DAY OF THE WEEK, THE TENTH DAY OF THE MONTH OF TAMUZ, FIVE THOUSAND SEVEN HUNDRED AND FIFTY-FOUR, CORRESPONDING TO THE NINETEENTH DAY OF JUNE, NINETEEN HUNDRED AND NINETY-FOUR, IN THE CITY OF DALLAS, TEXAS, AND IN THE PRESENCE OF LOVING FAMILY AND FRIENDS, NATALIE DEANNE HAUSMAN, DAUGHTER OF MICHAEL AND LENORA HAUSMAN, JOINED TOGETHER IN THE SACRED BOND OF MARRIAGE WITH SCOTT ISAIAH WEISS, SON OF MARK AND MARILYN WEISS.

AS TWO FLAMES COME TOGETHER, EACH WITH ITS OWN SPARK, EACH WITH ITS OWN ENERGY, THEY BECOME ONE. THE FLAMES DO NOT LOSE THEIR IDENTITY. INSTEAD, THEY CHALLENGE EACH OTHER TO BECOME ONE LARGER FLAME OF LIFE AND ACTIVITY, LIVING WITHIN THE WORLD THEY HELP EACH OTHER TO CREATE. WE WERE EACH SINGULAR FLAMES, EXPANDING AND SUBSIDING WITH EVER-GROWING ENERGY. ALONE, WE STOOD AS LIGHT TO THE SMALL WORLD THAT WE LIT UP AROUND US. NOW, AS WE COME TOGETHER, WE INCREASE THE AMOUNT OF LIGHT WE EXUDE AND, SO, THE AREA WE ILLUMINATE.

IN THE TRADITIONS OF OUR MOTHERS AND FATHERS, OUR GRANDMOTHERS & GRANDFATHERS, WE GIVE TO EACH OTHER OUR EVER-EXPANDING LOVE, OUR UNDYING FAITH & ETERNAL PASSION, WITH ALL OF OUR HEARTS, SOULS AND MINDS, BOUND TOGETHER IN LOVING PARTNER-SHIP. IN THE TRADITIONS OF THE JEWISH PEOPLE WHO HAVE PROGRESSED AND CHANGED THROUGH THOUSANDS OF YEARS OF EXISTENCE, WE SHALL CONSECRATE OUR HOME, LIVING WITH TOLERANCE OF CHANGE, PROGRESS, AND RESPECT. IN SO DOING, WE REMAIN FAITHFUL TO THE HONOR OF JUDAISM AND KEEP HER TRADITIONS IN OUR HOME AS WE ESTABLISH JEWISH LIFE FOR OURSELVES & OUR FAMILY.

WITH THE PASSAGE OF THE SEASONS WE SHALL SANCTIFY THE MOMENTS OF OUR JEWISH HERITAGE IN HOLIDAYS, OUR CHILDREN AND OUR FAMILY. WE SHALL SANCTIFY EVERY BREATH OF LIFE WITH THE BEAUTY OF OUR TRADITIONS THAT HELP US TO BUILD OUR SANCTUARY IN TIME. AND AT THE END OF THE WEEK, AS SHABBAT APPROACHES, WE SHALL GO OUT TO GREET HER AND INVITE THE PEACE OF THE SHELTER OF HER WINGS INTO OUR HOME.

ALL THIS WE TAKE UPON OURSELVES TO UPHOLD TO THE BEST OF OUR ABILITIES.

Wedding ketubah of Natalie and Scott Hausman-Weiss, June 19, 1994, featuring images of San Francisco's Golden Gate Bridge and UAHC Camp Swig, Saratoga, California. By Robert Saslow. (Also see color plate.)

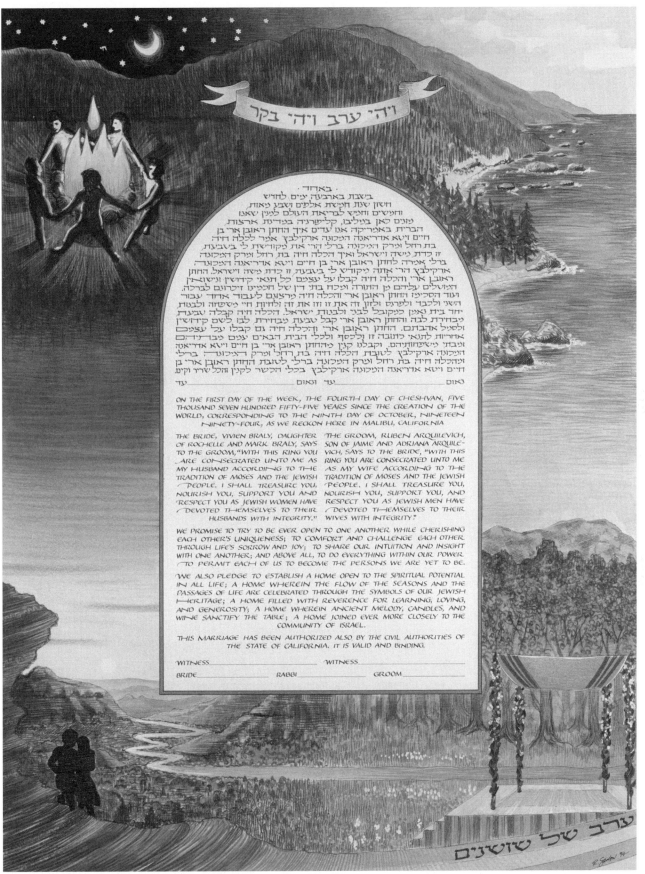

Wedding ketubah of Vivien Braly and Ruben Arquilevich, October 9, 1994, featuring images of
the northern California coast, Big Sur, Camp JCA-Shalom in Malibu.
By Robert Saslow. (Also see color plate.)

Wedding ketubah of Linda Schack and Kevin Kaiserman, August 29, 1998, featuring images of Yosemite Valley.

By Robert Saslow. (Also see color plate.)

Wedding ketubah of Annette Taub and Terrance Stinnett, June 29, 1991, featuring images of Mount Diablo, northern California.

By Robert Saslow. (Also see color plate.)

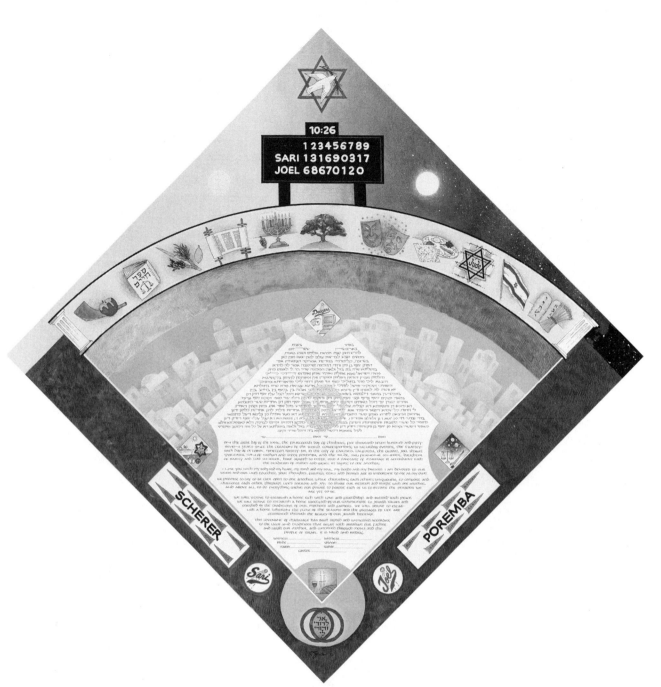

Wedding ketubah of Sari Scherer and Joel Poremba, October 26, 1996, inspired by their love of the Los Angeles Dodgers. By Robert Saslow. (Also see color plate.)

Thirty-third anniversary ketubah for Irene and Howard Levine, June 10, 1994, featuring images of California grapes.
By Robert Saslow. (Also see color plate).

Wedding ketubah of Joanne Cohen and Michael Shapero,
September 5, 1999, featuring images of
California redwoods in the Santa Cruz Mountains and
vineyards at Congress Springs Winery in Saratoga, California.
By Robert Saslow.

CHAPTER 8

JEWISH LEADERS AND THE
MOTION PICTURE INDUSTRY

FELICIA HERMAN

One could fill several library shelves with the numerous books that tell the story of the Jewish men (and, infrequently, women) who helped to build the American motion picture industry in the first half of the twentieth century. Harry and Jack Warner, Samuel Goldwyn, Louis B. Mayer, Irving Thalberg, Adolph Zukor, David O. Selznick: these are the figures who populate discussions of Jews and the motion picture industry—even though for many of these men, the fact that they had been born Jewish was almost incidental to their lives and to their work.

The story of the Jewish moguls, however, is not the only story of Jews and the motion picture industry. In fact, a host of Jewish communal leaders were active within the industry in this period, hoping to police the public image of American Jewry by exercising a measure of control over cinematic representations of Jews and Jewish issues. Their story has gone largely untold, and this is the way they wanted it: those Jewish leaders who were most active within the industry were justifiably afraid of strengthening the antisemitic allegation that "the Jews" controlled Hollywood and were using motion pictures to manipulate American audiences. Thus they kept their dealings with the industry quiet and out of the public eye, hoping to accomplish their communal goals without drawing unnecessary attention to themselves, their mission, or the relationships they were forming with Jews in the film industry.

Although Jewish leaders' goals were national and even international, their methods were local. And because of their proximity to and personal and professional connections with the film industry's most powerful figures, the leaders of California Jewry, especially in Los Angeles, became the primary representatives of organized Jewry within the industry. This method of drawing upon person-to-person connections with industry executives

was often quite successful, for although the industry's Jews generally de-emphasized their own Jewishness, the alarming increase in domestic and foreign antisemitism in the 1920s, '30s, and '40s posed a direct threat to the motion picture industry (because it was so heavily identified with Jews), to the industry's Jewish leaders, and to American and world Jewry in general. This precarious situation led Jews in the industry to a greater openness to overtures from Jewish communal leaders.

This essay explores the evolution of the relationship between California's Jewish leaders and the industry from the late 1920s to the years immediately after World War II. It traces the formalization of this relationship in a series of committees created to give the Jewish community an official voice within the industry, demonstrating the centrality of California's Jewish leaders to the Jewish communal effort to wield influence over films with Jewish characters or subjects. A central theme that emerges from this exploration is that, more often than not, the Jewish leaders closest to the industry were guided by fear and anxiety: they recognized the power that motion pictures held in American culture, and they feared the ways that films might endanger the safety of American Jewry. It was this fear that shaped the official relationship between American Jews and the film industry.

There are several reasons why the period between the 1920s and the 1940s witnessed the blossoming of the relationship between American Jewish leaders and the motion picture industry. First, this period encompassed the heyday of the studio system, which concentrated the industry's power into the hands of a few men, most of whom were Jewish, and many of whom were open to Jewish communal overtures if the moment were right. Even more importantly, however, throughout this period motion pictures

Los Angeles Breakfast Club featuring Louis B. Mayer and Marco H. Hellman, June 24, 1927.
Courtesy of the Western States Jewish History Archive.

were not protected under the constitutional guarantee of free speech. In 1915, the U.S. Supreme Court unanimously decided that motion pictures were "a business, pure and simple" and thus were subject to regulation like any other industry. Until 1952, when the Court reversed itself and found that films constituted a form of speech, censorship of motion pictures was legal, acceptable, and, to many minds, necessary. Most film reformers were concerned with what they perceived to be the immorality of motion pictures, but pressure groups of every conceivable stripe coalesced at one time or another to protect their cinematic image. Jewish organizations, therefore, felt no qualms about trying to shape the content of films relevant to their community. Although they disavowed censorship per se, they nonetheless believed in their right to suggest, rather than dictate, particular changes to films.

Finally, these were decades of crisis for American Jews: rising rates of domestic and foreign antisemitism convinced Jewish leaders of the urgency of exerting some sort of control over the portrayal of Jews and Jewish issues in motion pictures. In the 1920s, Henry Ford published diatribes against the Jews in his widely circulated *Dearborn Independent;* in the 1930s, Jews were blamed for the depression, accused of wielding too much power in the Roosevelt administration, and attacked publicly by antisemitic demagogues like Father Charles Coughlin and William Dudley Pelley; and the tumult of World War II awakened widespread intolerance, with American antisemitism reaching its peak during the war years. All three

decades were characterized by gentleman's agreements and quotas placing certain neighborhoods, companies, hotels, universities, and social clubs off-limits to Jews. One 1939 survey discovered that 20 percent of Americans believed there was "likely to be a widespread campaign" against Jews in the United States, and a striking 12 percent of Americans said that they would actively support such a campaign. By 1946, 64 percent of Americans reported having heard criticism of the Jews in the previous six months. With other contemporary observers of the film industry, including well-respected sociologists and communal activists, many Jewish leaders believed there was a direct correlation between the images audiences saw on screen and the attitudes and behaviors they then adopted. Just as moral reformers asserted that licentious films would create real-life licentiousness, Jewish leaders were certain that antisemitic or fulsomely philosemitic, or pro-Jewish, films would spark or strengthen antisemitism.

While the 1920s, '30s and '40s saw the most fruitful cooperation between Jews and the industry, the official inception of Jewish community–film industry relations can actually be dated back to 1913, with the founding of the Chicago-based Anti-Defamation League of B'nai B'rith (ADL). Several of the first American films—brief, black-and-white, silent vignettes—drew upon stereotypes of Jews long established in other media: Jews as money lenders, blackmailers, firebugs, and whiteslavers. The ADL was founded, in part, to stop these negative images, which it called the "most pressing problem" facing American Jews.

Warner Brothers Theater, Hollywood Boulevard and Wilcox Avenue, Hollywood.
Courtesy of the Western States Jewish History Archive.

In 1913 and 1914, its national secretary, attorney Leon L. Lewis (who would become an influential figure in the relationship between Jews and the industry in later decades), conveyed the ADL's dissatisfaction with antisemitic images to local theater owners, to regional, state, and national censorship boards, and to the filmmakers themselves. Lewis did achieve a modicum of success in convincing early filmmakers like Carl Laemmle, William Fox, Sigmund Lubin, and Thomas Edison to try to avoid spreading negative stereotypes of Jews in their films.

These early successes established the ADL as the unofficial Jewish communal voice within the industry. This role was formalized only after Cecil B. DeMille's silent screen epic *The King of Kings* (1927) sparked a nationwide Jewish debate over Jewish images on screen and the responsibility of Jewish organizations to control them. As soon as it

heard that DeMille was planning a film that would depict the last days, crucifixion, and resurrection of Jesus, the ADL involved itself in the film's production, fearing that the film would promulgate the particularly intractable stereotype of the Jew-as-Christ-killer. And it called upon its representatives in Los Angeles for help. By the late 1920s, turning to Los Angeles Jewry for help with the film industry was a foregone conclusion: most of the industry had already moved to sunny southern California, where the weather was almost always conducive to filming outdoors, and where a variety of topographies—ocean, mountain, desert—were all within a short drive. At the same time, Jews were also beginning to move west for their health, to flee the congestion of the northeastern urban areas, and to seek the same warmth and sunshine that drew other immigrants. Los Angeles' Jewish population

Albert Einstein and Rabbi Edgar F. Magnin, 1931.
Courtesy of Jacob Rader Marcus Center of the
American Jewish Archives.

that would one day draw hundreds of Jews and non-Jews to hear his sermons each week. He also began to take an interest in motion pictures. In a sermon delivered on Sukkot in 1915 and covered widely in the Stockton papers, Magnin lambasted D. W. Griffith's film *Birth of a Nation* (1915) for its racist depictions of African Americans: the film was "vicious in its influence, dangerous, and the last act of persecution hurled at a persecuted people. . . . One cannot leave the portals of the theater without being imbued with prejudice." Magnin's interest in motion pictures only intensified once he moved to Los Angeles in 1915 to become a rabbi of Temple B'nai B'rith. With industry leaders in his congregation and, soon, among his close friends, Magnin became one of the greatest and most vocal defenders of the industry and its Jewish members. Neal Gabler, in his book *An Empire of Their Own: How the Jews Invented Hollywood*, dubbed Magnin "the rabbi to the stars," and indeed he was, presiding over many of the weddings and funerals of the most influential Jews in the motion picture industry. He also frequently published positive articles and editorials about the industry in the *B'nai B'rith Messenger*, where he was an editor. But perhaps the most tangible manifestation of his relationship with the industry's Jews remains today in the very walls, windows, and floors of the temple building on Wilshire Boulevard that Magnin raised the funds to build in the 1920s. The Warner brothers donated a series of murals for the walls; Mr. and Mrs. Louis B. Mayer—three stained glass windows; Mr. and Mrs. Irving Thalberg (the former Norma Shearer, whom Magnin converted)—the decoration for the domed ceiling; Carl Laemmle—part of the chandelier, and so on.

Magnin, therefore, was seemingly the best person to help to shape the Jewish content of *The King of Kings*. He later asserted that he had done all he could to convince DeMille to refrain from producing the film altogether, but when that effort failed, he had settled for trying to minimize the film's negative portrayal of Jews. As an example, Magnin noted that he had convinced DeMille to remove the line, "His blood be upon you and your children," the verse from the Gospel of Matthew that had condemned future generations of Jews for the crime of deicide. But because he was no doubt too busy to attend to the daily vicissitudes of the film's production, Magnin was soon succeeded by three lesser-known rabbis and Jewish educators who were less successful with DeMille: Henry Radlin, Ernest Trattner, and Jacob M. Alkow. Radlin and Trattner

increased from 2,500 in 1900 to 70,000 in 1929, while the city's overall population jumped from 102,000 to 1,238,000 in that same period. When the ADL heard of DeMille's plans, therefore, it called upon the most logical man to serve as its liaison to DeMille: Rabbi Edgar Fogel Magnin of L.A.'s Temple B'nai B'rith.

Born in 1890 in San Francisco and a grandson of I[saac] Magnin of department store fame, Edgar Magnin was descended from German Jews and attended the predominantly German Hebrew Union College in Cincinnati. At the age of twenty-four, as a freshly ordained Reform rabbi, he returned to California to assume a pulpit in Stockton. In his fifteen months in the small, sleepy town, Magnin began to develop the characteristics that would eventually bring him national renown: an informal, congenial personality, a strong interest in the wider, non-Jewish community in which he lived, and a lively and accessible oratorical style

The noble Pontius Pilate (Victor Varconi), reluctant to harm Jesus, looks askance at the
Jewish High Priest Caiaphas (Rudolph Schildkraut) in Cecil B. DeMille's version of the passion, The King of Kings *(1927).*
Courtesy of Museum of Modern Art Film Stills Archive.

later confided that they themselves left the position because DeMille was unwilling to heed their advice. Alkow, for his part, remembered that although he had convinced DeMille to shoot scenes offering glimpses of Jewish daily life in the Galilee and Jerusalem and of Jesus teaching in a synagogue, DeMille eventually eliminated these scenes from the final version of the film. Thus, the primary villains of *The King of Kings* remained the Jews: Judas Iscariot (Joseph Schildkraut), the dark, greasy-haired and large-nosed Pharisees, and, most of all, Caiaphas (Rudolph Schildkraut), the High Priest, whose characterization New York rabbi Stephen S. Wise described as "a five and ten cent Shylock" and a "vindictive, savage, bloodthirsty monster." The film's intertitles described Caiaphas as a man "who cared more for Revenue than for Religion—and who

saw in Jesus a menace to his rich profits from the Temple," while Pontius Pilate (Victor Varconi) appears as a moral leader and reluctant tool of the Pharisees. Jesus (H. B. Warner) is presented as a saintly miracleworker and the film mutes his, his mother's, and his disciples' Jewishness.[1]

Once *The King of Kings* was released, there was, understandably, a nationwide Jewish outcry over the film's negative depiction of Jews—and over the ADL's apparent inability to prevent it. The Jewish press was quite vocal on the subject: more than a dozen papers around the country carried articles or ran editorials criticizing the film's anti-semitism and, frequently, the ADL's apparent impotence in the situation. Some of the most vitriolic criticism came from another California rabbi, the fiery young Louis I. Newman, who used his regular column in the Portland,

Oregon, Jewish newspaper *The Scribe* to denounce both the film and the ADL. Three years younger than Magnin, Newman came from the East Coast, although he had attended U.C. Berkeley as a graduate student. He eventually finished his degree at Columbia University while working at the Free Synagogue under the charismatic Rabbi Wise. When, at thirty-one, Newman returned to San Francisco to become the rabbi of that city's flagship Reform congregation, Temple Emanu-El, he brought with him what historian Fred Rosenbaum has called a "strident, positive expression of Jewish identity in the face of antisemitism and assimilation." Indeed, like Wise, Newman was an outspoken and uncompromising activist, writer, and orator who did not shy from public conflict. He and Wise also shared an antipathy for the elite and decorous organizations like the ADL and its parent B'nai B'rith, which were run by and catered to the conservative, middle- and upper-class descendants of central European Jewish immigrants to America. They particularly objected to the ways that elite Jewish organizations responded to antisemitism—through discreet, behind-the-scenes diplomacy, rather than through vocal public protests, which Newman, Wise, and Wise's American Jewish Congress preferred.

The King of Kings provided Newman (and Wise as well) with an excellent opportunity to criticize the ADL. Newman argued that, once Magnin and the other Los Angeles rabbis realized they could not prevent all of the film's anti-Jewish content, the ADL should have launched a national public protest against the film. Magnin, a member of the ADL, argued instead that the Jewish community should refrain from publicly protesting *The King of Kings* because protests would only increase the film's publicity and appear as if Jews were criticizing Christianity. Passionately disagreeing with this point, Newman published numerous articles denouncing the film, spoke out against it from his pulpit, encouraged liberal San Francisco ministers to sermonize against it, and convinced the Board of Rabbis of Northern California, on which he sat, to issue a public condemnation of it. Other San Francisco rabbis on the Board—Sherith Israel's Jacob Neito, Temple Sinai's Rudolf Coffee, and Temple Beth Israel's Elliot Burstein—also criticized the film in their sermons and published condemnatory articles in the local Jewish paper *Emanu-El*. The Board, in fact, was one of only two regional rabbinical boards to speak out against the film.

Although Newman argued that the collective protests of northern California's clergy did hurt the film's box of-

fice success in San Francisco, *Variety* reported that while business "was not of the record-breaking type" during the film's three-week engagement there, *The King of Kings* still "more than held its own." Newman and his San Francisco colleagues were vocal figures in *The King of Kings* debate, but San Francisco seemed very far from Los Angeles in the 1920s, and San Francisco's Jewish leaders enjoyed no special access to the industry. They did not seem to possess advance or insider information about the film, and they proved unable, in the end, to shape *The King of Kings* in any significant way. Jewish leaders in Los Angeles, on the other hand, possessed much greater power. Magnin and the other Jewish consultants to *The King of Kings* may not have been able to eradicate all of the film's antisemitism, but because they were local and were involved with the film in an official capacity, they nonetheless had an opportunity to voice their opinions to DeMille in person and, as Magnin and Alkow indicated, to shape the film somewhat.

The future promised even greater access to the industry for Los Angeles' Jewish leaders: distressed at the negative publicity surrounding *The King of Kings*, the industry's trade organization, the Motion Picture Producers and Distributors Association (MPPDA), named the ADL's parent organization, B'nai B'rith, as the official Jewish representative to the industry (a job it delegated to the ADL). The ADL considered this agreement a "victory for all [its] years of striving" to improve cinematic representations of Jews, while the MPPDA hoped that it would prevent future problems by endowing future films with a Jewish communal imprimatur. The ADL entrusted Leon Lewis with the creation of the new MPPDA–ADL committee. After years in Chicago as the ADL's national secretary and after being wounded in World War I, Lewis had moved to the more temperate climes of Los Angeles for his health. There he remained active in B'nai B'rith and the ADL. In fact, it is his voluminous correspondence with national ADL leaders that offers one of the most important sources for the history of the relationship between Jews and the motion picture industry in the 1920s, '30s, and '40s. As the records reveal, Lewis first approached comedian Eddie Cantor to serve on the MPPDA–ADL committee, and although Cantor agreed, it soon became clear that his frequent and often lengthy trips to New York prevented him from serving effectively. Lewis therefore replaced him with Reform rabbi Isidore Isaacson of Temple Israel, who served on the committee with Lewis and the ubiquitous Rabbi Magnin. But

Three Pharisees (one wearing tefillin*) check the time so they can catch Jesus
in the act of violating Jewish law by healing on Shabbat in* The King of Kings *(1927).
Courtesy of Museum of Modern Art Film Stills Archive.*

the MPPDA–ADL committee operated only sporadically in the late 1920s, consulting with the industry on only a handful of films with Jewish content.

Hitler's rise to power in Germany and a contemporaneous rise in domestic antisemitism caused the ADL to revive the MPPDA committee in late 1933—and, ultimately, to seek out an even closer relationship with the industry. The ADL had three main concerns in the 1930s. First, long-simmering tensions over the morality of motion pictures had finally come to a boil, with important repercussions for Jews. Would-be film reformers had tried to control the moral content of films since the inception of the industry. Because "Hollywood" had long been synonymous in many reformers' minds with "Jews," attacks on the industry also frequently revealed an undertone of antisemitism. Thus in the 1930s, film reformers drew upon a rhetoric that

stretched back decades as they argued that immoral films were the result of the inherent immorality of the Jews who made them. "Certain it is," declared Los Angeles Catholic bishop John J. Cantwell, "that if . . . Jewish executives had any desire to keep the screen free from offensiveness they could do so." The Methodist paper *The Churchman* attacked the "shrewd Hebrews" for their "meretricious methods" of "selling crime and shame" on screen; and Joseph Breen, the man who would eventually direct the Production Code Administration, the industry's self-censorship body, asserted to a colleague in 1932 that the Jews in the film industry "are simply a rotten bunch of vile people with no respect for anything . . . [who] seem to think of nothing but money making and sexual indulgence." Unwittingly adopting a kind of blame-the-victim stance, the ADL in the 1930s wanted to convince Jews in the industry that by producing films that reformers deemed immoral, they were potentially causing American antisemitism.

The ADL's other major concerns in the 1930s were Nazism and American antisemitism. The ADL continued to believe that films with antisemitic images would plant or reinforce antisemitism in filmgoers, especially those who had little contact with real Jews. As national director Richard Gutstadt explained in reference to a 1934 film based on a Broadway play with a ignominious Jewish protagonist: "in New York City, where [the play ran], it would do no perceptible harm. As a motion picture, however, shown to millions throughout the country, particularly large groups in the hinterlands who have but a vague understanding of Jews, I am afraid it would do a great deal of harm." This was especially important, he added, because of the increased threat to world Jewry since Hitler's rise to power. Throughout the 1930s, therefore, the ADL worked to ensure that American films did not promulgate antisemitism in any way. At the same time, however, the ADL acted on the seemingly paradoxical notion that films that were explicitly anti-Nazi or pro-Jewish were also dangerous. The latter types of films, ADL leaders believed, strengthened the notion that "the Jews controlled Hollywood" and were using films as vehicles for Jewish propaganda.

The ADL would never have been able to address any of its concerns effectively were it not for the creation of a new organization sympathetic to its goals, the Los Angeles Jewish Community Committee (renamed the Community Relations Committee after World War II; referred to here as the LAJCC). In July 1933, at the behest of the ADL, Leon Lewis created a Los Angeles anti-defamation committee, the forerunner to the LAJCC. The anti-defamation committee boasted some of the most influential Jews in Los Angeles—people who, Lewis discovered, were more interested in their local problems with antisemitism than with the national anti-defamation agenda. From the start, however, Lewis's committee clashed with a similar committee headed by the local B'nai B'rith lodge president, Harry Graham Balter. Lewis (and the ADL national office) disliked Balter's desire for publicity, and after some disagreements over funding, Lewis resigned from B'nai B'rith and founded the LAJCC in March 1934 with the backing of the ADL's national director. The LAJCC drew on the membership of the previous anti-defamation committee and ultimately consisted of local representatives from all of the major national Jewish organizations as well as other local Jewish leaders. Philosophically and methodologically, the LAJCC closely resembled the ADL: it was a group of self-appointed notables, largely of central European descent, who preferred a quiet, behind-the-scenes approach to anti-defamation work. The LAJCC also shared the ADL's fear of antisemitic films and overly philosemitic or anti-Nazi films, and it proved to be the most important agent for voicing Jewish concerns about these films to the film industry.

The relationship between the LAJCC and the motion picture industry developed out of the perceived need for and drama of the LAJCC's primary work in its earliest years: the top-secret mission of ferreting out Nazi sympathizers in the Los Angeles area. Southern California, as Lewis put it, had become a "hot-bed" of Nazi activity in the months after Hitler had come to power. Lewis planted non-Jewish undercover agents in local pro-Nazi organizations, and these spies reported back to Lewis about the groups' methods, propaganda, and sources of "moral and financial support." Acting on this information, Lewis worked behind the scenes at such organizations as the Disabled American Veterans (DAV) and the American Legion to promote "Americanism" resolutions which would repudiate fascist discrimination policies, recognize fascism's threat to American democracy, and emphasize "American" values of brotherhood, tolerance, and religious equality. Lewis, the LAJCC, and the ADL always believed that it was more effective to have a non-Jewish organization such as the DAV or the Legion promote positive ideas about equality than for Jews simply to defend themselves against antisemitic attacks. This method, they hoped, would create an atmosphere where non-Jewish Americans would not tolerate attacks on their Jewish neighbors.

Lewis realized early on that a powerful and largely untapped financial resource for this and other work lay in his own backyard: the wealthy Jews in the film industry. In November 1933, he and several prominent members of the Los Angeles anti-defamation committee met with executives at MGM, Warner Bros., and other studios to solicit funds. They were immediately successful: a little over half the committee's budget for 1933 and 1934 came from Jews in the film industry, and the percentage rose to almost 70 percent of the LAJCC's funding in 1934–1935. Relations with industry leaders only deepened after the creation of the LAJCC. No doubt anticipating the benefit of strong connections to the industry, the LAJCC appointed Mendel

Silberg, a prominent entertainment lawyer with many clients and friends in the industry, as its chairman. Then, only a week after the LAJCC's founding, it created a Motion Picture Committee, composed of prominent Jewish studio executives like Irving Thalberg, Harry Cohn, Jack Warner, and Joseph Schenck. Lewis and the Motion Picture Committee met monthly, discussing issues of concern to the Jews in the industry and to the Jewish community in general. Although the opinions of the Jewish film moguls on this subject are almost impossible to track down, it seems clear from their response to Lewis's work that the need to fight Nazism and antisemitism inspired many Jews in the industry to support Jewish communal work for the first time. They appeared particularly interested in the investigations of Nazi sympathizers that the LAJCC was carrying out in Southern California—and even in the studios themselves. Perhaps, as filmmakers, the industry executives were also attracted to the drama of the LAJCC's spy activities. Whatever their reasons, worldwide and domestic antisemitism made many Jews in the industry "conscious of their background, and heritage, and history," as entertainment lawyer and LAJCC leader Martin Gang put it. "Otherwise," he concluded, "in a free society, they might never have done so."

From the outset of the LAJCC's Motion Picture Committee, Lewis declared its direct connection to the industry "a great deal better" than the MPPDA–ADL committee had established in the wake of *The King of Kings*. As the ADL's national director Richard Gutstadt put it, Jewish communal leaders now had access to the "sanctum sanctorum."

The LAJCC's connections proved invaluable for offering Jewish leaders a means of voicing their concerns to the industry. Lewis became the point-man for Jewish communal relations with the industry: whenever the ADL or other Jewish organizations had questions about a specific film or wanted to convey a particular message to filmmakers, they called upon Lewis and the LAJCC. So, for example, to bring Jewish leaders' concerns about the film morality issue to Jewish filmmakers, Lewis arranged a meeting between Gutstadt and members of the Motion Picture Committee in July 1934. Gutstadt discussed the necessity of keeping the screen entirely free from antisemitism as well as the ADL's concern that the film morality debate was hurting the public image of American Jews. In response, the industry executives promised to make a "determined and sincere effort . . . to remove all causes of criticism" of the industry. Gutstadt left California satisfied.

The LAJCC's connections to the industry also proved invaluable when it came to films with antisemitic or overly anti-Nazi or pro-Jewish content. The LAJCC kept a watchful eye over films with potentially negative Jewish content. Two of the many examples of the LAJCC's efforts in this area demonstrate the effectiveness of the networks the organization was building within the industry. In the summer of 1934, at the ADL's behest, Lewis asked LAJCC chair Mendel Silberg to look into a proposed MGM film about the two thieves crucified alongside Jesus, *The Two Thieves*. Silberg was MGM chief Louis B. Mayer's personal counsel, and as Lewis told the ADL, "I believe that we need have no fear as to the outcome." (The film was never made.) Later that year, the ADL advised Lewis of Monogram's plans to produce *The Great God Gold* (1935), which "purports to be a story of receiverships" and thus should be "carefully watched" by Lewis. Lewis asked Sam Wolf, an attorney at the small studio, to investigate. Wolf told him that he would "take an immediate and active interest" in the film, and in March 1935, the ADL reported that due to "constant negotiations" in Los Angeles and New York, "the picture is entirely free from any unfavorable Jewish portrayal." The studio also planned to ship a special print of the film to the ADL's office in Chicago for previewing, and the producers assured the ADL that any material the preview committee found objectionable would be eliminated.

The LAJCC trained the same watchful eye on films that they believed were too overtly anti-Nazi or pro-Jewish. Throughout the 1930s, Leon Lewis used his contacts in the industry to gather insider information about a film project entitled *Mad Dog of Europe* which, had it been made, would have been a stinging indictment of Hitler. Lewis and Gutstadt worried that if the film were produced it would invite charges of Jewish propagandizing, since all of its would-be producers were Jews. The LAJCC and ADL cooperated with MPPDA officials, who were concerned about the film's effect on European markets for American films, and together they were successful in preventing its production. Then there was the somewhat more delicate project of trying to keep material that was too philosemitic off film screens. While eliminating any traces of antisemitism from film screens was a clear and understandable goal, the effort to stop overly positive images of Jews was more difficult to explain. In 1934, in reference to a film the ADL feared would be too pro-Jewish, Gutstadt explained the effort in this way:

[T]he world attributes to the Jewish people a dominant influence in the motion picture industry. With so many interests vigilant in the attempt to find basis for criticism, it is unwise to furnish material for such criticism of our people. . . . All that we are really concerned with is the sounding of a word of caution, if it be possible, in order that any [film] dealing with Jewish characters shall be so treated as to be freed from any possible charge of fulsomeness or propaganda.

Several years later, when the ADL heard that Warner Bros. was planning to make *The Life of Emile Zola* (1937), which would focus on the Dreyfus Affair, Gustadt asked the LAJCC's Mendel Silberberg to call his contacts at Warners to ensure that the film would pursue a "proper middle course" and would "not err in leaning too far in either direction"—that is, that it would portray Jewish characters neither in an antisemitic light nor in an "unduly favorable" manner "not justified by the story, and possibly savoring of propaganda." Later historians would criticize what they perceived as the film's downplaying of the antisemitic motivations of the Dreyfus Affair, but in 1937, neither the ADL nor the LAJCC found any fault with this approach.

Although the LAJCC served as the primary Jewish representative to the film industry throughout the 1930s, it was never actually elected to this position, nor did it necessarily represent the majority of Jewish opinion on particular films or Jewish issues. Like the ADL had been earlier, the LAJCC was simply the organization closest to the industry, and it acted according to its own philosophy of and methods for responding to antisemitism. Disagreement surfaced, as it had in the past, when other Jewish organizations expressed their own opinions about particular films or when the Jewish press applied less conservative and stringent criteria in responding to films with Jewish or anti-Nazi content. This dissension was apparent in the case of *Mad Dog of Europe,* whose "pro-Jewish propaganda [*sic*]," Lewis surmised, was being supported in some way by Rabbi Wise's American Jewish Congress. And at least two Jewish papers criticized the kinds of fears that led to the prevention of the film's production. The producers "got cold tootsies," sighed a columnist in the *B'nai B'rith Messenger,* complaining that "profits come ahead of RIGHT." The Minneapolis–St. Paul *American Jewish World* reported sympathetically on producer Al Rosen's charges that the industry was being intimidated by German officials, who threatened that the film would have negative re-

percussions both for German Jewry and for the market for American films in Nazi-dominated parts of Europe. Neither of these papers seemed aware of the cooperation that Jewish groups were giving to the battle against the film.

To screenwriter Ben Hecht, however, a Hollywood insider who became a passionate fundraiser for Zionist causes and who took a dim view of the conservative, fearful views of ADL and LAJCC leaders, the activities of the handful of Jewish leaders who were trying to play an active role in the motion picture industry were not only obvious but despicable. In 1944, Hecht published *A Guide for the Bedeviled,* biting criticism of these Jewish leaders and of the Jews in the industry with whom they cooperated:

> Oversensitive Jews, overnervous Jews, Jews frightened at the crude reminders of their own immigrant beginnings, Simple Simon Jews, hoping to blot out all consciousness of Jews in their country by breaking all the mirrors they could—these worked mightily, and are still dizzily employed, in the exorcising of the Jew from literature and the stage. The movies and the radio suddenly won the battle for them—chiefly the movies—for here there were mainly Jewish potentates to influence; potentates as full of Simple Simonism as any of the mirror breakers.

Hecht was correct in arguing that the Jewish leaders closest to the industry shared the viewpoint of the Jewish leaders of the industry: both groups were afraid of the antisemitic backlash that might follow films seeming to propagandize for Jewish causes. Yet it is almost impossible to say whether these fears were justified. But it is certain that such fears, appropriate or not, shaped the Jewish relationship to the film industry throughout the 1930s.

Nor did these fears decline during World War II. The LAJCC and ADL did soften their stance against explicit anti-Nazi films, since fighting the Nazis was now national policy and no longer bore the stigma of being a particularly Jewish battle. For example, both Lewis and Joseph Roos, the man who would succeed him at the LAJCC, praised the film *Hitler's Children* (1943), which revealed the brainwashing and violence at the heart of indoctrination into the Hitler Youth. And the ADL recommended to its regional offices *None Shall Escape* (1944), which depicted the violence and mass deportations attending the Nazi invasion of a Polish village, despite its customary reservations about one aspect of the film: Apparently, in one Brooklyn theater, a scene in which a rabbi is shot by

FELICIA HERMAN

Emil Bruckner (Skippy Homeier) shocks his American family's German housekeeper, Frieda (Edit Angold),
with his unrepentant Nazism in Tomorrow the World *(1944).*
Courtesy of Museum of Modern Art Film Stills Archive.

the Nazis had provoked applause from some audience members, after which a "minor riot" ensued in the theater. Such responses, however rare, convinced Jewish leaders that their fear of antisemitic backlash against certain film content was justified.

The only type of film that Jewish leaders closest to the industry could recommend without reservation in the 1930s and 1940s was one that promoted "American" ideals of tolerance and democracy in general, without drawing special attention to discrimination against Jews. Thus, the LAJCC cooperated heavily with Warner Bros. to publicize its 1944 short *It Happened in Springfield,* the true story of an innovative intercultural education program in Springfield, Massachusetts. The next year, the LAJCC awarded Warner Bros. president Harry Warner a place on its Honor Roll of Men of Good Will for his work promoting such education programs on screen and in real life. For *Tomorrow the World,* a 1944 United Artists film about a German

boy who comes to live with his family in America and there learns the difference between Nazism and Americanism, Lewis and the LAJCC created what became a widely-used educational program to accompany showings of the film to schoolchildren. The LAJCC also helped to fund a major study on the film's effect on young viewers.

In 1946, however, a situation not unlike that surrounding *The King of Kings* two decades before altered the LAJCC's role within the industry. Like *The King of Kings,* the film *Abie's Irish Rose* (1946) provoked criticism of its negative depiction of Jews and also prompted a national Jewish inquiry into the failure of Jewish organizations to stop such dangerous images. Just after the end of the war, Bing Crosby, one of the most popular actors of the day, produced a remake of the once-popular play and film about an Irish-Jewish intermarriage, *Abie's Irish Rose.* No doubt encouraged by the success of his recent films *Going My Way* (1944) and *The Bells of St. Mary's* (1945),

As Father Whelan (Emory Parnell) looks on, Solomon Levy (Michael Chekov) tries to explain to Patrick Murphy (J. M. Kerrigan)
why their children cannot marry in Abie's Irish Rose *(1946), a film which drew much fire for its stereotypical portrayals*
of both Jews and Irish-Americans.
Courtesy of Museum of Modern Art Film Stills Archive.

both of which featured him as a Catholic priest and traded gently on religious humor, Crosby probably believed that *Abie's Irish Rose* bore a message of religious tolerance—an argument made by some observers of the original 1920s play and film. The remake was a monumental misjudgment of the historical moment, however. Neither of Crosby's Catholic films had drawn on ethnic stereotypes in quite the way that *Abie's Irish Rose* did. Reinvigorating vaudeville-era stereotypes of Jews and the Irish, the film featured rich Jewish clothiers and lawyers with strong Yiddish accents, always on the lookout for shopping bargains and frequently guilty of ignorant malapropisms. The central Irish Catholic figure is similarly stereotypical: a stocky alcoholic quick to pick fights and raise his fists. Such stereotypes seemed out of place in postwar America: for years, the country had been infused with the rhetoric that Americans of all races, religions, and nationalities needed to work together to defeat the bigoted and intolerant Nazis. Moreover, caricatures of Jews were particularly ill-timed given the recent horrors of the Holocaust, and the vaudevillian tropes did not resonate with 1940s audiences, because the real-life immigrants they lampooned no longer occupied a prominent place in the American psyche. (No one faulted Crosby for anything more than

FELICIA HERMAN

poor judgment, however; his reputation as a promoter of religious tolerance kept him immune from charges of malicious intent.)

Understandably, *Abie's Irish Rose* found a stiff-armed reception from film critics and groups dedicated to overcoming group differences. Jewish organizations and the Jewish press were among the film's most strident critics. The ADL, LAJCC, and American Jewish Committee all registered complete disapproval of the film, as did several organs of the Jewish press. The character of the bargain-hunting, overdressed, accented, parochial Jewish immigrant not only embarrassed postwar Jews, but was exactly the sort of image that Jewish organizations had been working for decades to erase from American popular culture. Its reemergence after the war sparked intense fears of the damage such an image could cause: *Abie's Irish Rose* "packs more racial venom than a Gerald L. K. Smith meeting," stated the *California Jewish Voice,* while the (B'nai B'rith) *National Jewish Monthly* asserted that the film would "reinforce, if it does not actually create . . . outright prejudice."

The fact that a film like *Abie's Irish Rose* could be produced at all galvanized the major national Jewish organizations to examine the status of the Jewish community's relationship with the film industry. Apparently, the regular system whereby LAJCC members offered advice during a film's production process had not been employed in this case: perhaps because the LAJCC had few connections to Crosby's production company neither the film nor the script were available for the LAJCC to preview before the film's release. And although ADL representatives in Los Angeles had "endeavored continuously to dissuade the producers from showing this film" after it had been finished, their advice had gone unheeded. Because the work of the LAJCC, the primary liaison to the film industry, had always been carried out quietly through informal and personal communications, few people, even among Jewish leaders, were aware of the extent of the LAJCC's work with the motion picture industry since the early 1930s. The release of *Abie's Irish Rose* only strengthened the impression that no one was at the helm of Jewish relations with the industry. Therefore, the two-year-old National Community Relations Advisory Committee (NCRAC)—an umbrella group made up of the ADL, American Jewish Committee, American Jewish Congress, Jewish Labor Committee, Jewish War Veterans, the (Reform) Union of American Hebrew Congregations, and eighteen community relations committees from around the country—decided to step in. NCRAC had been founded as a coordinating agency for the Jewish defense organizations that had both multiplied and expanded their operations during the war. After the war, it followed those organizations into the realm of community relations where, instead of focusing on countering negative images of Jews, organizations worked more generally for interreligious, intercultural, and interracial understanding. Entering the motion picture field was a necessary aspect of this work, NCRAC believed. "Inasmuch as the effects upon group attitudes exerted by motion pictures were a matter of national concern to the Jewish community," an executive committee member stated in 1947, "there should be some national instrumentality whereby a coordinated approach could be made to the motion picture industry."

Consequently, in December 1946, having arrived at a negative appraisal of *Abie's Irish Rose,* NCRAC's Committee on Mass Approach (later renamed the Mass Media Committee, the Committee on Motion Pictures, and then the Motion Picture Project) began its study of the history of the relationship between the Jewish community and the motion picture industry. In March, a subcommittee report revealed that primary responsibility for this work lay with the LAJCC, which in NCRAC's view was merely a local organization without a mandate to represent the entire Jewish community. NCRAC therefore began negotiations with the LAJCC to bring the local group's work under NCRAC's aegis. These negotiations were not altogether smooth, for much was at stake: over the years, the LAJCC had obtained unprecedented access to the men who ran the most powerful vehicle of American popular culture. It had forged a workable, unobtrusive system of contact with important figures in the industry, not least through its own Motion Picture Committee. LAJCC chair Mendel Silberberg tried to convince NCRAC that although the LAJCC had not kept other Jewish organizations apprised of all of its actions over the years, it had been "quietly and in most instances, effectively" handling the problems that had arisen almost daily in the film field for over a decade. He warned that if too many people from "various organizations" began to exert new and disorganized pressure on the industry, industry executives might rebel and refuse to accept advice from any Jewish group at all. The MPAA (successor to the MPPDA) agreed when NCRAC turned to it for guidance: Jewish groups would be best served, the

MPAA argued, if they would officially consolidate their relationship with the industry into one body, as they had informally done through the LAJCC.

NCRAC acknowledged the need for this unified Jewish voice, and it recognized that the LAJCC had both the experience and connections necessary to work effectively within the industry. It especially wanted to capitalize on the LAJCC's broad web of connections to the Jewish film executives who, NCRAC's leaders soon realized, were fearful of "the charge of Jewish domination" of Hollywood and were not the easiest men to get along with. NCRAC then devised a compromise whereby the LAJCC became part of the NCRAC Mass Media Committee but continued to serve as the link between NCRAC and the industry. In addition, NCRAC and the LAJCC agreed to hire one person as the professional liaison to the industry. This person worked in close concert with the LAJCC but officially reported to NCRAC. The men who came to occupy this role over the next few decades—John Stone, William Gordon (son of actress Vera Gordon), and Allen Rivkin—were all chosen for their intimate knowledge of the industry as well as their close ties to L.A.'s Jewish community.

As antisemitism waned after the war, and as Jewish communal leaders and the Jews in the industry slowly became less fearful of explicit Jewish film content, the NCRAC Motion Picture Project evolved into the Jewish Film Advisory Committee (JFAC), which offered advice and information for filmmakers planning to include Jewish material in their films. In the mid–1970s, JFAC director Allen Rivkin asserted that disseminating factual information about Jews was a much more useful project than previous efforts to try to prevent negative Jewish stereotypes. He told a reporter in 1975 that, in the thirteen years that he had directed the JFAC, the committee's efforts to prevent what it considered to be unsympathetic material "ha[d] never really gotten anything." He was unable, for example, to change what he considered to be the negative Jewish content of *Goodbye, Columbus* (1969), *Goodbye Again* (1968), *Lepke* (1975), or *Jesus Christ Superstar* (1973). He had, however, provided many answers to an extraordinary range of questions from film and television creators: questions about Jewish history and ritual, the Holocaust, Jewish genetic diseases, the spelling and definition of Yiddish words, Israeli geography, and so forth. In fact, the JFAC became a well-known fount of Jewish information within the film and television industries, differing from its predecessors by publicizing its existence, emphasizing its Jewish particularity, and encouraging the inclusion of particular Jewish themes and content in films and television programs.

While Rivkin believed that the Jewish community was best served in the 1970s by the JFAC's public, positive work as an information agency within the film industry, the Jewish communal leaders who had interacted with the industry in the 1920s, '30s, and '40s were constrained by their fears of strengthening an already powerful antisemitic tide that was slowly sweeping over the world. Unlike the Jewish executives who have come to dominate the popular imagination, the Jewish leaders who worked without fanfare within the industry had an explicitly Jewish goal in mind: to try to protect the Jewish public image by preventing the many types of film content that might reflect negatively upon Jews. This national goal was pursued through local methods: California's Jewish leaders, especially in Los Angeles, developed and managed the relationship of the Jewish community with the film industry from the late 1920s on. Their intimate understanding of the workings of the industry, their variety of contacts within the industry, and their ability to use these contacts quickly and unobtrusively made them indispensable. Whether one agrees with the caution and fear that underlay their actions, one thing is clear: the efforts of Rabbi Magnin, Leon Lewis, and the members of the LAJCC resulted in a strong, effective Jewish voice within one of the most powerful mass culture industries of the first half of the twentieth century.

Directory of Sources

The most important sources for this article were various archival collections pertaining to the ADL, LAJCC, and NCRAC. The American Jewish Historical Society in New York holds some ADL material, as well as the NCRAC papers and the papers of Stephen S. Wise (useful for *The King of Kings*). The Urban Archives Center at California State University, Northridge, holds the LAJCC papers, which they catalogue as the Jewish Federation–Council of Greater Los Angeles Community Relations Committee Collection. The Jacob Rader Marcus Center of the American Jewish Archives in Cincinnati holds some early ADL material (especially in the papers of Rabbi David Phillipson), the (at present uncatalogued) papers of Rabbi Edgar Fogel Magnin, and an oral history interview with Magnin conducted by Malca Chall for the Regional Oral History Office, University of California, Berkeley. The MPAA Production Code Administration Papers, at the Margaret Herrick Library of the Center for the Study of the Motion Picture in Los Angeles, also came in handy, especially its *Mad Dog of Europe* collection.

For American Jewish newspapers from this period, I relied on the libraries of Brandeis University, the Jewish Theological Seminary of America, and the American Jewish Periodical Center at Hebrew Union College in Cincinnati.

Relevant secondary sources include Steven Alan Carr's *Hollywood and Antisemitism: A Cultural History up to World War II* (New York: Cambridge University Press, 2001) and Gregory D. Black's *Hollywood Censored: Morality Codes, Catholics and the Movies* (New York: Cambridge University Press, 1994), both of which discuss the antisemitic elements of film reform efforts; Neal Gabler's engaging group biography of the Jewish men who ran the Hollywood studios in this period, *An Empire of Their Own: How the Jews Invented Hollywood* (New York: Anchor Books, 1988), which also discusses Magnin, Silberberg, and the LAJCC; Fred Rosenbaum's *Architects of Reform:*

Congregational and Community Leadership, Emanu-El of San Francisco, 1849–1980 (Berkeley, Calif.: The Judah L. Magnes Memorial Museum, 1980) includes information about Rabbi Louis Newman; and Leonard Dinnerstein's *Antisemitism in America* (New York: Oxford University Press, 1994). The two best surveys of the Jewish image in American films are Patricia Erens, *The Jew in American Cinema* (Bloomington: Indiana University Press, 1984) and Lester D. Friedman, *The Jewish Image in American Film* (Secaucus, N.J.: Citadel Press, 1987).

NOTES

1. Magnin: *Jewish Daily Bulletin* 25 November 1927, 3, see also Isidore M. Golden, Official Statement of B'nai B'rith Anti-Defamation League on the "King of Kings," *B'nai B'rith Messenger* 9 December 1927, 1; Radlin and Trattner: *Detroit Jewish Chronicle* 25 November 1927, 1+; *Jewish Daily Bulletin* 16 November 1927, 2; Alkow: Jacob M. Alkow, *In Many Worlds* (New York: Shengold Publishers, Inc., 1985), 36, 41.

CHAPTER 9

CIVIL RIGHTS AND
JAPANESE AMERICAN INCARCERATION[1]

ELLEN EISENBERG

On March 6, 1942, the *San Francisco News* published an editorial supporting mass removal of Japanese immigrants and Japanese Americans. The editorial urged its readers to

> recognize the necessity of clearing the coastal combat areas of all possible fifth columnists and saboteurs. Inasmuch as the presence of enemy agents cannot be detected readily when these areas are thronged by Japanese the only course left is to remove all persons of that race for the duration of the war. . . . That is a clear-cut policy easily understood. Its execution should be supported by all citizens of whatever racial background, but especially it presents an opportunity to the people of an enemy race to prove their spirit of co-operation and keep their relations with the rest of the population of this country on the firm ground of friendship.

The *News* captured in this editorial the key arguments used by supporters of the removal policy: that nationals of enemy countries were a threat to the Pacific Coast, and that Japanese aliens and their descendants were a particular threat because their nationality was linked to their race. California Governor Culbert Olson explained this more crudely in his testimony before the House Select Committee on National Defense Migration (the Tolan Committee). Olson argued that refugees from European enemy nations should not be included in an evacuation order, but that all Japanese Americans should because "they all look alike," making it impossible to distinguish between the loyal and the disloyal. As the Governor explained, "The distinction between the Japanese and the Italian and German is the difficulty of telling who is who among the Japanese."

While the underlying racism of the removal and incarceration policies during World War II is now widely recognized, relatively few Americans spoke out against the policy at the time. Home to nearly three quarters of the mainland Japanese American population, California was central to discussions of these policies and was home to both its most active critics and most vocal supporters. While many Californians, influenced by longstanding prejudices against Asian Americans, swept up in wartime hysteria after Pearl Harbor, and eager to support the government and the armed forces, saw the mass removal and incarceration of Japanese Americans as necessary and even desirable, a well organized minority criticized the policy as racist and unfair.

In the midst of this conflict, the California Jewish community was notably silent. Despite the strong stance of the state's major Jewish communities on other civil rights issues, the organized Jewish community failed to defend Japanese Americans. At the same time, as mass removal and incarceration became a popular cause in California, Jewish organizations and leaders did not join the chorus of voices endorsing the policy.

While Jewish community leaders and the press frequently expressed their strong commitment to fighting for the civil rights of African Americans and other minorities, they distanced themselves from the Japanese American issue. Even as the Jewish community actively defended European enemy aliens and argued that they were loyal, it remained largely silent on the actions taken against the Japanese American community.

The community silence on this issue resulted from a conflict between the primary goals of the Jewish community at the time: supporting the war effort in order to defeat Nazism and save European Jewry, and fighting

Notice of removal to "all persons of Japanese Ancestry."
Courtesy of the Bancroft Library, University of California, Berkeley.
(1967.014G-A651 vol. 57)

antisemitism at home by emphasizing Jewish patriotism and promoting equal acceptance of *all* Americans. While fighting prejudice directed at African Americans could be connected easily to supporting the war effort, criticizing the mass removal policy, deemed a military necessity by the federal government, could not. Examination of the Jewish press in California makes clear that when the policy created a conflict between support for the war effort and the anti-prejudice campaign, the former took precedence, resulting in silence on the Japanese American issue.

While the organized community maintained silence, a few prominent Jewish leaders joined other Californians in opposing mass removal. Most of these exceptional individuals were motivated, at least in part, by their special sensitivity to the dual-loyalty issue. The California Jewish leaders who were the most prominent critics of the policy shared another ideological commitment: they were anti-Zionists who believed that Jewish nationalism threatened the status of American Jews by making them vulnerable to charges of dual loyalty.

In the aftermath of Pearl Harbor, public attention in California quickly came to focus on the perceived threat of the state's large Japanese American population. Even as newspapers published unfounded accounts of spy activity and, in historian Roger Daniels's *Concentration Camps: North America,* "spewed forth racial venom against all Japanese," some public officials and journalists made an effort to calm the public and defend the rights of Japanese Americans. For example, Governor Olson signed a December 29th press statement issued by the Northern California Committee on Fair Play for Citizens and Aliens of Japanese Ancestry (the Fair Play Committee), which called upon Californians to "cooperate actively in ensuring fair play and security to all law-abiding Japanese residents." Likewise, both the *San Francisco Chronicle* and the *Los Angeles Times,* despite printing stories that fanned the hysteria, called in December and January for calm and emphasized the loyalty of most Japanese Americans.

At the same that time they were calling for calm, California newspapers repeatedly published unsubstantiated reports of sabotage and fifth column activity. As the federal government moved toward a policy of removing all Japanese Americans from the Pacific Coast, editorials emphasizing the loyalty of Japanese Americans were replaced by endorsements of mass removal. By the time the Tolan Committee hearings began in late February, newspaper editors and public officials who had earlier supported more limited measures were advocating removal of all Japanese Americans. Governor Olson, for example, removed his name from the Fair Play Committee's roster, and instead, as we have seen, testified in favor of the policy. Historian Gary Okihiro has demonstrated a strong swing in public opinion between December and February toward mass removal.

The pro-removal rhetoric was built on strong anti-Asian sentiment that had existed in the state for decades. From the 1870s, California had played a central role in lobbying for the Chinese Exclusion Act and other laws restricting Asian immigration. San Francisco segregated Chinese school children in the nineteenth century, and attempted to segregate Japanese children in the first decade of the twentieth century. In 1913 California's Alien Land Law, which prevented aliens ineligible for citizenship from owning land, became a model that was emulated by other western states.

Despite the strong history of anti-Asian sentiment in California and the growing antagonism toward Japanese Americans evident in both the press and the testimony at the Tolan Committee hearings, some did speak in opposition to the policy. In the San Francisco hearings, and to a lesser extent in Los Angeles, a small but vocal minority of witnesses questioned the need for mass removal. Among these were a representative of the ACLU, a union official, and members of the Fair Play Committee, a group of academics and intellectuals based in Berkeley. These witnesses testified to the loyalty of most Japanese Americans, cautioned that violations of their liberties could set a dangerous precedent, and argued that they should only be evacuated and interned on a selective basis. As A. L. Wirin, of the Southern California ACLU, explained,

> We realize that during a time of war emergency many liberties which ordinarily are permitted have to be circumscribed during the war. We feel, however, that there must be a point beyond which there may be no abridgement of civil liberties and we feel that whatever the emergency, that persons must be judged, so long as we have a Bill of Rights, because of what they do as persons, and not because of what race that person is a member of. We feel that treating persons because they are members of a race constitutes illegal discrimination which is forbidden by the fourteenth amendment whether we are at war or at peace.

Joining the civil libertarians in opposing mass removal and incarceration were several members of the clergy. During the San Francisco hearings, representatives from the First Christian Church of Oakland, the Berkeley Society of Friends, and Presbyterian and Methodist missionary groups testified that they opposed mass evacuation, citing the dangers of discrimination and the loyalty of Japanese Americans. Likewise, in Los Angeles, representatives of the American Friends Service Committee, three Protestant missionaries and a Buddhist priest stated their opposition to the policy.

Individual Jewish Californians also protested the policy through their words or actions. Some Jews in the Boyle Heights section of Los Angeles, for example, looked after the homes of Japanese neighbors who were

ELLEN EISENBERG

forced to relocate. During the Tolan Commission hearings in San Francisco, Louis Goldblatt, secretary of the California State Industrial Union Council in San Francisco (a CIO affiliate) joined religious and university leaders in questioning the need for mass removal and incarceration. Making one of the most impassioned pleas heard by the commission, Goldblatt argued that using racial or ethnic characteristics to determine loyalty compromised American values and could lead to a slippery slope. "Where is this to end, Mr. Tolan?" he asked,

> Italians will be the next to be evacuated, then the Germans. Why stop with the Germans? According to the present Federal order Hitler could stay in San Francisco in a prohibited area and one of German nationality would have to leave because Hitler is an Austrian. So it will extend to the Austrians. It will go to the Hungarians, to Bulgarians, to Finns ... These are countries, many of them, which have declared war on us. Where is the mark to be drawn?
>
> And, Mr. Tolan, if we follow such a procedure we can land in only one place. We will do a perfect job for those who want to sabotage the war effort. We will have the American people at each other's throats.

Despite the protests of individual Jewish Californians like Mr. Goldblatt, who spoke out as representatives of secular organizations, the large and prominent organized Jewish communities of San Francisco and Los Angeles were notable for their silence. In San Francisco—a city where Jews had played leading roles in civic affairs since its founding—no Jewish organizations presented testimony at the hearings. In Los Angeles, a representative of the Jewish Club of 1933, an organization of Jewish refugees, spoke only to the particular situation of German "enemy aliens," without drawing parallels to Japanese Americans. Likewise, the rabbis of Los Angeles' largest congregations, Temple Israel and Congregation B'nai B'rith (the Wilshire Boulevard Temple), and the president of the Los Angeles section of the National Council of Jewish Women appeared as members of an interfaith group testifying before the Tolan Committee. The group called for selectivity with regard to internment of European "enemy aliens," while at the same time expressing confidence in the Army and supporting the notion that some Japanese Americans presented a real danger to the community. The group made no clear statement opposing mass evacuation and incarceration of Japanese Americans.

The failure of the organized Jewish communities of California to speak out against the mass removal and incarceration of Japanese Americans is particularly striking when this silence is contrasted with their vocal stance on other civil liberties questions at the time. The San Francisco and Los Angeles Jewish communities, as well as smaller communities in other California cities, had strong records on civil rights issues. The major Jewish newspapers, for example, frequently published editorials advocating for African American civil rights and condemning racism and discrimination. Similar statements were often heard from the pulpits of California's congregations and from Jewish organizations such as the B'nai B'rith. Given this record, the silence on the Japanese American question requires exploration. To understand the community's response, it is necessary to look closely at both its words and its silences in the face of these events.

In contrast to the saturation coverage in the mainstream press, the Jewish press in San Francisco and Los Angeles maintained a near total silence on the controversy over Japanese Americans. San Francisco's *Emanu-El and the Jewish Journal* and Los Angeles' *B'nai B'rith Messenger* covered both the war and civil rights issues extensively, but did not mention Japanese Americans.

Emanu-El's first edition after Pearl Harbor was its special Chanukah edition, published on December 12. The issue included many war-related stories on topics such as how to achieve unity, the Nazis, the situation in France, Palestine and Zionism as solutions to the plight of Jews in Europe, local Jews serving in the armed forces, and Russian war relief. It also included two editorials rallying support for the war effort under the headlines "Americans Unite!" and "Jews Unite!" While *Emanu-El*'s coverage tended to focus on those war issues related to Jewish interests, several articles dealt with more general wartime themes. However, none even touched on what was already becoming a principal focus of their hometown press: the question of the loyalty of the large Japanese American community that made its home in San Francisco.

Subsequent issues of *Emanu-El* throughout the winter and early spring followed the pattern set by the Chanukah edition. In addition to focusing extensively on general and Jewish war issues, the paper also devoted considerable space to advocacy of civil rights and condemnation of racial and religious discrimination. Yet, even in proclaiming the importance of civil liberties and the equality of all Americans, the paper assiduously avoided any mention of

Japanese Americans. An editorial on December 19, 1941, ti-tled "Risks of Repression," for example, reminded readers of the intolerance during the Great War, when there were widespread attacks on German Americans, and urged them to avoid this danger. Similarly, several stories in early January relayed statements made by Catholic leaders against intolerance. While the stated message of these sto-ries was captured well in the January 16, 1942 headline, "Social Stability Demands End of Race Hate," no mention whatsoever was made of Japanese Americans who were the objects of increasingly vitriolic attacks in the Califor-nia press at that time. While *Emanu-El* did not join these attacks, neither did it defend Japanese Americans. The February 6 issue, for example, contained an article head-lined, "Roosevelt Asks Resistance to Racial Prejudice and Intolerance," but the editors chose not to apply the president's plea to the Japanese American situation in their city. On February 27, just eight days after the issuance of Executive Order 9066, and following a week of extensive coverage of the Japanese question and the San Francisco Tolan hearings in the mainstream press, *Emanu-El* pub-lished an editorial emphasizing the need to cooperate with all defense efforts, along with a statement characterizing discrimination as a "fifth column" activity that aided the enemy. The pairing of these two admonitions at this par-ticular time—and the failure to mention the Japanese Americans whose plight is the obvious context for them—suggests the tension surrounding the issue.

This tension was displayed even more vividly in stories on enemy aliens. Because German Jewish refugees were classified as enemy aliens, the Jewish press naturally took a strong interest in the restrictions affecting them. When discussing this issue, the paper often made the case that that the "enemy alien" label was inappropriate for such ref-ugees, and that they should be exempt from restrictions. Yet, because enemy alien stories in the California press fo-cused almost exclusively on Japanese Americans, it re-quired a deliberate effort to write about alien issues with-out including that group. *Emanu-El* regularly published articles and opinion pieces on various rulings and restric-tions on enemy aliens, but mentioned only Italians and Germans. Likewise, when the paper reminded readers that "enemy aliens" were not really enemies, it referred only to Europeans. For example, the March 13 edition carried both a front-page article and an editorial on the topic of enemy aliens, without ever mentioning the Japanese. The article assured readers that German "enemy aliens," who were de-scribed as "friends," were likely to be subject only to regis-tration. The editorial, titled "Friendly Enemy Aliens," urged aliens to accept any inconvenience necessary due to the war emergency. Here, the editors pointed out to read-ers that "friendly enemy aliens" included not only German refugees, but also anti-fascist Italians, who, like the Ger-mans, were loyal to the United States. No mention was made of the Japanese. In such articles the "enemy alien" label was always placed in quotation marks, to signify the inappropriateness of that label for European refugees. By specifically questioning this label only as applied to Ital-ians and Germans, the editors implied that it was not problematic when used to describe Japanese Americans. Despite this implication, the paper, unlike many main-stream California newspapers, never specifically endorsed the restrictions on Japanese Americans.

Even news stories were carefully framed to avoid the Japanese American issue. On December 26, 1941, for exam-ple, *Emanu-El* published a news story headlined "FBI Steps In." Here, the paper reported the arrest of German sympathizers, emphasizing that those rounded up were pro-Nazi antisemites. *Emanu-El* did not mention that the FBI arrested a large number of Japanese Americans during these raids. By reporting only the arrest of Nazi sympa-thizers and not the Japanese Americans, the paper kept the story focused on a clear theme: that fascists are both anti-semitic and anti-American. Given the Jewish community's interest in fighting antisemitism, the pairing of antisemit-ism with fascism and anti-Americanism was a useful, and frequent theme.

The clearest suggestion that *Emanu-El* may have had a deliberate policy of avoiding mention of Japanese Ameri-cans comes in a March 27, 1942 opinion piece by Monroe Deutsch. Deutsch, provost and vice president of the Uni-versity of California, Berkeley, and a prominent member of Temple Emanu-El, was a Fair Play Committee board member, and active in the campaign to defend Japanese Americans. Yet when his statement on the rights of enemy aliens was published in *Emanu-El,* either he or the editors chose to avoid specific reference to Japanese Americans. Under the headline "Rights of Enemy Aliens," Deutsch made a case for tolerance and calm, and urged compliance with "whatever mass evacuation is determined upon by the authorities." Consistent with Fair Play Committee policy after the mass removal had been ordered, he went on to

ELLEN EISENBERG

argue that evacuation should be followed immediately by investigations to determine individual loyalty, so that only those found disloyal would be detained in the long run. While the specifics of this plea made clear that the context for Deutsch's article was Japanese American incarceration, he referred specifically only to German and Italian refugees, without ever mentioning the Japanese.

Wartime coverage in Los Angeles' *B'nai B'rith Messenger* followed a similar pattern to that in *Emanu-El*. The *Messenger* published numerous articles on Jews and the war, antisemitism, civil rights, and alien restrictions, while carefully avoiding mention of Japanese Americans.

In reporting on the alien restrictions, the *Messenger* published articles on December 19, 1941 and January 16, 1942 questioning the "enemy alien" label as it applied to German refugees. In both cases, the editors assured these refugees that they need not fear the restrictions. The only mention of Japanese aliens in this entire period came in a January 20 article when the *Messenger* reported the number of Italians, Germans, and Japanese affected by new registration requirements for aliens. The same story went on to report that Attorney General Biddle had "seconded the President's plea not to dismiss 'loyal enemy aliens.'" According to the story, Biddle "said it was stupid not to use the skilled technicians of German and Italian birth who had lived in this country for many years."

On March 13, the *Messenger* published an editorial headlined "Enemy Aliens as America's Friends," that was similar to the one that appeared in *Emanu-El* on the same day. At a time when "enemy alien" had become a synonym for Japanese American (whether alien or citizen) in the secular press, the *Messenger* article mentioned only Italians and Germans. Again, the implication of questioning of the enemy alien label only when applied to Italians and Germans was that the label *was* appropriate for Japanese Americans. Still, the *Messenger,* while failing to oppose the policy, also refrained from endorsing it.

Like *Emanu-El,* the *Messenger* published numerous articles on civil rights issues but avoided linking them to Japanese Americans. The paper published an article emphasizing the importance of tolerance and the dangers of discrimination during National Brotherhood Week in its February 13 issue, for example, without mentioning the Japanese issue that was receiving front-page coverage in the Los Angeles press at the time. On February 27, it printed a lengthy sermon that sharply criticized prejudice

in all forms as damaging to the country. Despite the fact that the sermon was published as the Tolan hearings were taking place, this plea for tolerance failed to mention the fate of Japanese Americans.

In the *Messenger,* the paper reported that while the Los Angeles Council of Social Agencies had adopted a statement "expressing confidence" in the handling of the matter by federal authorities, "it emphatically opposed the indiscriminate forcible mass evacuation of entire minority groups, citizens and aliens alike." Using the stereotypical language common in the era, the article went on to inform readers that "The *Messenger* agrees with the statement. In times such as these, when emotions are prone to become inflamed, it is necessary, indeed vital, to avoid action based on hysteria. We believe that the danger of real alien enemies, whether of foreign or native birth, whether yellow or white, can be handled without desecrating those fundamental principles for which we are fighting."

Even as it published this singular, clear editorial condemnation of "forcible mass evacuation of entire minority groups, citizens and aliens alike," the *Messenger* demonstrated tension over this issue. First, while the commentary used phrases like "citizen and alien alike," and "whether yellow or white," which clearly were references to Japanese Americans, it refrained from directly mentioning that group. In addition, the placement of the article contrasted sharply with the front-page story of the same issue, "Enemy Aliens as America's Friends," which singled out Italians and Germans as friendly aliens. The more inclusive editorial ran on page four of the paper, as one of four brief editorials sharing less than two columns of space on the page. As with *Emanu-El's* publication of Deutsch's opinion piece, the *Messenger* was taking a clear stand but doing so cautiously, without fanfare, and without violating what appears to have been an editorial policy to avoid specific mention of Japanese Americans.

The wartime coverage in both papers strongly suggests that their editors felt uneasiness, or even tension, over the Japanese American issue. Their clear condemnations of discrimination and forcible mass internment contrast with their reluctance to specifically defend Japanese Americans. The sources of this tension can be found in the conflict the issue created between two of the Jewish community's fundamental goals, its support of the war effort and its commitment to fighting antisemitism at home.

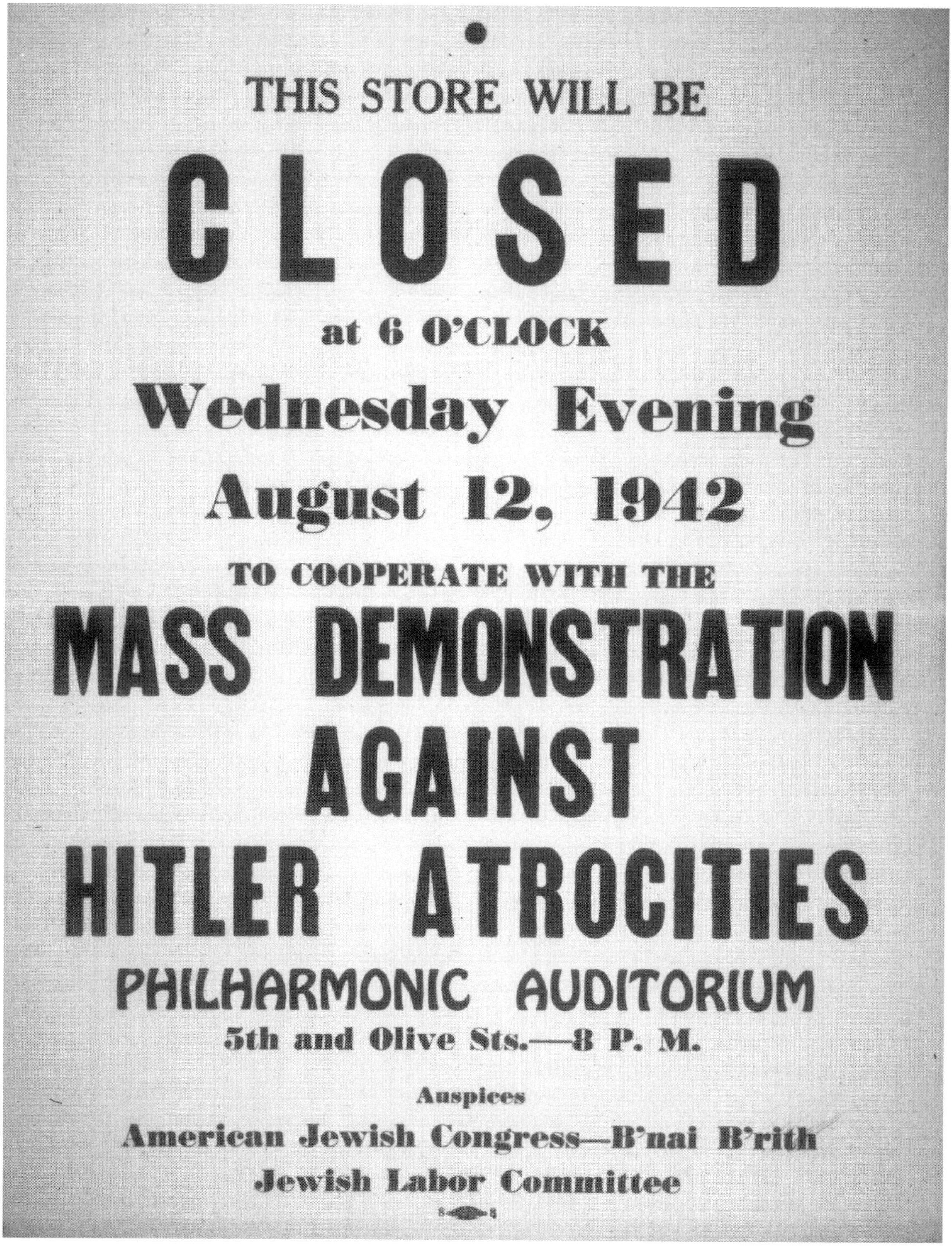

THIS STORE WILL BE

CLOSED

at 6 O'CLOCK

Wednesday Evening

August 12, 1942

TO COOPERATE WITH THE

MASS DEMONSTRATION

AGAINST

HITLER ATROCITIES

PHILHARMONIC AUDITORIUM

5th and Olive Sts.—8 P. M.

Auspices

American Jewish Congress—B'nai B'rith

Jewish Labor Committee

8 ◆ 8

Store closing sign, Los Angeles August 12, 1942.
Courtesy of Skirball Cultural Center, gift of Rabbi William Kramer.

As the extensive coverage of the war, and particularly the plight of European Jews, makes clear, support of the war effort in order to defeat Nazism and save European Jewry was the most important priority of American Jews. Supporting the war effort meant supporting all measures deemed necessary by the federal and military authorities. Questioning alien restrictions that military authorities deemed necessary smacked of undermining the war effort.

Along with support of the war effort, the battle against antisemitism at home was a second, central goal of Jewish communities in California and throughout the United States. While California had a remarkable record of tolerance and acceptance toward Jews in the nineteenth and early twentieth centuries, the rise of the KKK in the West in the 1920s and of vocal antisemites such as Father Coughlin during the depression led to increased concern among California Jewish leaders about antisemitism. One strategy to counter growing antisemitism was to emphasize the equality of all and to condemn all forms of discrimination. Defending the rights of other minority groups, like African Americans, was seen as a defense of the rights of all. This fight against prejudice was clearly a high priority of both California Jewish papers, and they consistently cast discrimination and intolerance as threats to democracy and to the war effort.

Historians Cheryl Greenberg and Marc Dollinger have demonstrated that national Jewish organizations avoided or ignored the inherent conflicts in the Japanese American incarceration issue, but the proximity of Californians to the issue made it difficult for them to ignore. Close examination of the March 13, 1942 edition of the *Messenger* demonstrates the conflicts created by this issue. The editorial endorsing the Council of Social Agencies' condemnation of "forcible mass evacuation of entire minority groups" is literally sandwiched between one editorial urging support for the war effort and another entitled "Defend the Negro." Here, editors called upon readers to support the rights of African Americans, and tied that support directly to the war effort: "People die for their land when they know it is their land. Can any American be unaware of the utmost need in this war of the skill, the energy and the devotion of 10,000,000 Negroes? Equally, can any American deny the devastating effect on the morale and the loyalty of these Negroes if they are to be cut off from the liberties for whose survival we are fighting?"

The Jewish community was able to clearly link its support for the war effort to its fight against prejudice when it defended the rights of African Americans, condemned antisemites and fascists, or called for tolerance and acceptance. Yet taking a position against the "military necessity" of incarcerating Japanese Americans would pit one communal goal against another. The community silence on Japanese Americans indicates that, for the majority of the Jewish community, the war goal predominated when the two came into conflict.

In their silence, these Jewish communities were far from atypical. As government policy in favor of evacuating and incarcerating all Pacific Coast Japanese Americans solidified, relatively little opposition surfaced. Few of the liberal groups that might have been expected to take a stance against mass incarceration did so. The national ACLU, for example, "adopted a policy statement recognizing the constitutionality of the wartime internment program and worked with government officials to modify its harshness." Strong ties between liberal organizations and the government, along with compelling reasons for supporting the war effort, worked against taking a critical stance on this wartime policy. As historian Judy Kutulas explained in her analysis of ACLU policy, "National officers, trusting the Roosevelt administration and its policies, worked with sympathetic bureaucrats and assumed that the New Dealers would protect individual liberties as best they could during a war emergency."

For local organizations on the West Coast, the front line of emerging policy, it was harder to ignore the issue. The Northern California ACLU, for example, broke with its national office over the issue, and took on several cases challenging alien restrictions and the removal and incarceration policy despite the loud objections of the national ACLU office. Likewise, while few raised their voices in opposition to the policy, the majority of those who did publicly object were located on the West Coast, particularly in San Francisco. The lead organization in defending Japanese Americans was the Committee on National Security and Fair Play organized by prominent individuals associated with the University of California at Berkeley. The committee, which advocated examination of the loyalty of individuals, rather than mass evacuation, included the sitting president of the University of California system, Robert G. Sproul, former UC president David P. Barrows, and former dean of Berkeley's School of Commerce, Henry F. Grady.

While no California Jewish organizations testified or otherwise spoke out for Japanese Americans during the winter and spring of 1942, two influential San Francisco Jews were early and prominent members of the Fair Play Committee. Monroe Deutsch, provost and vice president of UC Berkeley, and a leader at Temple Emanu-El, and Rabbi Irving Reichert of Emanu-El both served as a board members of the Fair Play Committee throughout the war and signed its original articles of incorporation as well as the statements it submitted to the Tolan Committee. As alien restrictions evolved, the Fair Play Committee moved from advocating selective (rather than mass) evacuations to urging fair treatment and rapid return, as well as countering anti-Japanese propaganda.

In September of 1942, Deutsch and Reichert, like the other Fair Play Committee board members, submitted testimonials on behalf of Japanese Americans. Deutsch's opposition to the policy was clearly influenced by his personal contacts at Berkeley. Fellow administrators and faculty members who had enjoyed close contact with Japanese Americans, particularly Nisei students, joined him in taking leadership roles on the committee, and several, including Deutsch, worked to help Nisei students transfer from Berkeley to universities outside the exclusion zone. In his testimonial, Deutsch cited his long experience on the Berkeley campus working with Japanese American students and emphasized their acceptance among the larger student population. He wrote, "As one who has lived almost all his life in California and has seen a great deal of the Japanese population, I feel able to express a considered judgment on them. I have never had occasion to doubt the loyalty of any of those with whom I have been in contact; I have found them hard working, devoted, and law abiding." Reichert's position was likely influenced by his long association with the Northern California ACLU and involvement in civil rights issues. His testimonial emphasized that "Many of the interned Japanese are persons of unquestioned loyalty to our country and uncompromising hostility to the Axis cause. We on the Pacific Coast, who have known Japanese, can bear witness to the sterling character and integrity of many of them. Heroic measures and exceptional precautions were required after Pearl Harbor to minimize fifth column activities. This resulted inevitably in grave injustices to American citizens of Japanese ancestry."[2]

Rabbi Reichert used some of his personal connections in the California Jewish community to enlist support for the Fair Play Committee. Committee correspondence records show letters from Reichert recruiting Rabbi Edgar

Magnin of the Wilshire Boulevard Temple in Los Angeles to the Fair Play advisory board in April of 1943, for example. Rabbi Magnin had been a member of the County of Los Angeles Committee for Church and Community Cooperation when it testified before the Tolan Committee on the danger presented by Japanese Americans in the community. Despite this, Reichert had good reason to think Magnin would be sympathetic to his cause. Magnin's Good Will Sabbath Sermon, which was broadcast on his weekly radio program and published on the front page of the *Messenger* on February 27, 1942, was a powerful statement in favor of tolerance. In the sermon, titled "Labels That Are Libels," the Rabbi argued strongly against prejudice in all forms. It was irrational to "condemn a whole group of people by reason of the faults or sins of some of them," he wrote. Referring to the Jewish experience in Nazi Germany he noted, "history has demonstrated that in times of crisis minorities are always picked on by crooked politicians and unscrupulous statesmen." Again using Jews in Germany as an example, Magnin went on to argue that "prejudice against any group of people is harmful not only to that group, but to the majority of the citizens of any country," and that such prejudice undermines unity and democracy. Magnin concluded with a plea to judge people by their individual acts rather than by their ethnic origin, and to hate nobody.

Reichert's recruitment effort was successful, and Magnin agreed to serve on the board of the Fair Play Committee beginning in 1943. Rabbi Magnin, in turn, recruited Judge Benjamin Schineman, who served on the board briefly. Shortly afterward, Rabbi Iser L. Freund of San Jose joined the committee and helped to organize a branch in that city.

While much of Monroe Deutsch's recruitment activity on the committee centered on academic contacts, he, like Reichert, occasionally called on his co-religionists for support. In 1944, Sergeant Ben Kuroki, a Nisei, addressed the Commonwealth Club in San Francisco. As president of the Commonwealth Club, Deutsch wrote a telegram to Undersecretary of War John McCloy saying that Kuroki "Deeply moved all. Earnestly urge he remain in this area as (he) can help true American democracy mightily." After the speech, Deutsch wrote to several individuals, including fellow Emanu-El congregant, Daniel Koshland, urging them to write letters to Secretary of War Henry Stimson, "commenting on Sergeant Kiroki's speech, if you heard it, and your belief that all Americans regardless of ancestry, including those of Japanese descent should as promptly as the military situation permits be granted their full rights as citizens." Koshland complied, writing a letter that warned Stimson, "The forces of bigotry and racial hysteria are so vocal on the Pacific Coast that I cannot refrain from expressing my views. If we win the war and fail to preserve the rights of our own citizens, irrespective of race, creed, or ancestry, we will only have brought forth a monster which may destroy us all. May I therefore respectfully request that the War Department do its utmost to grant full rights to all American citizens as soon as the military situation permits such action." Koshland's letter echoed one sent to Stimson by Deutsch himself, urging full restoration of Japanese Americans' citizenship rights: "As Abraham Lincoln pointed out that our nation cannot exist half slave and half free, so it cannot exist with various classes of citizens whose rights fall into different categories."

Deutsch likely felt a high degree of confidence when he urged Koshland to write. Deutsch and Koshland were not only fellow congregants and board members at Rabbi Reichert's Temple Emanu-El, but also activists in the San Francisco chapter of the anti-Zionist group, the American Council for Judaism (ACJ). That Reichert, Deutsch and Koshland, the three most prominent Jews to play active roles in the Fair Play Committee, were all anti-Zionists is significant. Their anti-Zionist ideology provided them with a different perspective on what was in the interest of American Jewry, and enabled them to defend the Japanese with less sense of conflict than their co-religionists.

While opposition to Zionism was widespread among assimilated, Reform Jewish communities such as San Francisco's from the late nineteenth century on, political Zionism had grown increasingly popular in the United States during the third decade of the twentieth century. As European Jewry became increasingly threatened by the rise of Nazism, and as East European Jews and their descendants came to represent a larger portion of the American Jewish community, the swing toward Zionism even began to influence Reform circles. During the 1930s, the Reform Central Conference of American Rabbis (CCAR) moved from anti-Zionism, to non-Zionism and official neutrality, and finally to sympathy to Zionism. In early 1942, the CCAR endorsed the formation of a Jewish army in Palestine.

As the CCAR underwent this transition, those holding fast to the anti-Zionist position felt increasingly under

siege. After the Jewish army decision, many of these dissenters came together to form the ACJ in 1942. Basing their ideology on the Classical Reform assertion that Judaism is a religion and not a nationality or race, ACJ members argued that political Zionism would both sap the religious basis of Judaism and lead to accusations of dual loyalty. As ACJ president Lessing Rosenwald explained in the June 1943 issue of *Life* magazine, Zionism was based on the racist theories that were fueling Nazism in Europe. The result, according to Rosenwald, "must inevitably be that here in America, or for Jews elsewhere, the question of dual allegiances will be raised by men who, in critical times, lack discrimination and understanding."

San Francisco proved to be a hotbed of ACJ activity. By 1945, San Francisco section members made up about a third of the national membership. Under the leadership of Rabbi Irving Reichert, Temple Emanu-El provided the ACJ with some of its most prominent members. Monroe Deutsch served as the local section president. Daniel Koshland, a Levi Strauss Company executive and member of one of the community's founding families, served on the executive board. Hattie Hecht Sloss, the wife of former California Supreme Court Justice Marcus Sloss, served along with Rabbi Reichert as a vice-president.

The fact that the most outspoken Jewish community leaders on the issue of Japanese American removal and incarceration were ACJ leaders was not simply a product of social connections. Rather, ACJ anti-Zionist ideology made them particularly sensitive to the issue of dual loyalty. The mass evacuation of Japanese Americans on the basis of dual loyalty accusations seemed to prove exactly what the ACJ preached: that ethnic groups with perceived ties to other nations are vulnerable to accusations of disloyalty. While evidence has not yet surfaced to indicate that either Reichert or Deutsch, the two ACJ activists who were most involved in the Committee for Fair Play campaign, ever made explicit the connection between anti-Zionism and defense of Japanese Americans, the parallel focus on dual loyalty and the coincidence in timing of the two campaigns suggest a clear connection.

Reichert had been quick to speak out against attacks on Japanese Americans. On December 13, 1941, the Shabbat following Pearl Harbor, Reichert presented a sermon titled "The Price of Freedom," which was reprinted in his congregation's newsletter, the *Temple Chronicle* the following Friday. In the sermon, Reichert emphasized the need for all racial groups to unite behind the war effort. He elaborated:

I said all racial groups in our country. That brings up immediately the question of the groups of Axis extraction. There has already been an outcropping of hysteria in our country and community . . . Already there have been unpardonable attacks and outrages upon American citizens of Japanese parentage whose loyalty to our country is as unyielding and assured as that of President Roosevelt himself. While, to be sure, we must zealously be on our guard against fifth columnists and saboteurs and traitors, by the same token we must not commit the unpardonable offense of visiting upon the heads of the innocent the crimes of the guilty in lands from which they came but from which they have long since disassociated themselves. And we Jews, who have for nineteen centuries suffered persecution because of the alleged conduct of some of our forbears in Judea 1900 years ago, ought to be among the first to cry down the unjust persecution of the foreign-born in our midst whose patriotism is equal to ours.

That Reichert's concern for Japanese Americans was directly related to his concerns about Jewish nationalism became clear two months later. During the final week of February, Reichert published in the Temple newsletter a statement explaining his refusal to support the formation of a Jewish army in Palestine. Reichert argued that Jews in Palestine should fight "as Palestinians in a Palestinian Army and let us in America, Jew and Gentile alike, contribute our strength as Americans." Reichert then expressed his hope that the Jewish army would not succeed, lest it create the perception of the Jew "as a ubiquitous nationality within every nation where they dwell, unified in a higher allegiance to the soil of Palestine and its nationalistic claims than to the countries whose protection and freedom they enjoy on terms of equality with their fellow citizens." Reichert's statement appeared less than a week after the Tolan Committee hearing in San Francisco, a hearing in which the Fair Play Committee defended Japanese Americans against dual loyalty accusations and argued that they were loyal only to the United States.

Reichert's concerns about the perils of dual citizenship were confirmed not only by the incarceration of Japanese Americans, but also by subsequent attacks on dual loyalties in the California legislature. For example, during the 1943 legislative session, Senate Joint Resolution 3 memorialized Congress to remove U.S. citizenship from all those holding dual citizenship in any other country, and to make those holding dual citizenship ineligible for U.S. citizenship. As a board member of the Fair Play Committee, Reichert was kept apprised of such legislative attacks in California and other western states.

Legislative attacks on dual loyalty such as California Senate Joint Resolution 3 reinforced anti-Zionist fears. While the majority of Jews in America—and in California—believed by 1942 that the solution to the problem of European Jewry was to defeat Nazism and settle refugee Jews in Palestine, ardent anti-Zionists like Reichert, Deutsch, and Koshland believed that Zionism would only result in more "Jewish problems." They believed that the Zionist program had the potential to lead American Jews down the path of Germany—to the perception of American Jews not as Americans but as a foreign element. The incarceration of Japanese American citizens along with Japanese aliens seemed to confirm their worst fears. For these anti-Zionists, with their heightened sensitivity to the dual loyalty issue, defense of Japanese Americans took on more importance than it did for others in the Jewish community. While a few Jewish leaders, most notably Rabbi Magnin, who did not share these anti-Zionist views, lent nominal support to the Japanese American cause, they were far less active and consistent in this cause than Reichert and Deutsch.

Rabbi Reichert and Monroe Deutsch, two of San Francisco's most prominent Jews, committed themselves to working on behalf of Japanese Americans through the Fair Play Committee, but they were not representative of California's Jewish community. The community's strong stance in favor of civil rights was outweighed by its commitment to supporting the war and to countering the antisemitism that a defense of Japanese Americans may have inflamed. It is clear that Reichert and Deutsch's position was not shared widely within the Jewish community—or even within Temple Emanu-El, despite its strong anti-Zionist contingent. While Reichert's December 13, 1941 sermon defended Japanese Americans, there was no further mention of the issue in the *Temple Chronicle* during this period. While continuing his activities on the Fair Play Committee, Reichert refrained from making further statements in the *Chronicle* about Japanese Americans, and there is no evidence that Rabbi Reichert made any particular effort to enlist his congregation in this cause.

Indeed, despite the public nature of the Rabbi's involvement with the Fair Play Committee, he downplayed that involvement within the Jewish community. When Reichert presented his annual report to his congregation in late January of 1942, he catalogued his activities for the past year, listing speeches given, organizations that he was involved in, and so on. He discussed the challenges that the war would bring to the community. Yet he never mentioned that he was a founding member of the board of the Fair Play Committee.

The community's determination to avoid the Japanese American issue despite the strong stance taken by individuals like Reichert remained visible even after the war was over. A 1947 document from Temple Emanu-El titled "Highlights of the Activities of Rabbi Irving F. Reichert . . . July 1, 1930–December 31, 1947," lists a wide variety of Rabbi Reichert's activities, both within the temple and in outside groups. Of the rabbi's years on the board of the Fair Play Committee, it is noted only that he played a role in 1941 in the organization of "the Fair Play Committee for purpose of protecting the rights of Chinese citizens and aliens." Even in 1947, the wartime incarceration of Japanese Americans was an issue that many California Jews thought was best avoided.

The decision to incarcerate all Japanese immigrants and their descendants on the Pacific Coast was clearly based on race prejudice. Many of the small number of Jewish community leaders who publicly recognized this racism and actively worked against it were motivated in part by the special sensitivity to the dual loyalty issue that was essential to their anti-Zionist ideology. For the majority of Jews in California and for the organized Jewish community as a whole, evidence of tension over this issue suggests that it was difficult to ignore the conflict between the mass removal and incarceration policy and the public stance of the community against prejudice and intolerance. While this discomfort prevented the community from endorsing the policy, its criticisms were veiled and indirect. Faced with a conflict between fighting prejudice and supporting the war effort that was so critical to the very survival of their European brethren, the California Jewish community deemed the war effort a higher priority.

Directory of Sources

Readers wishing to view the testimony before the Tolan Committee will find these proceedings published as *Hearings Before the Select Committee Investigation National Defense Migration* (Tolan Committee Hearings) House of Representatives, 77th Congress, Second Session, Los Angeles and San Francisco, part 31. The records of the Pacific Coast Committee on American Principles and Fair Play are available at The Bancroft Library, University of California, Berkeley (BANC MSS C-A 171). The Magnes Museum, also in Berkeley, holds many useful records on the California Jewish community, including several collections of Rabbi Irving Reichert's sermons and microfilm of San Francisco's *Emanu-El and the Jewish Journal* and Los Angeles' *B'nai B'rith Messenger.*

Analysis of mainstream press response to the crisis can be found in Gary Okihiro's "The Press, Japanese Americans, and the Concentration Camps" (*Phylon*, 1983), Lloyd Chiasson's "Japanese American Relocation During World War II: A Study of California Editorial Reaction" (*Journalism Quarterly*, 1991), and several of Roger Daniels's works, including *Prisoners without Trial*, Hill and Wang (1993) and *Concentration Camps: North America Japanese in the U.S. and Canada During WWII*, R. E. Krieger (1981). Judy Kutulas provides an outstanding analysis of the responses of liberals, and specifically of the fight within the ACLU over how to respond to internment, in "In Quest of Autonomy: The Northern California Affiliate of the American Civil Liberties Union and World War II" (*Pacific Historical Review*, 1998). For analysis of the response of the American Jewish community to the crisis, see Cheryl Greenberg's "Black and Jewish Responses to the Japanese Internment" (*Journal of American Ethnic History*, 1995) and chapter four of Marc Dollinger's *Quest for Inclusion*, Princeton University Press (2000). Further information on Rabbi Irving Reichert is available in Fred Rosenbaum's *Architects of Reform: Congregational and Community Leadership, Emanu-El of San Francisco*, Magnes Museum (1980) and *Visions of Reform: Congregation Emanu-El and the Jews of San Francisco 1849–1999*, Magnes Museum (2000). Fred Rosenbaum's article "Zionism vs. Anti-Zionism: The State of Israel Comes to San Francisco" in *Jews of the American West*, Wayne State University Press (1991) should be consulted for information on anti-Zionism in California. Thomas Kolsky's *Jews Against Zionism: The American Council for Judaism, 1942–1948*, Temple University Press (1990) provides a complete history of the anti-Zionist organization, the American Council for Judaism.

Photographic images of the removal and incarceration of Japanese Americans can be found in the Bancroft Library's collection, of War Relocation Authority photographs of Japanese American evacuation and resettlement. Many of these photographs can be viewed online, in the California Digital Library, accessible from the Bancroft Library's web-site.

The author gratefully acknowledges The Bancroft Library for granting permission to quote from the records of the Pacific Coast Committee on American Principles and Fair Play and to reproduce the photo of the Civilian Exclusion Order that appears in this essay.

NOTES

1. "Internment" is the term that has commonly been used to describe the mass removal of the first- and second-generation Japanese Americans from the Pacific Coast, and their subsequent incarceration. Historian Roger Daniels argues that "internment" is a misnomer for what happened to Japanese Americans during World War II. Internment is a legal process under which approximately 8,000 Japanese nationals, 2,300 Germans, and a few hundred Italians were arrested and held in detention. These individuals were singled out because their activities or associations were viewed as suspicious by the government. Internees, who were nearly all adult males, had the right to appeal their detention. It is important to distinguish this process from the mass removal and incarceration of the entire Japanese American population on the Pacific Coast, under which citizens and aliens—men, women and children—were forced from their homes into detention, based solely on their ancestry. For further discussion of this terminology, see Roger Daniels "Words Do Matter: A Note on Inappropriate Terminology and the Incarceration of Japanese Americans," in *(Dis)Appearances: Japanese Community in the Pacific Northwest,* Louis Fiset, ed. (forthcoming, University of Washington Press).

2. Testimonials of Monroe Deutsch and Irving Reichert, Folder 63, Pacific Coast Committee on American Principles and Fair Play records, BANC MSS C-A 171, The Bancroft Library, University of California, Berkeley. Correspondence among Jewish members of the Fair Play Committee is available in Boxes 1 and 2 of this collection. Additional documents, referenced later in this paper, that were sent by the committee to Rabbi Reichert and other committee members are from Folder 60 of this collection.

ELLEN EISENBERG

CHAPTER 10

JEWS AND CATHOLICS
AGAINST PREJUDICE

WILLIAM ISSEL

Introduction

On August 12, 1957, Mayor George Christopher presided over the swearing-in ceremony for the seven members of San Francisco's new Commission on Equal Employment Opportunity (CEEO). Approved by the Board of Supervisors after more than a decade of lobbying by civil rights activists, the CEEO became the first such agency in a major California city. Three years later, the commission ceased operations when the state pre-empted its duties, after the California Fair Employment Practice Act of 1959 went into effect. The twenty-year period prior to the passage of the state FEPC act witnessed a world torn asunder by war and cold war, a world in which the practice and preservation of civil rights and civil liberties stood as a central issue in world affairs and domestic politics. In San Francisco, site of the dramatic signing of the Charter of the United Nations at the War Memorial Opera House on June 26, 1945, the campaign for civil rights took center stage in municipal politics and policy making. Jewish and Catholic participation during these years deserves attention as a successful experiment in liberal civil rights coalition building in the urban West during the World War II and early cold war period.[1]

During the late 1930s and early 1940s, Jews and Catholics in San Francisco shared the nationwide outrage at the murderous consequences of Hitler's European and North African wartime regime and the postwar repression practiced by Stalin in Poland, Hungary, and other Soviet satellite countries. As historian Stuart Svonkin has pointed in his recent book *Jews Against Prejudice: American Jews and the Fight for Civil Liberties,* Jews had a particular interest in civil rights and civil liberties coalition building during and after World War II. In San Francisco, such a coalition, op-

erating on the assumption that no one can be safe unless everyone is free, emerged in the late 1930s. Jews played the leading roles in the effort, but the coalition also included Catholic liberals, as well as those who were neither Jewish nor Catholic. The white liberals coalesced with racial and ethnic defense organizations in the early 'forties and created an interracial council that revitalized the civil rights movement in the Bay Area. The Bay Area Council Against Discrimination began its work in early 1942, making San Francisco one of the first cities in the nation to establish a citywide interracial and multiethnic civil rights organization during the war years. According to Hilda Taba, who conducted interracial human relations workshops throughout the nation during the late 1940s and 1950s, some four hundred civic unity councils sprang up during the war years, but nearly all of them expired without tangible accomplishments by the end of the 1940s. But the civic unity movement proved successful in San Francisco. The San Francisco Council for Civic Unity, which succeeded the Bay Area Council Against Discrimination in 1944, made legislative gains in the 'forties and 'fifties and it created the institutional and ideological foundation for the later civil rights work of the 1960s.

*San Francisco's Tradition of Jewish
and Catholic Participation in Civic Life*

The city's tradition of religious toleration played a role in shaping the nature of Jewish and Catholic participation in the civil rights movement in the 1940s and 1950s. To Americans today, influenced by events since the 1960s, San Francisco may seem "naturally" tolerant and liberal. In fact, until after World War II San Francisco—for all its vaunted reputation as a raucous wide-open port city—did not welcome racial diversity, gays, lesbians, or political radicals any more than did the rest of urban America. The city's reputation for religious toleration was well deserved, however. In 1931 San Francisco Archbishop Edward Hanna received the annual American Hebrew Award for the Promotion of Better Understanding between Christians and Jews in America. In 1950, Earl Raab visited San Francisco and interviewed residents for one in a series of articles on "The American Scene" for *Commentary,* the monthly magazine of the American Jewish Committee. "San Francisco, for cities of its size," Raab concluded, "is the nation's 'white spot' of anti-Jewish prejudice" with a "startling poverty of anti-Semitic tradition." Raab described how Jewish residents had created a remarkably assimilated, and unusually secular, community while they forged a century-long record of business, professional, and cultural achievement. Historians have subsequently described how Jewish and Catholic participation in business and political leadership set the urban West apart from the rest of the nation generally, and San Francisco may well have perfected the model.

The Activists and Their Coalition

The San Francisco civil rights coalition during this period originated in and received its greatest support from the liberal center. When judged by such criteria as the sources of financial support for the civil rights coalition, outspoken advocacy by official representatives of religious institutions, and willingness to accept leadership positions in legislative work, the conclusion is unmistakable. Jews played the leading roles and Catholics occupied secondary roles in the 1940s and 1950s. The coalition depended on the fundraising talents of members of established families, such as Levi Strauss executives Daniel E. Koshland, Sr., and Walter A. Haas, Sr. Two Jewish philanthropies provided grants for operating expenses in the first years: the Columbia Foundation and the Rosenberg Foundation. Postwar Jewish migrants to the city also excelled in drumming up financial support, particularly Fairmont Hotel owner Benjamin H. Swig and Rabbi Alvin I. Fine of Temple Emanu-El, who arrived in 1946 and 1948 respectively.

The liberals believed that well-meaning men and women could put aside their different class, religious, and ethnic loyalties in the interest of civic pride and national progress. Their goal was not to "change the system" but rather to make incremental reforms in the system. They

Benjamin H. Swig, chairman of the board
of the Fairmont Hotel, about 1960.
*Courtesy of the San Francisco History Center,
San Francisco Public Library.*

sought to protect Americans in the exercise of their constitutional rights and to improve the everyday lives and future opportunities of thousands of disadvantaged and underprivileged Americans. The liberals saw themselves as building upon the work of the previous Progressive Era and New Deal reform generation, and several of the founders of the civil rights coalition began their public careers as Progressive Era activists.

The Progressive Era heritage appears clearly in the origins of the Survey Committee, a 1930s Jewish defense association that produced offshoots that supported African American, Asian, and Mexican American civil rights during and after World War II. In 1937, Judge M. C. Sloss, Jesse Steinhart, Walter A. Haas, Sr., and Daniel E. Koshland, Sr., established a San Francisco branch of the American Jewish Committee's Survey Committee. Sloss, the son of one of the city's most influential Jewish business leaders in the late nineteenth century, served on the California Supreme Court from 1906 to 1919. Sloss, Steinhart, Haas, and Koshland brought in their contemporary, Eugene Block, to direct the daily affairs of the Survey Committee. Block was a journalist who had started his career as a protégé of the Progressive activist Fremont Older, editor of the muckraking afternoon paper, the *San Francisco Bulletin*. The Survey Committee, together with the B'nai B'rith Anti-Defamation League and a newly established branch of the American Jewish Congress, launched a counterattack on the local Nazi Bund and other antisemitic organizations. Then Japanese relocation threatened the liberties of Issei and Nisei residents, debates intensified over citizenship status for Chinese residents, and wartime migration brought nearly a 1,000 percent increase in the African American population of San Francisco. Activists in the Survey Committee, the International Institute, and other local groups addressed themselves to the protection of civil rights generally. The Bay Area Council Against Discrimination began its work in 1942 and was active until 1944. Mayor Roger D. Lapham established a Mayor's Civic Unity Committee in 1944, which operated parallel to the Council for Civic Unity (CCU) for several months and then disbanded. The CCU then began a more than twenty-year period of work with local and state African American, Asian American, and Mexican American organizations on behalf of racial equality in education, employment, and housing.

Daniel E. Koshland, Sr., Eugene Block's associate in the Survey Committee, later characterized Harold J. Boyd as "the real founder of the Council for Civic Unity." Boyd, the city's controller in 1940, was born in 1890, but whereas Block grew up in the French American Jewish community, Boyd came of age in the Irish American Catholic Mission district. A labor union activist as well as a city official, and a "champion of the underdog" since the Progressive Era, Boyd stirred the community when he made an outspoken public speech at the Treasure Island Golden Gate Exposition in 1939 condemning Nazi attacks on Jews and Catholics. Boyd assumed leadership in the local Citizens Committee for Democratic Freedom in North Africa, the Bay Area Committee of the National Committee Against Persecution of the Jews, and the local branch of the National Conference of Christians and Jews (NCCJ).

The president of the NCCJ during the war years, Catholic manufacturer Frederick J. Koster, also began his career in the Progressive Era, serving as president of the local chamber of commerce. He also played a leading role in establishing the Law and Order Committee of 1916, following the Preparedness Day Parade bombing that killed ten and wounded forty people on Saturday July 22, 1916. A

Harold J. Boyd, controller of the city and county of San Francisco, September 28, 1944. Courtesy of the San Francisco History Center, San Francisco Public Library.

businessmen's association dedicated to eradicating violence, eliminating class enmity, and banning all collective bargaining agreements produced by "duress or coercion," the Law and Order Committee operated according to the principles of Pope Leo XIII's labor encyclical. Koster's California Barrel Company developed a reputation for fair management practices, including establishment of the eight-hour day, and the Coopers' Union honored him with a certificate of appreciation at the height of local hysteria about the 1916 bombing. During the 1930s, he championed New Deal labor reforms and vigorously condemned fascism and Nazism.

Party loyalties did not keep supporters of the civil rights movement of the 'forties and 'fifties from coalescing on behalf of local and state legislation. As Benjamin Swig recalled in a 1978 interview: "In those days there wasn't so much stress [among liberals] on whether you're a Democrat *or* a Republican. So I went to anybody I knew [when I was raising money]." The founders of the Jewish Survey Committee possessed impeccable Republican party credentials, as did Catholic Frederick J. Koster, whereas Harold Boyd prided himself in being a New Deal Democrat. Nonetheless, Walter A. Haas, Sr., who like Koster presided over the local chamber of commerce, regarded Harold Boyd as "a special friend."

Robert and Lucy McWilliams, both left of center Democrats, brought a Catholic point of view to the civil rights coalition during the 'forties. Superior Court Judge Robert L. McWilliams, who like Koster was active in the local chapter of the NCCJ, took his law degree from UC Berkeley. He began his career at the high point of the Progressive Era as an assistant district attorney before opening his own practice and teaching at Hastings Law School and the San Francisco Law School. Among the many students influenced by his commitment to Catholic principles of social justice, future governor Edmund G. (Pat) Brown is the best known. Both Judge McWilliams and his wife Lucy frequently publicized their support for interfaith cooperation and for civil rights legislation. Lucy McWilliams, an honorary member of the Hadassah Zionist organization, also served as the vice-chairman of the Democratic State Central Committee. In 1935 she led a campaign to establish healthy migrant worker camps in the Pescadero and Half Moon Bay farms in San Mateo County. In 1942 she chaired the Bay Area Council Against Discrimination, and in 1944 she served as one of the founders of the Council for Civic Unity.

During the latter half of the 1930s and the first years of the 1940s, a new and younger contingent of white liberal activists joined the older veterans of the Progressive Era in the civil rights coalition. Some, as mentioned earlier, were neither Jewish nor Catholic, but they all brought to the coalition a political consciousness forged in the heat of New Deal debates over the failure of American capitalism and the use of government policy to secure the American dream for all. Many had embraced the socialist cause before the war. When they moved to what Arthur M. Schlesinger, Jr., in 1947 called "the vital center," their work expressed a continued commitment to economic equality as well as racial justice.

Three leading activists in the coalition typified this process. David Selvin moved from work at the Pacific Coast Labor Bureau to the Jewish Survey Committee and then became the executive secretary of the Bay Area Council Against Discrimination. Selvin, a Jew, grew up in Utah,

Earl Raab, San Francisco
Jewish Community Relations Committee.
Courtesy of the Western States Jewish History Archive.

sensitive about his minority status and sympathetic with those forced to live on the margins of society. Edward Howden worked for the San Francisco Planning and Housing Association and the California Housing Association, and after three years of military service became the director of the Council for Civic Unity. Earl Raab, who worked with Eugene Block in the Jewish Community Relations Council, also represented this new, younger cadre of civil rights activists. Like the Council Against Discrimination, the Community Relations Council evolved from the Jewish Survey Committee. Raab's writings, sometimes co-authored with political sociologist Seymour Martin Lipset, reached a national audience, and he also chaired the Bay Area Human Relations Clearing House.

Neither Selvin nor Earl Raab, also of Jewish background, grew up in an actively religious household. Each of them, however, drew upon the tradition that represented the Jews as a people with an historical destiny to alleviate suffering and to right wrongs. They used their academic training in research and writing, Selvin at Berkeley and Raab at City College in New York, to further the cause of economic justice and racial and religious freedom. Howden grew up in Oakland, attended University High School near the Oakland-Berkeley border and then graduated from the University of California. Howden found himself drawn to the liberal activism of Harry Kingman and Ruth Kingman. Harry Kingman served as general secretary of Stiles Hall on the Berkeley Campus, the only location where members of the Young Communist League could meet. Born in China, the child of Protestant missionaries, Harry Kingman counseled hundreds of future activists about the importance of protecting civil liberties and civil rights. Harry and Ruth worked as partners, and they directly inspired Howden as well as Yori Wada, a Japanese American student who would go on to become the director of San Francisco's Japantown YMCA and to a long career as a civil rights activist and a stalwart liberal Democrat. In September 1958, Edward Howden left the Council of Civic Unity to head the new city CEEO and then a year later was appointed by Governor Brown to head California's Fair Employment Commission. At the same time, Harry and Ruth Kingman established their Citizen's Lobby in Washington, D.C., with Daniel E. Koshland, Sr., serving as treasurer. Both Harry and Ruth Kingman and Edward Howden worked closely with Clarence Mitchell, director of the Washington, D.C. division of the NAACP in the lobbying campaign to pass what became the 1964, 1965, and 1968 Civil Rights acts.

San Francisco's large and active communist community developed an ambivalent relationship with the liberal civil rights movement. Communists worked with liberals on civil rights during the period of the "popular front" line of World War II and before the cold war. This common front approach was evident in the Bay Area Council Against Discrimination in 1942 to 1944, in Mayor Roger D. Lapham's Civic Unity Committee in 1944, and in the first two years of the Council for Civic Unity in 1944 and 1945. Devout Catholic anti-Communists such as attorney Maurice Harrison and Paulist priest Rev. Thomas F. Burke, served on these committees. So did Communist party officers and activists such as Oleta O'Connor Yates and Aubrey Grossman. They investigated rumors of an impending race riot in Hunters Point (it never happened), and they listened to complaints filed by black tenants against the city's Housing Authority (the discriminatory policy was eventually outlawed).

Tensions developed in late 1945 and 1946 and the common front collapsed. The party line changed and forbade cooperation with liberal reformers, and the party's credibility suffered as knowledge of Soviet repression of civil liberties increased. Liberals distanced themselves from Communists by declaring that their determination to eradicate racial injustice did not call into question their loyalty to America. For these reasons and because of the social and ideological changes in the city's African American community after the war ended, the coalition experienced a variety of tensions and challenges during the years of its most widespread appeal. Many on the left and on the right as well remained outside the liberal coalition, opposed to its reformist principles, critical of its legislative strategies, determined to eliminate its influence.

The Principles That Activated the Coalition Builders

In 1938, Elliot M. Burstein, rabbi at Temple Beth Israel from 1927 to 1969, and Saul E. White, rabbi at Beth Sholom from 1935 to 1983, founded the northern California branch of the American Jewish Congress. Then they organized a boycott of German goods in protest against Nazi repression. Burstein and White stood out as outspoken advocates of the establishment of a Jewish state in a Jewish community that generally eschewed Zionism. The principles of freedom and self-determination central to their work earned White and Burstein a wide following among civil rights activists. Both men appeared frequently before non-Jewish audiences and spoke to local radio audiences. Rabbi White developed a close personal and professional relationship with Howard Thurman, minister of the Church for the Fellowship of All Peoples, a pioneering Protestant interracial church in the heart of the Fillmore district.

Burstein's sermons and lectures from the late 1930s and the years of World War II exemplify the ideological connection linking the defense of Jewish freedom, the struggle of the Allies against the Axis powers, and the campaign for civil rights. On March 27, 1937, a year after Hitler demilitarized the Rhineland and seven months after the Anschluss with Austria, Burstein presented a lecture to the radio audience of station KFRC on "Slavery in Modern Times." The rabbi exhorted the audience to "eternally give battle to every robber of human freedom" and argued that the story of Moses leading his people out of Egypt was everyone's heritage, not just that of the Jews. "The story of the Exodus is a warning to be eternally

Rabbi Saul E. White, spiritual leader of Beth Shalom.
Courtesy of the Western States Jewish History Center,
Judah Magnes Museum.

vigilant against all lash-masters . . . that is why we regard with dismay the mushroom growths of fascistic movements in the world today." Speaking at Odd Fellows Hall on "What is Americanism" ten days after Hitler opened the Balkan campaign and the day before Yugoslavia surrendered to the Nazis, Burstein anticipated the civic unity council efforts that marked the war years. "There is still plenty of prejudice against the [N]egro, the Jew, the Catholic. As long as this exists, our democracy will be sick and needs a good dose of tolerance. But even tolerance is not enough. Tolerance is arrogance. Our Americanism should include definite efforts made to unite all Americans on their common tasks and to urge groups not to capitalize on their differences."

On June 30, scarcely a week after Adolf Hitler danced for joy before photographers after forcing a humiliating armistice on France, Rabbi Burstein addressed an audience at the First Methodist Church. "The Christian-Jewish answer to the World's Crisis," he insisted, is to stand up to the "force, trickery, ruthlessness . . . of Communism, Nazism, or fascism . . . We must not, if we value our democ-

racy and liberties they allow us, employ their tactics . . . We must bend over backwards and give sympathy and love in greater measure than ever. . . . World conditions are such that shortly they will demand tremendous sacrifices from all of us. But the greatest sacrifice of all is a subjugation of passion to reason. We must not lose our wits. We must fight not with hate and vengeance, but with a calm sense of a serious duty to perform."

By the summer of 1944, one month after the Allied invasion of Normandy, Burstein spoke on "Religion and Democracy" over radio station KSFO. He suggested that "the religious idea . . . that humanity is one great family—a family of equals in its own eyes and the eyes of God . . . will not be established unless the democratic idea is first established." In a democracy, "man must at least respect his neighbor, his person, his opinions, his wants and his rights. If this cannot be achieved positively by persuasion, it can at least be achieved negatively by legislation."

Burstein summed up his talk about the link between religion and democracy with a call for "not love of neighbor, but an understanding of, a sympathy with, a healthy respect for, our neighbor." Social theorist Horace Kallen had for years popularized this model of social relations as "Pluralism" or "Democratic Pluralism." As Burstein explained, "Discrimination or attacks against any group anywhere, no matter what its beliefs, origin, or skin pigmentation, is an attack against humanity as a whole."

Burstein's endorsement of pluralism found an echo in the sermons and lectures of Paulist priest Rev. Thomas F. Burke, pastor of Old St. Mary's Church and brother of Monsignor John J. Burke, the general secretary of the National Catholic Welfare Conference and a prominent national spokesman on Catholic social justice matters. Archbishop John J. Mitty, whose term of office extended from 1935 to 1961, frequently delegated Burke to represent the archdiocese at interfaith gatherings. Burke's 1937 Thanksgiving Day sermon at the Civic Auditorium, under the auspices of the NCCJ, urged San Franciscans to "gather for common interests and for common action" against "bigotry and intolerance and bitterness and war."

By the time Father Burke died in 1947, his prewar message about the need for pluralism as the basis for cooperation to protect "the very soul of America" had an even greater appeal to liberal Catholics and Jews. Earl Raab recalls how when he involved himself in the civil rights coalition in 1951, he did so because "I had a great interest . . . in strengthening democracy in this country,

WILLIAM ISSEL

Archbishop John J. Mitty, Adrien Falk of the Community Chest, and Mrs. Harold Ringrose of the Catholic Social Service Agency, February 5, 1947.
Courtesy of the San Francisco History Center, San Francisco Public Library.

coming out of the experiences of the 1930s for the Jews. . . . My underlying philosophy, and this related to my main interest in Jewry, was that the important objective of [this work] was to strengthen democratic pluralism . . . and civil rights demonstrated this principle at the time more than anything."

How the Liberal Coalition Operated and What It Accomplished

In the spirit of Rabbi Burstein's conviction that "our big positive guns are persuasion and education" and if that failed, then "negatively by legislation," the civil rights liberals used the Council for Civic Unity to educate and inform the public and lobby for new civil rights laws. The Council adopted an inclusive strategy, bringing together representatives of established groups and new organizations. From Chinatown came Henry Shue Tom, executive secretary of the Chinatown YMCA, and Lim P. Lee, a lawyer and Democratic Party activist who became San Francisco postmaster in 1967. The Chinese American Citizens Alliance sent Kenneth Fung, a San Francisco-born attorney, three-term president of the organization, and its Washington, D.C., lobbyist for immigration law reform. The Council also worked with Robert B. Flippin of the National Association for the Advancement of Colored People (NAACP) and

Seaton W. Manning of the city's new branch office of the National Urban League, established in 1946.

During and after the war, new migrants to the city added their voices and energy to the emerging coalition. Terry A. Francois, an African American Catholic, and 1940 graduate of Xavier University in New Orleans, moved to San Francisco after his discharge from the Marine Corps in 1946. Francois immediately immersed himself in civil rights activity. In 1950, with a Hastings law degree in hand, he joined the boards of directors of both the local NAACP and the national Catholic Interracial Council. He and his law partners Loren Miller and Nathaniel Colley carried the NAACP suit against the city housing authority that culminated in the banning of its so-called "neighborhood pattern" policy of segregation. Francois served as NAACP local president and with Edward Howden and Irving Rosenblatt he conducted the negotiations with the San Francisco Employers' Council in 1957 that resulted in their endorsement of the city CEEO ordinance. In 1964 Terry Francois became the first African American to serve on the Board of Supervisors when Mayor Shelley appointed him to that position.

Mayor George Christopher appointed Francois to the new city CEEO in 1957, where he served with Peter E. Haas, the son of one of the founders of the Jewish Survey Committee. The son and the father, incidentally, disagreed about liberal civil rights legislation: "I remember big arguments with my father," Haas recalled in 1992, "[he] said you can't legislate these things. You can't legislate morality." Richard L. Sloss, son of another of the four men who organized the Jewish Survey Committee, served on the board of the Urban League after World War II and brought his liberal point of view to his work on behalf of its projects. In his lay sermons at various synagogues during the 1940s and 1950s, Sloss returned again and again to the importance of eradicating prejudice and fostering pluralism, as in this 1948 talk. "Differences in thinking are not only inevitable, they are healthy signs of freedom of the mind; but they need not, and should not, become the basis for groundless suspicions and unreasoning distrust. Let no man believe unkind generalizations about groups other than his own."

Richard Sloss belonged to the Temple Emanu-El congregation. Alvin Fine, a staunch liberal from Cincinnati who arrived in San Francisco in 1948, served as senior rabbi at Emanu-El until 1964. A native of Portland, Oregon, Rabbi Alvin Fine quickly moved to the center of the

Terry Francois, Mayor John Shelley, and Chief Administrative Officer
Thomas J. Mellon, August 24, 1964.
Courtesy of the San Francisco History Center,
San Francisco Public Library.

Mayor George Christopher and the
Council for Equal Employment Opportunity.
Courtesy of the San Francisco History Center,
San Francisco Public Library.

civil rights coalition, playing an active public role in a variety of initiatives, including the campaigns to establish a city and state FEPC.

Rabbi Fine also took active leadership in the National Council of Christians and Jews. Throughout the 1950s, quietly and with considerable tact, he nudged Archbishop John J. Mitty to place the church actively in the forefront of interfaith cooperation and civil rights reforms. One instance is particularly revealing of Fine's strategy. When the criticism over Harry Truman's appointment of an ambassador to the Vatican made headlines across the country in late 1951 and early 1952, the local NCCJ met behind closed doors for a confidential discussion of how to limit the damage to interfaith relations in San Francisco. When several of the Protestant representatives "vehemently" declared their opposition to Truman's action, Rabbi Fine "told [them] that he didn't think it was any of their business whether the Vatican was a State or not a State." Archbishop Mitty's representative to the meeting, superintendent of Catholic schools Father James N. Brown, confided to Mitty that while Fine's arguments expressed "the Jewish attitude toward religion in the public schools . . . he is one of the Zionists who does not believe in a Church-State set up there."

The Vatican ambassador controversy, and the concurrent battle over whether tax monies should be allowed to support Catholic schools, underscored the longstanding mutual suspicions between the Catholic Church and Jewish and Protestant organizations that persisted during this period. Archbishop Mitty, who had served as bishop in Salt Lake City from 1926 to 1932, brought to San Francisco considerable experience in negotiating interfaith tensions. He facilitated the practice of "mixed marriages" between Catholics and non-Catholics, and he led the successful campaign to reform the Church's national policy so as to allow such marriages to take place in parish churches. During and after World War II, Mitty received a crescendo of requests from Protestant and Jewish organizations and Catholic laymen for greater interfaith cooperation and support for domestic civil rights. The archbishop allowed the formation of an Interracial Communion League at St. Benedict the Moor Church in 1952. Father Bruno Drescher, the pastor of the church, which stood in the heart of the Western Addition African American community, was a civil rights stalwart who served on the CCU board. However, attempts to obtain Mitty's approval for a citywide Catholic Interracial Council did not succeed until 1960.

WILLIAM ISSEL

Senior Rabbi Alvin Fine of Temple Emanu-El.
Courtesy of the Western Jewish History Center,
Judah Magnes Museum.

Given his experience in Salt Lake City, where he had co-existed with the Mormon majority as well as expanded efforts to make converts to Catholicism, Mitty responded to calls for interfaith cooperation with ambivalence. He was determined to refuse a forum to unfriendly liberal and left-leaning Protestant and Jewish ministers and rabbis who might vilify the Church because of its support for Spain's General Francisco Franco. "Catholics" as he put it in a confidential letter, should not be placed "in a compromising position." Additionally, "There is the possibility that the ordinary rank and file of the people may begin to feel, as a result of these meetings, that one faith is as good as another." The archbishop resolved his ambivalence in a way that typified his administrative practice generally. He made almost no public statements whatsoever about either the interfaith movement or the civil rights movement. At the same time he delegated to trusted priests and laymen the authority to act on behalf of the archdiocese. Mitty began this policy in 1941 and did not change course during the nearly twenty years following. He explained to a colleague on the faculty of Holy Redeemer College that

he had been influenced by the opinions of "a very splendid Catholic judge" and "a very splendid Catholic lawyer." No doubt he referred to Judge Robert L. McWilliams and attorney Maurice A. Harrison, both of whom were on close personal terms with the archbishop. "Their opinion," he confided, "makes me a bit slow in condemning these meetings." Besides, "the big difficulty I foresee in not giving some participation in these meetings is the possibility of a charge of un-Americanism."

The question of how to define and practice Americanism took center stage in American political culture during these years. The Jewish community, heterogeneous in outlook, debated the question of whether support for a Jewish homeland in Israel could be compatible with loyalty to America. The Catholic community, heavily Irish American, questioned whether racial prejudice and discrimination could coexist with its profession of Christianity.

Amid these tensions and ambiguities, the most *public* Catholic *institutional* support for the civil rights movement in San Francisco during these years came not from archdiocesan priests but from priests associated with particular religious orders. The activism of Father Thomas F. Burke, whose Paulist order might be expected to take the vanguard on these matters given its program of interfaith cooperation, has already been noted. In addition, the Jesuit University of San Francisco developed institutional relationships with the NAACP and the Urban League during the first decade after the war, and these relationships increasingly brought Catholic lay and clerical civil rights activists together with a variety of African American leaders. The connection came about largely through the initiative of Father Andrew C. Boss, the director of the University's Labor-Management School. Boss grew up in a blue-collar working-class family in the city's Mission district. By the late 1940s, like Earl Raab, who first clashed with the Communist left during his student days at City College of New York, Boss was a principled anti-Stalinist as well as a firm advocate of civil rights. The Labor-Management School opened its doors in the spring of 1948, after Boss and Father Hugh A. Donohoe decided that the city needed a Catholic alternative to the California Labor School, because Communist party members dominated the administration and the curricula of the California Labor School. Donohoe wore several hats. In the late 1930s he began a twenty-five-year service as chaplain to the Association of Catholic Trade Unionists. During the war years he edited the official newspaper *The Monitor*. In 1948 the archbishop appointed him auxiliary bishop and delegated him to represent the archdiocese on the board of the Council for Civic Unity.

During the decade between the founding of the school and the passage of the city and state FEPC laws, Father Boss opened the pages of the School's periodical, *Labor Management Panel*, to articles by local African American leaders. He also organized conferences to expose discrimination in employment and generate support for Fair Employment legislation. The USF events provided a forum for opponents of liberal civil rights legislation as well as an opportunity for its supporters to spread their gospel. In an April 1951 Institute on Minority Group Employment, for instance, Adrien Falk, then president of the California Chamber of Commerce, criticized the legislative approach and called for voluntary job training and skill development initiatives by employers. Falk, a confidant to mayors Roger Lapham and George Christopher, would persist in this argument all the way to the passage of the city ordinance in 1957.

One of the Labor-Management School's civil rights programs, a panel discussion broadcast on radio station KNBC in January 1954, featured D. Donald Glover, industrial relations secretary of the city's Urban League. Judge Sylvester McAtee, another panelist, raised the issue of the Communist party's influence in the civil rights movement. John F. Henning, a 1939 St. Mary's College graduate, then research director of the California State Federation of Labor, also appeared on the program. In August 1957, Henning would join Peter Haas and Terry Francois on the city FEPC, and in 1959 Governor Brown appointed Henning the director of the California Department of Industrial Relations. Now Henning bristled at McAtee's claim that "FEP legislation provides the ideal opportunity for propaganda by . . . Communists . . . who wish to create racial animosities, and employer-employee conflict." Henning responded: "On this matter of associating the drive for racial justice in this country with any Communist purpose. The Communist apparatus must be opposed if democracy is to survive but to exploit the issue and associate the campaign for racial justice with the Communist movement is actually the last refuge of those who are morally sterile and philosophically bankrupt."

The state FEPC bill passed five years later, on April 16, 1959. The campaign to pass the legislation began with the Bay Area Council Against Discrimination and the Civic Unity Council in the early to mid–1940s. Then in 1953,

John Henning, Archbishop John T. Mitty, and
Sylvester Andriano, October 25, 1956.
Courtesy of the San Francisco History Center,
San Francisco Public Library.

the Civic Unity Council and its Southern California counterparts, the California State Labor Federation and the Jewish Labor Committee, all working with the NAACP's 1953 "Fight for Freedom" program, revived the campaign. Augustus Hawkins and Byron Rumford, African American members of the California state assembly, saw the bill through the legislature. C. L. Dellums of the Brotherhood of Sleeping Car Porters, the uncle of future congressman Ron Dellums, served as chair of the labor, minority, and religious coalition. White liberals William Becker and Max Mont from the Jewish Labor Committee managed the day-to-day operations. By the time the state FEPC began its work in 1959, the liberal coalition desegregated San Francisco's public housing projects, won an anti-discrimination clause in urban redevelopment housing policy, and successfully campaigned to establish the city CEEO.

Conclusion

Jewish and Catholic activism in a centrist political coalition during the 1940s and 1950s moved the civil rights agenda further toward the goal of full equality for all San Franciscans. Jews and Catholics campaigned for civil rights as part of a broad coalition, but Jewish and Catholic activism during this period, as this account makes clear, should not be read as a narrative of a golden age of interfaith cooperation. Nor should the degree of success of the interracial civil rights coalition be exaggerated. All the same, the moderate goals and measured successes of the campaign should be acknowledged. The white liberal Jews and Catholics who participated in the civil rights movement of the

1940s and 1950s prepared the ground for an expansion of interfaith cooperation, as well as for further legislative victories at the state and local levels during the 1960s. The 1960s saw Catholic activists moving into full partnership with Jews rather than continuing as secondary players. Liberal Catholics established a local branch of the Catholic Interracial Council in 1960, and the archdiocese established an official Social Justice Commission in 1964. In the same year, Father Eugene Boyle, a diocesan priest, brought together Protestant, Catholic and Jewish activists in a San Francisco Conference on Religion, Race, and Social Concerns. The new organization publicized and expanded upon the work of existing groups such as the Council for Civic Unity, the NAACP, and the Urban League. Also in 1964, the state's fair housing legislation of 1959 faced the challenge of Proposition 14, an initiative measure designed to block government bans against discrimination. The new archbishop, Joseph T. McGucken, forthrightly defended fair housing, and two citizen's groups, Catholics Against Proposition 14 and Californians Against Proposition 14, campaigned against the measure. When California voters overwhelmingly endorsed the proposition, Earl Raab of the Human Relations Clearing House and John Delury of the new Catholic Interracial Council worked on behalf of the ultimately successful legal campaign to overturn the voter mandate in the courts.

In 1964, Mayor John F. Shelley, a former state senator and U.S. congressman whose early career as a labor union activist included a charter membership in the Association of Catholic Trade Unionists, proposed to the city Board of Supervisors a permanent Human Rights Commission. The Board established the Commission on July 13, and Shelley quickly appointed the fifteen commissioners, including Rabbi Alvin Fine, Earl Raab, and Sister Rose Maureen Kelly. Father Eugene Boyle and Daniel E. Koshland, Sr., served on the advisory council. The Commission's chairman, Edgar D. Osgood, and its director, Frank A. Quinn, took office after serving in the same positions in the Council for Civic Unity. Quinn had been associate director of the NCCJ during the early 1950s and then worked as a field officer among Native Americans in California for the American Friends Service Committee before succeeding Edward Howden at the CCU. The new Commission wielded subpoena power and it soon developed a national reputation as an aggressive advocate of racial, religious, gender, and sexual orientation equality in education, employment, and housing.

Archbishop Joseph T. MCGucken receives the first regional Human Relations Award of B'nai B'rith from Samuel L. Fendel, May 23, 1963.
Courtesy of the San Francisco History Center, San Francisco Public Library.

Directory of Sources

Several recent books provide well-researched narratives of events across the nation useful for background to this chapter. See Gulie Ne'eman Arad, *America, Its Jews, and The Rise of Nazism* (Bloomington: Indiana University Press, 2000), Marc Dollinger, *Quest for Inclusion: Jews and Liberalism in Modern America* (Princeton: Princeton University Press, 2000), Stuart Svonkin, *Jews Against Prejudice: American Jews and the Fight for Civil Liberties* (New York: Oxford University Press, 1997), and Cheryl Greenberg, "Negotiating Coalition: Black and Jewish Civil Rights Agencies in the Twentieth Century," in Jasck Salzman and Cornel West, eds., *Struggles in the Promised Land: Toward a History of Black-Jewish Relations in the United States* (New York: Oxford University Press, 1997). Earl Raab's 1950 article, "There's No City Like San Francisco," can be found in *Commentary* 10 (October 1950):369–378, is indispensable, as are Moses Rischin, ed., *The Jews of the West: The Metropolitan Years* (Waltham, Mass.: American Jewish Historical Society, 1979), and Moses Rischin and John Livingston, eds. *Jews of the American West* (Detroit: Wayne State University Press, 1991). Collections of private papers and oral histories of Benjamin H. Swig, Alvin Fine, and rabbis Saul White and Elliot Burstein are located at The Western Jewish History Center of the Judah Magnes Museum in Berkeley, California. The Bancroft Library of the University of California at Berkeley, including the San Francisco Labor Council Records; San Francisco Council for Civic Unity Records; California Federation for Civic Unity Records; and National Association for the Advancement of Colored People Western Region Records, and the correspondence files in the Chancery Archives of the Archdiocese of San Francisco, located at St. Patrick's Seminary in Menlo Park, also contain extensive records essential to this topic.

NOTES

1. In accordance with the style and aims of this series, citations have been omitted from this essay. A fully annotated version can be obtained from the author at Department of History, San Francisco State University, 1600 Holloway Avenue, San Francisco, CA 94132.

CHAPTER II

FROM MINYAN TO MATRICULATION

LAWRENCE BARON

The history of San Diego's Jewish community has been relatively neglected because the city's Jewish population remained small until it experienced a belated growth spurt after 1970. Like other spots with natural harbors along the California coast, San Diego attracted its first Jewish settlers in 1850 with the dual promises of commercial opportunity generated by the gold rush and religious tolerance afforded by California statehood the same year. In this period, San Diego's Jewish immigration resembled that of other boom towns. A core of Jewish settlers arrived in the town and founded the first Jewish congregation in Southern California in 1861. The opening of a direct link to the transcontinental railroad in 1885 expanded the city's general population to thirty-five thousand and the Jewish community to three hundred by 1887, providing sufficient membership to erect Beth Israel, the first synagogue in San Diego in 1889. Unfortunately, the railway line to the east was washed out by a flash flood, depriving San Diego of direct access to the transcontinental railroad. The city's population plunged to sixteen thousand by 1890, and the number of Jews declined even more steeply to an estimated 110 by 1905.

The bursting of San Diego's economic bubble in the 1880s led to the cancellation of two attempts to establish a state college there toward the end of the decade. Nevertheless, land developers and municipal leaders continued to pursue their goal to locate a normal school in San Diego to enhance the city's allure to families seeking a hometown with an ample supply of professionally trained teachers to staff the local elementary schools. In this regard, San Diego lagged behind San Jose, Los Angeles, and Chico, which already had such normal schools. In 1897 the California legislature and governor approved the charter and funding for the San Diego Normal School, which began offering classes in temporary quarters in the fall of the following year. Paralleling the city's economic recovery and population growth to nearly forty thousand inhabitants by 1910, the normal school's enrollment jumped from 91 to 400 in the same period.

In this period, Jewish women in California were more likely to seek a career before marrying than their female co-religionists in the larger Jewish population centers on the East Coast and in the Midwest. Greatly outnumbered by Jewish bachelors who tended to delay becoming engaged until they gained business contacts and expertise or college degrees in bigger cities, local Jewish women often attended public and normal schools to support themselves financially as teachers before they married. During its first decade, 90 percent of the students at San Diego Normal School were women. The lists of the first graduates from San Diego Normal School indicate that the first Jewish graduate from the school was a woman, likely either Grace Baker of the Class of 1900, Lily Lesen of the Class of 1902, or Elsie Davidson of the Class of 1903, all of whom resided in or near San Diego. (An early but undated synagogue membership roster from Beth Israel includes families named Baker, Davidson, and Lesen.)

Henrietta Rose, daughter of San Diego's legendary Jewish developer Louis Rose, taught in the city's public schools from 1895 to 1940 and enrolled in courses occasionally at the Normal School to upgrade her pedagogical skills. She remained single, perhaps because she achieved financial independence as the sole heir to her father's fortune in 1881 and learned early in her teaching career that the board of education routinely fired women teachers when they married. She also led an active civic life as a leader of the women's auxiliary to the local Masonic Lodge.

Though both the general and Jewish population of San Diego increased between 1910 and 1940, the city remained relatively small compared to Los Angeles and San Francisco in this period (see table 1). In 1921 the status of San Diego State Normal School was elevated to that of a state teacher's college with a four-year curriculum. The enrollment at the school burgeoned from 203 in 1920 to 1,250 students by 1930. This growth necessitated building a bigger campus on Montezuma Mesa, where the university is still located. Approximately 90 percent of the 1,220 students who attended the new campus in 1931 came from the San Diego metropolitan area and commuted to their classes. Only twelve of them listed their religious affiliation as "Hebrew." This small Jewish enrollment reflected the size of San Diego's Jewish community. Jewish male students in California usually gravitated to more prestigious colleges and universities in Los Angeles and San Francisco, which possessed larger Jewish communities on campus and in the surrounding metropolitan areas (see table 2).

From 1928 on, the most visible Jewish presence at San Diego State was Professor Abraham P. Nasatir. Not only did Nasatir distinguish himself as an outstanding teacher and prolific scholar of the history of South America and Spanish colonialism in North America, but also as an Orthodox Jew. It may be that his traditional piety facilitated his acceptance by students, 75 percent of whom were affiliated with some religious denomination. The Jewish students who attended the college in the 1930s and 1940s believe that the respect Nasatir enjoyed among his students and peers prevented any overt manifestations of antisemitism on the campus. Starting in 1932, Nasatir opened his home for a daily *minyan* for male students who wanted to *daven* before they went to classes. Bernard Lipinsky, who attended the college during the 1931–1932 school year, fondly recalls that Nasatir sometimes asked his students to buy him a movie ticket for Saturday matinees because he observed the tradition of not carrying money on *shabbat*. Nasatir taught at San Diego State until 1974 and authored eighteen books during his career. In 1985 the university established the Nasatir Professorship in Modern Jewish History. A year later the eastern wing of the old Humanities-Social Sciences Building was renamed Nasatir Hall. When he died in 1991, the donations made in his memory were dedicated to funding an annual Nasatir Lecture on American Jewish History.

The one form of antisemitic discrimination that existed at San Diego State in the 1930s was the exclusion of

TABLE 1.

Los Angeles, San Diego, San Francisco General, and Jewish Population Growth, 1910-1940

City	1910	1920	1930	1940
Los Angeles, general pop.	319,198	576,673	1,238,048	1,504,277
Los Angeles, general pop.	5,795	43,000	65,000	225,000
San Diego, Jewish pop.	39,578	74,683	147,987	203,341
San Diego, Jewish pop.	110	n. a.	2,000	3,000
San Francisco, general pop.	416,912	506,676	634,394	634,536
San Francisco, Jewish pop.	25,000	30,000	35,000	50,000

TABLE 2.

Jewish Student Percentage of Total Enrollment at California Universities and Colleges During the 1930s

School	Percentage of Student Body Composing Jewish Students
University of California, Los Angeles	11.23%
University of Southern California, (Los Angeles)	8.12%
University of California, Berkeley	7.41%
Los Angeles Junior College	4.67%
California Institute of Technology (Pasadena)	3.18%
Stanford University (Palo Alto)	2.87% (had Jewish quota)
San Diego State Teachers College	1.00%

Jews from fraternities and sororities, a common practice on American campuses until the 1960s. Charlotte Fried-Schultz, class of 1941, remembers that when her sister pledged a sorority, she was told that the chapter could not accept any other Jews without special permission from its national headquarters. Likewise, Sol Schultz, Class of 1941, believes that Bob Breitbard, a popular varsity football player, was blackballed from joining the fraternity of his choice by an individual member who disliked Jews.

If Jewish students at San Diego State wanted to socialize with Jews their own age, they had to join local Jewish organizations. In 1931 Jewish males in their late teens and early twenties founded the Alpha Beta chapter of Aleph Phi Pi which described itself as an "off-campus social fraternity." It drew much of its leadership from former and

LAWRENCE BARON

Abraham Nasatir, professor of history,
San Diego State University, 1928–1974.
Courtesy of Lipinsky Institute for Judaic Studies Archive,
San Diego State University.

current San Diego State students. In 1938 Bernard Lipinsky served as its chancellor and Bob Breitbard as its vice-chancellor. Another member was Lipinsky's friend Sol Price, Class of 1934, the future owner of the wholesale chain of Price Club stores. Lipinsky and Breitbard also acted as officers for B'nai B'rith's youth organization, Aleph Zadik Aleph. Similarly, female Jewish teenagers formed a local chapter of the B'nai B'rith Junior Girls Auxillary in 1933, which hosted an annual Charity Ball starting in 1936. In that year, Ida Friedman, Class of 1940, held the office of president of the group.

The 1940s proved to be a mixed blessing for San Diego State College and its Jewish student body. On the one hand, enrollment dropped from a high of 2,077 students in 1940 to a low of 860 in 1943 as many students joined the Armed Forces. This decrease prompted a reduction in faculty from 112 to 60. On the other hand, the rapid expansion of war-related industries and military and naval bases in and around San Diego sparked a population spurt enlarging San Diego's general population to 334,387 and Jew-

ish population to 6,000 by 1950. Many new Jewish residents initially visited San Diego as marines, sailors, and soldiers on their way to the Pacific front and moved to the city after 1945 to take advantage of the mild climate and the educational and employment opportunities resulting from the GI Bill and the federal contracts with factories producing military equipment and arms. Since their social security benefits and union pensions were portable, many senior citizens joined this Sunbelt migration whose postwar impact was more pronounced in Los Angeles and Miami. While it grew at a slower pace than those cities, San Diego was evolving into a metropolis, too. San Diego State's enrollment swelled to over 4,000 by 1947 with the Jewish student body reaching nearly 100. A poll of 64 Jewish students in 1947 indicated that 75 percent of the men and 55 percent of the entire group had served in the Armed Forces in some capacity during World War II.

To meet the demand for more courses, the college hired 170 new faculty members in the immediate postwar years. Three of these professors, Ernest Wolf, Harry Ruja, and Oscar Kaplan, were committed Jews. Along with Abe Nasatir, they supported the Jewish students' bid to gain the sponsorship of the San Diego Jewish Federation, the local B'nai B'rith lodge, and its Women's Auxiliary for the establishment of a Hillel chapter. Temple Beth Israel hosted the opening ceremonies for the Hillel chapter on September 30, 1947, with 650 people from the campus and the community attending to hear the keynote address by the president of Brandeis University, Abraham Sachar. He told the crowd that "understanding of our Jewish heritage gives a feeling of confidence and pride to our youth so that they no longer will accept defensive apologetics."

The first act of San Diego State's Hillel was to petition the registrar to reschedule registration for the fall semester so it did not coincide with the High Holy Days. Yet this was still a time when the goal of mainstream American Jewish groups was building ecumenical coalitions rather than pursuing a parochial Jewish agenda. Accordingly, the Hillel chapter of San Diego State amended its charter to admit gentile members (with the proviso that they couldn't serve as officers), established an interfaith scholarship fund, jointly celebrated Hanukah and Christmas with Christian student groups, and conducted an annual Interfaith Seder that included New Testament passages that referred to the observance of Passover by Jesus and his Apostles.

As the GI Bill diversified the student body at San Diego State, the restrictive admission policies of the school's

Don't Say We Didn't Warn You!

WE'RE TELLING YOU NOW TO RESERVE

TUES., SEPTEMBER 30, 1947 -- 8 p. m.

FOR SAN DIEGO'S MOST OUTSTANDING EVENT!

Installation of San Diego State College

HILLEL

SPONSORED BY

LASKER LODGE — B'NAI B'RITH — BIRDIE STODEL

Temple Beth Israel ❖ 3rd and Laurel, San Diego

DR. A. L. SACHAR

GUEST SPEAKER

Director National Hillel Foundations
President National Hillel Commission

___

Famous Lecturer, Educator, Author

___

☆ Speakers

    ☆ Entertainment

        ☆ Refreshments

If you miss it . . . You'll regret it!

Acorn Press—San Diego, Calif.

Hillel installation poster, 1947.
Courtesy of Lipinsky Institute for Judaic Studies Archive, San Diego State University.

fraternities and sororities came under fire in 1948. Moved by arguments that discrimination by race or religion could no longer be tolerated after Christian whites had fought alongside "Negroes" and Jews during the war, the Associated Student Council authorized a review of all student organizations to determine if they discriminated against minorities. The fraternities and sororities lobbied vigorously against changing their membership criteria, in the end, a student referendum approved the status quo by a vote of 1,225 to 721.

In the same year, however, San Diego State's students elected the first Jewish president of the Associated Student Council, Duane Kantor. Rejecting numerous offers to join one of the college's fraternities, Kantor stayed out of the fray over Greek membership policy to avoid polarizing the campus along religious lines. For the same reason, he declined to endorse the founding of a Jewish fraternity that was being promoted by his classmates Bob Levy and Larry Solomon. In the following year, their efforts led to the formation of a local fraternity named Beta Tau. In 1951 it affiliated with the national Jewish fraternity Zeta Beta Tau. Abe Nasatir became its faculty advisor. Two more Jewish fraternities subsequently chartered chapters at San Diego State, Alpha Epsilon Pi in 1970 and Sigma Alpha Mu in 1983.

Jewish women students eventually sought their own sorority as well. In the early 1960s, a local Jewish sorority named Alpha Epsilon recruited members and in 1963 affiliated with the national Jewish sorority Alpha Epsilon Phi. Harry Ruja acted as its faculty advisor. Judy Gumbiner, Class of 1966, admits that she pledged Alpha Epsilon Phi "as a way to meet other Jews and identify Jewishly." Yet she hardly segregated herself from the rest of campus life. The Associated Student Council named her Woman of the Year three times in a row for her service on the council. Alpha Epsilon Phi folded as part of a general decline of the Greek system in the 1970s for several reasons: students wanted their own apartments; the state mandated the abolition of discriminatory policies by campus groups; and student radicals perceived the Greek system as outdated and racist.

Even though the majority of students at San Diego State were politically conservative like the San Diego electorate in general, the campus was not immune to the forces of student radicalism in California, which culminated in the founding of the Berkeley Free Speech Movement in 1964. In 1959 the University of California system had abolished mandatory faculty loyalty oaths and an-

nounced that it allow speakers representing a broad spectrum of political views to address campus audiences. In 1960 a San Diego State chapter of the American Civil Liberties Union and a student organization, the Committee for Student Action, which dedicated itself to stimulating political debate on campus, were founded. The Committee for Student Action tested the limits of campus tolerance by inviting George Lincoln Rockwell, the leader of the American Nazi party, to talk at the college's Open Air Theater on March 8, 1962. Drawing a crowd of over two thousand, Rockwell launched into a diatribe against blacks and Jews, charging that the Holocaust had not occurred and that Jews were "loyal to Moscow or Israel" and promoted racial integration. When a Jewish physical education major named Ed Cherry climbed on stage to refute these calumnies, Rockwell blocked his access to the microphone. Cherry then punched Rockwell. A melee ensued in which students pelted Rockwell with rocks and eggs and vandalized his car. The incident garnered national publicity and resulted in disciplinary actions being taken against Cherry and two other students. The leaders of Hillel sent a letter to the college newspaper "regretting that Rockwell was not allowed to speak without interruptions," but expressing sympathy with "the actions of the student who was carried away by his emotions."

During the 1960s, San Diego State's growth kept pace with that of the city. The city's population approached 700,000, with the Jewish community numbering 12,000 by 1970. San Diego State College's enrollment rose from 10,700 in 1960 to 25,500 ten years later with full-time faculty positions increasing from 475 to over 1,000. The size of the Jewish student body was approximately 1,000 by 1968. A poll conducted among faculty and students in that year revealed considerable support for offering a minor in Jewish studies.

The Jewish pride generated by Israel's stunning victory in the Six Day War of 1967 and student and faculty pressure to offer academic programs in African American, American Indian, Chicano, and Women's studies in the late 1960s benefited the movement to institute a Jewish studies program at San Diego State. Rabbi Israel Weisfeld, the director of the San Diego Bureau of Jewish Education, taught courses in Hebrew and Judaism during the 1969–1970 school year for the nominal salary of one dollar to prove they could attract sufficient enrollments, and they did. A group of faculty members formed a Jewish issues forum called Yavne in 1969. Nine professors agreed to teach Jewish studies courses in the formal application for the minor in 1970. Following the approval of the minor that spring, Irving Gefter was hired in a tenured position to teach Hebrew and the Jewish heritage survey course. The next year Ita Sheres joined the faculty to teach courses on the Bible and modern Jewish literature.

By 1972 the state legislature recognized that San Diego State College had in effect become a comprehensive university awarding masters degrees and joint doctorates. Brage Golding, the first president to take the helm of the university, was Jewish. Golding detected no antisemitism directed toward him during his presidency, which lasted until 1977. This lack of animosity was all the more remarkable considering there were events like the Yom Kippur War of 1973, the 1974 United Nations resolution condemning Zionism as racism, and the related gasoline shortages and price increases caused by OPEC's oil embargo, which could have fueled an antisemitic backlash on campus.

The 1970s also marked a time when more Jewish students became concerned with issues of their ethnic and religious identity. Zionist idealism prompted Ray Belser to start a Jewish commune in the college area and eventually to make *aliyah* to Israel in 1973 where he joined fifty other North American Jewish students to found Garin Hagolan, a kibbutz in the northern Golan Heights. Chabad House opened near campus in 1970. Its Friday night services left Lorie Geddis, Class of 1972, with warm memories of "traditional shabbat dinners with lots of kosher wine and stories of the Baal Shem Tov late into the night." She was also deeply influenced by the university course "Pathways through the Bible" taught by Rabbi Samuel Penner. Hillel continued to be a focal point of Jewish student activity. Donna Kanter, Class of 1974, reminisces that "Hillel became my social life, my daily volunteer work, and connected me to Judaism in a way that years of practice, religious school, and even B'nai B'rith Girls hadn't." In January of 1976 Hillel moved into its present building and renamed itself the Jewish Campus Center because the San Diego Jewish Federation and not the national Hillel organization subsidized the rental and eventual purchase of its new quarters. The center hired Rabbi Jay Miller as its director in 1977.

By the 1980s the Jewish enrollment at San Diego State soared to over three thousand. The San Diego metropolitan area had over thirty thousand Jewish residents. Even though San Diego State continued to attract more students, reaching a peak enrollment of almost thirty-six thousand by 1987, state budget allocations decreased in the late 1970s as a consequence of the passage of Proposition

Thirteen. which capped property tax rates. Threats of drastic reductions in the funding of the California State University gradually crippled the Jewish studies program, which had depended on faculty members from other departments—which now hesitated to release professors to teach specialized Jewish studies courses. In the 1983–1984 school year, only four of the fourteen courses that counted towards the Jewish studies minor were offered. Pressure for the university to solicit private donations to fund the program emerged from the Jewish Campus Center, the Jewish Student Union, and Jewish faculty members. The university's development office began to approach potential contributors in 1983. Concerned faculty drafted a letter in 1984 informing San Diego Jewry that the "potential is here for an academically strong and enriching program that will communicate the vibrancy of Jewish culture to students and the public at large."

In response, the university hired Professor Jacob Goldberg of Tel-Aviv University to be a fundraiser for the Jewish studies program. Howard Kushner of the history department assisted Goldberg on behalf of San Diego State's faculty. What galvanized prominent local Jews to help fund Jewish studies was their consternation over the invitation of Louis Farrakhan to lecture at the university under the auspices of the Associated Students. President Thomas Day attempted to appease both sides by defending Farrakhan's right to appear on campus while convincing Jewish philanthropists that endowing the Jewish studies program would discredit his antisemitic tirades by educating people about Jews and Judaism. Day won over Bernard and Dorris Lipinsky, who announced a major donation in 1985 for endowing a permanent chair in modern Jewish history and an annual visiting Israeli professorship. Thus, the Lipinsky Institute for Judaic Studies opened in the Fall of 1985.

The topography and climate of San Diego county resembled that of Israel and other Middle Eastern countries. Like the nations bordering the Mediterranean Sea, the county possessed a temperate coastal strip adjacent to a ridge of mountains and an interior desert with a saltwater lake and irrigated farming plots in its eastern interior. The creation of the Fred J. Hansen Institute for World Peace at the university, and the signing of the Camp David accords between Israel and Egypt in 1979 enabled the school to become directly involved in fostering peaceful cooperation between Israel and neighboring Arab countries. Appointed the director of the Hansen Institute in 1979, retired professor Robert Ontell sent letters to Menachem Begin and

Bernard and Dorris Lipinsky
Announcement of the Endowment for the establishment of the
Lipinsky Institute for Judaic Studies, January 1985.
Reprinted with permission of The Daily Aztec,
San Diego State University.

Anwar Sadat suggesting that Egypt and Israel meet with American agricultural specialists in San Diego to improve the efficiency of growing crops in arid conditions. In 1982 the Institute received a five-million-dollar grant from the United States Agency for International Development to fund this plan. Before there were diplomatic contacts between the Palestine Liberation Organization and Israel, Ontell brought dovish Israeli and Palestinian politicians on campus to address private audiences of Arab and Jewish Americans about how to resolve the conflict between Israel and the Palestinians. Under the sponsorship of the Hansen Institute in the 1990s, representatives of Israel, Egypt, Jordan, Morocco, Oman, the Palestinian Authority, Qatar, Tunisia, and Turkey have cooperated with each other on practical matters like desalinization of water, water conservation, and the genetic engineering of crops requiring less moisture.

At the regional level, growing student enrollments and community attendance for the courses and public programs of the Lipinsky Institute for Judaic Studies reflected a westward shift in both Jewish settlement patterns and the academic institutionalization of Jewish studies. Between 1950 and 1990, the proportion of the American Jewish population residing in the western states rose from 7 percent to 24 percent, surpassing the Midwest as the second largest concentration of Jews outside of the Northeast. The influx of Jews and the enrollment of many of their children in colleges and universities in the West has served as the catalyst for the creation of new Jewish studies departments and programs and the expansion of existing ones. Los Angeles blazed the trail in this process with the founding of the University of Judaism in the late 1940s and the merger of a branch of the Hebrew Union College with the Jewish Institute of Religion in 1957. Both schools have since achieved the status of rabbinical seminaries for their respective denominations. Likewise, highly regarded Jewish studies degree programs have emerged at the University of California campuses of Berkeley, Los Angeles, and San Diego, and at private schools like the Claremont School of Theology, the Graduate Theological Union, and Stanford University.

In 1994, Lipinsky Institute director Lawrence Baron created the Western Jewish Studies Association, emulating the Midwestern Jewish Studies Association, an organization founded in the 1980s partly as a protest against the Association for Jewish Studies' decision to hold its annual conference in Boston. Many interpreted the AJS policy as a refusal to acknowledge the proliferation of Jewish studies programs outside the Northeast. When the AJS leadership rebuffed his proposal to alternate conference sites to make attendance more accessible and affordable for Jewish studies scholars in the Midwest and West, Baron convened the first meeting of the Western Jewish Studies Association in San Diego in 1995. Subsequent conferences have been held in Colorado Springs, Denver, Los Angeles, Phoenix, Seattle, and Tucson. Responding to requests from both the Western and Midwestern Jewish Studies Associations, the AJS held its 1999 conference in Chicago and met in Los Angeles in 2002.

The symbiosis of San Diego's Jewish community and the Lipinsky Institute culminated in the fall of 2000. Commemorating the one-hundred-fiftieth anniversary of Jewish settlement in San Diego, the thirtieth anniversary of the Jewish Studies Program at San Diego State, and the

Jewish History Society of San Diego and Lipinsky Institute for Judaic Studies sign Memorandum of Understanding, December 1999. From left to right, Professor Lawrence Baron, JHSSD President Stanley Schwartz, SDSU Dean Paul Strand. Courtesy of Jewish Historical Society of San Diego Archives and Lipinsky Institute for Judaic Studies Archive, San Diego State University.

twentieth anniversary of the Jewish Historical Society of San Diego, the Lipinsky Institute and Jewish Historical Society honored people who had made important contributions to San Diego and San Diego State Jewish history. The ceremony was preceded and followed by tours of the Jewish Historical Society of San Diego Archives housed in the Lipinsky Institute's Snyder Judaic Studies Reading Room.

Town-gown relations are often characterized by antagonism between partying students, controversial academics, and staid communities whose tranquility and values are threatened by both. The relationship between what Jewish studies programs teach and the political and religious priorities of the local Jewish population have suffered from similar tensions. Yet this generally has not been the case at San Diego State. In older Jewish communities on the East Coast or in the Midwest, Jewish settlement and the creation of Jewish educational institutions like day schools, community centers, and yeshivot usually preceded the introduction of secular Jewish studies programs at private and public universities. In San Diego the pattern was different. The period of most rapid Jewish population growth occurred between 1970 and 2000 when it skyrocketed from twelve thousand to eighty thousand. While the San Diego Jewish community busily erected a new community center, additional synagogues, and day schools, the Jewish studies program at San Diego State had the opportunity to fill the niche for adult education. The Lipinsky Institute's weekly New Perspectives in Judaic Studies Lectures, annual Glickman-Galinson Symposium on Modern Israel, and outreach lectures to community groups by the Visiting Israeli and Nasatir professors and other Jewish studies faculty have thrust San Diego State to the center rather than the margins of Jewish communal education in the city.

Directory of Sources

Archives of the Jewish Historical Society of San Diego and the Lipinsky Institute for Judaic Studies, Judaic Studies Reading Room, 363 Love Library, San Diego State University.

Gerson, Ronald. *Jewish Religious Life in San Diego, California, 1851–1918.* Thesis. Hebrew Union College-Jewish Institute of Religion, 1974.

Kramer, William M., Stanley and Laurel Schwartz, eds. *Old Town, New Town: An Enjoyment of San Diego Jewish History.* Los Angeles and San Diego: Western States Jewish Historical Association, 1994.

Marcus, Jacob Rader. *To Count a People: American Jewish Population Data.* Lanham: University Press of America, 1990.

Moore, Deborah Dash. *To the Golden Cities: Pursuing the American Jewish Dream in Miami and L.A.* New York: The Free Press, 1994.

Pourade, Richard. *The History of San Diego.* 7 Vols. San Diego: Union-Tribune Publishing Company and Copley Books, 1964–1977.

Starr, Raymond. *San Diego State University: A History in Word and Image.* San Diego: San Diego State University Press, 1995.

Acknowledgments

The author dedicates this article to the memory of Bernard Lipinsky (1914–2001), and thanks him, as well as Donald Harrison, Stan and Laurel Schwartz, Raymond Starr, and Jackie Tolley for sharing their knowledge about San Diego Jewry and San Diego State University.

CHAPTER 12

120 YEARS OF WOMEN'S ACTIVISM

AVA F. KAHN AND GLENNA MATTHEWS

Bella Abzug of New York was the second Jewish congress-woman. The first was California's Florence Prag Kahn of San Francisco. Kahn's achievement is just one of the many significant firsts for California Jewish women. From Kahn's mother, Mary Goldsmith Prag, serving on San Francisco's 1922 board of education, to Dianne Feinstein and Barbara Boxer in the United States Senate, Jewish women have played high-profile roles in shaping California's political culture. With a remarkable 44 percent of California women serving in the House of Representatives between 1920 and 1990 being Jewish, there are innumerable reasons for interest in this subject and just as many questions to ask about Jewish women's history in the state. This essay is a first attempt to propose a few answers, but more importantly to explore Jewish women's political history.

One reason for this leadership position may be traced to a general acceptance of Jews in California, a state where Jews helped found new "instant cities" and local governments. In other parts of the United States, during the country's founding years, Jewish participation in the American political process was fraught with obstacles. In the early colonial period, only Jews in South Carolina could vote or hold public office, and the colony rescinded this privilege in 1721. After the Revolutionary war, with the adoption of the United States Constitution, Jews obtained full federal citizenship including office-holding privileges. However, this was not always recognized by states. Although they steadily gained rights, by 1790 Jews could participate in the elective process in only five states. Most states allowed Jews into political life soon thereafter, though there were still a few exceptions. Until 1826, to hold public office in Maryland, for example, one had to take a Christian oath. In North Carolina, Jews remained ineli-

1992 campaign button to elect
Barbara Boxer and Dianne Feinstein to the U.S. Senate.
Courtesy of the Skirball Cultural Center and
Gerald M. and Carolyn Z. Bronstein.

gible for public office until 1868, while New Hampshire, until 1877, required that its governor and members of the Senate and House of Representative be Protestant.

Jews always had the franchise in California. From the state's inception in 1850, Jews enjoyed membership in the community-at-large. Without a Protestant hegemony, due to its multiethnic gold rush beginnings, California saw American-born Jews and immigrants alike helping found the state's many Anglo-based institutions. Soon after their arrival, Jews began to obtain positions of community leadership, becoming town and federal officials, judges,

Justice Harry A. Lyons, California State Supreme Court, 1851–1852.
Courtesy of Western States Jewish History Archive.

and state representatives. Abraham C. Labbat, a Sephardic Jew from Charleston, was elected alderman in San Francisco in 1851, and both Solomon Heydenfeldt and Henry A. Lyons served on the State Supreme Court of California during the state's first years. In 1853, representing San Francisco, Elkan Heydenfeldt (Solomon's brother) and Isaac N. Cardozo (Uncle of Benjamin N. Cardozo who later would be an associate justice of the United States Supreme Court) served in the California Assembly. The first of many Jews to serve Los Angeles, M. L. Goodman, a merchant, sat on the first city council in 1850. Maurice Kremer served as treasurer of Los Angeles County from 1859 to 1865.

By the late nineteenth century, Jews in San Francisco had assumed prominent roles in political life. In 1894 Adolph Sutro was elected mayor of San Francisco, becoming one of the first Jewish mayors of a large city. In 1898, only forty-four years after statehood, voters in the city's Fourth District chose Julius Kahn to serve in the United States Congress.

Jewish women, however, were not going to let men take all the leadership positions. Working for community betterment since the state's early days as members of benevolent societies, organizers of charitable events, and later as hospital volunteers, club women, and activists, Jewish women by the late nineteenth century moved from self-help organizations into the public sphere. Some Jewish women joined clubs that were more political than social, while others became activists for causes they believed in. Many women worked behind the scenes.

Three women who began their activities in the nineteenth century, well before California women received the vote in 1911, were especially significant. Mary Goldsmith Prag, Hannah Marks Solomons, and her daughter Selina Solomons all took leadership roles working for women's suffrage and women's rights. Their lives demonstrate the different paths taken by Jewish women in the fight for equality.

Prag, the daughter of a *shochet* (ritual butcher), arrived in San Francisco from Poland with her family in 1852 when she was five years old. Nurtured both by the Jewish and the general community, she would go from high school teacher and administrator to activist for teachers' and women's rights. The first Jewish woman in California to hold public office, Prag served on the San Francisco Board of Education for over twelve years, beginning at age seventy-five. Earlier, Prag had campaigned for equal pay for male and female teachers, secured the right to work for married teachers, and begun the movement to establish California's pension system.

Receiving a Jewish education under San Francisco's first rabbi, Julius Eckman, and a secular education in San Francisco's public schools, Prag was well prepared for public life. She used her knowledge of both fields in pressing for a pension plan for California's teachers. In her 1892 address to the Association of California Teachers, Prag stressed that California should follow the lead of Germany and other European countries by enacting a teacher's pension plan. After describing the European plans in detail, she concluded her address by paraphrasing Proverbs 31 "A Woman of Valor," stating that if California had such legislation "her children, and her teachers will rise up and call her blessed."[1] She believed, furthermore, that California should set an example for other states to follow.

A teacher's pension was only one issue where Prag thought that Californians should lead the way. She was an active participant in the annual Woman's Congress

Rabbi Julius Eckman of Temple Emanu-El, 1854–1855.
Courtesy of Western States Jewish History Archive.

sponsored by the Pacific Coast Association from 1894 to 1897. At the 1896 meeting on woman and government, Prag's well-received address entitled "The State" was reported in the *San Francisco Call* (May 7, 1896). Prag discussed the history of governments in world civilizations and the role of social and political institutions, tracing the history of democracies from the Greeks onward and suggesting that giving women the right to vote would be the only logical outcome of this process of democratization. For, she concluded, "the people are the State," and therefore, the will of the people must lead the way. While Mary was appointed and not elected to office, her daughter, Florence Prag Kahn, was elected to the United States Congress in 1925, succeeding her husband, Julius Kahn.

Also working as an activist was Hannah Marks Solomons, who was born in Poland to Jews who had fled Germany, grew up in Philadelphia, and was raised by her aunt and uncle after the death of her parents. In 1853 she traveled to gold rush San Francisco to marry a man chosen for her by her brother, Bernhard Marks, but upon arrival refused her suitor. To support herself she taught at the religious school of Temple Emanu-El and in the public schools, becoming the only woman and youngest school principal in San Francisco. In 1862 she married Seixas

Solomons, the grandson of Gershom Mendes Seixas, a Revolutionary patriot, a Sephardi Jew from a prominent family who moved his congregation out of New York during the War of Independence and was one of fourteen clergymen to officiate at George Washington's 1789 inauguration. Seixas Solomons joined the gold rush to California; active in Jewish and community life, he was a founding member of congregation Emanu-El, B'nai Brith and a member of the 1856 Vigilance Committee. For her part, Hannah, serving as an example for her children, especially her daughters, was a leader in Jewish and secular women's activities, activities which enlarged many women's spheres of influence. A member of the California Club, Hannah worked to support civic projects in all neighborhoods of the city and for suffrage. And she represented all of San Francisco's Jewish women at an 1888 meeting to decide if women should serve on the local board of education.

In 1868, Hannah was president of the first Jewish fundraising fair in San Francisco, the Ladies Fair Association of Temple Emanu-El, which supported the Orphan's Home where she also taught. With other Jewish women, she was a founder of the Women's Educational and Industrial Union of San Francisco which worked across class lines to improve the lives of working women. Hannah served as the organization's president in 1891, bringing with her the financial support of the Jewish community. Prominent donors included Levi Strauss, Jewish-owned businesses such as the Alaska Commercial Company, and Jewish women of San Francisco's elite, such as Mrs. Daniel (Clara) Meyer. Hannah wrote in her 1891 president's report that the Union believed in not the "patronizing of poor women by rich ones; not a handing down of benefits from women on one plane of life to a woman on another, but a true union of women for mutual help and sympathy—for united progress and advancement—each helping each." The WEIU offered classes to "promote the educational interests of women." To this end, college student Jessica Peixetto (later to become the first woman full professor at the University of California, Berkeley) offered an English class, while her mother conducted a singing chorale. The WEIU also provided a training ground for Hannah Solomon's daughter Selina, who served as chair of the Committee on Social Affairs, where she learned how to organize entertainment, establish a library, and plan social functions—skills which she soon brought to the suffrage movement.

All of Hannah's children were high-achievers. Adele became a doctor, Lucius a lawyer, Theodore an explorer and journalist, Leon a professor, and her first-born Selina a suffragist and author. Born in San Francisco in 1862, Selina possessed her family's characteristics of leadership abilities and forcefully held beliefs. Learning organizational skills from her mother, Selina put all her energy into the suffrage movement, which she chronicled in her 1912 book, *How We Won the Vote in California*. Serving as one of the leaders of the movement, she organized and served as president of the Votes-for-Women Club, which met in downtown San Francisco. A headquarters for the suffrage movement, the club offered a place where women could rest, read, and have lunch. Attracting both working women and shoppers, this club raised money and offered plays, lectures, and literature about suffrage. In support of the movement, Selina wrote a play, *The Girl from Colorado*. Produced several times before the 1911 election, the play is a comedy with a message of women's suffrage. When confronted with the argument that suffrage would destroy order in the home, Selina replied, we "intend to have a voice in our own government. If you men continue to withhold it from us . . . we will take it." On October 10, 1911, the men of California voted to allow women to vote in all elections. California became the sixth state in the nation to allow women to vote.

The next question for women was how they would express their vote. Except for a few notable men who were born or had spent significant time in the American South, for the most part, San Francisco Jews had a sixty-year tradition of supporting the Republican party. Viewed as entree into acceptance in American society, it was the party of most German Jews and business, and the party had a history of speaking out against antisemitism on foreign soil. In most American cities before the New Deal, Jews voted Republican, and especially in San Francisco, with the Jewish-Republican coalition lasting until the 1950s. In Los Angeles, however, the party shift came earlier. As Los Angeles attracted a larger proportion of eastern European immigrants who joined the Democratic party, Jewish party affiliation became more balanced in the southern part of the state. But Jewish women could be found in many places on the political spectrum.

Besides the suffrage activist, another category of pioneering activist includes women in the trade union movement, some of whom engaged in electoral politics. Of the abundant names, some of the most important women were Rose Pesotta, an organizer for the International Ladies Garment Workers Union in Los Angeles in the 1930s

Selina Solomons, pictured in How We Won the Vote in California, *published by the New Woman Publishing Co., 1912.*

and Elaine Black Yoneda, a Communist party labor activist in San Francisco during the same period. One of many women with significant impact was Jennie Matyas, another ILGWU leader.

Born to a large Orthodox family in Transylvania in 1895, Matyas came to the United States with her family when she was ten. She later recalled in an interview that the family emigrated not because of religious persecution but because they were desperately poor. Though she reported in the same interview that she had lost her belief in conventional religion as a young adult, she also explained, paying tribute to her religious background, "We believed in God and the justice that God dispensed."[2] In New York she longed for an education but at age fourteen she had to go to work in a garment factory. Three years later she became active in the garment worker's union, most of whose members were either Jewish or Italian. She also became a Socialist. A few years later, following the

From left to right, Florence Prag Kahn, a son, a grandson, Mary Goldsmith Prag.
Courtesy of Western Jewish History Center of the Judah Magnes Museum.

Russian revolution, Communists began to come into the ILGWU in sufficient numbers that Matyas felt compelled to withdraw. After a period of exploring the country, she eventually married and settled in San Francisco. She still kept aloof from the union, however, believing there was too much Communist party influence.

Then two things changed in her life. First, she became a New Dealer after listening to President Franklin Roosevelt's inaugural speech in 1933. Then, a meeting with ILGWU president David Dubinsky during an AFL (American Federation of Labor) meeting in San Francisco in 1934 brought her back within the union fold. She became a full-time organizer for the ILGWU in San Francisco and enjoyed many successes, including in Chinatown. As a labor leader she also threw herself into electoral politics, working hard for the winning candidacy of Cul-

bert Olson as governor of California in 1938. During World War II she was on an advisory committee to the War Manpower Commission, and when the war ended she won election as a national vice-president of the union. Along the way, she even managed to acquire a bachelor's degree in economics, cum laude, from the University of California at Berkeley. She had come a long way indeed from the dirt poor village in Transylvania.

The First Jewish Congresswoman

With this context of mobilized women in the community of California Jewry, the first Jewish woman to serve in Congress was a San Franciscan, Florence Prag Kahn. Kahn was also one of the first women in Congress to leave a substantial legislative legacy. Representing one of two districts in San Francisco from 1925 to 1937, the Republican Kahn was the person city leaders turned to when they wanted to get something done.

Born to Conrad Prag and Mary Goldsmith Prag in 1866, Florence had in her mother an impressive model of female leadership, as we have learned. She also received the excellent advice from her mother that she should attend the newly established University of California, from which she graduated in 1887, among only seven women and thirty-three men to do so that year.

Like her mother, Florence became a teacher. In 1898 she married a rising Republican politician, Julius Kahn. Elected to Congress the same year, Julius and Florence moved to Washington. Florence served as her husband's secretary and regularly attended House sessions to follow debates. When Julius died in 1924 (he had been in Congress for all but two years during their marriage), Florence was well prepared to take his place. Elected in a closely contested race, when only a tiny handful of women had served in the House, Kahn quickly established herself as capable and trustworthy and in 1929 became the first woman to serve on the House Armed Services Committee. With this key appointment, she sponsored much important legislation for the San Francisco Bay Area, including the bill securing federal approval to build the Bay Bridge linking San Francisco and Oakland, a measure opposed by the U.S. Navy.

The immense popularity of Franklin Roosevelt contributed to Kahn's defeat in 1936, but not before she had carved out a name for herself as an effective representative. Indeed, one of her obituaries in 1948 referred to her "occasionally frightening talents for ramming through legislation," quite a summing up for a woman politician at the time.

As for her Jewish identity, it was clearly important to her success in many ways. First, she had a long and close affiliation with San Francisco's Temple Emanu-El, going back to childhood. Secondly, as a young matron she belonged to such Jewish women's organizations as San Francisco's Philomath Club and Emanu-El sisterhood. And at a time when antisemitism was manifest in both overt and subtle ways, she frequently—and banteringly—called attention to her religious identity. Her maiden speech in Congress in April 1926 exemplified this point. Before addressing her subject, support for reapportionment in favor of the nation's cities, she quoted from the Book of Numbers in the Bible. She humorously implied

Florence Prag Kahn, representative from California, shown at the microphone during the spelling bee between capital newspaperwomen and wives of Washington's official families, with Eleanor Roosevelt seated at right, May 21, 1934. Courtesy of Western States Jewish History Archive.

that inasmuch as her co-religionist Moses had conducted the world's first census, she saw herself as especially qualified to speak out on the issue.

Florence Prag Kahn was the first prominent Jewish woman to hold elective office in California, but many others followed her. In fact, of the nine California women who served in the House between 1920 and 1990, four were Jewish.

The Second Wave of Electoral Success

The latter part of the 1930s and the war years saw Jewish women's public influence primarily in the ranks of organized labor, as we have seen in the case of Jennie Matyas. Then in the early 1950s came another breakthrough figure in elective office: Los Angeles' Rosalind Wiener Wyman. At a time when the city council was all-male, she won election to that body—when she was twenty-two years old.

Born in 1930, Rosalind Weiner attended the University of Southern California and majored in public administration, graduating in 1952 with the goal of attending law school. But in 1950 she had a life-altering experience: she had volunteered in the senatorial campaign of Helen Gahagan Douglas and had found herself as the candidate's driver and, hence, possessor of a front row seat for observing Douglas's grace under the fire of Richard Nixon's vicious attacks. In an interview during the late 1970s, Wyman expressed her admiration for Douglas as an inspirational figure. Meanwhile the young woman was part of the Democratic club at USC that also included future State Assembly speaker Jesse Unruh and future congressman Philip Burton. Indeed, her mother, Sara Weiner, worked with the Democratic Women's Forum. Surrounded by politicians, Wyman decided to run for the Los Angeles County Democratic Central Committee in 1951. She and six other young people put together a slate and focused their energy on the heavily Jewish Beverly-Fairfax area because they anticipated a high voter turnout there. Wyman won, and a couple of years later found herself interviewing potential candidates for a slot on the city council. The experience convinced her she should announce for the seat herself—less than a year after she had graduated from college.

Wyman astonished everyone by placing first in the primary with the help of zealous young people. For the general election in April 1953 many Jewish leaders helped her raise money for her victorious campaign. In 1954 she married fellow Democratic party powerhouse Eugene Wyman. In addition to her three terms on the council, she has had a career of hard work for the Democratic party and various Jewish causes. Of the latter she has explained that her Jewish identity came less from her upbringing than from her realization as an elected woman that she had a responsibility to the community.

About the time that Wyman was making waves in Los Angeles, another Jewish woman who would scale unprecedented heights, San Francisco's Dianne Feinstein, was beginning to display the leadership qualities that would carry her into high office. As an undergraduate at Stanford University in the early 1950s she was vice-president of her class and a memorable figure on campus. Born Dianne Goldman in 1933, she attend a Jewish school and then the Convent of the Sacred Heart. While at the Catholic school, she made so strong an impression on the father of one of her classmates, Edmund G. "Pat" Brown, who was first attor-

ney general and then governor of California, that he would subsequently appoint her to a state board dealing with parole issues, an appointment that launched her career in public life. Those who met her when she was young recall that she was explicit about her political ambitions, certainly an unusual trait in those years. She graduated from Stanford in 1955, won a Coro Foundation fellowship to study public policy upon her graduation, and won election to the San Francisco Board of Supervisors for the first time in 1969. As for her Jewish identity, she has said, "For my family and me, Temple Emanu-El has been more than just the 'Temple in our backyard.' It has been a house of learning, a house of worship and the home of a warm and loving community with whom we have been privileged to share . . . our lives."

Another prominent Democratic woman, one who has held no elective office herself but has helped many others to win office, also began to be active in the 1950s. Ann Alanson Eliaser, born Ann Wertheim in San Francisco in 1926, married at nineteen and settled down to the life of a young married woman. In 1956 her friend Sue Lilienthal recruited her to volunteer for the campaign of Adlai Stevenson, and her life has never been the same since. Eliaser conceived the idea of affixing the candidate's name to various small items, such as pieces of jewelry, as a fundraising device. So successful was this that she soon launched a campaign to raise money from small contributors, a campaign known as Dollars for Democrats. Before long, she developed a reputation as one of the party's truly formidable fundraisers—though she told an interviewer that she hated dealing with money. Her explanation for her success was that her family raised her to be very self-disciplined. Besides, she said, "[y]ou know as well as I that Jews are trained from the time they're able to understand anything the need to give—the obligation to give." Her career has included being Democratic National Committeewoman from California from 1965 to 1968, a position from which she resigned to support the candidacy of Eugene McCarthy for president. It has also included a personal acquaintance with most of the top Democrats in the country for many decades.

Another powerhouse for the Democratic party lived in southern California. Carmen Warschaw was born in Los Angeles in 1917. The daughter of Russian immigrant parents, she grew up in a Jewish household that encouraged her to seek a career and firmly supported the Democratic party. After receiving a degree in social work from the

University of Southern California, she became a field worker for the State Relief administration. During college she had become a member of the Young Democrats, along with her future husband Louis Warschaw.

When the Warschaws established a home in Los Angeles in 1948, they founded the Los Feliz–Vermont Democratic Club. From there Carmen moved into community leadership positions, becoming president of the Democratic Women's Forum and a delegate to many Democratic national conventions, acting as chair of Women's Activities for Adlai Stevenson and Women for Kennedy.

On the state level, during the 1950s and 1960s Warschaw became a member of both Democratic and nonpartisan committees. She was a member of the State Board of Social Welfare and the State Fair Employment Practices Commission and, in 1960, chaired the women's division of the State Central Committee. In 1976 she was the first woman appointed to the Little Hoover Commission.

In 1964 Carmen Warschaw was appointed by President Johnson to the National Citizens Advisory Committee for Community Service. Warschaw attributes her high degree of commitment to Democratic causes to her parents' strong interest in politics. She was proud of their achievements as first-generation Americans, and as Jews. Although she is not religious, she identifies with her Jewish heritage, and sees it as a source of her intellectual abilities. Besides political organizations, Warschaw was a member of several Jewish associations, including the Community Relations Committee of the Jewish Federation, and was a board member of the Pacific Southwest Regional Anti-Defamation League. The political work of women like Warschaw helped to establish a path for later Jewish women to follow.

The 'Sixties as Incubator

It is hardly news that the decade that saw so much protest and so many social movements coming into being, including feminism, should have politicized many Jewish women. We do not yet have a book dealing with this important subject at the national level, though it is clear that many of the most significant feminist leaders—Betty Friedan, Gloria Steinem, and Bella Abzug come to mind—are Jewish. Clearly that pattern held for California as well. It is impossible in this brief compass, however, to do more than sketch a few details of the picture.

Any account of the 1960s in California must, of course, begin with the student movement at the University of California at Berkeley, from the first stirrings of protest against the House Un-American Activities Committee in the late 1950s through the Free Speech Movement in 1964 and on to the demonstrations about People's Park in 1969. It is not that there were not important student movements at many other California campuses, but the Free Speech Movement and its attendant publicity functioned almost like "the shot heard round the world" for its era in that it helped precipitate events elsewhere. And when one examines the Free Speech Movement, one immediately notices that two of the outstanding leaders were Jewish women— Bettina Aptheker and Jackie Goldberg. Aptheker, the daughter of the Communist intellectual, Herbert Aptheker, typifies the many Jewish activists in the 1960s who were called "Red Diaper Babies," the sons and daughters of radical activists of the 1930s. Goldberg, too, came from a working-class, politicized background in Los Angeles. Leaders in the 1960s, both women have continued to play high-profile roles, Aptheker as a professor of Women's Studies at UC Santa Cruz and Goldberg in electoral politics, first on the Los Angeles school board, then the city council, and, as of 2001, in the state assembly.

Remarkably, three Jewish women who were friends, roommates, and Jewish sorority sisters (Delta Phi Epsilon) at Berkeley in the 1960s have all become important politicians in California in subsequent years: Goldberg, Dion Aroner, as of 2002 Democratic caucus chair in the assembly, and Susan Davis, first-term congresswoman from San Diego. Aroner shared her recollections of a Jewish woman's becoming politicized in those years.

Born Dion Schwartz in San Francisco in 1945, Aroner recalls attending religious school at Temple Emanu-El as a child. She also recalls that her parents were not especially observant, though a great-grandfather had been a talmudic scholar. One of her strongest memories is of her neighborhood at Seventh and Lake, a wonderful block featuring, among other residents, a rabbi, a cop, a lesbian couple, and a doctor. So plentiful were the children from these diverse households, remarked Aroner, that *San Francisco Chronicle* columnist Herb Caen wrote about it. We would argue that Aroner's childhood embodies what made the experiences of so many California Jews relatively positive: rootedness in the Jewish community while having a broad range of contacts outside it as well.

When she was in junior high school, her family moved to Los Angeles. After graduating from University High

*Dion Louise Aroner for California State Assembly
campaign literature, 1994.
Courtesy of Dion Aroner and Glenna Matthews.*

School, Aroner opted to attend Berkeley because her older brother had. She arrived on campus in the fall of 1962 and chose to major in political science. But her real political education came in the course of discussions with her first roommate, Jackie Goldberg. "We used to have terrible arguments," Aroner remembers. "I was so naive in those days."

The second source of her political education came while learning to function in the profession she chose after graduation from UC Berkeley, which was social work. She had taken one social welfare course in college and "knew the alphabet soup." Her activism began within a very short time of her hiring because she had to fight to defend the interests of her clients. Toward the end of her first year she joined Service Employees International Union (SEIU), Local 535 and soon became a leader of her chapter. In 1970–71, at age 26, she became statewide president, the first woman in the position and the youngest to serve at that level. About this time she "discovered Sacramento." Ronald Reagan was governor, and she needed to defend the interests of both the welfare clients and the professionals. She went from SEIU leadership to working for Alameda County Supervisor Tom Bates, then to working for California *assemblyman* Tom Bates, and then went on to replace him in the Fourteenth Assembly District in 1996. She became one of the most respected members of the assembly. Asked how she would account for her commitment to

social justice, she singles out the influence of her mother, Doris Schwartz, who held many leadership roles, from president of the PTA to president of Mt. Zion Hospital Auxiliary. "My mother was the queen of volunteers; I was raised to give something back to the community."

The true number of women who became publicly active in these years would be impossible to calculate. Some ran for elective office, like Dianne Feinstein and Carol Ruth Silver in San Francisco. Some became active in their unions. Some prepared themselves for a life of feminist scholarship, a position from which they could influence younger women to become involved. And with the founding of the National Women's Political Caucus in 1971, those interested in electoral politics per se had the first-ever organization explicitly designed to encourage women to run for office. Many Jewish women were active in various chapters in California, and many of these would in turn run for office.

The Year of the Woman and Beyond

In 1992, the so-called "Year of the Woman," something quite extraordinary happened: California voters elected two Jewish women from the Bay Area, Barbara Boxer and Dianne Feinstein, to the U.S. Senate. It was an unprecedented development in the nation's history for a state to have two women senators, let alone two Jewish women senators.

Dianne Feinstein had gone from being chair of the San Francisco Board of Supervisors to being the city's mayor after the tragic assassination of George Moscone in 1978. She served as mayor for nine years and then ran unsuccessfully for governor against Pete Wilson in 1990. Though she lost, she ran a credible race and established herself as one of the best-known politicians in the state.

Barbara Boxer, born in 1940, won election to the Marin County Board of Supervisors in 1977 and to the U.S. House of Representatives in 1982. More liberal than Feinstein, she had catapulted to national prominence by leading a charge of congresswomen in an "assault" on the Senate in late 1991 to protest the treatment of witness Anita Hill during Clarence Thomas's U.S. Supreme Court appointment confirmation hearings. The Hill-Thomas confrontation had dramatized the difficulties of obtaining justice for a woman from a legislative body of ninety-eight men and two women. It also created momentum to bring more women into high elective office.

Feinstein was an odds-on favorite in 1992, while Boxer's candidacy seemed more uncertain. But Feinstein's wholehearted embrace of Boxer's campaign, with two joint appearances, helped give legitimacy to Boxer's candidacy. Furthermore, Boxer received a gift from the state's Republican voters in the primary in that they nominated Bruce Herschensohn as her opponent, a conservative candidate whose positions were to the right of the California mainstream. In consequence, both women won.

The years since have seen both Feinstein and Boxer winning re-election and their being joined in Washington by a number of Jewish women representing California in the House, including, currently, Susan Davis and Jane Harman. As we have seen, Dion Aroner has a leadership position in the State Assembly in 2002. In short, 120 years of activism have made it possible for Jewish women to be viable candidates for every single elected office in California.

In addition, the tradition of Jewish women's leadership in the trade union movement, with a spillover effect in the realm of electoral politics, continues. As of 2002, one of the country's outstanding labor leaders is San Jose's Amy Dean, who heads the South Bay Labor Council. Elected to her current post in 1994 while still in her early thirties, Dean was the youngest person in the country ever to fill so distinguished a position. Since then her leadership has drawn high praise and has reinvigorated the South Bay labor movement. She helped elect candidates both to the San Jose City Council and to Congress. In an interview in December 1998 Dean spoke of the influence of religious upbringing: "My religious background was very formative and laid the foundation for me to do the work that I do today," explaining that she meant the ethical code of Conservative Judaism.

Conclusion

What has led to this amazing achievement for Jewish women in California? We note that most of the women whose careers we examined identified themselves as Jews, and many attributed their political activities, whether Democrats or Republicans, to their Jewish upbringing. Several believed that their ethnic identity influenced their political actions. This is especially evident in the relationship between mothers and daughters. In the nineteenth and early twentieth centuries, Mary Goldsmith Prag and her daughter Florence both spoke of their Jewish values and of the need to work for a better society. In

the twenty-first century, Dion Aroner spoke of following in the footsteps of her mother who worked as a volunteer, while Aroner herself wanted to have a larger impact and work for pay.

We also believe that much of the success of Jewish women in California is due to the state itself. One advantage for California Jewish women, for example, was the University of California at Berkeley, attended by a striking number of the women discussed in this essay. The university gave them an almost free, good education, and offered the example of such firsts as Jessica Peixotto (Ph.D. in sociology), who became the first woman appointed the rank of full professor at Berkeley. Furthermore, because of California's multicultural foundation, Jewish men succeeded early on in politics and this standard foreshadowed the successes of Jewish women. (A concrete example is the Kahn family: there was little question when Julius Kahn died that his wife Florence would succeed him.) And with this model, the future for Jewish women in California's political life became firmly established.

Directory of Sources

Several important books served as bibliography for this chapter and will provide additional context for the reader. For those interested in Jewish women's history and politics see: Glenna Matthews, Linda Witt, and Karen Paget, *Running As a Woman: Gender and Power in American Politics* (New York: The Free Press, 1993); Glenna Matthews, "'There is No Sex in Citizenship': The Career of Congresswoman Florence Prag Kahn" in Melanie Gustafson, Kristie Miller, and Elisabeth Perry, eds., *We Have Come to Stay: American Women and Political Parties, 1880–1960* (Albuquerque: Univ. of New Mexico Press, 1999); Glenna Matthews and Ava F. Kahn, "Florence Prag Kahn," in *Jewish Women in America: An Historical Encyclopedia*, Paula E. Hyman and Deborah Dash Moore, eds. (New York: Routledge, 1997); Ava F. Kahn, "Mary Goldsmith Prag," and "Hanna Marks Solomons," in *Jewish Women in America: An Historical Encyclopedia*, Paula E. Hyman and Deborah Dash Moore, eds. (New York: Routledge, 1997). Prag's life is further chronicled in Ava F. Kahn, *Jewish Voices of the California Gold Rush: A Documentary History 1849–1880* (Detroit: Wayne State University Press, 2002) and "To Journey West: Jewish Women and Their Pioneer Stories," in *Jewish Life in the American West*, Ava F. Kahn, ed. (Los Angeles: Autry Museum of Western Heritage, 2002); Celia

Morris, *Storming the Statehouse: Running for Governor with Ann Richards and Dianne Feinstein* (New York: Scribners, 1992); William Toll, "From Domestic Judaism to Public Ritual: Jewish Women of the American West," in *Women and American Judaism: Historical Perspectives,* Pamela S. Nadell and Jonathan Sarna, eds. (Hanover: Brandeis University Press, 2001); M. K. Silver, "Selina Solomons and her Quest for the Sixth Star," in *Western States History,* Summer 1999; Mae Silver and Sue Cazaly, *The Sixth Star: Images and Memorabilia of California Women's Political History 1868–1915* (San Francisco: Ord Street Press, 2000); Rose Pesotta, *Bread upon the Waters,* John Nicholas Beffel, ed. (New York: Dodd, Mead, 1944); and for the life of Elaine Black Yoneda see: Vivian McGuckin Raineri, *The Red Angel: The Life and Times of Elaine Black Yoneda* (New York: International Publishers, 1991). For more about Jews in California politics see: David G. Dalin, "Jewish and Non-Partisan Republicanism in San Francisco, 1911–1963 in *The Jews of the West, the Metropolitan Years,* Moses Rischin, ed. (Waltham, Mass.: American Jewish Historical Society for the Western Jewish History Center of the Judah L. Magnes Memorial Museum, Berkeley, 1979); Judy Yung's *Unbound Feet: A Social History of Chinese Women in San Francisco* (University of California Press, 1995), a study of Chinese women in San Francisco, also provides context for several of the Jewish women involved in San Francisco politics.

NOTES

1. The manuscript collections of the Bancroft Library, the Western Jewish History Center of the Judah Magnes Museum, and the California State Library were essential for this chapter. Especially see Mary Prag, "Should the State Pension Teachers?" Address delivered at the California State Teachers' Association (San Francisco: Frank Eastman & Co., Printers 1892), at the California State Library; the Selina Solomons collection and the *WEIU Third Annual Report.* 1891–1892:14 at the Bancroft Library; and the Julius and Florence Kahn Collection at the Western Jewish History Center for both Florence Prag Kahn and Mary Goldsmith Prag.

2. This chapter greatly benefited from the work of interviewers at the Regional Oral History Office at the Bancroft Library at the University of California at Berkeley. The following interviews were quoted from directly: "Jennie Matyas and the I.L.G.W.U.," Interview conducted by Corinne Gilb, 1957, p. 23; "'It's a Girl': Three Terms on the Los Angeles City Council, 1953–1965" Rosalind Wyman conducted by Corinne Gilb (the comments about fundraising are on pp. 23, 24 also p. 14); "From Grass-Roots Politics to the Top Dollar: Fundraisings for Candidates and Non-Profit Agencies," an interview with Ann Alanson Eliaser conducted by Malca Chall, p. 71f, 183. This chapter also benefited from "A Southern California Perspective on Democratic Party Politics," an interview with Carmen Harvey Warschaw, conducted in 1977–1978 by Malca Chall.

CHAPTER 13

THE COUNTERCULTURE

MARC DOLLINGER

For an incredible thirty-two hours in early October 1964, Jack Weinberg sat in the back seat of a police car surrounded by hundreds of students in the middle of UC Berkeley's Sproul Plaza. Weinberg, a Jewish civil rights leader, faced prosecution for violating a new university policy forbidding political activities on campus. In an impressive show of support, proponents of free speech prevented authorities from removing Weinberg, or the automobile, from its precarious spot. One by one students approached the vehicle, removed their shoes, carefully climbed onto the roof, and used the police cruiser as a personal soapbox to protest the university's ill-fated decision. While student leaders showed some goodwill by reimbursing the police department $455.01 for damage to its car, they capitalized on Weinberg's experience to launch a Free Speech Movement (FSM) that would redefine popular attitudes toward campus life, youth culture, and civil disobedience.

This well-known protest punctuated the impressive role California Jews played in the social reform movements of the postwar era. In the civil rights struggles of the 1950s and early 1960s, Jewish college students journeyed south to register voters, lobbied for enactment of a new federal civil rights law, and joined organizations committed to realizing racial equality. Across the state, Jews signaled their interest in social change by offering Democratic presidential candidates overwhelming support. In the 1960 election that gave John F. Kennedy a razor-thin victory over Californian Richard Nixon, Los Angeles Jewish voters rewarded the Massachusetts senator with an impressive 83 percent of their votes. Lyndon Johnson's popularity rivaled that of his mentor, Franklin D. Roosevelt, when 90 percent of Jewish Angelenos endorsed him and his plans for a Great Society. Even in defeat, 1968 Demo-cratic party nominee Hubert Humphrey polled 85 percent of the Jewish vote.

In northern California, Berkeley Jews constituted a majority of the Free Speech Movement's steering committee even though Jews made up just 3 percent of the overall population and 10 percent of those attending college. Approximately half of California's progressive Peace and Freedom Party claimed Jewish ancestry, while a 1971 poll of UC Berkeley freshmen discovered that 58 percent of the Jewish students considered themselves "leftist," more than double the response rate for non-Jews. When the American Council of Education wanted to know the single best predictor of campus activism, it concluded: "Jewishness." In the years following the free speech protests, California Jewish college students led the movement to end U.S. involvement in Vietnam, joined Native American and Latino activists in their struggles for civil equality, and eventually launched the most impressive ethnic revival in American Jewish history.

Just three years after Weinberg's arrest, California Jews, along with their co-religionists across the country, faced an entirely new political climate that destroyed most of their old alliances and challenged Jewish commitment to countercultural ideals. Lyndon Johnson's signatures on the landmark Civil Rights Act of 1964 and Voting Rights Act of 1965 ended the movement for racial equality and hastened a public feud between Jewish leaders and a new generation of black activists. Black Power advocates charged Jewish liberals with paternalism, purged them from leading civil rights organizations, and invoked age-old antisemitic canards in a series of high-profile confrontations. The advent of quota programs in education and government hiring alienated Jewish liberals who feared an end to their impressive social mobility. In the months after Israel's

*Jack Weinberg seated in the back seat of a police car,
Sproul Plaza, UC Berkeley, October 1964.
Courtesy of Howard Harawitz.*

victory in the 1967 Six Day War, many of the Jewish community's one-time political allies, including the leading New Left organization Students for a Democratic Society (SDS), embraced the Palestinian cause and condemned Israel as an "imperialist aggressor."

As Los Angeles rabbi Harold Schulweis explained, "Pulpits and pews in the '70's resonate to messages different from those of the '50s and '60s." California Jews who traveled to Mississippi to help African Americans in the early 1960s ventured to the Soviet Union in support of Jewish "refuseniks" a decade later. Once secular Jews donned *kipot* and *talitot* as they created new-age California-style *yeshivot*. Students at the University of California stopped protesting in Sproul Plaza and chose instead to export their political activism to Israel as participants in the college's new study abroad program. Throughout the state and across the country, Jews slowed

their intra-group efforts in favor of Jewish-centered activities. Jewish leaders stopped asking if their proposals were "good for America" and focused instead on whether a particular policy was "good for the Jews."

Ironically, California Jews responded to the new historical developments by emulating the black nationalist ideology of their newfound detractors. When young African Americans argued that "black was beautiful," they gave California Jews an unintended gift: the ability to fashion the nation's respect for ethnic diversity into a powerful tool for Jewish education, observance, and communal survival. California Jewish leaders borrowed a page from the Black Power handbook and turned inward, focusing renewed attention on the particular needs of the Jewish community. At a time when California Latino students rallied around the Chicano movement, the Golden State's indigenous tribes occupied Alcatraz Island in the San Francisco Bay, and the Black Panthers marched in the streets of Oakland, California, Jews launched a movement to aid Soviet Jews, redefined modes of religious worship, and revitalized a moribund Jewish organizational establishment. Combining elements of secular liberal activism, Jewish tradition, and local California culture, young Jews in the Golden State created one of the most important countercultural movements in American history.

As the California counterculture revitalized Jewish life, the Jewish community's sacred commitment to social integration and American accommodation appeared to weaken. For Rabbi Schulweis, the renewed emphasis on Jewish particularism undermined the very foundation of Jewish civil equality: "The Enlightenment vision of a constantly progressing universal society calling for Jews to involve themselves in the battle for social justice," he lamented, "is now interpreted as suicidal." California Jews struggled to balance their desire for greater Jewish consciousness with their love of American democratic ideals. They wanted the ability to express themselves as Jews just as they searched for new ways to build bridges with Californians of other racial and ethnic backgrounds.

Despite the concerns of Schulweis and others, California Jewish leaders fashioned a wide-ranging social movement that emulated the era's new ethnic activism while it protected the Jewish community's reputation as consensus-minded Americans. California Jews clung to their liberal optimism, continuing a generations-long search for non-Jewish allies, even as many ethnic Americans abandoned an accommodationist political approach. When the Bay

Area Council for Soviet Jewry looked for ways to free Jews under Communist rule, it invoked cold war themes. Founders of a yeshiva in San Francisco called on larger countercultural assumptions as they wrote their educational curriculum and established their rules of governance. Across the Bay in Berkeley, leaders of the new havurah movement searched for common ground between Jewish tradition and California popular culture.

When the California counterculture began in the early 1960s, secular Jews took a much greater role in social activism than their more traditional co-religionists. Whether in civil rights protests or the burgeoning Free Speech Movement, unaffiliated Jews illustrated the counterintuitive nature of California Jewish politics. "Radicalism rose substantially as religious orthodoxy declined," social scientists Stanley S. Rothman and S. Robert Lichter discovered, "Reform Jews were more radical than Orthodox or Conservative Jews . . . in fact, unaffiliated Jews were even more radical than non-religious students." Secular Jewish Californians joined the New Leftist group Students for a Democratic Society and followed in the tradition of their parents and grandparents who associated with the Socialist and Communist parties, organized the needle trades, and led the union movement through the New Deal years. Traditional Jews, committed to close-knit residential patterns and an Orthodox lifestyle, eschewed the public policy arena in favor of their own educational programs. In a pattern that would repeat itself across the country, one's leftist political orientation rarely correlated to one's level of religious observance.

The secular nature of the California Jewish counterculture manifested itself most powerfully when Berkeley's politically minded reform activities weakened and a new countercultural movement emerged in the Haight-Ashbury district of San Francisco. For this new generation of youth, focused efforts to create political change gave way to experimental drug use, sexual promiscuity, and vows to "turn on, tune in, and drop out." At UC Berkeley, four out of five Jewish freshmen polled in 1970 acknowledged illicit drug use. The collectivist mentality that inspired mass protests at the University of California evolved into a narcissistic individualism committed to achieving higher levels of personal consciousness. Eastern religious styles enjoyed great popularity among Californians and especially among Jews. Surveys of various New Age movements revealed that between 15 and 18 percent of Hare Krishnas and 6 to 8 percent of Unification "Moonie"

Outside the San Francisco YMCA, Summer 1970. Bruce Pither, very top with headband, Kathy Pither, second row, second from right. Courtesy of Kathy and Bruce Pither.

Church members came from Jewish backgrounds. California Jews also joined the Church of Scientology and attended self-actualization seminars such as EST (Erhard Seminar Training) in disproportionate numbers. Some Jewish Californians merged the socialist spirit of the Israeli kibbutz with the values of the counterculture by establishing their own communes in the rural sections of northern California. While few Jewish Californians actually dedicated their lives to communal living, 55 percent of the Jewish freshmen at Berkeley indicated a willingness to live on a commune compared to only 37 percent of the non-Jewish freshmen.

The Berkeley-centered political activists and the Haight-Ashbury counterculturalists joined together for a brief moment when opposition to U.S. policy in Southeast Asia united the two otherwise disparate groups. Free speech activists viewed President Johnson's escalation of the Vietnam conflict as another example of a bureaucratic and capitalist nation-state waging war for its own economic benefit. Counterculturalists across the Bay in San Francisco adopted a pacifist stance, popularizing the 1960s slogan "make love, not war." Together, they led the antiwar movement, marching in the streets of Oakland during "Stop the Draft" week and participating in acts of civil disobedience. When national Jewish organizations adopted what one official called "a deliberate silence" on the issue of Vietnam, young California Jews demanded action. While some protests, most notably the draft resistance efforts, failed to garner popular support, Jewish activists celebrated when two national organizations, the AJCongress and the Union of American Hebrew Congregations,

MARC DOLLINGER

called for an end to the Vietnam conflict. In the Spring of 1966, the AJCongress joined a broad coalition of religious, civic, and educational organizations to create "Negotiation Now," a group determined to bring the warring factions to the peace table. Three years later, the AJCongress determined "that the ultimate objective must be self-determination of the Vietnamese people" and called for "fully democratic elections in which all Vietnamese can participate freely." When the United States expanded the war into neighboring countries, the northern California division of the AJCongress called for "immediate withdrawal of United States forces from Cambodia and Vietnam."

U.S. foreign policy in this era proved especially problematic for Jews. Young California Jewish idealists opposed American actions in Vietnam and took to the streets as the leaders of the anti-war movement. But, their opposition to Vietnam-style cold war anti-Communism complicated support for Israel. "How can one be a "hawk" in the Middle East and a "dove" in Vietnam?" the head of the AJCongress asked in 1968. President Johnson, irate over Jewish opposition to his Vietnam policy, went so far as to summon the Jewish community's national leadership to the White House for a rather frank discussion of American Jewish interests. Show more support for my policy in Southeast Asia, the commander-in-chief inferred, or I will weaken my support for Israel.

Jewish pacifists, whether born of the San Francisco-based counterculture or the Berkeley-centered anti-war political movement, faced a unique "Catch 22" when they filed for conscientious objector status from the U.S. armed forces. While the armed forces recognized an individual's right to object on religious grounds, they also required that a potential conscript make a statement affirming that his faith community opposed *all* types of war. For Quakers and those of other denominations who did not discriminate between different types of wars, the regulation proved irrelevant. For Jews, whose religious tradition allowed individuals to distinguish between just and unjust wars, the policy threatened to discriminate against Jewish anti-war activists in ways not faced by Americans of other faiths.

Draft-age Jews appealed to their rabbinic leaders and to the legal divisions of national Jewish organizations to challenge the government edict. The Conservative movement's Rabbinic Assembly passed a resolution recognizing "the right of the conscientious objector to claim exemption from military service, in any war in which he cannot give his moral assent" and pledged themselves "to support

Israel Emergency Rally, Hollywood Bowl, Los Angeles, June 11, 1967.
Courtesy of the Archives of the
Jewish Community Library of Los Angeles.

him in his determination to refrain from any participation in it." The Reform movement's Central Conference of American Rabbis concluded that "conscientious objection to military service is in accordance with the highest interpretation of Judaism" while Rabbi Roger E. Herst, the director of Urban Affairs of San Francisco's Jewish Community Relations Committee, published a "Conscientious Dissent from a Jewish Point of View."

Jewish activists endured more ostracization when white New Leftists and black militants sided with the Palestinians after the 1967 Six Day War. While Jewish Californians lauded Israel's democratic values and importance in U.S. foreign policy, the SDS, which had boasted a 50-percent-Jewish delegate count at its 1966 national convention, equated Zionism with "imperialist racism." In Chicago, the 1967 Labor Day National Conference for New Politics passed a resolution condemning Israel for creating an "imperialist Zionist war." Even leading mainline Christian organizations refused to support Israel in the critical days of the war.

In Oakland, a group of African Americans called the Black Panthers offered a wake-up call to Americans by arming themselves and marching in the city's streets. After Panther leader Eldridge Cleaver went to Algiers and defended the leading PLO group, Al Fatah, in a September 1969 article, Jewish Liberation Journal writer Itzhak Epstein responded, "Let it suffice to say that the Panthers have declared themselves to be the enemies of my people's national aspirations, and supporters of those who want to commit genocide against us. Whatever justice there is in the Panthers' own struggle, I must view them from now on as my enemies." For Jewish activists, it became nearly impossible to maintain either a collegial or political relationship with anti-Zionists.

For Jews, the Panthers' embrace of the Palestinian cause unraveled a generations-long commitment to liberal idealism. "Even if I were a super-altruistic liberal and campaigned among the Jews to support the Panthers' program," Epstein argued, "I would justifiably be tarred and feathered for giving aid and comfort to enemies of the Jews. I would rather it were not this way, but it was you who disowned us, not we who betrayed you." A 1970 Louis Harris poll revealed that 25 percent of African Americans agreed that "the Black Panthers represent my own personal views." Among blacks under twenty-one years of age, the number jumped to 43 percent. Almost two-thirds of the respondents indicated that the Black Panthers gave them "a sense of pride."

On the national scene, Stokely Carmichael, elected chair of the Student Non-violent Coordinating Committee in 1965, pioneered the Black Power movement and presided over a series of white purges that forced Jewish civil rights activists out of many national organizations. Even as Martin Luther King, Jr., delivered his famed August 1963 "I Have a Dream" speech on the steps of the Lincoln Memorial in Washington, D.C., his influence as an accommodationist liberal interested in maintaining an interracial alliance had already peaked. Ethnic nationalism and identity politics emerged as the strategies of choice for Americans intent on preserving their particular group's cultural autonomy. Whites would never influence black civil rights organizations as they once had nor, as California Jews soon demanded, would non-Jews divert Jews from the sacred task of rebuilding an educated, traditional, and committed Jewish community.

Mainstream California Jewish leaders responded to black militancy with trepidation. In a 1964 letter, Stanley Jacobs of the Anti-Defamation League's (ADL) Bay Area office reported that the black leadership "take the position that Jewish leaders are identified with the white community and therefore not to be trusted." Jacobs, while noting the absence of any violent confrontations between blacks and Jews in his northern California district, acknowledged "a disengagement between NAACP, Urban League, and others with JCRC, ADL, and AJC, the agencies which formerly worked more or less closely with such groups." Ja-

cobs concluded that the "entire attitude of Negro leadership . . . is one of distinct coolness and even indifference toward the Jewish agencies" and recommended that the ADL "do little more than it presently is doing until the present battle situation clarifies."

Leftist California Jews offered surprising support for the Black Panther and other radical non-Jewish social reform movements, which they considered important voices for social change. The Jewish Liberation Movement, a Berkeley-based student group, backed the Black Panther party in its early days by sending delegates to its annual conference in Oakland. In the Spring of 1968, Berkeley Hillel and the Union of Jewish Students urged their co-religionists to "stay to hear [Black Panther leader] Bobby Seale" following a Soviet Jewry demonstration. The UJS also invited Seale to speak at their "radical high holiday service." When some black leaders criticized Jewish landlords for unethical business practices, Harold Schulweis, then the spiritual leader of Congregation Beth Abraham in Oakland, demanded that his congregants "leave the ghetto." Invoking the rabbinic injunctions against *genevat daat* (stealth of mind) and *onaat d'varim* (oppression by words), Schulweis explained that "there is always an alternative to complicity with evil. The alternative for the Jew is to get out. GET OUT. This is no way for Jews to make a living."

In larger political developments, the local affiliate of the AJCongress backed the 1969 Indian occupation of Alcatraz Island in San Francisco Bay. "As concerned citizens," the AJCongress pleaded, we "urge the San Francisco Board of Supervisors and the office of the Mayor to use all means within their power to help alleviate these deplorable conditions that exist for the Indian residents of our community." They called for creation of an educational and cultural center "that could assist in developing some of the practical solutions so necessary in helping this most deprived of all minorities." In the middle of the festival of Chanukah, AJCongress officials journeyed to Alcatraz to "break bread" with the Native American protesters. "Chanukah," one official explained, "commemorates the victory of Judah Maccabee over the Syrians in the second century B.C. and symbolizes one of man's first attempts to gain national liberation." The same year, the Young Adult chapter of San Francisco's AJCongress visited Delano, California, as guests of the United Farm Workers (UFW). Phil Veracruz, vice-president of the UFW Organizing Committee, invoked labor Zionist ideals when he proposed

MARC DOLLINGER

creation of a retirement village similar to the Israeli kibbutz. In the San Fernando Valley north of Los Angeles, Jewish activists inscribed Isaiah's admonition, "Thou shalt not eat the fruit of the oppressed" in both English and Yiddish when they picketed a Jewish-owned supermarket for violating a UFW-led boycott on table grapes.

Jewish undergraduates at Berkeley searched for ways to reconcile their Zionist inclinations and still respect the concerns of their non-Jewish political allies. While they took care to assert Israel's right to exist, Berkeley's Union of Jewish Students (UJS) also affirmed the right of Palestinian Arab refugees to self-determination. They backed creation of a Palestinian "socialist republic" and called on the Jewish state to withdraw from the West Bank and Gaza Strip for "moral reasons." The Radical Zionist Alliance (RZA) sponsored a Rosh Ha'shanah rally in Wheeler Auditorium that attracted an interracial and interfaith crowd of over two hundred. Echoing the UJS theme, the RZA affirmed that "no just and lasting solution to the Arab-Israel conflict can occur without the mutual recognition of the right to self-determination of the Jewish people and the Palestinian-Arab people."

For Jewish students associated with the campus's Hillel organization, though, the UJS' combination of Jewish and leftist politics did not mix. They challenged the UJS for criticizing Israel and questioned its Zionist commitment. Tensions between the UJS and Hillel came to a head in April 1968 when the leftist group organized an "anti-Israel Day" on Berkeley's Sproul Plaza. When the acting head of the UJS condemned Israel as "an aggressor and imperialist," the Hillel students bolted. "It appears to have been the turning point in the relations between the two groups," one observer noted, "Hillel now viewed the UJS with open suspicion and growing hostility, rather than with curiosity." That same year, UC Berkeley Jewish student leader Sherman Rosenfeld helped create the Radical Jewish Union (RJU), a response in part to what Rosenfeld described as "the anti-Israel posture of the New Left."

The dispute between Hillel and the UJS captured a much larger dilemma facing activist Jews in the 1960s: support for their one-time leftist allies seemed to demand a repudiation of Jewish interests and communal priorities. Most student leaders rejected that characterization and searched for new ways to express radical political ideas in a Jewish context. As Rosenfeld argued, "We believe that to be Jewish and to be radical are not mutually exclusive. . . . The basis of our radicalism is our belief in Judaism." The

Berkeley student activist explained that his generation felt "a cultural identification with Jewish history and art as well as with radical politics" and, given the broader social embrace of ethnic awareness, admonished his co-religionists "to come around and learn to accept their own distinct identity." As Rosenfeld's RJU colleague David Biale explained in a 1970 Jewish Radical article, "to reject the politics and mass culture of WASP America is at once a radical and Jewish act; radical because it calls for a complete reassessment of our place in this society; Jewish because we see the need for that reassessment comes directly from the fact that we are Jews."

While some Jewish leaders continued to support secular political causes, most California Jews responded to the political changes in the late 1960s by turning inward and focusing on issues and concerns of particular interest to Jews. As Theodore Bikel, the famed actor and Jewish activist, lamented in a 1967 visit to Berkeley, "many young Jews turn to Buddhism or other Eastern cults to find a hook on which to hang their spiritual coat. Look first," he implored, "in your own attic." Jewish student leaders at Berkeley emulated models established by black nationalists and set out to mold the new American respect for ethnic identity into a powerful force for Jewish education and continuity. "This new Jewish generation," Bay Area Jewish leader Irving Solomon explained, "found that the Blacks of their generation were finding their Black identity, the Chicanos were finding their Mexican identity, the Chinese, the Japanese, et cetera. All of them reaching for their own ethnic identities." For Solomon, 1960s-era ethnic activism signaled the end of the proverbial American melting pot and the emergence of a new group-centered national consciousness. "You cannot belong to anything," Solomon argued, "without identity." In a stunning departure from the consensus-building liberal ideals of civil rights workers, Solomon concluded that Jews "could not share in the Black or any other identity." As Rabbi Schulweis explained in 1975 from his new congregation in Los Angeles, there was "a convergence of diverse interests rallying around the flag of 'Jewish self-interest,' from lower middle class Jews, blue collar, working class Jews, disillusioned ex-Marxists, Lubavitchers, JDL'ers, and celebrators of ethnic particularism."

Berkeley students responded to the growing strength of identity politics by embarking on impressive Jewish-centered protest movements that invoked strategies from an earlier, more secular, era. "Since the world today is composed of national units exclusively," Berkeley's Radical

Jewish Union affirmed, "no people can hope to achieve liberation outside its national framework." The RJU published its own Jewish newspaper, organized an ongoing discussion group to engage issues of Jewish interest, created the Soviet Jewry Action Group and the Israel Affairs Committee, and opened Café Tel Aviv, a social club for interested Jewish students. It also sponsored a table on Sproul Plaza that carried information on Israel but also included material on black/Jewish relations and the plight of migrant farm workers.

Even those more interested in spirituality than political change invoked countercultural language to attract Jewish support. When Berkeley's Hillel sponsored "An Encounter with Chabad Chassidism" in 1970, for example, it acknowledged in its program description that "Opposing the 'establishment' had become for many, almost a way of life." Hillel noted Jewish student concerns "about the loss of individuality," "the hypocrisy of much of contemporary morality" and promised that "the Encounter will deal with the insights Chabad Chassidism can offer." Hillel also sponsored a "paint in" that encouraged Jewish students to take advantage of "free expression on the walls of Hillel," offered seminars on Hasidism, and classes on Hebrew.

Two years later, the Jewish student center expanded its education program when it opened the "Free Jewish University." Instead of following the typical "free university" model that offered populist classes to educate the masses, the FJU boasted such Jewish topics as "Soviet Jewry" and "Issues in Jewish Mysticism." For their program brochure, FJU founders elected to place an illustration of Hasidic children with the caption "the freshman class of the Berkeley Free University" and another image of an elderly Hasidic man with the title, "a graduate student of the Berkeley Free Jewish University." Far from the days when Jewish students looked to King and Gandhi as their philosophical mentors, the post–civil rights generation of California Jews looked back to seventeenth-century Poland for their inspiration.

The Jewish community's turn inward led Berkeley's new Jewish leftist movement to focus its early reform efforts on the Jewish organizational establishment. When the San Francisco Jewish Federation threatened to close the community's Brandeis Jewish Day School in 1971, students from the RJU joined with activists from the Labor Zionist group *Habonim*, the San Francisco Jewish Liberation Project, and the Stanford Union of Jewish Students, as well as with Bay Area Jewish educators and youth lead-

ers, and created the Jewish Education Coalition (JEC). They appealed to the San Francisco Jewish Federation to increase its support of Jewish educational programs and, paraphrasing Nation of Islam leader Malcolm X, threatened "to make public, by any means at our disposal, all the evidence of the Federation's refusal to adequately educate its children." "We are young Jews," they wrote in a broadside titled *A Challenge to Federation Priorities*, ". . . concerned that the kind of Jewish education people of our generation are receiving is turning them away from Judaism." In a biting critique of Jewish organizations and the people charged with running them, they listed "swimming pools and high paid Jewish bureaucrats" under the heading "WHAT WE DON'T WANT" and "New Jewish projects and Jewish actions" as "WHAT WE WANT."

They charged the Federation with obstruction of Jewish education and demanded the "right to quality Jewish education," funding of "innovative ideas," youth activities, and public debate. JEC leader Sherman Rosenfeld demanded greater democratic accountability within the Federation movement. In a May 7, 1971 letter to the Jewish Student Press Service, Rosenfeld wrote that "although the community *views* the Federation as public, the Federation itself considers it to be a 'private organization' made up of Jewish philanthropists and responsible to these donors." Underscoring Federation control of the Bureau of Jewish Education and the community's newspaper, the San Francisco *Jewish Bulletin,* Rosenfeld could only conclude that "the SF Jewish community is *not* democratic; it is run by a group of wealthy individuals who, by and large, do *not* respond to the community's greatest welfare need—the need to be educated. Such individuals apparently define their Jewishness in terms of the checks they write, not in terms of real commitment to Jewish values."

When Federation officials failed to meet the student demands, the JEC called for an April 30 sit-in at San Francisco Federation Headquarters. In a departure from earlier FSM-style protests, organizers emphasized that their sit-in was "not a mere physical occupation" but would be conducted along traditional Jewish lines. They celebrated shabbat and engaged in Jewish study. "There is a new Jewish youth—committed to Jewish life," the JEC argued, "—*not* assimilation and showpieces. Hidden beneath the empty edifices of synagogues and Sunday schools, we have discovered an almost forgotten but vibrant tradition." While their sit-in failed to change Federation policy, JEC activists did bring important institutional questions to the fore. As the outgoing president of Los Angeles' Federation would acknowledge eight years later, "Federations generally had the attitude years ago that they were secular Jewish institutions. That's a contradiction in terms, of course, but that's what they believed. They saw their responsibility as providing for the health and welfare needs of Jews. . . . Now we've come to recognize that Jewish life can't be compartmentalized, can't be divided into welfare on the one hand and Judaism on the other."

In the international arena, young California Jewish activists turned away from Vietnam War protests and focused attention instead on the plight of Soviet Jews. For California Jews disillusioned by the breakup of the black-Jewish alliance but still committed to progressive causes, the Soviet Jewry movement emerged as the emblematic American Jewish cause of the contemporary era. The Bay Area Council of Soviet Jewry grew as a national leader in efforts to save Jews behind the Iron Curtain. Local rabbis held vigils, organized rallies, and some endured arrest by handcuffing themselves to the gates of the Soviet Embassy on Green Street in San Francisco. UC Berkeley students, in tacit condemnation of American Jewish silence during the Shoah, proclaimed, "We will not be guilty of the crime of silence."

Leaders of the Soviet Jewry movement also borrowed a page from the African American civil rights strategy book, imitating the style, technique, and rhetoric of earlier liberal protests. Just as Martin Luther King, Jr., sought white liberal support by casting the civil rights struggle in universalist terms, leaders of the Soviet Jewry movement called on an all-important accommodationist theme, anti-Communism, to link Jewish interests with those of the larger Christian majority. By focusing on Soviet human rights abuses, Jewish activists not only helped their eastern European brethren but also took advantage of American cold war opposition to the Communist state. In 1972, Senator Henry Jackson of Washington rallied seventy-six colleagues to co-sponsor legislation tying U.S. economic incentives to the human rights records of Communist nations. An April 1972 House resolution calling on "the Soviet government to permit the free expression of ideas and the exercise of religion by all its citizens" passed by a 360–0 vote.

The Student Struggle For Soviet Jewry estimated that 28 percent of its activists had participated in the civil rights movement. When asked why American Jews should protest the condition of Soviet Jews, Jacob Birnbaum, the organization's founder, responded, "Many young Jews

Rabbi Graudenz (second from left), Cantor Simon Cohen (third from left), Morris Goldstein (sixth from left), Rabbi Gumbiner (seventh from left), Rabbi William Dalin (eighth from left), Rabbi Harold Schulweis (ninth from left), Rabbi Sam Broude (fifth from right), Rabbi Abrams, speaking, at the East Bay (Berkeley/Oakland) Rally for Soviet Jews. Courtesy of American Jewish Historical Society.

today forget that if injustice cannot be condoned in Selma, USA, neither must it be overlooked in Kiev, USSR." One of the earliest meetings, a Conference on the Status of Soviet Jews held in October of 1963, counted civil rights leader Martin Luther King, Jr., Supreme Court Justice William O. Douglas, and labor leader Walter Reuther as sponsors. In one high-profile protest, the 1974 "Freedom Ride" from Washington, D.C., to Seattle, Jewish leaders invoked memories of the 1962 civil rights bus protests to draw parallels between the oppression of blacks in the American South and Jews in the Soviet Union. "With its peaceful tactics," William Orbach explained, the Soviet Jewry movement "satisfied the needs of those who could not subscribe to the student militancy of the late 'sixties."

Just as the JEC and the Soviet Jewry movement emulated the earlier style of secular political protesters, other Bay Area Jewish groups internalized aspects of the Hippie movement, embarking on what would become a national campaign for greater Jewish spirituality, tradition, and religious meaning. In 1968, Rabbi Shlomo Carlebach opened his San Francisco "House of Love and Prayer" as a Jewish-centered alternative to the secular counterculture. In the spirit of the times, the religious leader appealed to "hippies and drop-outs" of "a generation already involved with Eastern religion, psychedelics, and astrology." He wanted his disciples to know, in true countercultural language, that "when you walk in, someone loves you; when you walk out, someone misses you."

As much as Carlebach and the other organizers of the House of Love and Prayer embraced the counterculture's emphasis on personal growth, they focused their efforts on creating a Jewish-centered experience. Rejecting the assimilationist posture of the times, Carlebach's disciples lamented those who were "nominally Jews" and invoked traditional Jewish sources to bring wayward souls back to the faith. The California counterculture, they believed, diverted too many young Jews from the meaningful traditions of their ancestors. "Our children joined with these others in seeking a society in which they could belong," one House leader explained, "They sought it in new music, the new (old) dress, the odd dress, the new politics, the new religions, and the new mind expanders, the drugs." Mainstream Jewish leaders, he lamented, stood "hopelessly by on the sidelines, bemoaning the loss of our children, but doing little more than wailing and wringing our hands over the loss of this generation which has rejected our values or lack of values."

As one of the House's first residents proclaimed, Rabbi Carlebach "completely changed my life." A student at San Francisco State University, this newfound Jewish soul acknowledged that he rarely studied, smoked marijuana, and took acid trips. "I was looking," he explained, "for a way to get beyond all the boredom and ugliness and hatred I saw in the world around me, to experience real beauty and truth. That's why I took drugs." Once he began his studies at the House of Love and Prayer, he rejoiced, "I can get high without drugs. Our great rabbis and teachers have been getting high for centuries on Torah and prayer." Other students expressed their newfound Jewish identities by journeying to Israel. Two House of Love and Prayer alumni announced their intention to make *aliyah* and create an Israeli version of the San Francisco alternative yeshiva. Eventually more than two dozen fellow graduates joined them in the Jewish state.

Six years after Carlebach opened the House of Love and Prayer, a group of East Bay Jews attended a series of seminars led by Lubavitch-trained rabbi Zalman Schachter. They were inspired by Schachter's love of Jewish life, emphasis on prayer and spirituality, and desire to welcome unaffiliated Jews into the religious fold. With help from their newfound rebbe, they formed Berkeley's Aquarian Minyan and set out to create a symmetry

Invitation to the Aquarian Minyan's High Holy Days worship services, 1976. Illustration by Susan Aftersut, Sara Sheidelman, and Yehudit Goldfarb. Courtesy of Yehudit and Reuven Goldfarb.

between the celebratory hasidic style of Jewish observance and the self-actualization mentality of many Bay Area Jews. The popularity of the Aquarian Minyan, and the challenges it faced, captured the essence of the California Jewish counterculture. It stood as an inward-directed Jewish institution focused on combating assimilation and strengthening levels of Jewish education and observance. It also borrowed in large measure from the secular values of San Francisco's progressive communities. In the Aquarian Minyan, worshippers could reconnect with their Jewish roots without compromising many of the era's larger political and social ideals.

In a sharp break from the universalist ideals of an earlier era, organizers of the Aquarian Minyan sought a prayer community devoted to Jewish tradition and practice. As one of the Minyan founders, Yehudit Goldfarb, noted, "we were taught the structure that underlies the [worship] service and given permission to play with it." In its founding documents, the Minyan professed commitment to Torah, the Jewish people, and the Divine. Organizers of this new experiment in religious observance wanted to create a "native Jewish spiritual community" based on legendary Hassidic rabbi Kook's precept of "making new the holy, and making holy the new." The Minyan embraced Rav Schachter's use of Jewish mysticism as a tool to redirect Jewish souls involved, as another Minyan founder Reuven Goldfarb explained, with "Eastern spiritual paths, psychedelics, encounter work, and other cleansing therapies, both physical and cognitive."

Leaders of the Aquarian Minyan also understood the need for creative change in Jewish religious life. The experiences of the 1960s social protest movements taught them the need for gender equality, democratic leadership, consensus-style organization, physical contact, alternative approaches to conventional questions and, in some cases, the unsanctioned use of mind-altering substances. While they adopted the Hebrew word *minyan* in their name to denote a Jewish-centered sense of community, they opted to call themselves the "aquarian" minyan because that word "implied the acceptance of the unconscious, non-rational parts of our being" and "set up a distinction between those Jewish groups in which ten men constituted a minyan and a group which believed every living being could be part of a minyan if the intention for 'connection' existed." They also employed guided meditation, intimate discussion groups, and dyads, which, according to another minyan leader, "enabled the participants to confront and befriend their inner selves."

Born in the midst of the feminist movement, the Aquarian Minyan rejected the male-centered practices of traditional Judaism and instead articulated an egalitarian approach to Jewish life. While Orthodox Judaism, and even many Conservative-movement synagogues, refused to allow women to read Torah or lead the congregation in prayer, the Minyan believed that "each individual has the potential and the function to act as spiritual leader." Organizers of the Aquarian Minyan extended their critique of mainstream Judaism by eschewing a formal synagogue building and praying instead in members' homes, where they believed they could achieve a stronger sense of community. While some first-time visitors to Minyan services reacted with occasional aloofness, the Aquarian leadership encouraged its membership to touch and embrace one another as yet another tool for better social relations and stronger community building.

Ironically, the Minyan's own desire to mix Jewish tradition and the California counterculture eventually led to

Aquarian Minyan founders Yehudit and Reuven Goldfarb, 1976. Courtesy of Yehudit and Reuven Goldfarb.

Aquarian Minyan by Jeffrey (Gabe) Dooley. Courtesy of Yehudit and Reuven Goldfarb.

some communal discord. Just as the Aquarian Minyan grew from its ability to marry larger cultural changes to its own Jewish-centered goals, the Berkeley experiment in progressive Judaism faltered when the religious culture of Bay Area Jewish life turned away from the consciousness-raising emphasis of the countercultural era.

As early as 1977, the Minyan suffered from the same sort of apathy that plagued traditional Jewish institutions. In a painful parallel to mainstream synagogue life, more than half of the Minyan's membership attended only High Holiday services. A few volunteers handled the lion's share of Minyan responsibilities. Frequent appeals for aid in the Minyan newsletter failed to light any fires. As Minyan leader Jacob Picheny blasted in a 1977 letter to the membership, "The center is not holding." Citing the group's own desire to embrace countercultural values, Picheny considered the possibility that his worship community had fallen victim to its own naïve ideals. "Perhaps the absence of a committed core in the Minyan," he wrote, "is an outcome of the loose and undemanding way we've functioned since the beginning. Perhaps on the seesaw between individual needs and group needs we've most often tilted the first way."

Other members took aim at some of the secular counterculture's most sacred institutions. Sandra Josephine Lee (Levi) pointed out that while the Minyan claimed to be a Jewish group, its members adhered to an unwritten code of conduct that discouraged worshippers from questioning the teachings of certain rabbis or gurus, the use of astrology and fortune telling, and, as Levi described, "the use of certain Hindu or other eastern chants which are often chanted to various gods and goddesses." She took particular offense at members who used drugs during the worship service: "if you use a drug that is going to put your head in a strange place," she pleaded, "please remember that your behavior will tend to put other people in a strange place also, whether they want to be there or not." In the spirit of a Minyan policy that permitted only vegetarian food out of respect for people's varying levels of kashruth, Levi asked that all communal worship embrace Jewish beliefs, rather than "a hodge podge of Sufism, Hinduism, fire breathing, etc., which is either offensive, prohibited or uncomfortable to those of us that lean toward traditional Judaism."

Karen Iris Bogen, then a student at Berkeley's Graduate Theological Union (GTU), shared Levi's concerns. "What is this 'new age consciousness' people talk about in the Minyan?" Bogen asked. According to the GTU student, it was not, as many Minyan members believed, a vehicle to "get high" on Judaism. Prayer, she believed, should be centered more on the opportunity "to interact socially and religiously with others." As Bogen posed in rhetorical fashion, "Religion can be a 'high'; but isn't it—or wasn't

it—intended to be an ethical imperative?" For Levi, Bogen, and other dissatisfied worshippers, the Aquarian Minyan had lost sight of Judaism's very essence. As Bogen concluded, "I would very much like to see the public values of morality, kindness, and manner brought back."

Other California religious leaders created similar types of Jewish countercultural experiences. In August, 1977, Rabbi Hanan Sills combined the learning-centered posture of the House of Love and Prayer, the experiential style of the Aquarian Minyan, and the pioneering spirit of the Zionists when he created a one-week kibbutz experience in California's Mendocino county, located two hours north of San Francisco. While he boasted activities that included yoga, organic gardening, improvisional theater, silk screening, a gestalt group, and evening campfires, Rabbi Sills sought a particular Jewish emphasis. His week's theme, "Joys of Jewishing and Connecting with Our Jewish Roots," reflected the larger countercultural shift towards heightened ethnic identity. He included sessions on the mystical traditions of Kabbalah, davening, Hassidic dancing, Yiddish music, and Jewish feminism. As the rabbi explained, he wanted to create "a place to have a Jewish experience on the land for those of us who don't want to go to Israel to get that connection."

By the 1970s, the Jewish-centered California counterculture developed from a group of small, independent efforts typical of the Aquarian Minyan, the HLP and the California Kibbutz experience into larger, better-organized alternative religious bodies. The California synagogue, once an institution of scorn to disaffected countercultural Jews, embraced many of the movement's most appealing creations, including its hallmark innovation, the havurah. In Los Angeles, Rabbi Schulweis pioneered the havurah at Valley Beth Shalom, where membership rocketed to more than 900 families after the new rabbi's arrival from Oakland. "The synagogue community has got to prove itself as having something to say in relationship to the moral, spiritual, and intellectual needs of a very new kind of Jewish hunger," Schulweis explained, "and that's what the chavurah structure—small groups, within the synagogues— makes possible." For Schulweis, the particular demographic profile of California Jews made the havurah experiment much more successful. "You've got at least 150,000 Jews concentrated in this [San Fernando] Valley area," he argued, "There is tremendous mobility, a shriveled extended family, and a sense of loneliness that's very marked, and all that encourages innovations such as

Hagigah, the Jewish Workshop in the Arts, UAHC Camp Swig, 1990.
Courtesy of Don May.

Bumper sticker for CAJE,
photographed by Lelo Carter
Courtesy of Skirball Cultural Center, gift of Adele Lander Burke.

chavurot." According to the Los Angeles rabbi, California Jews enjoyed a position "on the sharp edge of life." What happened in the Golden State, he observed, "happens back East five to ten years later."

The Reform movement's Camp Swig in Saratoga and the Conservative movement's Camp Ramah in Ojai embraced the turn inward as well. Jewish music replaced popular American folk songs. Counselors became *madrichim*,

and *rashei eidah* (unit heads) focused each session on a particular Jewish educational theme. Zionism emerged as a major component in California Jewish camping when Camp Swig invited a group of Israelis from Kibbutz Reim to design and build a new agricultural collective on a piece of undeveloped camp property. In Los Angeles, the Bureau of Jewish Education created a year long camp-style ninth-grade program called *Havurat Noar*. While students attended their religious schools for regular weekly instruction, every six weeks they journeyed to Camp Hilltop in Malibu for a weekend of experiential Jewish living and learning. According to longtime Havurat Noar leader Eddie Friedman, the high school program proved well suited to the geographic isolation of Los Angeles Jews. "We have a whole bunch of little communities, each with its own temple and its own school," he explained, "I think that camping is much more important to us than to other communities. . . .

Camps," he explained, "help to compensate for our geographic dispersion."

Just as many of the radical activists of the 1960s eventually accommodated to a more mainstream lifestyle, the Jewish counterculture lost strength when moderate Jewish organizations co-opted some of its most important innovations. In one sense, the California Jewish counterculture fell victim to its own creativity and imagination. As the movement's leaders offered wayward Jews a sense of meaning and purpose, they opened up broad new programmatic possibilities for synagogues, Jewish Community Centers, and their affiliated groups. Havurah membership forms are now included in most synagogues' new membership packets.

Informal Jewish education, pioneered in the experiential world of Jewish summer camping, has become a staple of Jewish day schools, supplemental schools, and even senior citizen elderhostel programs. The pathbreaking Jewish educational group CAJE reflected the embrace of mainstream Judaism when it changed its name from the Coalition for *Alternatives* in Jewish Education to the Coalition for *Advancement* in Jewish Education. The Reform movement has already opened its second California summer camp, Camp Newman in Santa Rosa, while officials from Camp Ramah continue to look for ways to meet the incredible demand for their limited bunk space. For many contemporary Jewish youth raised with summer camping, Israel programs, and a heightened sense of their own ethnic identity, the California counterculture may seem a distant memory. For a 1960s generation of social reformers intent on changing the ways Jews express their Judaism, though, the younger generation's unwitting embrace of their movement's goals stands as the greatest, and most powerful, sign of its success.

Directory of Sources

Most of the primary source documents for this chapter can be found in the Aquarian Minyan, Hillel Foundation, and Jewish Radical collections of the Western Jewish History Center located at the Magnes Museum in Berkeley. The American Jewish Historical Society archives at the Center for Jewish History in New York City also house materials from the California Jewish counterculture. Students of the California counterculture may wish to consult Stanley S. Rothman and S. Robert Lichter, *Roots of Radicalism: Jews, Christians, and the Left* (Transaction Publishers, 1996), Thomas Piazza, "Jewish Identity and the Counterculture," appearing in Charles Y. Glock and Robert N. Bellah, editors, *The New Religious Consciousness* (University of California Press, 1976). The University of California, Berkeley, has initiated an ambitious web-based research archive titled, "The Free Speech Movement Project," that can be accessed at the following url: http://www.lib.berkeley.edu/BANC/FSM/.

CHAPTER 14

CONTEMPORARY ART GLASS

A PHOTO ESSAY FEATURING THE STAINED GLASS OF DAVID AND MICHELLE PLACHTE-ZUIEBACK

The personal and professional lives of stained glass artists David and Michelle Plachte-Zuieback mirrored the journey of many Jewish California counterculturalists. Born and raised in Los Angeles, David and Michelle rejected the middle-class comforts of west Los Angeles and the San Fernando Valley in favor of a forty-acre parcel of undeveloped land an hour's drive from the town of Willits, itself located 150 miles north of San Francisco in California's Mendocino County.

Without electricity or running water, the Plachte-Zuiebacks built a homestead, created a stained glass studio, and began their lives as professional artists. In their early career, David and Michelle focused on secular themes, incorporating motifs of California grapes into a window for a Willits restaurant, teaching art in the local public schools, and spearheading grant proposals for the city government.

In the summer of 1983, the Plachte-Zuiebacks joined the staff of UAHC Camp Swig's Hagigah workshop in the Jewish arts. At once teaching high school–age Jewish youth the art of stained glass and immersing themselves in experiential Jewish life, the Plachte-Zuiebacks, joined now by daughter Becky, started a twenty-year camp career that brought them and their students from simplistic windows comprising repeating Star of David panes to complex art glass capturing themes of social justice, Jewish identity, and classical text.

Eventually, David and Michelle moved from Willits to the much larger town of Santa Rosa where they joined a community of Jewish artists and participated in Simcha Sunday, a Sonoma County celebration of Jewish life. They began work on a series of synagogue installations that in-

cluded Rabbi Harold Schulweis's Valley Beth Shalom in Encino, California, Temple Emanu-El in San Diego, Congregation Beth Am in the Los Altos Hills, and the Shirley Levine Beit Midrash on the Northridge campus of the Heschel Day School.

With these commissions, the Plachte-Zuiebacks brought aesthetic meaning to the larger California Jewish turn inward. Whether at the congregational birthplace of the California havurah movement or within one of Los Angeles' first community day schools, David and Michelle's artistry captured a larger movement from secularism to tradition and revealed the powerful impulse that returned many California Jews to a more educated and identified form of Jewish expression.

In the contemporary era, the Plachte-Zuieback's career has changed focus yet again. After completing synagogue window installations in locations as varied as Nashville, Tennessee, Paramus, New Jersey, and Fayetteville, North Carolina, David and Michelle have started work on their first major church installation. Drawing on their knowledge and experience in synagogue art glass, the Plachte-Zuiebacks interfaith work makes important connections between different religious groups. The universalist ideals that first drew David and Michelle to embrace a countercultural life in Willits now brings them into dialogue with their Christian neighbors as they search for ways to visually represent Christian theology for a new generation of churchgoers.

On the pages that follow, you will find a representative sample from the Plachte-Zuieback's artistic journey. (See also the color plates.)

Hurwitz residence, Beverly Hills, 1978. This work focused on the theme of bougainvillea flowers and is typical of the floral style the Plachte-Zuiebacks developed during their early days in Willits. Courtesy of Michelle and David Plachte-Zuieback.

(Also see color plate.)

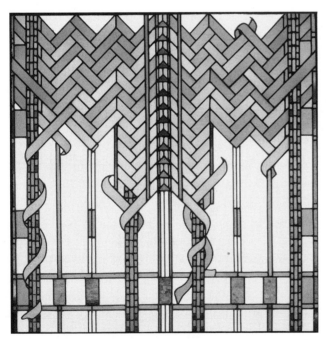

Signer residence, Beverly Hills. Completed in 1984 for the home of a Hebrew Union College professor and rabbi, this forty-eight-inch-square panel bears the inscription, "Yesh M'ayin" (literally, "something from nothing"), a term describing a medieval theory of the origin of the Universe. Courtesy of Michelle and David Plachte-Zuieback.

(Also see color plate.)

One of many windows created by campers at UAHC Camp Swig, "Jewish Identity" expresses the individual creativity of more than 150 young people. This composition represents a view of the giving of the Ten Commandments at Sinai as seen from beneath the fringes of a tallit while the first shema *illuminates the landscape. Courtesy of Michelle and David Plachte-Zuieback and UAHC Camp Swig. (Also see color plate.)*

Study at Valley Beth Shalom, Encino, 1997. A pomegranate, symbol
of the Torah, splits open and spills books, including a page of Talmud
and a Hebrew alphabet, dotted with honey to make learning sweet.
The Talmud page was rendered by silk screening high-fire glass
enamels directly onto the glass before firing them in the kiln. Painted
dichroic glass creates the seeds within the pomegranate.
Courtesy of Michelle and David Plachte-Zuieback.
(Also see color plate.)

"Divine Spark," Congregation Beth Am, Los Altos Hills, California,
1999. Lightning occurs when the heavens touch the earth.
In this interpretation of Redemption and the splitting of the
Red Sea, lightning flashes, a pillar of cloud looms, and a rolling sea
separates. Sound ripples the crackling atmosphere in a moment of
elemental power. In the open position, set for worship, a new
stained glass setting is created, representing the elements of
Revelation: earth, fire, air, and water. Six hundred-thirteen
dichroic stars are spread, like sparks, from the tips of the flame
that is a letter shin. It is the cauldron of Creation, the tip of
Mount Sinai, an image of the presence of God.
Courtesy of Michelle and David Plachte-Zuieback.
(Also see color plate.)

Back of "Divine Spark," Congregation Beth Am, Los Altos Hills.
The three-dimensional character of this installation is evident
when viewed from the exterior. The desert rock of Sinai and
the elemental shin-shaped flame stand out against the
background of lightning and darkness.
Courtesy of Michelle and David Plachte-Zuieback.

Lopati Chapel, Valley Beth Shalom, Encino, 1992.
This symbolic composition on the theme "It is a tree of life to
them who hold fast to it" consists of fifteen stained glass panels,
two sandblast-carved ark doors, and two eternal lights.
Courtesy of Michelle and David Plachte-Zuieback.
(Also see color plate.)

CHAPTER 15

SHLOMO BARDIN'S "ERETZ" BRANDEIS

BRUCE J. POWELL

*At a ripe old age, he was still full of plans and dreams and goals and he had a whole list of
unfinished dreams ahead of him. — Rabbi Jack Riemer, BCIer, 1947*

The life and dreams and accomplishments of Shlomo Bardin are bound up with the legacy he bequeathed to California—the Brandeis Collegiate Institute, House of the Book, Camp Alonim, all part of the Brandeis-Bardin Institute. Perhaps Bardin chose Southern California because of the unending sunshine that enabled him to operate programs year-round. Or perhaps it was the ready availability of Hollywood money. I believe, however, that Bardin saw among the people of postwar Los Angeles a willingness to pioneer; he saw a community unlike the deeply rooted East Coast Jews. In Los Angeles, he found people willing to take chances, to build, to dream, to plant their own unique roots.

Bardin's dreams touched the lives of thousands of American Jews and shaped the vision and dreams of some of California's most distinguished Jewish leaders. His story is a fascinating odyssey leading to the thirty-one-hundred-acre grounds of the Brandeis-Bardin Institute in Simi Valley, California, a place so large that it has its own zip code. According to California law, the Institute director may perform weddings and is also the postmaster. It is, perhaps, the largest piece of Jewish community–owned real estate in the world, outside of Israel. Bardin's story and the continuing legacy of Brandeis-Bardin in California is one in which Jewish values, formed upon the backdrop of tumultuous world events and a loving and rich Jewish home, found fertile ground under the California sun where, in 1947, all was possible.

*Dr. Shlomo Bardin, founder of the Brandeis Institute.
Courtesy of the Brandeis-Bardin Institute.*

Bardin's Life and Times

Shlomo Bardin's life spanned a time that witnessed the complete transformation of the modern world. The impact of the Russian revolution, two world wars and the building of the State of Israel were writ large upon the soul and psyche of one Russian Jew, who was determined to take part in that transformation, and who subsequently left a mark upon the Jewish world, and especially upon the Jews of California, that he never imagined possible.

At the turn of the twentieth century, life for the Jews in Russia was, at best, precarious. Czar Nicholas had little concern for what befell the Jews. Pogroms were often a matter of course in smaller towns, and discrimination against Jews was the norm in the cities. Many Jews chose to emigrate to America, and thousands more would follow over time. A few, imbued with the Zionist fervor of the day, traveled the more dangerous path to Palestine.

Into this milieu Shlomo Bardinstein was born in Zhitomir on December 3, 1898. Fortunately for young Bardinstein, his family was financially comfortable. His father, Hayim, owned a distilling business, while his mother, Menia, played the conventional role of housewife and homemaker. From all accounts, Shlomo grew up in a stable, loving family setting. Bardin's parents also appeared to be Jewishly knowledgeable. Jewish wisdom, values, practice and law informed matters of substance. Bardin often explained that even though his father was in the distilling business, there were few drunks among the forty thousand Jews of Zhitomir. Bardin credited this fact to the strong Jewish values that seemed to permeate the Jewish community at the time. Indeed, as this brief history unfolds, the values Bardin learned and incorporated into his own life would eventually find their way to his creation of BCI—the Brandeis Collegiate Institute (formerly known as the Brandeis Camp Institute)—thirty years later.

Bardin's family had a powerful Zionistic passion. His first language was Hebrew, followed by Yiddish and Russian. Like most Jewish boys in those years, Bardin received a multifaceted education. The early morning would find all of the Jewish boys attending the local *heder*. Here they learned the classical Hebrew texts including Bible, Talmud, and Midrash. By age seven, Bardin could quote biblical sources by heart. Achievement in Jewish learning was respected and prized by the community.

After heder, Bardin attended the secular Russian school where he acquired general knowledge and skills. For most Jews, the secular school was of secondary importance to Jewish learning, but even more important to Bardin were the values he learned in his parents' home. He often spoke of these values to his students. For example, at age nine he learned that life was a "trust." Our physical bodies and our time on this earth were for a special purpose. It was therefore incumbent upon each human being to find that purpose and to act accordingly. Wasting a life violated the most basic covenant between humankind and God. Bardin also learned that just as the earth was on loan to humans and must be returned, so too our lives were "on loan" from God and must be returned in perhaps better condition than when we received them.

Bardin's education in Jewish values extended to every aspect of his life. His parents taught that "happiness" was not an "act of life," but a mode of living. One did not seek happiness as one sought after a particular commodity. One experienced happiness by living a certain "way." This path or way could be found in the richness of Jewish life and tradition, in the context of a well-ordered life. Haphazard, undirected living would not bring happiness; purposeful, deliberate actions created a satisfied existence.

From his home and community, Bardin inherited the meaning and beauty of the Jewish Sabbath. Fridays were spent shopping, cooking, cleaning, and making all necessary preparation. Bardin often explained that his home never smelled "neutral." One could tell the day of the week from the odors emanating from his mother's kitchen. The Sabbath ambience was, literally, in the air.

Saturday morning the family would walk to *shul* (synagogue). The men and women sat separately, the women taking their places in the balcony while the men prayed below. Bardin saw this arrangement as a very practical matter. The Russian Jewish tradition dictated that only the married men would wear the *tallit* (prayer shawl) during the service. This would allow the women sitting above to identify the unmarried men. In this way, mothers with unwed daughters would discuss with the matchmaker who might be a suitable candidate for the *huppah* (wedding canopy). Telling this story forty years later at BCI, Bardin reminded the campers that there were no "old maids" in Zhitomir.

Bardin seemed to take great pride in the nearly one hundred percent rate of marriage in his town. He believed that it was a characteristic of a community that truly cared about its citizens. No one should be alone; partnership and companionship were a universally held

BRUCE J. POWELL

value and it was the community's task to ensure that everyone who wanted could benefit from this value in a very real way.

For Bardin, caring also extended to the dead. He grew up in a community where many of the most prominent Jews in his town participated in the *hevra kadisha* (holy society for the purpose of burying the dead under Jewish law). It was both an honor and a sacred responsibility to ensure a proper and respectful burial for those who died. No commercial burial service was available. Caring for those who could not return the favor stood paramount as a Jewish value and had a great impact upon Bardin's future vision of education and life. He carried this powerful theme with him in his formulation of BCI.

Young Bardin also learned the value and importance of strength. When word of an ensuing pogrom reached his family, all of the women and children would be shipped off to the nearby town of Berditchev until the danger passed. Berditchev, also a town filled with Jews, was safe from pogroms. There were large numbers of Jewish thieves who lived in the town, and these men were armed and willing to fight against the rampaging peasants. For this reason, Berditchev was never attacked. Bardin realized that Jews who were willing to fight back could live in relative peace. He carried this lesson with him during his years in Palestine, and even during the early days of establishing BCI in California. He often told the campers that he would sleep with a rifle under his bed just in case some local antisemites in Simi Valley might decide that the Jews ought not own so much land in "their" neck of the woods.

As was the case with most young Russian Jewish intellectuals in the early 1900s, Bardin was involved in the heated debates about whether or not socialism would be the answer to the Jews' desire for free and equal access to all facets of Russian life. Most believed it was the only salvation for the Jews in a time of often rabid antisemitism, discrimination, and physical attacks against Jews.

Two years after the Russian revolution in October 1917, twenty-one-year-old Bardin and his friends recognized that communism would offer no help for the Jews. In 1919 he and his group left for Palestine. Between 1919 and 1928, Bardin spent six years in Palestine working on a kibbutz or teaching Hebrew in small development towns, two years studying at the University of Berlin, and one year at London University.

In addition to the educational and administrative expe-rience Bardin gained during this period, he also formed important insights into the value and meaning of a university education. He discovered that at none of the universities he attended, which totaled four in different lands, was moral education an important factor. He often quipped that someone could be a Ph.D. and an S.O.B. at the same time. On a more serious note, he often pointed out that in Germany, where university learning was at its highest level, many of Hitler's elite advisors and policy makers held doctorates from German universities.

In 1928, Bardin arrived in the United States from Palestine in order to pursue masters and doctoral degrees at Teachers College of Columbia University. Bardin was exposed to perhaps the most important American educators of this century including John Dewey and George Counts, who were to have a profound influence on young Bardin, as we shall see in his later work.

Bardin made his first social contacts at the International Students House at Columbia. There he encountered a variety of students with different backgrounds and religions. Bardin recalled that there were a number of Jews among the foreign students who continually tried to hide their Jewishness. Bardin was perplexed by this behavior. He discovered that by accenting his own Jewishness, he was better able to relate to students of differing religions and ethnicities. Indeed, making strength out of Judaism's unique values system earned Bardin both respect and trust. These encounters also planted for Bardin the question of why Jewish students were "in flight" from their Judaism. Finding the answer to this question would form the basis of Bardin's work in developing BCI.

Bardin's ideas and vision earned him a speaking engagement at the Faculty Club of Columbia University in 1930. In his speech he claimed that Americans did not believe in *education*. Rather, they believed in organized *schooling*, in *measuring* and *shaping*. He argued that schools must create an atmosphere and discipline under control of teachers who have high ideals and values, and who should bring students up to those ideals. Success did not mean, "succeed"; instead, it implied results in values, ideals, and positive behaviors.

Bardin also found a great dichotomy in the American system. On the one hand, he saw that the American people have a great and lasting faith in education, while, at the same time, they place the educational system in the hands of immature teachers. He saw the genius of the system to be in its structure, while inside the schools he found chaos, muddled thinking, blurry purpose, weak mission, and general lack of direction.

He concluded his speech by proposing that the humanities should take a central place in the curriculum. Science, he argued, tells us nothing of life or how to behave; it does not provide meaning, just description and application of technology. For Bardin, science was amoral, and therefore antithetical to a "good" education. Later in his life, Bardin would formulate the basis for a residential Jewish preparatory high school where Judaism informed and shaped the core of a humanities curriculum. He would argue that just as Christianity formed the humanities core for the great American prep schools such as Phillips Exeter and Andover, so too might Judaism serve this purpose within a Jewish high school.

This radical notion would have to wait sixty years before finding direct application with the formation of several dozen Jewish high schools in America at the turn of the twenty-first century. In Los Angeles, as the first headmaster of the Milken Community High School and the founding head of school of New Community Jewish High School, I have integrated many of Bardin's ideas into the educational fabric of those two institutions. Today, Milken Community High School, with over eight hundred students in grades seven through twelve, and the New Community Jewish High School stand, in part, as the living reality of many values taught to me at BCI and Camp Alonim.

It is no surprise that these two Jewish high schools have developed within the vibrant California landscape. The pioneering spirit that existed subsequent to World War II remains to this day. Great Jewish California leaders such as Rabbi Isaiah Zeldin and Rabbi Harold Schulweis in the greater L.A. area, philanthropists Noah Alper and Bobby Lent in northern California, and Anne Jaffe in San Diego, have all built upon that spirit. Almost miraculously, by fall 2002, there will be six full-service Jewish high schools along the fertile coast of California.

Impressed by Bardin's vision and insights, Professor George Counts took Bardin under his wing and introduced him to the Danish Folk High School (DFHS). With the help of Columbia University, Bardin traveled to Denmark to observe first-hand the workings and philosophy of this unique Danish invention. This visit would be a seminal event in Bardin's educational thinking.

The Danish Folk High School was designed to help preserve Danish culture and values against the historical backdrop of powerful German cultural incursions into Denmark during the mid 1850s. The school serviced Danish farm boys of high-school age during the cold Danish winters when farm work was impossible to conduct. They attended these schools for three or four months, where they were exposed to Danish folk art, music, dance, and drama within the context of Christian values and practices. The DFHS model would become the template for Bardin's later design of the BCI program.

Bardin finished his doctorate in education at Columbia in 1932. His dissertation, *Pioneer Youth in Palestine*, published as a book by Bloch Publishing Company in New York dealt with the pioneering youth *aliyah* movement in Palestine as well as with the philosophy of A. D. Gordon, the great nineteenth-century thinker. Gordon believed that the only salvation for the Jews of Europe was to return to Palestine and perform physical labor upon the land. He believed that middle-class European Jewish decadence had to be overcome. To this end, Gordon was one of the founders of *Degania*, the first kibbutz in what would later become the State of Israel. In founding the Brandeis-Bardin Institute, Bardin attributed great influence to Gordon's famous dictum, *Torah im derech eretz*—the learning of *Torah* while engaged in physical labor. Bardin would even integrate physical labor at BCI as an essential part of the educational experience.

Louis D. Brandeis: The Conversation

Bardin's tenure at Columbia afforded him the opportunity to meet many notable people. In 1931, according to an unpublished history of Bardin by Benjamin Herson, Bardin attended a dinner party where he met Mable Walker Willowbrandt, deputy attorney general in the Hoover administration. Herson explained that Willowbrandt "recognized in Bardin a kindred spirit" to then Supreme Court Justice Louis D. Brandeis. She was insistent that the two should meet, and that very evening she telephoned Brandeis at his home in Massachusetts. One week later, Bardin held the first of what was to become a long series of meetings over the next ten years with the great Justice Brandeis.

At their first meeting, Brandeis posed a number of troublesome questions. "How does one stop the flight of young American Jews from identifying with their people, their heritage, their culture?" "How do you make the great ethical heritage of Judaism meaningful and relevant to them?" Bardin recalled that Brandeis was convinced that

Jews who would not or could not identify with their culture and history were maladjusted human beings. He argued that this maladjustment was not good for Judaism, nor was it healthy for America. "To be good Americans," he told Bardin, "we must be better Jews." Herson elucidated Brandeis's concern more fully:

> The question of continuity, of transmitting the Jewish heritage to the new generation of young Americans, deeply concerned Justice Brandeis during those critical years (prior to World War II). His own life was a drama of self-discovery as Jew and Zionist. It was becoming clear as the decade unfolded that American Jewry was destined to play a crucial role in the struggle for Jewish survival.

Even though Bardin shared Brandeis's concern for the American Jew, much work still remained to be accomplished in Palestine. Herson explained that the pioneering spirit in Bardin beckoned him to return to Palestine. Bardin believed himself in no position to answer Brandeis's call.

Bardin returned to Palestine in 1932, with his wife Ruth Jonas Bardin, and began breaking new educational ground. (Bardin met his wife when he was engaged by the Jonas family of New York to tutor their daughter Ruth, in Hebrew. This job was arranged for Bardin by Dr. Samuel Dinin, one of the founders of the University of Judaism and the Bureau of Jewish Education in Los Angeles.)

Greatly impressed by the structure and success of the Brooklyn Technical High School he had visited in New York, Bardin founded the Haifa Technical High School in 1933, based upon the Brooklyn model. The need for well-trained technicians for the building of Palestine's budding industrial enterprises was a top priority at that time.

In 1938, Bardin was also instrumental in founding the Haifa Nautical School, the first such institution to teach Jews how to be seamen. Bardin convinced David Ben-Gurion that the Jews must be prepared to operate their own ships and ports. Dependency upon others might spell disaster for the barely surviving *yishuv* (Jewish settlement) economy in Palestine. As Herson observed, "In those early pioneering labors, Bardin was already manifesting those attributes of character which made him an iconoclast and seeker of new pathways in the field of education."

During subsequent visits to America, Bardin met regularly with Brandeis. Bardin would expound upon his great progress with his schools in Palestine, and Brandeis would continue to explain the problem of Jews in flight from themselves in America. This conversation continued over eight years, and it was not until the outbreak of World War II that circumstances began to dictate Bardin's future course.

On a trip to New York with his family in 1939, Bardin was unable to return to Palestine because of the outbreak of the war in Europe. Herson noted "it was then that Bardin decided to take up the challenge (of Brandeis) to do something for the American Jew."

At first, Bardin wanted to enter the industrial sector for purposes of making money. Immediate financial security and success seemed to be a priority at the time. Seeing the folly of this choice, Bardin's wife Ruth and their good friend Manya Shochat, a founder of K'far Giladi in Palestine, conspired with Brandeis to keep Bardin in the field of education.

Bardin finally agreed to accept Brandeis's challenge and approached the jurist with a plan that encompassed the elements of the Danish Folk High School and Palestinian kibbutz reset within the American summer camp environment. Bardin would assemble a group of college-age students for a one-month exposure and exploration of Jewish art, music, drama, and dance, and to the rich intellectual, cultural, and religious traditions of Judaism. Impressed by the plan, Brandeis called it "a laboratory for living Judaism," and offered to raise the funds needed for the camp. In 1941, the Summer Camp Institute (renamed Brandeis Camp Institute after Brandeis's death in the fall of 1941, the name was changed again in 1976 to Brandeis-Bardin Institute after Bardin's death) opened its doors at a Young Judea campsite near Amherst, New Hampshire.

The Brandeis-Bardin Institute: History and Programs

After a successful start on the grounds of the Young Judea in New Hampshire, Bardin reported back to Brandeis on what had transpired during the summer. Brandeis, understanding the need for ongoing financial support, pledged half the program's budget and agreed to raise the rest from East Coast sources. Five weeks after Bardin and his head counselor, Gisela Warburg, reported to Brandeis, the great justice passed away in September 1941. Bardin received permission from Brandeis's wife to rename the camp the Brandeis Camp Institute (BCI).

In 1943, a gift from Abraham Goodman of New York

Shlomo and Ruth Bardin with sons David and Hillel at the Brandeis Camp Institute, Winterdale, Pennsylvania, 1943. Courtesy of the Brandeis-Bardin Institute.

made it possible for BCI to vacate its rented facilities and move to its own grounds in Winterdale, Pennsylvania, in the Pocono Mountains. Here, the vision that Bardin had synthesized from the ideas of the Danish Folk High School, kibbutz, and American summer camp, took firm root. Success of the initial project prompted, as Herson called it, "an empire-building mood," and thus plans for expansion of the project unfolded.

Inspired by the effect of BCI upon their daughter, Julius and Molly Fliegelman of Los Angeles urged Bardin to locate a second BCI in California, which opened in 1947. A third camp was also proposed and opened in Hendersonville, North Carolina, in 1948.

As the decade of the 1940s drew to its dramatic close, the American Jewish community began to realize its own prominence in world Jewish affairs. More and more American Jews needed to synthesize their own identity and purpose in the United States. The Zionist movement, which had been in the forefront of the struggle for Jewish survival, faced a difficult paradox with the establishment

"Eretz (land of) Brandeis!"
Courtesy of Hannah R. Kuhn, photographer. (Also see color plate.)

BRUCE J. POWELL

First aliyah in California, 1947.
Courtesy of the Brandeis-Bardin Institute.

of the State of Israel in 1948. The Zionist primary goal of Jewish statehood in Palestine had been achieved. What purpose were they now to serve? These events were important to the shaping of the program at BCI. The early Zionist concerns of the camp no longer existed, now replaced by the more urgent demands for intelligent Jewish leadership in the United States.

Finding the financial burdens of operating three camps simultaneously too expensive, Bardin and the Zionist Organization of America (ZOA), under whose auspices Bardin had been receiving part of his funding, decided to close down the Winterdale and Hendersonville sites, establishing permanent headquarters in California. The camp made this move so that the program could expand into a year-round operation without sacrificing the quality of the program, especially during the winter months. In 1950, believing that the purposes and philosophy of BCI and the ZOA had drifted apart, Bardin decided to incorporate BCI as an independent, nonprofit entity. Herson be-

lieved that this incorporation marked a "a new and vigorous phase in its history."

BCI and BBI in California

The California camp has a unique and interesting history, one tightly bound up with the life and times of Southern California from 1947 to the present. Bardin and Julius and Molly Fliegelman, prominent Los Angeles business leaders, searched for an appropriate piece of land for the camp, one that would be within two hours of the Jewish population of greater Los Angeles at the time. In 1947 they came upon a twenty-two-hundred-acre parcel in Simi Valley, northwest of the city and about an hour's drive from Beverly Hills. Interestingly, the land and buildings were owned by the Brew 102 Beer Company, and used as a retreat center for its employees. With the financial help of Joseph Foster (of Foster Grant sunglasses fame), Bettie and Joseph Rifkind, and many others, the land was purchased.

BCIers in California, 1947, with Bardin standing on the right. McElroy and Fisher Photo.
Courtesy of the Brandeis-Bardin Institute.

The rolling hills on the property reminded Bardin of the Judean wilderness in the "Land of Israel." Perhaps in some way Bardin saw this land as "Israel writ small." As time would show, Bardin made the right choice. Most participants in any of the many BBI programs seem to be drawn to the land itself in a way that often compels a return visit, furthering the programs and the vision unique to BBI. Bardin had, indeed, found "*eretz* (land of) Brandeis!"

The first problem for the new site arose immediately. In 1947, Simi Valley had yet to gain access to water from Los Angeles so that a fresh water supply had to be found on the premises. This was no easy task. According to some accounts, thirty-nine wells were dug without any luck, and additional financial resources had to be found before the digging could continue. Finally, on the fortieth attempt (although this *fact* is perhaps more legend than fact), Herson explains, the "earth responded and the whisper of a hidden spring was discovered on the western boundary of the property." This discovery allowed the first BCI *aliyah* (session) to commence in July of 1947.

It is interesting to note that Bardin employed the term "aliyah," a term generally reserved for "going up" or emigrating to the State of Israel. My sense is that the word *aliyah* itself bound the BCI participants to Israel. Perhaps he also felt that one's participation in the program was a form of a spiritual "going up." For many who moved to California after World War II, their move to the Golden State was, indeed, a "going up," a move toward a pioneering enterprise, a new life in a land of endless material and spiritual opportunity.

The early faculty and staff of the Institute established the California camp as the undisputed home of BCI. Raiken Ben-Ari (1898–1968) was the drama director at BCI (and subsequently at Camp Alonim, the children's division of the Brandeis-Bardin Institute), for more than two decades. As a young man, Ben-Ari was very involved in the New York Yiddish Theater and was one of the founding members of *HaBimah* Theatre Company. Later he became drama coach to actors including Marlon Brando. He joined with Bardin in the late 1940s and served as an important artistic and Jewish influence at BCI.

BRUCE J. POWELL

Max Helfman (1901–1963) served at BCI and Camp Alonim for nearly twenty years as the director of music. In California, Helfman found "open ears" and fresh thinking. Instead of having to fit into established traditions, the California context allowed him to create anew. His efforts enabled BBI to develop a unique collection of Jewish musical arrangements. Helfman's music, often original to BBI, fulfilled Bardin's desire not to identify with any extant Jewish denomination or movement. In Bardin's view, BBI needed to remain independent of the established Jewish community and thereby become a true, pluralistic, nondogmatic, nonjudgmental meeting ground for all Jews and all Jewish ideas. Helfman's arrangements, original pieces, and especially his liturgical creations are still used at BBI today, and many are in use throughout the Jewish world.

In 1959, Bardin discovered Dani Dassa, a young Israeli dancer studying with Martha Graham in New York. Bardin convinced Dani to move to Los Angeles with his wife Judy, and to establish a superior Israeli dance program for BBI. Over time, Dani's brilliant choreography, powerful personality, teaching expertise, and clear understanding of Jewish texts, history, and Israeli life created a deep culture of Israeli folk dance at BBI, and ultimately made Israeli dance a staple of Jewish life in all of Southern California.

Dani Dassa reminded me in a recent conversation that Dr. Bardin had challenged him "to teach Judaism through the legs because the legs move, and the mind remains static." Today at BCI, and especially at Camp Alonim, the dance program holds a central place in the life of the Institute. It is truly a wonder to behold Friday nights during the summer programs of Camp Alonim, where 350 campers aged eight to fifteen, counselors-in-training, and staff dance together to the music of traditional and contemporary Israeli songs. The Israel folk dancing not only touches the Jewish souls of the participants, but in some almost magical way, creates a gentle culture where twelve-year-old boys show special respect and kindness to ten-year-old girls. The fact that virtually every boy of every age dances, is itself evidence of the power of dance to build community within a Jewish context. Today, many of those ten-year-old girls and twelve-year-old boys, now in college, have formed the backbone of an Israeli dance culture that has become a staple of Jewish life at Hillels on college campuses throughout California and the nation. This culture of dance embraces hundreds of synagogue-sponsored events, b'nai mitzvah celebrations, and weddings. Many leaders within the California Jewish community trace their

Raikin Ben-Ari drama workshop with Camp Alonim campers. Courtesy of the Brandeis-Bardin Institute.

passion for Jewish life to Israeli folk dance with Dani Dassa. (Dani's legacy of dance continues to this day under the able leadership of his son, David Dassa.)

With Ben-Ari, Helfman, and Dassa in place at the Institute, and with his ability to attract distinguished Jewish teachers and scholars to BCI, Bardin was poised to fulfill his educational dream. Under the guidance of powerful artists and teachers who reflected intellectual maturity and deep values, the ideas of the Danish Folk High School were transformed from Danish arts and culture, to Jewish art, culture, values, and history. Upon the twenty-two-hundred-acre setting, the ideas of A. D. Gordon and the Israeli kibbutz movement found fertile ground. And within the freedom of America and the structure of the American summer camp, the Institute possessed the tools to implement its special voice.

A history of the California camp must acknowledge the prodigious efforts of Bettie Rifkind of Beverly Hills. Bettie, and her husband Judge Joseph Rifkind, were prominent leaders in the Beverly Hills community. The Judge had made his fortune doing legal work for several Los Angeles-based oil companies, and Bettie, a native of Kansas, served in the traditional role of mother and homemaker. Bardin's introduction to the Rifkind family was, according to some, the single most important connection in securing the success of the California enterprise.

Bettie Rifkind served Bardin from the very beginning of the California enterprise by first helping to raise large sums of needed capital and later performing the necessary public relations tasks for the camp. She served as a volunteer until 1954, when she became a paid member of the BBI staff. Bettie "took care" of the thousands of details

Dr. Bardin with Bettie and Judge Joseph J. Rifkind at Bardin's seventieth birthday, December 15, 1968.
Courtesy of the Brandeis-Bardin Institute.

necessary to make things operate smoothly. Bardin depended on her for arrangement of menus, housing assignments for important guests, fund raising, supervision of Camp Alonim, cleanliness, catering special parties for donors, and dozens of other personnel and public relations details. Bettie become the "soft, gentle" alter ego to the more charismatic, brash Bardin. Indeed, they were a professional marriage made in heaven.

In 1950, wanting to use the camp facilities on a year-round basis, Bardin organized the first adult weekend institutes. Thirty or forty men, and later couples, would spend an inspirational shabbat (sabbath) at camp, and experience a mini-BCI. The adults would participate in Jewish song, dance, and drama, hear lectures from world-renowned scholars, and spend hours together away from phones, radios, and televisions within the warmth and camaraderie of a rich shabbat environment.

From these weekends Bardin formed the House of the Book Association (HOB) composed of several hundred couples who served as the Institute's financial backbone. HOB became a model and wellspring for adult Jewish education in the greater Los Angeles area. Today, most synagogues offer "scholar-in-residence" weekends either in the city or at a local campsites modeled upon the pioneering efforts of HOB.

In 1953, Bardin established Camp Alonim for Jewish children aged eight to sixteen. Alonim is, at its core, BCI for kids. Bardin used the same elements as those employed by the college and adult programs, translating them appropriately for children.

The programs of BCI, Camp Alonim, and House of the Book weekends all share common threads. First, Bardin was masterful in his use of the arts "to touch and to teach" Judaism. Jewish singing, drama, dance, and visual art are a

BCI staff in July, 1970. (Left to right) John Silo (drama), Shlomo Bardin, Chanan Eisenstadt (music), and Dani Dassa (dance).
Rothschild photo.
Courtesy of the Brandeis-Bardin Institute.

part of almost every program. At BCI, for example, college-age students select one of four arts workshops for their twenty-six-day encampment. Each Saturday night, the workshops share their art with the entire group during the *melaveh malka* (literally, escorting the Sabbath queen) celebration that occurs at the end of the Jewish Shabbat. These artistic moments, "performed" by amateurs in the warm setting of a nonjudgmental community, serve as powerful examples of Jewish education at its best.

Second, based upon ideas formed at Columbia University in the 1930s, Bardin understood that compelling content and deep knowledge in the hands of great teachers would, indeed, "touch and teach." To this end, the BCI and HOB programs introduce participants to great Jewish thinkers who are passionate and articulate about their subjects. Bardin brought to California teachers such as Abraham Joshua Heschel, Mordechai Kaplan, Irving (Yitz) Greenberg (who credits Bardin with giving him his start

on the national Jewish scene), Trude Weiss-Rosmarin, Leonard Fein, Elie Wiesel, and a host of other now-famous Jewish celebrities. He brought to California a level of Jewish teaching and content that helped to uplift and transform the local Jewish scene.

Third, Bardin understood that the educational environment, in this case a natural setting where the sounds, smells, and sights would create memory, were essential to a powerful learning context. Indeed, the "place" of Brandeis-Bardin is so compelling that it would succeed in creating strong personal and community ties even without a program. Bardin somehow knew that the piece of California real estate he had selected would become, in and of itself, intrinsic to the success of the Institute.

Bardin's personal passion and understanding of the power of the land itself allowed him to develop a close relationship with Rolfe and James Arness, owners of a thousand-acre ranch located on the western border of the

Institute. (James Arness, as most will recall, was the star of the long-running television show, "Gunsmoke.") Arness would often visit Bardin during sessions of Camp Alonim, signing autographs for the campers, and challenging Shlomo to barbecuing contests, with the campers deciding who cooked the best hot dogs.

When Arness was approached by a home developer to buy his land, he and his father decided that the land must, instead, become part of the Brandeis-Bardin Institute. Over many years Bardin had inspired and impressed James and Rolfe Arness, both non-Jews, with his vision and educational philosophy. In 1972, James Arness gave his entire 1000-acre ranch to the Institute with the single stipulation that Rolfe be allowed to live on the land until his death. The Arness gift is certainly the largest single gift of land by a Jew or non-Jew to a Jewish institution in the history of California, and perhaps in the history of the United States. Today the Institute encompasses 3,100 acres of mostly undeveloped land and, thanks to James Arness, is permanently shielded from encroachment by the "outside" world.

A question arises as to why such a gift was made in California? Why hadn't this happened in the East? Perhaps the wide-open spaces of Southern California and the special relationships that form among those who respect and love the land lead to open minds, greater acceptance of those from all walks of life, and shared values, especially in the realm of natural preservation. James Arness and Shlomo Bardin shared this common California passion.

Bardin's Legacy

By the time of his death in May 1976, Dr. Bardin had created a precious legacy for the Jewish community of Southern California, and, some would argue, the Jewish world. The pioneering spirit of Los Angeles and Southern California just after World War II seemed an ideal match for Bardin's personality and vision. Everything seemed possible, and Bardin made those possibilities reality. He became part of the early L.A. pioneers that included Rabbi Edgar Magnin of Wilshire Boulevard Temple, Rabbi Max Nussbaum of Temple Israel of Hollywood, Jack Warner of Warner Brothers Studios (who donated used dressing rooms from his studio lot to the camp for housing), and Rabbi Isaiah Zeldin, who built his own synagogue and educational empire in the hills of Bel Air. Indeed, Bardin's contacts included virtually the entire pantheon of Los Angeles Jewish leadership of the 1940s, '50s, and '60s.

Gerald Bubis, founder of the Irwin Daniels School of Jewish Communal Service at Hebrew Union College in Los Angeles, credits Bardin with shaping the postwar Jewish Federation leadership of Los Angeles. Bardin provided a special enclave where community leaders could "recharge" their Jewish batteries, fill their spirits, and reinvigorate their vision of Jewish life.

Indeed, many of the powerful and visionary Jewish leaders to this day credit Brandeis-Bardin with helping them to become better leaders, as well as personally enriching their lives as Jews. Larry and Barbie Weinberg, major supporters of AIPAC, Barbie Weinberg as the first woman president of the Jewish Federation in Los Angeles, and powerful leaders on the California and national Jewish scene for the past thirty-five years, count BBI as one of their spiritual homes. Willard and Rita Chotiner, noted L.A. builders, Bettie and Ira (z'l) Weiner, real estate developers, Sidney Eisenstadt, prominent L.A. architect, Rabbi Alfred Gottschalk, past president of Hebrew Union College and builder of Hebrew Union College in Los Angeles, Ruth and John Rauch, real estate developers and founders of the Center of Jewish Culture and Creativity, and Steve Broidy, the great philanthropist most identified with Cedars-Sinai Hospital, all point to BBI as a center of Jewish empowerment and spirit.

Norman Corwin, a pioneer and creative genius of early radio entertainment, says of Bardin: "He did more to awaken an understanding of Judaism in me than a squadron of rabbis, meaning no disrespect to the reverends." Corwin was not the only entertainment luminary who was "touched" by Brandeis-Bardin. Max Laemmle, relative of Carl Laemmle, founder of Universal Studios and pioneer in the area of studio tours, became a major force both at BBI and in shaping the Southern California landscape. The Laemmle theaters in Los Angeles are known for hosting the Israeli film festival each year, as well as providing access to high-quality films for L.A. audiences. Gregg Laemmle, Max's grandson, fills the Laemmle legacy at BBI by serving on the board of directors of the Institute, and continuing in the family business.

Bardin also attracted to the Institute great writers and artists who worked in Hollywood, such as Michael Blankfort, creator of the television series "Broken Arrow," a very popular show for its time, and Mischa Kallis, creator of dozens of Hollywood movie sets. Bardin rekindled in Blankfort a connection to his Jewish roots in Brooklyn by inspiring him to write Jewish plays for performance at the camp. Among them was "Maimonides," a play that was used for more than thirty years to introduce new participants at the adult weekend institutes to this important figure in Jewish history. Blankfort's reattachment to Judaism was perhaps greatly enhanced as well.

In the same way, Bardin invited Mischa Kallis to serve as BCI's artist-in-residence for several of the summer sessions. He used his prodigious artistic skills to create wonderful Jewish art, which, to this day, adorns many of the walls at BBI. Both Blankfort and Kallis were important forces in shaping the artistic community of Los Angeles, and there is no doubt of BBI's impact upon their work.

The BBI tradition of attracting secular artists continues. People such as Lucas Richman, assistant conductor of the Pittsburgh Philharmonic, and David Low, master cellist and important force within the community of studio musicians in Los Angeles, both credit BBI with their intimate involvement in Jewish life, and in their efforts to use their musical talents to create Jewish musical statements.

Bardin also shaped much of the Jewish life of Los Angeles' medical community. Drs. Max Bay and Ludwig Strauss (both now deceased), prominent surgeons on the staff at Cedars-Sinai Hospital in Los Angeles since the mid–1940s, helped to recruit many physicians to attend an adult-weekend Institute at Brandeis-Bardin. In addition, while Dr. Bay served as the Institute president for ten years, Dr. Strauss took charge of recruiting doctors to serve in residence at camp for one-week stints during the summer sessions of BCI and Camp Alonim. During these weeks of voluntary service, the doctors were invited to attend lectures at BCI. Over time, the doctors were so moved by what they heard and saw at BCI and Camp Alonim that they, too, were "touched" by the Jewish spirit of the Institute, often infusing their own Jewish lives at home with greater participation in and observance of Jewish life.

The BBI experience was often so powerful that many of the adults who attended the weekend programs would return home determined to create study groups and send their children to BCI and Camp Alonim. Dr. Strauss and his wife Ada, with Bardin's guidance, formed what some would argue is Los Angeles' first independent study group, meeting monthly to review and analyze Jewish texts. The Strauss group, called Achedet Rishon (the First One), begun in 1967, still meets. This early version of a havurah inspired similar groups throughout the Los Angeles area and later influenced the establishment of the havurah groups in Boston and New York.

Over time, Bardin touched thousands of Jewish children and adults with his powerful, transformational magic that we know today as the Brandeis-Bardin Institute. Many of those thousands who experienced BCI, Camp Alonim, or HOB programs went on to major lay and professional leadership roles in the local and national Jewish world. They, in turn, "touched" thousands more with the beauty, meaning, and purpose of Jewish life.

Perhaps Rabbi Donniel Hartman, who spent six summers in residence at BCI after Bardin had passed from the scene, captures best the enduring influence and power of Brandeis-Bardin:

> We live in a community whose members expend a tremendous amount of energy reflecting on whose Judaism they accept and who accepts their Judaism. We seem to spend insufficient time on whether we accept our Judaism and whether we have created a Judaism worthy of acceptance. It is here that Brandeis-Bardin emerges as a unique institution. In a spirit of pluralism and openness, it challenges people to build a vibrant and serious Jewish life. Utilizing philosophy and the arts, it incorporates joy and meaningfulness as the foundation of a Judaism worth living.
>
> In a certain sense Brandeis-Bardin is an anachronism. It is out of touch with the "hot" debates and discussions permeating our community: from antisemitism, to "will there be one Jewish people in the year 2010?"
>
> "All" it cares about is that in the year 2010 Jews will have different Judaisms, each being vibrant and profound. It is on such anachronisms that our future depends.

Today the legacy of leadership shaped by Brandeis-Bardin, a quarter century after Bardin's death, continues. Dr. Bardin's core educational belief was "to touch and to teach." He argued that the "touching" (through Jewish arts and inspirational Jewish ideas) was for life. He believed that Jews were obligated to participate and to lead in the repair of the world. It was the covenant of the Jew to care, to be a mensch, to uphold the eternal values of Judaism that over half of humanity uses as the basis of its moral civilization.

Today, the Brandeis-Bardin Institute stands not as a final Jewish destination, but rather as a nonjudgmental, transdenominational Jewish celebration, an unselfish catalyst, a unique portal through which a Jew may touch

One of Bardin's dreams, the "House of the Book," on the Brandeis-Bardin campus, dedicated on July 22, 1973.
Designed by Sidney Eisenshtat, its dedication plaque reads: "'Come ye and let us go up to the mountain of the Lord,'
ancient words of Isaiah and Micah."
Courtesy of Hannah R. Kuhn, photographer. (Also see color plate.)

the Jewish past and create the Jewish future. Under the able leadership of Rabbi Dr. Lee Bycel, the legacy is in good hands.

Postscript

Shlomo Bardin did not approve of birthday celebrations. He would often say, "Birthdays? Not a Jewish idea." Rather, Jews celebrate one's *yahrzeit,* the day of death. Only then, he would argue, can we measure the achievements of a person's life.

It has been more than a hundred years since Bardin's birth. His life and deeds have transformed the lives and deeds of three generations. It would be difficult to imagine a California Jewish community without the influence of Brandeis-Bardin. The Jewish ethos, especially of Los Angeles, continues to reverberate with Israeli folk dance, scholar weekends at synagogues, thousands involved in havurot (study and social groups), rabbis who found their Jewish direction at BCI, and the existence of two Jewish community high schools educating future generations of Jewish leadership.

BRUCE J. POWELL

CONTRIBUTING AUTHORS

Lawrence Baron is the director of the Lipinsky Institute for Judaic Studies and the Nasatir Professor of modern Jewish history at San Diego State University. He is the founder and current president of the Western Jewish Studies Association.

Marc Dollinger, co-editor of *California Jews,* serves as the Richard and Rhoda Goldman Chair in Jewish studies and social responsibility at San Francisco State University. He is author of *Quest for Inclusion: Jews and Liberalism in Modern America.*

Ellen Eisenberg is professor of history at Willamette University in Salem, Oregon. Her published work includes *Jewish Agricultural Colonies in New Jersey 1882–1920* and several articles on Jewish communities in the American West.

Felicia Herman received her Ph.D. from Brandeis University, where she wrote her dissertation on the relationship between the American Jewish community and the motion picture industry from the 1910s to the 1940s. She has published several articles on that subject, as well as on the history of synagogue sisterhoods and the films of Barbra Streisand. She is currently a program officer at Jewish Life Network/Steinhardt Foundation.

William Issel is professor of history at San Francisco State University. He teaches courses on American social history and American religion, and he is the author or co-author of numerous works on the social and political history of San Francisco.

Ava F. Kahn, co-editor of *California Jews,* is a historian of western Jewish life, served as the visiting scholar at the California Studies Center, University of California, Berkeley and has taught in the Jewish Studies programs of the University of California at Davis and San Francisco State University. Her publications include *Jewish Voices of the California Gold Rush: A Documentary History 1849–1880* (Wayne State University Press, 2002) and *Jewish Life in the American West: Perspectives on Migration, Settlement and Community* (Heyday Books, Berkeley, 2003).

David Kaufman is assistant professor of American Jewish studies at the Hebrew Union College–Jewish Institute of Religion in Los Angeles and author of *Shul with a Pool: The "Synagogue-Center" in American Jewish History.*

Glenna Matthews is a visiting scholar at the Institute of Urban and Regional Development, University of California, Berkeley. The author of a number of books and articles about women's history and California history, she has most recently completed *Silicon Valley, Women, and the California Dream.*

Bruce Phillips is professor of sociology and Jewish communal service at Hebrew Union College, Los Angeles. He is a member of the National Technical Advisory Committee that guided the 1990 and 2000 National Jewish Population Surveys.

David and Michelle Plachte-Zuieback are nationally recognized stained glass artists, specializing in the design and fabrication of stained and etched glass panels for ecclesiastical architecture. As teachers, Michelle and David are recipients of the California Arts Council Grant for Arts in Education and have been artists in residence at UAHC Camp Swig Institute for Living Judaism annually, since 1983.

Bruce Powell is head of New Community Jewish High School in West Hills, California. He is also founder and president of Jewish School Management, a national consulting firm that works primarily with start-up Jewish high schools throughout the United States. He has been instrumental in founding two other Jewish high schools in the greater Los Angeles area. Dr. Powell teaches graduate courses in education at the University of Judaism in Los Angeles.

Naama Sabar serves as the Joanne and Jaime Constantine Chair and professor of education at Tel Aviv University and is the author of *Kibbutzniks in the Diaspora.*

Robert Saslow earned his degree in two-dimensional art from California State University, Northridge, and was featured in the San Francisco Jewish Museum's exhibition, "Illuminations."

Amy Hill Shevitz teaches American Jewish history and religious studies at California State University, Northridge, and modern Jewish history at the University of Judaism, Los Angeles. She lives in Venice, California.

Steven Windmueller is the director of the Irwin Daniels School of Jewish Communal Service at Hebrew Union College–Jewish Institute of Religion in Los Angeles. He has written extensively on issues related to Jewish public policy concerns. In 1999, he completed a study on Latino-Jewish relations in Los Angeles, funded by a grant from the John and Dora Haynes Foundation.

BIBLIOGRAPHICAL ESSAY

When *California Jews* was first contemplated, the editors and authors were all aware of the pioneering work of Moses Rischin and John Livingston in *Jews of the American West.* This 1991 collection of essays was the first scholarly work to acquaint readers with Jews in the far West. Its introduction and eight chapters were written by authorities in regional history. California Jewish history is the subject or part of the subject of several of the essays. In many ways this book and Rischin's *The Jews of the West, the Metropolitan Years,* a series of short studies including an introduction by Moses Rischin and essays by Peter Decker (San Francisco) and Mitchell Gelfand (Los Angeles), set the benchmark for this volume.

While several books have presented the parts of the California Jewish history with text and historical images, few have covered the breadth of the state's landscape and differing voices. *Jewish Life in the American West: Perspectives on Migration, Settlement and Community,* edited by Ava F. Kahn, explores the entire western United States with scholarly essays and images. While it concentrates on the region as a whole, this volume sheds light on the life of women in nineteenth-century California and merchants in some of California's cities. *Our City: The Jews of San Francisco,* by Irena Narell, is an illustrated history centered on San Francisco's Jewish elites. It is useful for family genealogies and photographs, most of which come from the families themselves or the Western Jewish History Center of the Magnes Museum in Berkeley. Many of the photographs that are in family hands were published for the first time in this book and are quite wonderful. Other books tell the history of the larger West in which California is a small part. *We Lived There Too* by Kenneth Libo and Irving A. Howe provides a documentary and pictorial history of Jews in the westward movement from 1630 to 1930. Harriet and Fred Rochlin's *Pioneer Jews: A New Life in the Far West* describes the years from 1500 to 1912 in thematic chapters, including "Gold and Other Discoveries" and "Humdingers." This fine work is an excellent look at individual Jews who shaped the history of the West including California.

From Mark Twain to the gold rush era onward, California has been a topic of interest for authors of fiction and historians alike, and also for historians of the Jewish experience. In 1978 Robert E. Levinson chronicled the Jewish men and women who "went to see the elephant," in *The Jews in the California Gold Rush.* This was the first widely distributed book to look closely at Jews of the mining country and the secular and Jewish communities they established. Joining this book, the recently published *Jewish Voices of the Califor-*nia *Gold Rush: A Documentary History 1849–1880* by Ava F. Kahn provides first-person accounts of the era through letters, images, diaries, and newspaper articles of both gold rush country and San Francisco. However, neither book explores more than a small region nor is able to place the region in statewide context.

In the decades after the gold rush, California Jews migrated to cities such as Sacramento, San Francisco, and later Los Angeles. This was a time of community and synagogue building. Historian Fred Rosenbaum documented much of this history in his *Visions of Reform: Congregation Emanu-El and the Jews of San Francisco, 1849–1999;* Emanu-El, while not typical, is one of the state's premier congregations. Founded in 1851, this elite Reform congregation was central to the development of a distinct California Reform Jewry. Rosenbaum's book, though not a history per se of the congregation, tells the story of its development through individual biographies of its eleven primary spiritual leaders, allowing the reader to learn about the type of rabbi that the congregation would choose to hire. Rosenbaum took another approach to community history in his 1976 book *Free to Choose: The Making of a Jewish Community in the American West—the Jews of Oakland, California,* which tells the story of the merchants who formed Oakland's first benevolent societies and synagogue. Oakland's community is known for its relationship with San Francisco, and for two of its most renowned children—Gertrude Stein and Judah Magnes.

In 1970 Max Vorspan and Lloyd P. Gartner co-wrote the *History of the Jews of Los Angeles.* This pathbreaking book was one of the first Jewish community histories to be written by serious historians for a general audience. While a good introduction to the Jewish history of Los Angeles, it is dated by today's social history standards. What it does exceptionally well is document the early history of the city that today houses one of the world's largest Jewish communities. Vorspan and Gartner describe the first hundred years of Jewish community life in chronological order, telling the story of Jewish businesses, prominent men and women, relationships between Jews and non-Jews, local politics, and the founding of congregations and social, fraternal, and educational organizations. Los Angeles's first rabbi, Abraham Edelman, was unusual in his ability to unite German and Polish members of his community and form a single congregation. B'nai B'rith (today known as Wilshire Boulevard Temple) remained under his leadership until 1884 when the congregation hired a Reform rabbi and adopted a new prayer book and other attributes of the early Reform movement.

In recent years contemporary works of the period have been re-published; they tell of a California long forgotten. I. J. Benjamin's *Three Years in America 1859–1862* is singularly important for California Jewish history. Benjamin spent almost two years in California and the West chronicling the different Jewish communities. While his descriptions of western life before his arrival in 1859 are hearsay, for the most part they seem accurate. Benjamin's records are extremely significant, as some of the original documentation of congregational life has been lost over the years. A traditionally observant Jew with a particular point of view, Benjamin's conclusions must be considered in context. Harriet Lane Levy's *920 O'Farrell Street: A Jewish Girlhood in Old San Francisco,* reissued by Heyday Books, is a wonderful autobiography of a young Jewish girl growing up in San Francisco in the late 1800s. Levy writes about community life, family life, Sherith Israel, and the differences between the German and the Polish communities. Her book also provides insight into the life of Levy's neighbor, young Alice B. Toklas. Also recently rediscovered, *Western Jewry: An Account of the Achievements of the Jews and Judaism in California,* first published by Congregation Emanu-El and reissued by Henny Hollander Bookseller, is a history of San Francisco institutions and a "mug" book of prominent people. Its value is in its photographs and short biographies. The early chronicler of Jewish Los Angeles, Harris Newmark's *Sixty Years in Southern California, 1853–1913* is a family history as well as a history of Los Angeles Jewry. It is a detailed book, a mix between a chronology and an autobiography describing Newmark's childhood in West Prussia, his immigration, and his sixty years in Southern California. If one is interested in very specific areas of Los Angeles life, one should look at all publications of the Southern California Historical Society, especially the *Legacy* series published as journals of the Southern California Jewish Historical Society. For the west as a whole, it is important to consult *Western States Jewish History* (formerly, the *Western States Jewish Historical Quarterly*), founded in 1968 by Norton B. Stern and William M. Kramer for the purpose of documenting western Jewish life.

INDEX

Abie's Irish Rose (film), 105–7, *106*

Abrams, Rabbi, *161*

Abzug, Bella, 150

Achedet Rishon group, 183

African American—Jewish alliance: black militancy, 157–58; civil rights movement, 110, 113, 115, 117, 125; demise of, 154–55; urban politics, 57, 59

Aftersut, Susan, *162*

Agudath Achim-Bikur Cholim synagogue, Chicago, 7

Alacon, Richard, 59–60

Alaska Commercial Company, 145

Alcatraz Island occupation, 158

Aleph Phi Pi organization, 136–37

Aleph Zadik Aleph organization, 137

Alien Land Law, 112

Aliyah, 178

Alkow, Rabbi Jacob M., 98–100

Allgemeine Zeitung des Judenthums (General Journal of Judaism), 30

Alper, Noah, 174

Alpha Epsilon Phi sorority, 139

Alpha Epsilon Pi fraternity, 139

Alta California (daily newspaper), 30, 44, 47

American Civil Liberties Union (ACLU), 14, 112, 117, 139

American Council for Judaism (ACJ), 12, 119–20

American Friends Service Committee, 112

American Israelite (newspaper), 37, 41

Americanization, xii, 3–5, 40–41, 81, 84–85, 131

American Jewish Committee, 107, 124–25

American Jewish Congress, 100, 104, 107, 125, 127, 156–58

American Jewish World (newspaper), 104

American Jewish Year Book (Szold), 1

Andriano, Sylvester, *132*

Anti-Defamation League, 14; civil rights movement, 125, 158; motion picture industry, 96–104, 107

Antisemitism, 12, 14, 34, 58, 101–2, 108, 117, 124, 140, 146. *See also* Prejudice and discrimination

Anti-Vietnam–war movement, xiii, 156–57, 161

Anti-Zionism, 12, 118–20, 157, 159

Aptheker, Bettina, 150

Aquarian Minyan, 162–64, *162–63*

Architecture of synagogues. *See* Synagogue architecture

Archives Israelite (newspaper), 30

Arness, James and Rolfe, 181–82

Aroner, Dion, 150–52, *151*

Arquilevich, Ruben, *89, color plate 4*

Arts and culture, 26; camping movement, 165, 178–81; contemporary art glass, 16, 167–70, *168–70, color plates 9–14*; Israeli dance, 165, 179; music, 165; temple architecture, 13, 40–56; wedding ketubot, *10, 16, 87, 88–94, color plates 2–8*. *See also* Motion picture industry

Assimilation, xii, 3–5, 40–41, 81, 84–85

Association of California Teachers, 144

Atlanta, Ga., demographics, 23

Baalei tshuva, 73–76

Bainbridge, William Sims, 25

Baker, Grace, 135

Balter, Harry Graham, 102

Bardin, Ruth Jonas, 175, *176*

Bardin, Shlomo, 16, 171–84, *171, 176, 178, 180, 181*

Baron, Lawrence, 15, 141, *142*

Barrows, David P., 117

Baruh, Aaron and Rosalie, 34, *35*

Bates, Tom, 151

Bay, Max, 183

Bay Area Committee of the National Committee Against Persecution of the Jews, 125

Bay Area Council Against Discrimination, 123, 125–27

Bay Area Council for Soviet Jewry, 155–56

Bay Cities Synagogue (Pacific Jewish Center), 73, *74*

Becker, William, 132

Ben-Ari, Raiken, 178, *179*

Bene Yeshurun synagogue (Cincinnati, Ohio), 47

Benevolent Societies, 30

Ben-Gurion, David, 175

Berkeley Free Speech Movement, xiii, 139, 150, 154–55. *See also* University of California

Berkeley Society of Friends, 112

Beta Tau fraternity, 139

Beth Abraham Congregation (Oakland), 158

Beth Am Congregation (Los Altos Hills), 167, *169–70, color plate 13*

Beth Israel Congregation (Los Angeles), 55–56, *56*

Beth Israel Congregation (San Diego), 51, *52*, 135

Beth Israel Congregation (San Francisco), 39, 56, 127

Beth Shalom. *See* Temple Beth Shalom

Biale, David, 159

Bickur Cholim synagogue, 47–48, *49*

Bikel, Theodore, 159

Birnbaum, Jacob, 161

Birth of a Nation (film), 98

Black Panthers, 157–58

Black Power movement, 154–55, 158

Blankfort, Michael, 182–83

Block, Eugene, 124–25

Bloom brothers, 68

B'nai B'rith Congregation (Los Angeles, Wilshire Blvd. Temple), 67, 98, 113; first synagogue, 48–49, *50*; second synagogue, 54–55, *55*

B'nai B'rith Messenger (newspaper), 98, 104, 113, 115, 118

B'nai B'rith organization: college organizations, 137; mining towns, 34; motion picture industry, 100; *National Jewish Monthly*, 107. *See also* Anti-Defamation League

Bogen, Karen Iris, 164

Boss, Father Andrew C., 131–32

Boxer, Barbara, 143, *143*, 151–52

Boyd, Harold J., 125, *125*, 126

Boyle, Father Eugene, 133

Boyle Heights (Los Angeles), 19, 61–62, *62*, 67–68, 112–13

Bradley, Tom, 59, *59*

Braly, Vivien, *89, color plate 4*

Brandeis, Justice Louis, 1, 16, 174–75

Brandeis–Bardin Institute, 16, 171, 175–84, *176–79, 179, 184, color plates 15–16*

Brandeis Jewish Day School, 160–61

Breen, Joseph, 101

Breitbard, Bob, 136, 137

Broidy, Steve, 182

Brooklyn Technical High School, 175

Brooks, Fanny and Julius, 31, Fanny, *32*

Broude, Rabbi Sam, *161*

Brown, Edmund G. (Pat), 126, 127, 149

Brown, Father James N., 130

Bubis, Gerald, 182

Bureau of Jewish Education, 160, 165

Burke, Rev. Thomas F., 127, 128, 131

Burstein, Rabbi Elliot M., 100, 127–29

Burton, Philip, 149

Bush Street Synagogue Cultural Center, 54

Butler, Miner Frederic, 41

Bycel, Rabbi Lee, 184

Caen, Herb, 150

California Fair Employment Practice Act of 1959, 123

California Jewish Voice (newspaper), 107

California Labor School, 131

Californians Against Proposition 14, 133

California State Assembly, 144

California State Federation of Labor, 132

California State Industrial Union Council, 113

Camp Alonim. *See* Brandeis–Bardin Institute

Camp Hilltop, 165

Camp JCA–Shalom (Malibu), *89*

Camp Newman (Santa Rosa), 166

Camp Ramah (Ojai), 165–66

Camp Swig (Saratoga), *88*, 165, *165, 168, color plates 3, 10*

Camping movement, 164–66, *165*, 175–81, *176–79*

Cantor, Eddie, 100

Cantwell, Bishop John J., 101

Cardozo, Benjamin, 144

Cardozo, Isaac N., 144

Carlebach, Rabbi Shlomo, 161–62

Carmichael, Stokely, 158

Carson, James H., 34

Catholic Interracial Council (National), 129

Catholic Interracial Council (San Francisco), 130, 133

Catholicism in California, 7; civil rights movement, 14–15, 123–34; Social Justice Commission, 133

Catholics Against Proposition 14, 133

Censorship, 95–96

Central Conference of American Rabbis (Reform), 119

Cherry, Ed, 139

Chinese Exclusion Act, 112

Chotiner, Willard and Rita, 182

Christopher, George, 123, 129, *130*, 132

Church for the Fellowship of All Peoples, 127

The Churching of America, 25

The Churchman, 101

Citizens Committee for Democratic Freedom in North Africa, 125

Citizen's Lobby, 127

City University of New York, 28

Civic Unity Committee (San Francisco), 125, 127

Civic Unity Council (San Francisco), 132

Civil Rights Acts, 127, 154–55

Civil rights movement, xiii, 14–15; African American–Jewish alliance, 110, 113, 115, 117, 125; California Fair Employment Practice Act of 1959, 123; Catholic–Jewish alliance, 123–34; Communist Party involvement, 127, 132; coverage in the Jewish press, 113–15; dual loyalty issues, 131; fair housing legislation, 133; intermarriage, 130; parochial school issues, 130

Cleaver, Eldridge, 157

Coalition for the Advancement of Jewish Education, *165*, 166

Coffee, Rabbi Rudolf, 100

Cohen, Joanne, *94*

Cohen, Samuel H., 30

Cohen, Simon, *161*

Cohn, Harry, 103

Cohn, Henry, *33*

College of Judaic Studies, xv

Colley, Nathaniel, 129

Columbia, Calif., 41

Columbia Foundation, 124

Commentary (magazine), 124

Commission on Equal Employment Opportunity (CEEO), 123, 127, 129

Committee for Student Action (San Diego), 139

Communist Party, 127, 132, 147, 161

Community buildings (Jewish), 19; *baalei tshuva,* 73–76; civil rights coalition, 123–34; federation giving, 25–26; fraternal societies, 34; gold rush, 29–39; Jewish institutions, 30–37, 68–70; kibbutzniks in California, 78–80, 85; Latinos in Los Angeles, 61; in Los Angeles, 57–64; neighborhoods, 26; Pacific Jewish Center, Venice, 73–76; practicing Americanism, 131; retirement communities, 70–71, *72*; in San Diego, 135–42; synagogue affiliation, 23–24; in urban centers, 38–39; in Venice, Calif., 65–76

Community Relations Council (San Francisco), 126

Comstock Silver Lode, 19

Concentration Camps: North America (Daniels), 112

Contemporary art glass, 167–70, *168–70, color plates 9–14*

Corwin, Norman, 182

Coughlin, Father Charles, 96, 117

Council for Civic Unity (San Francisco), 123, 125–30

Council for Equal Employment Opportunity (San Francisco), *130*

Counterculture era, 15, 154–66, *156*; homesteading, 167; religious affiliation, 25, 26. *See also Havurah* movement; Political involvement

Counts, George, 173, 174

Crane, William, 41

Cranston, Alan, 59

Crosby, Bing, 105–6

Daily Alta California. See Alta California

Daily Morning Chronicle (newspaper), 19–20

Dalin, Rabbi William, *161*

Daniels, John, 41

Daniels, Roger, 112

Danish Folk High School (DFHS), 174

Dassa, Dani, 179, *181*

Davidson, Elsie, 135

Davis, Susan, 150, 152

Day, Thomas, 140

Dean, Amy, 152

Dearborn Independent (newspaper), 96

Degania kibbutz, 174

Dellums, C. L., 132

Delury, John, 133

DeMille, Cecil B., 97–100

Democratic Party. *See* Political involvement

Deutsch, Monroe, 114–15, 118–19

Dewey, John, 173

DeYoung, Charles, 19–20

Dinin, Samuel, 175

Dollinger, Albert, 3–5, *4*, 5–6

Dollinger, Marc, 15, 117

Dollinger, Marcus (Mordechai), 3, *3*

Dollinger, Sara, *5*

The Dollinger Family's Journey to California (Saslow), *2, color plate 1*

Donohoe, Father Hugh A., 131
Douglas, Helen Gahagan, 149
Douglas, William O., 161
Drescher, Father Bruno, 130
Dual loyalty issues: in the civil rights movement, 131; during World War II, 119–20
Dubinsky, David, 147

East-Coast Jewish life: economic factors, 10; intermarriage, 26; political affiliations, 12; population rates, 20–23, 41
Eckman, Rabbi Julius, 41, 144, *145*
Economic factors: banking, 18; development, 12; East-Coast Jewish life, 10; kibbutzniks in California, 79–80, 83–85; mining, 18–19; population growth, 21; railroads, 19; nineteenth-century Jewish merchants, 17–19, 29–30. *See also* gold rush
Edelman, Abraham M., 54–56
Edelman, Rabbi Abraham Wolf, 48, 54
Edison, Thomas, 97
Education: about Nazism, 104–5; acting, *6;* adult education, 180–81; arts and culture, 178–81; camping movement, 175–81; fraternities and sororities, 136–37, 139; Jewish education, 159–61, 173–74; Jewish high schools, 174; Jewish organizations, 136–37; Jewish student enrollment, 136*t;* Jewish Studies programs, 15, 139–41; of kibbutzniks in California, 78, 82–85; moral education, 173–74; in San Diego, 135–42; teachers, 135, 144, 145, 148. *See also* University of California
Eidlitz, Leopold, 47
Einstein, Albert, *98*
Eisenberg, Ellen, 14
Eisenstadt, Chanan, *181*
Eisenstadt, Sidney, 182, *184, color plate 16*
El Capitan, 1
Eliaser, Ann Alanson, 149
Emanu-El Congregation (San Diego), 167
Emanu-El Congregation (San Francisco), xv, 31–32, *38*, 39, 100; American Council for Judaism (ACJ), 119; civil rights movement, 124, 129–30; first synagogue, *42–43; Temple Chronicle,* 119–20; Temple building, *38, 39, 41–47, 44–46,* 56; women activists, 145–46, 148, 149, 150
Emanu-El (newspaper), 100, 113–15
Emanu-El synagogue (New York, N.Y.), 47
An Empire of Their Own: How the Jews Invented Hollywood (Gabler), 98
England, Thomas, 41
Epstein, Itzhak, 157–58

Equality (journal), *11*
Ethnic issues: alliances, 57; Americanization, 3–5, 40–41, 81, 84–85, 131; ethnic activism, 15, 58–60, 63, 155–66; gold rush, 29; intermarriage, 26–27; multiculturalism, 1, 58; religious tolerance, 14–15, 123–24, 135, 143. *See also* Civil rights movement; Latinos; Prejudice and discrimination
Eureka Social Club, 35

Fair Employment Commission, 127, 132
Fair Play Committee, 112, 114–15, 117–21
Falk, Adrien, *129*, 132
Farmers and Merchants Bank, 18
Farrakhan, Louis, 140
Fein, Leonard, 181
Feinstein, Dianne, 143, *143*, 149, 151
Feminist movement, 163
Fendel, Samuel L., *133*
Fernbach, Henry, 47
Film industry. *See* Motion picture industry
Fine, Rabbi Alvin I., 124, 129–30, *131*, 133
First Christian Church of Oakland, 112
First Hebrew Congregation (Oakland), 49, 51, *51*, 56
Fliegelman, Julius and Molly, 176–77
Flippin, Robert P., 129
Florida demographics, 21, 22, 23
Ford, Henry, 96
Foster, Joseph, 177
Fox, William, 97
Francaviglia, Richard, 68
Franchise for Jews, 143
Francois, Terry A., 129, *130*, 132
Franklin, Lewis, 41
Fraternal societies, 34–35, 37
Fred J. Hansen Institute for World Peace (San Diego), 140–41
Free Jewish University (Berkeley), 160
Free Speech Movement (Berkeley), xiii, 139, 150, 154–55
Freund, Rabbi Iser L., 118
Friedan, Betty, 150
Friedman, Eddie, 165–66
Friedman, Ida, 137
Fried-Schultz, Charlotte, 136
Fung, Kenneth, 129

Gabler, Neal, 98
Galveston Project, 5
Gang, Martin, 103
Garin Hagolan Kibbutz, 140
Gartner, Lloyd, 67
Geddis, Lorie, 140
Gefter, Irving, 140

GI Bill, 137
The Girl from Colorado (Selina Solomons), 146
Glover, D. Donald, 132
Goldberg, Jackie, 150–51
Goldberg, Jacob, 140
Goldblatt, Louis, 113
Goldfarb, Reuven, 163, *163*
Goldfarb, Yehudit, 162–63, *162–63*
Golding, Brage, 140
Gold rush, 1, 29–39; boom towns, 41; forming congregations, 31–33; Jewish stereotypes, 34; maintaining Jewish traditions, 30, 33–38; migration to California, 10–12, 29–31; occupations of Jews, 17–18, 32–38; travel routes, 31
Goldstein, Morris, *161*
Goldwater, Michel, 38
Goldwyn, Samuel, 95
Goodbye, Columbus (film), 108
Goodbye Again (film), 108
Goodman, Abraham, 175–76
Goodman, Morris, 19
Gordon, A. D., 174, 179
Gordon, William, 108
Gottschalk, Rabbi Alfred, 182
Graduate Theological Union at Berkeley, 164
Grady, Henry F., 117
Graudenz, Rabbi, *161*
The Great God Gold (film), 103
Greenberg, Cheryl, 117
Greenberg, Irving (Yitz), 181
Griffith, D. W., 98
Grossman, Aubrey, 127
A Guide for the Bedeviled (Hecht), 104
Gumbiner, Judy, 139
Gumbiner, Rabbi, *161*
Gutstadt, Richard, 102, 103–4

Haas, Peter E., 129, 132
Haas, Walter A., Sr., 124, 126
HaBimah Theater Company, 178
Habonim, 160
Haifa Nautical School, 175
Haifa Technical High School, 175
Haight-Ashbury district (San Francisco), 156
Handlin, David P., 49
Hanna, Archbishop Edward, 124
Harman, Jane, 152
Harris, Emil, 19
Harrison, Maurice A., 127, 131
Hartman, Rabbi Donniel, 183
Hausman-Weiss, Natalie and Scott, *88, color plate 3*

Havurah movement, 15, 156, 164–66, 183

Havurat Noar, 165–66

Hawkins, Augustus, 132

Hebrew (newspaper), 35

Hebrew Union College–Jewish Institute of Religion (Los Angeles), 141

Hecht, Ben, 104

Helfman, Max, 179

Hellman, I. W., 18, 19

Hellman, Marco H., *96*

Henning, John, 132, *132*

Herman, Felicia, 14

Herschensohn, Bruce, 152

Herson, Benjamin, 174

Herst, Rabbi Roger E., 157

Heschel, Abraham Joshua, 181

Heschel Day School (Northridge), 167

Heydenfeldt, Elkan, 144

Heydenfeldt, Solomon, 144

Higham, John, 12

Hill, Anita, 151

Hillel: at Berkeley, 158–59, 160; at San Diego State University, 137, *138*

Hirsch, Baron de, 3

Hispanics. *See* Latinos

Hitler's Children (film), 104

Hollywood. *See* Motion picture industry

House of Love and Prayer (San Francisco), 161–62

House of the Book, *184, color plate 16. See also* Brandeis–Bardin Institute

Howden, Edward, 126–27, 129

How We Won the Vote in California (Selina Solomons), 146

Humphrey, Hubert, 154

Hurwitz residence, *168, color plate 14*

Immigration to California, xi–xii, 58; Americanization, xii, 3–5; of kibbutzniks, 77–86; of Russian Jews, xv; in Venice, Calif., 67–68. *See also* Migration to California

International Ladies Garment Workers Union, 146–47

Inventing the Dream (Starr), 66

Isaacs, Mark, 30

Isaacson, Isidore, 100

Iser, Alexander, 30

Israel, 1; emigration of kibbutzniks, 13–14, 77–86; political activism in the U.S., 155–57; 1967 Six Day War, 155, 157. *See also* Zionism

Israel Levin Center, Venice, Calif., 70–71, *72*, *73*

Issel, William, 14–15

It Happened in Springfield (film), 105

Jackson, Calif., 33–34, 41

Jackson, Henry, 161

Jacobs, Stanley, 158

Jacoby, Charles, 19

Jaffe, Anne, 174

Japanese American incarceration, 14, 110–22; coverage in Jewish press, 113–15, 118; Fair Play Committee, 112, 114–15, 117–21; notice of removal, *111;* store closing sign, *116;* Tolan Committee, 110–13

Japanese American Religious Federation (JARE), 53–54

Jesus Christ Superstar (film), 108

Jewish Bulletin (San Francisco), 160

Jewish Chronicle of London (newspaper), 30

Jewish Club of 1933, 113

Jewish Community Committee, 14

Jewish Daily Forward (newspaper), xiii

Jewish Education Coalition (JEC), 160–61

Jewish Federation of Los Angeles, 182

Jewish Historical Society of San Diego, 142, *142*

Jewish Home for Wayfarers, Boyle Heights, Los Angeles, *62*

Jewish Institute of Religion. *See* Hebrew Union College

Jewish Issues in Multiculturalism (Langman), 60

Jewish Journal (newspaper, Los Angeles), 59

Jewish Labor Committee, 107, 132

Jewish Liberation Journal, 157

Jewish Liberation Movement, 158

Jewish Radical, 159

Jewish Student Press Service, 160

Jewish Studies programs, 15, 139–41

Jewish Survey Committee (San Francisco), 124–25, *126*

Jewish War Veterans, 107

Jews Against Prejudice: American Jews and the Fight for Civil Liberties (Svonkin), 123

Jews of the American West (Rischin), 30, 44

Johnson, Lyndon B., 150, 154

Kahn, Ava, 15; wedding ketubah, *10, color plate 2*

Kahn, Florence Prag, 15, 20, 143, 147–48, *147*, 152

Kahn, Julius, 1, 20, 144–45, 148, 152

Kahn, Marvin and Bea, *9*

Kahn, Moses Aaron, 5–7, *7*

Kahn family, *9*

Kaiserman, Kevin, *90, color plate 5*

Kallen, Horace, *128*

Kallis, Mischa, 182–83

Kanter, Donna, 140

Kantor, Duane, 139

Kaplan, Mordechai, 181

Kaplan, Oscar, 137

Katz, Richard, 59–60

Kaufman, David, 13

Kelly, Sister Rose Maureen, 133

Kennedy, John F., 150, 154

Kesher Shel Barzel, 34

Ketubot. *See* Wedding ketubot

Keysor, Ezra R., 48–49

Kibbutzniks in California, 13–14, 77–86

King, Martin Luther, Jr., 158, 161

King, Thomas Starr, 45

Kingman, Harry and Ruth, 127

King of Kings (film), 97–100, *99, 101*

Kinney, Abbott, 65–67

Klein, Fannie, 68

Koshland, Daniel E., Sr., 118–19, 124, *125*, 127, 133

Kosmin, Barry, 21

Koster, Frederick J., *125, 126*

Kotkin, Joel, 59

Kuroki, Ben, 118–19

Kushner, Howard, 140

Labbat, Abraham C., 144

Labor Management Panel (periodical), 132

Labor movement, 146–48, 151–52, 158–59

Laemmle, Carl, 97, 98, 182

Laemmle, Gregg, 182

Laemmle, Max, 182

Langman, Peter, 60

Language use: English, 81, 84–85; Hebrew, 81, 84–85; Yiddish, 70–71, 73

Lansburgh, G. Albert, 56

Lapham, Roger D., 125, 127, 132

Laski, Samuel M., 34–35

Latinos, 13, 57–64; economic concerns, 60–61; links with the Los Angeles Jewish community, 61–63; Mexican–American Legal Defense Fund (MALDEF), 61; political concerns, 59–61

Lazard, Solomon, 19

Lee, Lim P., 129

Lee (Levi), Sandra Josephine, 164

Lent, Bobby, 174

Lepke (film), 108

Lesen, Lily, 135

Lesser, Isaac, 30, 34

Levine, Irene and Howard, *93, color plate 8*

Levi Strauss company, *62,* 145

Levy, Bob, 139

Levy, Daniel, 30

Lewin, Louis, 19

Lewis, Leon L., 97, 100–105, 108

Lichter, S. Robert, 156
The Life of Emile Zola (film), 104
Lilienthal, Sue, 149
Limerick, Patricia Nelson, 12
Linoberg, Emanuel and Pauline, 36–37, *37*
Linoberg, Louis, 37
Lipinsky, Bernard and Dorris, 136–37, 140, *141*
Lipinsky Institute for Judaic Studies (San Diego), 140–41, *141*, *142*
Lipset, Seymour Martin, 126
Local politics: ethnic tensions, 59–60; in Los Angeles, 57–64; in San Francisco, 144; in nineteenth-century mining towns, 19, 36–37; women's involvement, 148–52
Los Angeles, Calif.: after the gold rush, 38; annexation of Venice, 67; Board of Trade, 19; city council, 148–49; community activism, 57–64; International Ladies Garment Workers Union, 146; Jewish merchants, 17–18; kibbutzniks, 77–86; land development, 19; Latinos, 57–64; Milken Community High School, 174; New Community Jewish High School, 174; Pico/Robertson neighborhood, 74; police force, 19; population growth, 21, 23, 67; synagogue affiliation, 23–24; synagogue buildings, 67. *See also* Motion picture industry
Los Angeles Breakfast Club, *96*
Los Angeles Council of Social Agencies, 115
Los Angeles Dodgers, 92
Los Angeles Jewish Community Committee (LAJCC), 102–8
Los Angeles Jewish Federation Council, 59, 61
Los Angeles Times (newspaper), 112
Low, David, 183
Lowenberg, Ignatz, 68
Lubin, Sigmund, 97
Lyon, Moses J., 52–54, *54*
Lyons, Harry A., 144, *144*

Mad Dog of Europe (unmade film), 103–4
Magnin, Rabbi Edgar F., 55, 98–100, *98*, 108, 118, 120, 182
Main Street Revisited (Francaviglia), 68
Malcolm X, 160
Manning, Seaton W., 129
Marks, Bernard, 145
Marriage: during the gold rush, 35–36; intermarriage, 26–27; synagogue affiliation, 23–24
Marysville, Calif., 41
Massachusetts demographics, 22
Matthews, Glenna, 15

Matyas, Jennie, 146–47
Mayer, Louis B., 95, *96*, 98, 103
McAtee, Sylvester, 132
McCarthy, Eugene, 149
McCloy, John, 118
McGucken, Archbishop Joseph T., *133*
McWilliams, Carey, 21, 66
McWilliams, Robert and Lucy, 126; Robert, 131
Medved, Michael, 73
Mellon, Thomas J., *130*
Mexican–American Legal Defense Fund (MALDEF), 61
Meyer, Clara, 145
Meyer, Eugene, 31
Midwestern demographics, 20–23
Migration to California, 20–21, 23, 41; after World War II, 7, 21; gold rush, 10–12, 29–31; travel routes, 31. *See also* Immigration to California
Milken Community High School (Los Angeles), 174
Miller, Loren, 129
Miller, Rabbi Jay, 140
Mining towns, 19; Jewish merchants, 32–38; local politics, 36–37
Mishkon Tephilo Congregation, 68, *69*, *70*, 71, 73–76, *75*
Mitchell, Clarence, 127
Mitty, Archbishop John J., 128, *129*, *130*, 132
Mokelumne Hill, Calif., 41
Mondshine, Leo and Rose, and Charlie, *8*
Mont, Max, 132
Moore, Deborah Dash, 69
Motion picture industry, 12, 59, 95–109; antisemitism, 14, 95–96; Breakfast Club, *96*; censorship, 95–96, 101–2; relationships with the Jewish community, 95–96; representations of Jews, 95–109
Motion Picture Producers and Distributors Association (MPPDA), 100–102
Mount Diablo, Calif., *91*
Myerhoff, Barbara, 70–71, *72*

NAACP (National Association for the Advancement of Colored People), 127, 129, 131, 132, 158
Nasatir, Abraham P., 136, 137, *137*
National Catholic Welfare Conference, 128
National Committee Against Persecution of the Jews, 125
National Community Relations Advisory Council, 14, 107–8
National Conference of Christians and Jews (NCCJ), 125, 126, 128, 130

National Council of Jewish Women, Los Angeles, 113
National Jewish Data Bank, 28
National Jewish Monthly (periodical), 107
National Jewish Population Survey of 1990, 22, 28
National politics, 20, 143–44, 147–52
National Women's Political Caucus, 151
Native American protest movement, 158
Naturalization Certificate of Marcus Dollinger, *3*
Neito, Rabbi Jacob, 100
Nevada City, Calif., 34–36, 41
Nevada City Journal (newspaper), 34
Nevada Hebrew Society, 34
New age religion. *See* Religious practice in California
New Community Jewish High School (Los Angeles), 174
New Palestine Colony, Argentina, 3
Newman, Louis I., 99–100
Newmark, Harris, 19
Newmark, Joseph, 48
Newmark, M. J., 19
Nixon, Richard, 149, 154
Noah, Mordecai, 1
None Shall Escape (film), 104–5
Northern California ACLU, 117, 118
Number Our Days (Myerhoff), *70*
Nussbaum, Rabbi Max, 182

Oakland, Calif., 49, 51
The Occident (newspaper), 30, 34
Occupations of California Jews, 17–19; merchants, 17–19, 32–38; motion picture industry, 95; teachers, 135, 144–45, 148; in Venice, Calif., 67–69; in working class communities, 67–69
Ocean Front Walk (Venice), *66*, 68, 71–73, *72*
Ofir (Ophir), 1
Ohabai Shalome Congregation (San Francisco), 39, 45, 52–54, *54*
Okihiro, Gary, 112
Older, Fremont, 125
Old St. Mary's Church, 128
Olson, Culbert, 110, 112, 147
Ontell, Robert, *141*
Organizational roles of California Jews: federation giving, 25–26; synagogue affiliation, 23–24
Osgood, Edgar, D., 133

Pacific Jewish Center, 73–76, *74*
Pacific Ocean Park (Santa Monica), 67, 69, 71, 73

Palestinian cause, 155, 157–58

Patton, William, 45, 47, 53

Peixetto, Jessica, 145, 152

Pelley, William Dudley, 96

Penner, Rabbi Samuel, 140

Pesotta, Rose, 146

Philanthropy, 41; civil rights movement, 124; Jewish high schools, 174

Phillips, Bruce, 12

Physical characteristics of California, 1, 12–13

Picheny, Jacob, 164

Pico/Robertson neighborhood, Los Angeles, 74

Pioneer Youth in Palestine (Bardin), 174

Pither, Bruce and Kathy, *156*

Placerville, Calif., 33–34, 41

Plachte-Zuieback, Michelle and David, 16, 167–70, *168–70, color plates 9–14*

Poker Flat, Calif., 33

Political involvement: campus activism, 154–64; civil rights movement, 125–27, 132; ethnic activism, 58–60, 63, 155–66; liberalism, 26, 61; linkages with Latinos, 61–63; Nazism in California, 102, 114, 125, 139; party affiliations, 12, 13, 146, 154; radical leftists, 70; in San Diego, 139; sharing power with Latinos, 57–64; social activism, 58, 63; unaffiliated Jews, 156; voting patterns, 60–61; women's involvement, 15, 143–53

Population changes, 20–23; earliest Jews in America, 41; gold rush, 29, 38, 39n1; in Los Angeles, 13, 57, 58, 60–61; in the 1920s, 67; in San Diego, 135–42, 136*t*; in Venice, Calif., 71; World War II, xi–xii, 7, 137

Poremba, Joel, *92, color plate 7*

Powell, Bruce, 16

Prag, Conrad, 148

Prag, Mary Goldsmith, 143–45, *147–48,* 148, 152

Prejudice and discrimination: during elections, 59–60; in fraternities and sororities, 136–37, 139; during the gold rush, 29, 34; involving African Americans, 154–55; involving Asian Americans, 10, 14, 110, 125; involving recent immigrants, 58; Jewish stereotypes, 34, 96–97, 99, 106–7; in motion pictures, 95, 96–105; Nazism in California, 102, 114, 125, 139; Sunday Laws, 29. *See also* Japanese American incarceration

Press, Jewish, 37; immigration to California, 30; incarceration of Japanese Americans, 111–12. *See also* names of specific newspapers

Price, Sol, 137

Quinn, Frank A., 133

Raab, Earl, 124, 126–29, 131, 133

Racism. *See* Prejudice and discrimination

Radical Jewish Union (Berkeley), 159–60

Radical Zionist Alliance (Berkeley), 158–59

Radlin, Rabbi Henry, 98–99

Railroad, 135

Raitsits (Rice), Emile and Toba, 5, *7*

Rauch, John and Ruth, 182

Reagan, Ronald, 151

Real estate development, 66

Recreation, 66

Reichert, Rabbi Irving, 118–21

Reim Ahuvin (Ryhim Ahoovim) Congregation (Stockton), 43, *43*

Religious practice in California, 7, 26, 27*t;* Aquarian Minyan, 162–64; *baalei tshuva,* 73–76; Catholicism, 7, 14–15, 123–34; contemporary changes, 74–75; eastern religions, 26, 156, 159, 161–62, 164; *havurah,* 15; interfaith cooperation, 130–31; Jewish spirituality, 160, 161–65; of kibbutzniks, 81–82; ordination of women, 15, 75; Orthodoxy, 73–76; synagogue affiliation, 23–24, 75; tolerance, 14–15, 123–24, 135, 143; ultra-Orthodoxy, 85; unaffiliated Jews, 156. *See also* Synagogue architecture

Republican Party. *See* Political involvement

Retirement communities, 70–71, *72,* 137

Reuther, Walter, 161

Richman, Lucas, 183

Richman, Mitchell A., *10, color plate 2*

Rieff, David, 76

Rifkind, Bettie and Joseph, 177, 179–80, *180*

Ringrose, Mrs. Harold, *129*

Rischin, Moses, 30, 44

Ritzwoller, Selig, 37

Rivkin, Allen, 107–8

Rockwell, George Lincoln, 139

Roesnberg Foundation, 124

Roos, Joseph, 104

Roosevelt, Franklin D., 147, 154

Rose, Henrietta, 135

Rosen, Al, 104

Rosenbaum, Fred, 100

Rosenberg, Nathan, 49

Rosenblatt, Irving, 129

Rosenbloom, Isaac and Leah, 5

Rosenfeld, Sherman, 159, 160

Rosenheim, Aaron, 34

Rosenwald, Lessing, 119

Rothman, Stanley S., 156

Ruja, Harry, 137, 139

Rumford, Byron, 132

Russian Jewish immigrants, xv, 161, *161*

Sabar, Na'ama, 13–14

Sachar, Abraham, 137, *138*

Sacramento, Calif., 41

Saint Louis, Calif., 33

San Diego, Calif., 15, 51, 135–42

San Diego Bureau of Jewish Education, 139

San Diego Jewish Federation, 137

San Diego Normal School, 135–36

San Diego State University, 136–42; agricultural research, 140–41; Jewish Studies program, 15, 139–40

San Fernando Valley, Calif., 71; kibbutzniks, 79

San Francisco, Calif., 1; after the gold rush, 38–39; antisemitism, 12; Bay Area Council Against Discrimination, 123, 125, 126, 127; Catholic Interracial Council, 130, 132; Civic Unity Committee, 125, 127; Civic Unity Council, 132; civil rights issues, 123–34; Commission on Equal Employment Opportunity (CEEO), 123, 127, 129; Community Relations Council, 126; construction of synagogues, 41–47; Council for Civic Unity, 123, 125, 126–27, 129, 130; Council for Equal Employment Opportunity, *130;* early Congregations, 38–39; early Jewish community, 30; earthquake, 6; Fair Employment Commission, 127, 132; forming the first congregations, 31–33; gold rush, 29; Haight-Ashbury district, 156; Hebrew Benevolent Society, 37; Human Rights Commission, 133; Jewish Survey Committee, 124–25, 126; Jews in local politics, 144; Labor-Management School, 131–32; NAACP (National Association for the Advancement of Colored People), 131; National Conference of Christians and Jews (NCCJ), 125, 126, 128, 130; population growth, 21, 23, 38; synagogue affiliation, 23–24; Temple Emanu-El, *38,* 39, 43–47, *44–46;* traditions of religious tolerance, 14–15; Urban League, 129, 131, 132; Women's Educational and Industrial Union (WEIU), 145

San Francisco Bulletin (newspaper), 125

San Francisco Chronicle (newspaper), 19–20, 112

San Francisco Employers' Council, 129

San Francisco Jewish Federation, 160–61

San Francisco Jewish Liberation Project, 160

San Francisco News (newspaper), 110

San Francisco State University, xv

San Joaquin Republican (newspaper), 34

San Jose, Calif., 37, 47–48

San Leandro, Calif., 51–52

San Pedro, Calif., 19

Santa Cruz Mountains, *94*

Santa Monica, Calif., 67, 68, 71, 75

Sarna, Jonathan, 34

Saslow, Robert, 2, 16, 87, 88–94, *color plates 1, 3–8*

Schachter, Rabbi Zalman, 162–63

Schack, Linda, *90, color plate 5*

Schartz, Doris, 151

Schenck, Joseph, 103

Scherer, Sari, *92, color plate 7*

Schiff, Jacob, 5

Schineman, Benjamin, 118

Schlessinger, Arthur M., Jr., 126

Schneider, Anne, *8*

Schneider, Fannie and Hyman, 5

Schneider, Lil, *8*

Schneider, Rose, 5, *8*

Schultz, Sol, 136

Schulweis, Rabbi Harold, 155–56, 158–59, *161,* 164–65, 167, 174

Schwartz, Stanley, *142*

Schwartzman, Esther Kite, *71*

The Scribe (newspaper), 100

Secularism, 13

Seixas, Gersom Mendes, 145

Seligmann, Heinrich, 44

Selling, Ben, 38

Selling, Caroline and Philip, 38

Selvin, David, 126–27

Selznick, David O., 95

Service Employees International Union (SEIU), Local 535, 151

Shapero, Michael, *94*

Sheidelman, Sara, *162*

Shelley, John F. , 129, *130,* 133

Sheres, Ita, 140

Sherith Israel Congregation (San Francisco), 1, 31–32, 39; construction of synagogues, 41–42, *43,* 47, *48,* 56

Shevitz, Amy Hill, 13

Shochat, Manya, 175

Shomer HaTsair movement, 84

Shuls, 40, 55. *See also* Synagogue architecture

Sigma Alpha Mu fraternity, 139

Signer residence, *168, color plate 9*

Silberberg, Mendel, 102–4, 107

Sills, Rabbi Hanan, 164

Silo, John, *181*

Silver, Carol Ruth, 151

Silver, Herman, 19

Sloss, Hattie Hecht, 119

Sloss, Louis, 31

Sloss, M. C., 124

Sloss, Richard L., 129

Smith, Gerald J. K., 107

Solomon, Larry, 139

Solomons, Hanna Marks, 144, 145–46

Solomons, Seixas, 145

Solomons, Selina, 144, 145–46, *146*

Sonora, Calif., 36–38, *36, 37,* 41

South Bay Labor Council, 152

Southern California ACLU, 112

Southern demographics, 20–23

Soviet Jewry movement, xv, 161, *161*

Spiegel, Albert A., *59*

Sports, *11,* 83. *See also* Camping movement

Sproul, Robert G., 117

St. Benedict of the Moor Church, 130

Stained glass, 167–70, *168–70, color plates 9–14*

Stanford Union of Jewish Students, 160

Stark, Rodney, 25

Starr, Kevin, 66

State politics, 19–20, 144

State Supreme Court, 144

Steinem, Gloria, 150

Steinhart, Jesse, 124

Stevenson, Adlai, 149, 150

Stimson, Henry, 118–19

Stinnett, Terrance, *91, color plate 6*

Stockton, Calif., 34, 41, 43

Stone, John, 108

Strand, Paul, *142*

Strauss, Levi, 29

Strauss, Ludwig and Ada, 183

Student movement in California, 150

Student Non-violent Coordinating Committee (SNCC), 158

Students for a Democratic Society (SDS), 155, 156

Student Struggle for Soviet Jewry, 161

Summer Camp Institute. *See* Brandeis-Bardin Institute, Camp Newman, Camp Swig

Sutro, Adolph, 19, 144

Svonkin, Stuart, 123

Swig, Benjamin H., 124, *124,* 125

Synagogue architecture, 13, 40–56; American symbols, 47, *48;* expressions of Reform Judaism, 47–56; Gothic revival style, 42–43, 48–49; interiors, *45,* 47, *48;*

Jewish imagery, 45–51; Moorish style, 51; neo-colonial style, 43, *43;* onion domes, 43–44, 51; Renaissance Revival style, 51; Romanesque revival style, 45, 48, 55, *55;* Sephardic/Mediterranean style, 53–54, *54;* Stars of David, 45, 47–48, 51–52, 55, *55;* Ten Commandments, 45, 51–52. *See* specific congregations/temples

Szold, Henrietta, 1

Taba, Hilda, 123

Taub, Annette, *91, color plate 6*

Temple Beth Shalom (San Leandro), 51–52, *52*

Temple Israel, Los Angeles, 113, 182

Temple Sinai (Oakland), 56

Texas demographics, 21

Thalberg, Irving, 95, 98, 103

Nineteeth-century Jewish merchants, 17–19

The California Hebrew and English Almanac, 30

Thomas, Clarence, 151

Thurman, Howard, 127

Tolan Committee, 110–13, 118, 120

Tom, Henry Shue, 129

Tomorrow the World (film), 105

To the Golden Cities (Moore), 69

Touro, Judah, 41

Trade union movement. *See* Labor movement

Trattner, Rabbi Ernest, 98–99

The Two Thieves (film), 103

UAHC Camp Swig (Saratoga), *88,* 165, *165, 168, color plates 3, 10*

Union of American Hebrew Congregations, 107, 156–57

Union of Jewish Students (Berkeley), 158–59

United Farm Workers (UFW), 158–59

United Jewish Communities, 28, 61

United States Congress, 20, 143–44, 147–52

University of California, Berkeley, 15, 19; Berkeley Free Speech Movement, xiii, 139, 150, 154–55, *155;* drug use, 156; Graduate Theological Union, 164; Hillel activism, 158–59, 160; Jewish women in political roles, 152; Soviet Jewry movement, 161, *161*

University of Judaism (Los Angeles), 141

University of San Francisco, 131–32

Unruh, Jesse, 149

Urban centers: after the gold rush, 38–39; gentrification, 73; political activism, 63; urban renewal, 71–72. *See also* Local politics

Urban League, 158
Urban League (San Francisco), 129, 131, 132

Valley Beth Shalom Congregation, 164–65, 167, *169–70, 169, color plates 11–12*
Variety, 100
Venice, Calif., 13, 65–76
Veracruz, Phil, 158–59
Vietnam War, 156–57, 161
Vorspan, Max, 67
Voting rights, 127, 143, 145–47, 154–55
Voting Rights Act, 127, 154–55

Wada, Yori, 127
Warburg, Felix, 54
Warburg, Gisela, 175
Warner, Harry, 95, 105
Warner, Jack, 95, 103, 182
Warner Bros. Studio, 98, 104, *105*
Warner Brothers Theater, *97*
Warschaw, Carmen, 149–50
Weber, Charles, 43
Wedding ketubot, *10, 16, 87, 88–94, color plates 2–8*
Weinberg, Jack, 154, *155*
Weinberg, Larry and Barbie, 182
Weiner, Bettie and Ira, 182

Weisfeld, Israel, 139
Weiss–Rosmarin, Trude, 181
Wells Fargo Bank, 18
Western Jewish demographics, 20–23
Western Jewish History. See *Western States Jewish Historical Quarterly*
Western Jewish Studies Association, 141
Western States Jewish Historical Quarterly, 2
West Hollywood, Calif., 79
West Los Angeles, Calif., 68, 75
White, Rabbi Saul E., 127, *128*
Wiesel, Elie, 181
Willowbrandt, Mable Walker, 174
Wilshire Boulevard Temple (Congregation B'nai Brith, Los Angeles), 55, *55,* 182
Windmueller, Steven, 13
Wirin, A. L., 112
Wise, Rabbi Isaac Mayer, 37, 41, 47
Wise, Rabbi Steven S., 99–100, 104
Wolf, Ernest, 137
Wolf, Sam, 103
Wolf Brothers store, Sonora, Calif., *36*
Women: education, 135; gold rush, 35–37; kibbutzim, 83; Mishkon Tephilo Sisterhood, *70;* ordination, 15; political activism, 15, 143–53; suffrage, 145–47; as teachers, 135, 144–45, 148

Women's Educational and Industrial Union (WEIU), 145
World War II: antisemitism, 14, 96; civil rights movement, 123–29; dual-loyalty issues, 119–20; enemy alien issues, 114; growth of San Diego, 137; internment of Japanese Americans, 110–22
Wyman, Eugene, 149
Wyman, Rosalind Wiener, 148–49

Yates, Oleta O'Connor, 127
Yavne (Jewish Issues forum, San Diego), 139
Yiddish language use, 70–71, 73
Yi-Fu Tuan, 68
Yoneda, Elaine Black, 146
Yosemite Valley, *90*

Zeldin, Rabbi Isaiah, 174, 182
Zeta Beta Tau fraternity, 139
Zionism, 81–82, 119–20, 127, 176–77; attacks on, by the left, 157–59; camping movement, 165; in San Diego, 140. *See also* Anti-Zionism
Zionist Organization of America, 177
Zukor, Adolph, 95